Ireland and the Crusades

IRELAND AND THE CRUSADES

Edward Coleman, Paul Duffy and Tadhg O'Keeffe

EDITORS

FOUR COURTS PRESS

Set in 11.5 pt on 13.5 pt Centaur MT for
FOUR COURTS PRESS LTD
7 Malpas Street, Dublin 8, Ireland
www.fourcourtspress.ie
and in North America for
FOUR COURTS PRESS
c/o IPG, 814 N Franklin St, Chicago, IL 60610

© Four Courts Press and the various contributors 2022

A catalogue record for this title is available
from the British Library.

ISBN 978-1-84682-861-4

All rights reserved. No part of this publication may be
reproduced, stored in or introduced into a retrieval system,
or transmitted, in any form or by any means (electronic,
mechanical, photocopying, recording, or otherwise), without
the prior written permission of both the copyright owner
and publisher of this book.

Printed in England,
by CPI Antony Rowe, Chippenham, Wilts.

Contents

Illustrations		7
Abbreviations		9
Contributors		12
Preface		15

1	Ireland and the crusades: surveying the field *Edward Coleman*	19
2	Inspiring Irish crusaders: St Bernard's writings and Cistercian impact *Jean-Michel Picard*	38
3	Conquest as crusade: Ireland's invasion and a colonial plea to the papacy *Maeve Callan*	52
4	'Palmers' as ex-crusaders in Irish urban environments? The evidence of the *Dublin Guild Merchant Roll* *Catherine Swift*	70
5	Curtailing kings: Ireland, the Cathar Crusade and the cult of Simon de Montfort *Paul Duffy*	77
6	From the Boyne valley to the Holy Land: the crusading tradition of Geoffrey de Geneville and Jean de Joinville *Ciarán McDonnell*	91
7	The military-religious orders in Ireland: their patrons and their purpose *Helen J. Nicholson*	107
8	*Tuitio fidei?* The Irish Hospitallers at war *Paolo Virtuani*	121

9	The medieval hospital in Ireland: a comment on the crusader connection *Thomas Ivory*	129
10	Reconstructing the manor of Ballyman: the Poor Knights of Christ and the Temple of Solomon in the southern marches of Dublin *David McIlreavy*	136
11	Regal poise: the 'cross-legged' phenomenon on Irish effigy tombs during the age of the crusades *Dave Swift*	154
12	Crusading rhetoric and Anglo-Irish relations, *c.*1300–1600 *Kathryn Hurlock*	164
13	A Dublin 'crusader' *Emer Purcell*	178
14	Epilogue: commanderies, crusades, frontiers *Tadhg O'Keeffe*	183
	Bibliography	200
	Index	224

Illustrations

COLOUR PLATES
(between pages 128 and 129)

1.1 Papal bulla lead seal, John XXI (1276–7).

2.1 Carving of St Malachy.

2.2 Carving of St Bernard.

3.1 Pope Adrian IV.

4.1 *Dublin Guild Merchant Roll.*

4.2 Medieval burial under excavation in the graveyard of the Hospital of St John.

5.1 Fragment of Simon de Montfort's tomb at Carcassonne showing the great siege of Toulouse, 1218.

5.2 The Battle of Baziège from the manuscript of the Canzo de lo Crozada.

5.3 The Battle Well at Evesham.

6.1 Geoffrey de Geneville, as justiciar on the fourteenth-century *Waterford Charter Roll.*

6.2 Trim Castle and the Sheep Gate, the last remaining medieval gate of the town.

6.3 East range of the Blackfriary, Trim, established by Geoffrey de Geneville in 1263.

7.1 The ruins at Crooke, overlooking Waterford Harbour.

7.2 Baldongan church.

8.1 Glenmalure – where fitz Roger was defeated.

8.2 Remains of Kilteel preceptory.

9.1 St John's priory, Newtown Trim, Co. Meath.

9.2 View along the nave of St John's priory church, Newtown Trim, Co. Meath.

9.3 Plan of St Mary's, Chichester, showing nave as possible hospital.

10.1 Ballyman church.

10.2 CUCAP Archive No. BDP024 with possible double-ditched enclosure visible to the north of Ballyman Road.

10.3 Map showing suggested reconstruction of Ballyman and associated lands.

11.1 Conjectural drawing of St Peter's graveyard armoured burial.

11.2 Knight in relief at Hospital church, Co. Limerick.

11.3	Detail of rowel spur on the knight effigy at Christ Church cathedral, Dublin.
11.4	'The Brethren' double effigy at Jerpoint abbey, Co. Kilkenny.
11.5	Knights from Athassel tomb surround – currently housed at Cashel – showing cross-legged pose.
11.6	King Edward III from *Waterford Charter Roll* reclining against throne in cross-legged pose.
11.7	King receiving keys of the city from *Waterford Charter Roll*.
12.1	Thomas fitz Gerald, 10th earl of Kildare.
12.2	Hugh O'Neill, 1608.
12.3	Siege and Battle of Kinsale, 1601.
13.1	St Michan's church, Dublin, nave and tower.
13.2	Steps descending into the crypt at St Michan's church.
13.3	St Michan's crusader.
14.1	Conjectural plan of Hospitaller commandery at Kilmainham.
14.2	Conjectural reconstruction drawing of Hospitaller commandery, Kilmainham by Stephen Conlin. (Reproduced with kind permission of Dublin City Council Archaeology).
14.3	Hospital Church.

Abbreviations

AFM	*Annála Ríoghachta Éireann: Annals of the kingdom of Ireland by the Four Masters, from the earliest period to the year 1616: edited from MSS in the library of the Royal Irish Academy and of Trinity College Dublin with a translation and copious notes*, ed. and trans. John O'Donovan, with an introduction by Kenneth Nicholls, 7 vols (Dublin, 1990)
AH	*Analecta Hibernica*
AI	*Archaeology Ireland*
BL	British Library
Callan, *Templars*	Maeve B. Callan, *The Templars, the witch and the wild Irish: vengeance and heresy in medieval Ireland* (Dublin, 2015)
Cart. Gen. Hosp.	*Cartulaire général de l'ordre des Hospitaliers de S. Jean de Jérusalem (1100–1310)*, ed. Joseph Delaville le Roulx, 4 vols (Paris, 1894–1906)
CCM	*Calendar of the Carew manuscripts preserved in the archiepiscopal palace of Lambeth, 1515–1624*, eds J.S. Brewer and William Bullen, 6 vols (London, 1867–73)
CCR, Edw. II:	*Calendar of the close rolls preserved in the Public Record Office, Edward II*, 4 vols (London, 1892–8)
CCR, Edw. III:	*Calendar of the close rolls preserved in the Public Record Office, Edward III*, 14 vols (London, 1896–1913)
CDI	*Calendar of documents relating to Ireland preserved in Her Majesty's Public Record Office, 1171–1307*, ed. Henry S. Sweetman, 5 vols (London, 1875–6)
CEPR	*Calendar of entries in the papal registers relating to Great Britain and Ireland: papal letters*, 23 vols (Dublin, 1893–2018)
CIRCLE	*A calendar of Irish chancery letters, c.1244–1509.* https://chancery.tcd.ie/content/welcome-circle
CPR, Edw. III	*Calendar of the patent rolls preserved in the Public Record Office, Edward III*, 16 vols (London, 1891–1916)
CPR, Henry III	*Calendar of the patent rolls preserved in the Public Record Office, Henry III*, 6 vols (London, 1901–13)
CSP Ire.	*Calendar of state papers relating to Ireland in the reigns of Henry VIII, Edward VI, Mary and Elizabeth*, eds H.C. Hamilton, E.G. Atkinson & R.P. Mahaffy, 11 vols (London, 1860–1912)
CSP Spain	*Calendar of state papers, Spain*, 13 vols (London, 1862–1954)

CSMA	*Chartularies of St Mary's abbey, Dublin with the register of its house at Dunbrody and Annals of Ireland*, ed. John T. Gilbert, 2 vols, Rolls series 80 (London, 1884)
DIB	*Dictionary of Irish biography*
EHR	*English Historical Review*
Falkiner, 'Hospital'	Caesar Litton Falkiner, 'The hospital of St John of Jerusalem in Ireland', *Proceedings of the Royal Irish Academy: Archaeology, Culture, History, Literature*, 26 (1907), 275–317
HI	*History Ireland*
Hurlock, *Crusades*	Kathryn Hurlock, *Britain, Ireland and the crusades, c.1000–1300* (London, 2013)
IHS	*Irish Historical Studies*
JEH	*Journal of Ecclesiastical History*
JIA	*Journal of Irish Archaeology*
JMH	*Journal of Medieval History*
JRSAI	*Journal of the Royal Society of Antiquaries of Ireland*
MGH	*Monumenta Germaniae historica inde ab anno Christi quingentesimo usque ad annum millesimum et quingentesimum, antiquitates, diplomata, epistolae, leges, scriptores* (multiple editors and places of publication, 1826–)
MRHI	Aubrey Gwynn & R.N. Hadcock, *Medieval religious houses: Ireland* (Dublin, 1970; new ed. 1988)
NMI	National Museum of Ireland
NMS	National Monuments Service of the Department of Housing, Local Government and Heritage
ODNB	*Oxford dictionary of national biography*
PL	*Patrologia Latina*, ed. J.P. Migne, 221 vols (Paris, 1844–64)
PRIA	*Proceedings of the Royal Irish Academy*
PRV	*Pontificum romanorum vitae, qui fuerunt inde exeunt saeculo ix ad finem saeculi xiii, ab aequelibus conscriptae, quas ex archive pontifici, Bibliothecae Vaticanae aliarumque codicibus, adiectis suis cuique ex annalibus et documentis gravioribus editae*, ed. J.M Watterich, 2 vols (Leipzig, 1862; repr. 1966)
RK	*Registrum de Kilmainham: register of chapter acts of the Hospital of Saint John of Jerusalem in Ireland, 1326–1339, under the grand prior, Sir Roger Outlawe, with additions from the times of his successors, Sir John Mareschall, Sir John Larcher and Sir John FitzRichard, grand priors of Ireland, edited from the Bodleian MS Rawl. B. 501*, ed. Charles McNeill (Dublin, 1932)

Rolls series	*Rerum Britannicarum medii aevi scriptores: chronicles and memorials of Great Britain and Ireland during the Middle Ages*, 253 vols (London, 1858–1911)
SMR	Sites and Monuments Record
TRHS	*Transactions of the Royal Historical Society*
UCD	University College Dublin
Wood, 'Templars'	Herbert Wood, 'The Templars in Ireland', *Proceedings of the Royal Irish Academy: Archaeology, Culture, History, Literature*, 26 (1907), 327–77

Contributors

Maeve Callan is professor of religion and women's and gender studies at Simpson College in Iowa. She earned her PhD and MA in religion at Northwestern University and her MPhil in women's studies from Trinity College Dublin. She has published two books, *The Templars, the witch, and the wild Irish: vengeance and heresy in medieval Ireland* (2014), and *Sacred sisters: gender, sanctity, and power in medieval Ireland* (2019). Her current research focuses on ethnic identity, religion and racism in the British Isles from 1000 to 1400.

Edward Coleman teaches medieval European history at University College Dublin. His research interests include the history of the crusades and he has previously published 'The crusader's tale' in Sparky Booker & Cherie Peters (eds), *Tales of medieval Dublin* (2014) and '"Powerful adversaries": the Knights Templar, landholding and litigation in the lordship of Ireland' in Martin Browne & Colmán Ó Clabaigh (eds), *Soldiers of Christ: the Knights Templar and the Knights Hospitaller in medieval Ireland* (2016).

Paul Duffy is a senior archaeologist with Irish Archaeological Consultancy, specializing in medieval and urban archaeology. He has led several landmark excavations in Dublin city and has been awarded Royal Irish Academy and Irish Research Council funding for a number of research projects. He has published widely on this work and was an editor of *Carrickfergus to Carcassonne* (2018), a volume detailing the involvement of Hugh de Lacy II in the Cathar Crusade.

Kathryn Hurlock is reader in medieval history at Manchester Metropolitan University, and has written widely on the impact of the crusades in Britain and Ireland. This includes her monographs on *Wales and the crusades, c.1096–1291* (2011) and *Britain, Ireland and the crusades, c.1000–1300* (2013), as well as articles on aspects of crusading culture in a number of journals and edited collections.

Thomas Ivory returned to academia after a long career in retail, and was awarded an MA in archaeology from UCD in 2016. He is now an Irish Research Council-funded PhD candidate in UCD School of Archaeology, where he is researching medieval hospitals in Ireland.

Ciarán McDonnell is a military historian specializing in identity, war and society. His PhD from Maynooth University examined Irish identity in the British military during the French Revolutionary Wars. His subsequent postdoctoral research at the Institute of Historical Research in London explored Jacobitism and the Irish Brigade in the French army. While working at the Blackfriary Archaeology Field School in Trim, Co. Meath, he began his research on the crusades, crusaders and medieval Ireland. He now works for Meath County Council and continues to publish both locally and internationally on topics from the medieval to the modern.

David McIlreavy is an archaeological director with Irish Archaeological Consultancy and holds master's degrees in both modern history and archaeology from Queen's University Belfast. He is a member of the Institute of Archaeologists of Ireland and his research interests include the development of the medieval settlement of Ulster. He is the founder and lead researcher of the Medieval Bray Project, a community research partnership exploring the development of the settlement of Bray, Co. Wicklow, throughout the medieval period.

Helen J. Nicholson is professor of medieval history at Cardiff University. She has published extensively on the military orders, crusades and various related subjects, including an edition of the Templar trial proceedings in Britain and Ireland (2011). She is currently studying the inventory and estate accounts from the Templars' estates in England and Wales during the years 1308–13, and is also writing a history of Queen Sybil of Jerusalem (1186–90) for Routledge's Rulers of the Latin East series.

Tadhg O'Keeffe studied in University College Dublin and the universities of Durham, London and Poitiers. He teaches in UCD where he is Full Professor of archaeology. He is a specialist in medieval European architecture.

Jean-Michel Picard studied at the University of Provence in Aix-en-Provence, at the University of Paris IV-Sorbonne, and at UCD. As a specialist in medieval languages, literature and history, he has published several books and numerous articles on Irish hagiographical literature, on Hiberno-Latin language, and on the history of contacts between Ireland and the Continent during the Middle Ages. He is professor emeritus in the UCD School of Languages, Cultures and Linguistics, and a member of the Royal Irish Academy.

Emer Purcell is a senior executive assistant in the Publications Office of the National University of Ireland. She has published widely on Viking Age Ireland and medieval Dublin. She co-edited *Clerics, kings and Vikings: essays on* *medieval Ireland* (2015) and *Text, transmission, and transformation in the European Middle Ages, c.1000–1500* (2018). She is also a coordinator of the Forum for Medieval and Renaissance Studies in Ireland (https://fmrsi.wordpress.com/).

Catherine Swift has postgraduate degrees in history, archaeology and Old Irish from UCD, Durham, Oxford and TCD. Her publications emphasize the European aspects of medieval Irish society and culture. She lectures in Irish studies and history in Mary Immaculate College, University of Limerick.

Dave Swift is a field archaeologist with a specialist interest in the military history and material culture of medieval Ireland and the Irish War of Independence among other periods. He is also a Viking/medieval artefact and post-medieval glass-vessel finds specialist. He periodically works in the film industry in various roles such as writer, historical advisor, choreographer, actor, armourer, props supplier and wardrobe provider. He is a member of the Society of Combat Archaeology, a panellist on the Heritage Council's Heritage in Schools Scheme, and a founder member of Claíomh, the leading professional Irish experimental archaeology and historical recreation group.

Paolo Virtuani is a graduate of Milan's Università Statale and obtained his doctorate in UCD, with a dissertation on the Knights Hospitaller in medieval Ireland. He has published on the subject with Four Courts Press and Taylor & Francis. He currently covers administrative and teaching roles in UCD.

Preface

The crusades – a broad term encompassing a disparate series of military expeditions, with the avowed intent of preserving/expanding Christianity and the orthodoxy of the Roman Church – were a quintessential phenomenon of moral and religious life in medieval Europe. Traditionally, Ireland's connection with the crusades has been seen to be slight. In recent years, however, new research has begun to replace this view with a more nuanced picture.

It could be argued that the concept of crusade, as first articulated by Pope Urban II on the 27 November 1095, would have needed little explanation in Ireland. Hagiography had fixed in the Gaelic consciousness of that age the heroic deeds of a multiplicity saints from earlier centuries who had established Christianity in an Ireland of non-Christian 'others' and then helped to reverse the dimming of Christianity's light across Europe after the fall of Rome. Moreover, if reports of the pope's speech reached Ireland, Urban's words might well have resonated with a population whose ancestors had experienced the violent incursions of non-Christians from the late eighth century. The record of these traumatic 'heathen' attacks in Irish sources finds a ready parallel in the pope's report of atrocities committed by Muslims in the East; the language and imagery used by Urban is uncannily similar to that of the Gaelic scribes describing the Viking raids:

> an accursed and foreign race, enemies of God, ... whose spirit was not steadfast with God have invaded the lands of those Christians [Greeks] and devastated them with the sword, rapine, and fire. Some of the Christians they have carried away as slaves, others they have put to death. The churches they have either destroyed or turned into mosques. They desecrate and overthrow the altars. They circumcise the Christians and pour the blood from the circumcision on the altars or in the baptismal fonts. Some they kill in a horrible way by cutting open the abdomen, taking out a part of the entrails and tying them to a stake; they then beat them and compel them to walk until all their entrails are drawn out and they fall to the ground. Some they use as targets for their arrows. They compel some to stretch out their necks and then they try to see whether they can cut off their heads with one stroke of the sword. It is better to say nothing of their horrible treatment of the women.[1]

1 Urban's speech was recorded by Robert of Rheims (d. 1122). See Oliver J. Thatcher & Edgar Holmes McNeal (eds), *A source book for mediæval history: selected documents illustrating the history of Europe in the Middle Ages* (New York, 1905), pp 518–21.

It is also worth recalling in this context that *Cogadh Gáedel re Gallaib*, the epic work of dynastic propaganda, recast the Battle of Clontarf (1014) as a great religious conflict between the Christian Brian Boru and a heathen race – the Norse. The work was probably written shortly after the First Crusade and it is possible that the anonymous author was influenced by the crusading ideal and the awakening sense of a Christian unity of purpose against a distinct 'other'. While it would be inaccurate to frame Clontarf as a crusade, the transformation of Dublin in the century after the battle from a place that was ambivalent about Christianity to the place which boasted the largest concentration of churches anywhere in Ireland is nonetheless worthy of note.

The arrival of the Anglo-Normans in the late twelfth century marked Ireland's first direct engagement with the new crusading culture that emerged in the late eleventh century. Among the aristocrats, soldiers and settlers who established the new Angevin lordship of Ireland were men who had been on crusade or who were destined to head out from Ireland on crusade (and perhaps never return). For almost all of them, the crusading experience was to be in the land of the greatest, most violent and longest-lived contestation between Christians and non-Christians: Outremer, the land to the east of Mediterranean, a Holy Land to all the protagonists, Christians, Muslims and Jews. However, crusading for Christ was also possible closer to home, and some – most famously Hugh de Lacy II, enemy of heretic Cathars – took that option. One wonders how many of the native-born (or, to use a cumbersome phrase for convenience, 'ethnically Gaelic') inhabitants of Ireland took to the seas also as crusaders, and whether they travelled alongside Anglo-Normans. One wonders also whether any of those same native Irish were struck by the irony of Knights Templar and Knights Hospitaller, iconic defenders of the faith and of the faithful in the Holy Land, putting down roots and fighting in Ireland of all places.

This collection of essays, written by researchers working in a number of disciplines, explores the place of medieval Ireland in the world of crusading. Recent years have seen renewed interest in Ireland in crusader culture in its broadest sense, and this is the third collection of essays in less than a decade to reflect that: *Soldiers of Christ: the Knights Hospitaller and the Knights Templar in medieval Ireland*, published in 2016, examined Ireland's relationship with the military orders of crusader origin, and *From Carrickfergus to Carcassonne: the epic deeds of Hugh de Lacy on the Albigensian Crusade*, published in 2018, focused on Ireland's connection with one of the crusades on European soil.[2] The scope of this

---

2 Martin Browne & Colmán Ó Clabaigh (eds), *Soldiers of Christ: the Knights Hospitaller and the Knights Templar in Medieval Ireland* (Dublin, 2016); Paul Duffy, Tadhg O'Keeffe & Jean-Michel Picard (eds), *From Carrickfergus to Carcassonne: the epic deeds of Hugh de Lacy on the Albigensian Crusade* (Turnhout, 2018).

Preface 17

volume is broad. In contributions which vary in size, geographical scope and investigative detail, it offers additional perspectives on the themes of the other two volumes, as well as new perspectives on other topics.

As Edward Coleman demonstrates in the opening chapter, Ireland's crusader history was for many years a neglected topic, but recent decades have seen renewed interest in the subject. His survey of the historiography contextualizes issues which are explored in the chapters that follow. The chapters are arranged in a general chronological order. A number of themes emerge from them.

The military orders, subjects of classic papers that were published simultaneously in the early twentieth century by Caesar Litton Falkiner and Herbert Wood, feature prominently in the modern discourse on medieval crusading. No modern scholar has contributed more to the study of these orders in Ireland than Helen Nicholson. Her chapter in this collection explores how the knights operated as agents of colonial government in Ireland but also as conventional and well-endowed monastics, exempt from taxes and dues on account of their responsibilities to their brethren and to the Christian mission in the Holy Land. Two other chapters address matters pertaining directly to the orders. Paolo Virtuani discusses the neglected matter of the military activities of the Hospitallers on the island, and documents their involvement in the military protection of the lordship. David McIlreavy examines an estate purported to have been a Templar possession in the southern marches of Dublin. His reconstruction of the estate's geography and economy illuminates the potential for further fine-grained studies of local landscapes. A third chapter in the collection is focused on a monument type popularly associated with one of the orders: the Hospital. Thomas Ivory examines the background to, and considers the validity of, this association, and he discusses hospital foundation by another monastic order with reputed links to the Holy Land, the Fratres Cruciferi or Crutched Friars.

The place of the Church in Ireland's crusader history is not confined to the two great military orders. Jean-Michel Picard examines the part played by the Cistercian order in the rise and transmission of the crusader ideal in western Europe, and offers a fresh perspective on the role of the Irish Cistercians in promoting that the crusading spirit among the island's warrior elite. Papal authority rather than monastic ideal takes centre stage in Maeve Callan's chapter, which considers the seismic event of the Anglo-Norman conquest through the lens of crusading ideology and rhetoric, then reaching its apogee in the kingdoms of Europe. Continuing the theme of the relationship between the Church and the concept of crusading in Ireland, Kathryn Hurlock's chapter explores the history of the late medieval Gaelic-Irish deployment of the language of crusading against the English, thus reversing the experience of their twelfth-century predecessors.

The names of many men who travelled from Ireland on crusade are recorded. Most travelled to the eastern Mediterranean, but Hugh de Lacy II, son of the first Anglo-Norman lord of Meath, joined the crusade against the Cathars of southern France. Paul Duffy, building on previous work on de Lacy's activities in France, charts in his chapter the presence of a cult of Simon de Montfort in Ireland and its likely origins in the crusader's milieu in Languedoc. Some individual Anglo-Norman families that settled in Ireland had strong crusader connections, and Ciarán McDonnell focuses on one such family in his chapter, tracing the motivations of the de Geneville brothers, Jean and Geoffrey, who participated in the the crusades of Louis IX of France and The Lord Edward (the Future Edward I of England), respectively. One can be certain that some of the individuals who were wealthy enough to be memorialized by effigial sculptures had been crusaders, but, unlike the Geneville brothers who are known to us from the documentary sources, the carved figures on the tombs are often unnamed. Dave Swift revisits and critically reappraises the often-repeated assertion that knights represented in death by effigies with crossed legs were former crusaders. A lot is known about crusaders whose families were not of aristocratic rank. Catherine Swift examines the possibility that former crusaders have been hiding in plain sight as 'palmers' in the *Dublin Guild Merchant Roll*. Dublin is home today, of course, to the most famous Irish 'crusader' – the mummified individual with crossed legs in the crypt of St Michan's church, Dublin. Emer Purcell reconstructs the history of the popular association of this mummy with crusading.

In the closing chapter, Tadhg O'Keeffe focuses on two well-studied themes in the study of the crusades: the archaeology of the military-religious orders, and the concept of the frontier. The scope for more work on both of these is discussed, thus closing the collection of essays by opening windows for future research.

In their totality, it is hoped that these contributions present a varied and compelling whole that ultimately shifts medieval Ireland closer in the historical imagination to the famed shores of Outremer.

1 / Ireland and the crusades: surveying the field

EDWARD COLEMAN

The crusades were for a long time an almost completely neglected aspect of Irish medieval history. However, in the last twenty years or so there has been a remarkable upsurge of interest that is reflected in the production of monographs, journal articles and edited collections on the subject. This essay will trace the main lines of research up until the present time and highlight some of the key publications. It will also offer some reflections on the question of why the history of Ireland's involvement in the crusades received so little attention until recently.

The modern historical investigation of Ireland and the crusades really dates from two articles, one might almost say companion pieces, on the crusading military orders by Caesar Litton Falkiner (Hospitallers) and Herbert Wood (Templars) that appeared at the beginning of the last century.[1] Herbert Wood (1860–1955) joined the Irish Public Record Office in 1884 and spent his entire career there as an archivist, becoming deputy keeper in 1921.[2] He is remembered particularly for his (extremely timely as it turned out) *Guide to the records deposited in the Public Record Office of Ireland*, published in 1919. After the destruction of the Four Courts in 1922, he produced a valuable appraisal of the loss of records and the potential for reconstruction based on guides, registers and calendars, including some that he himself had written.[3] For these achievements alone he 'deserves to be ranked as one of the country's greatest archivists'.[4] Wood's research into the history of Knights Templar in Ireland was characterized by the attention to detail and critical analysis of sources that might be expected of an experienced archivist. His essay was the first serious attempt to gather and make sense of the sources relating to the order in

---

1 Falkiner, 'Hospital', 275–317; Wood, 'Templars', 327–77. The complementary nature of the subject matter plus the fact that both essays were published in the same edition of the same journal points to a programmatic agenda on the part of the authors, the journal or both. In an acknowledgment appended to the end of his article, Falkiner stated that his 'friend Mr Herbert Wood of the Irish Record Office' had assisted him in finding out which Templar properties had passed to the Hospitallers on the suppression of the Order of the Temple, and he noted that Wood's article was in preparation. 2 H.G. Leask, 'Herbert Wood', *JRSAI* 86 (1956), 109. 3 Herbert Wood, 'The public records of Ireland before and after 1922', *TRHS* 13 (1930), 17–49, at 33–6. Were he alive today, Wood would certainly have approved of the recent project to reconstruct digitally the corpus of medieval Irish governmental records: *CIRCLE*. 4 Sean J. Murphy, 'Herbert Wood, archivist and historian (1860–1955)', https://www.academia.edu/41278716/Herbert_Wood_Archivist_and_Historian_1860–1955, unpublished paper, accessed 18 July 2020.

Ireland. He also identified a problem that historians of the Knights Templar all over Europe will readily recognize, given the romance and notoriety that still surrounds the order. Much of what had been written about the Templars, Wood observed, was 'chaotic, conflicting and unreliable'.[5] He also alluded to a further complicating factor in the study of the Irish Templars, namely that following the suppression of the order in 1312 and the handover of its properties to the Hospitallers, confusion often subsequently arose as to which localities originally belonged to which order.[6] Wood corrected some of the more egregious errors prevalent in antiquarian writing, e.g. the misinterpretation of Kilmainham, the principal Hospitaller preceptory, as a gift made by Strongbow to the Templars, and the mistaken identification of William fitz Roger as a master of the Temple, when in fact he was master of the Hospital.[7] Wood's careful scrutiny of the sources enabled him to accurately reconstruct the Irish patrimony of the Templars for the first time, beginning with Henry II's grant of lands in counties Dublin, Waterford and Wexford (c.1172–5); this grant included Clontarf, which was to become the Templars' principal seat in Ireland.[8] Wood estimated, on the basis of returns made for Edward III in 1328, that the value of the income and goods of the order in Ireland at the time of its suppression amounted to £716 16s. 6½d.[9] He found that the furnishings of their preceptories were very humble and that, surprisingly for a military order, they were 'poorly equipped with arms'.[10] Wood also provided a list of the Templar masters in Ireland, beginning in 1186 with Walter the Templar, that remains widely accepted and cited today (despite some speculative identifications).[11] A sizable part of Wood's essay concerns various episodes of judicial litigation in which the Templars were pitted against other individuals, churches, monasteries – and on occasion even the crown – in vigorous, and usually successful, defence of their lands, income and rights. This kind of record in fact comprises the bulk of the surviving evidence about the Poor Knights of Christ in Ireland up until their suppression in the early fourteenth century.

In contrast to Herbert Wood, Caesar Litton Falkiner (1863–1908) was trained not as an archivist but a lawyer. He had wide-ranging intellectual interests and wrote prodigiously on history, literature and biography. His essay on the Knights Hospitaller in Ireland was a rare excursion into the Middle Ages, as his research was mainly concerned with seventeenth- and eighteenth-century

---

5 Wood, 'Templars', 327. 6 Ibid., 362–3. 7 Ibid., 340, 361. 8 Ibid., 363–71. 9 Ibid., 348. 10 Ibid. 11 Ibid., 333. The extent of Irish possessions of the order is described by Wood in appendix A. Other appendices recover the post-suppression inventory of the preceptory of Clonoulty, Co. Tipperary, a grant of Matilda de Lacy to the Templars, and an account of the arrest, imprisonment, death and burial of Walter le Bachelor, who was master of the Templar order in Ireland between 1295 and 1301.

Ireland and the crusades: surveying the field

history. Although rather less thorough than Wood's analysis of the Templars, and written in a more colourful style, Falkiner's work remains an important reference point for the study of the Knights of St John in Ireland. In common with his fellow historian of the military orders, Falkiner too was careful to point out the errors of antiquarian writing, noting that Kilmainham was a Hospitaller priory from its foundation, contrary to the assertions of earlier authors such as Archdall, Harris and d'Alton, and he provides a detailed summary of the charter evidence in support of this interpretation.[12] He speculated that Strongbow might even have granted Kilmainham to the Hospitallers before he came to Ireland.[13] Like the Templars, the Hospitallers acquired lands, properties and rights in many areas of the island. Following the suppression of the Templars in 1312, Hospitaller holdings were increased further as they took over the possessions of their rival order.[14] However, Falkiner does not seem to have been aware of the existence of an important text – the *Registrum de Kilmainham (RK)* – which contains information about both the transfer of assets from the Templars to the Hospitallers, and the property portfolio of the Hospitallers in general, as well as arrangements regarding corrodians and the disposition and functions of buildings at Kilmainham.[15] As Wood did for the Templars, Falkiner, drew up a list of Hospitaller priors of Kilmainham, beginning with Hugh de Clahull in 1180; by the later Middle Ages this office was often occupied by scions of the leading Anglo-Irish families, such as the Butlers, fitz Geralds and Talbots. Falkiner's list of priors, which is not without its problems, is largely based on information contained in a manuscript of the Church of Ireland archbishop William King (1650–1729).[16] Falkiner also discussed the involvement of the Hospitallers in the grain trade and fresh-water fish farming, the latter being an activity that led to a famous clash with the citizens of Dublin over rights on the river Liffey.[17] He was the first to highlight their close engagement at the highest level with the administration of the Anglo-Norman lordship in roles such as justiciar, deputy justiciar, chancellor and treasurer, and he drew attention to their military service for the English crown against its enemies within Ireland, aspects of the order's activity in Ireland that have proved to be fertile ground for further research in more recent scholarship.[18]

---

12 Falkiner, 'Hospital', 276, 280. Consideration of Irish antiquarian writing about the crusades lies beyond the scope of this survey. However, it may be noted in passing that a number of widely accepted 'facts' about the crusading military orders in Ireland ultimately rest on studies from this era in the absence of surviving original medieval documentation.   13 Ibid., 283.   14 Ibid., 285–7; appendix I, 306–15.   15 Ibid., 290: 'No such admirable illustration of life in a fourteenth-century priory as is supplied by the "Account Roll of the priory of the Holy Trinity, 1337–1346" has been preserved to inform us how the Hospitallers of Kilmainham, lived, moved and had their being. We must therefore content ourselves with such occasional and unsatisfactory glimpses as the State papers give us of the life of the Hospitallers generally.'   16 Falkiner, 'Hospital', appendix II, 316–17.   17 Ibid., 280.   18 Ibid., 296–300.

Following the pioneering research of Wood and Falkiner, the study of Ireland and the crusades fell into abeyance for most of the rest of the twentieth century, save for a handful of localized publications.[19] An exception in this barren period was a reference work that attempted to gather to together for the first time historical data relating to the presence of religious orders in Ireland in the Middle Ages and relate it to topographical information in a comprehensive manner. This was Gwynn and Hadcock's *Medieval religious houses*, the aim of which was to provide a gazetteer with supporting documentation of all religious foundations in Ireland up until the dissolution of the monasteries.[20] The military orders were included as they were considered to be religious organizations. Gwynn and Hadcock produced a list of the possessions of the Templars and Hospitallers that represents an advance on the work of Wood and Falkiner as it gathered together all the known references in one place. It is also made some additions and amendments to the findings of the two earlier articles, utilizing source material published in the intervening sixty or so years. However, some of Gwynn and Hadcock's identifications have been questioned in more recent scholarship and their list of military order properties is now in need of revision and updating.[21]

The general lack of attention paid to the history of the crusades in Ireland over such a long period remains puzzling, however, bearing in mind that it is widely recognized that crusading was a hugely important activity in the Christian West during the twelfth and thirteenth centuries. Crusade was seen as a 'means of regenerating and reforming Christian belief; of creating a truly Christian society'.[22] It seems improbable that Ireland would have been unaffected by a movement of such magnitude.[23] How then is the dearth of studies to be explained?

It might in part have been a consequence of the scattered nature of the source material. Anyone seeking to uncover the involvement of Ireland in the crusades must search for evidence across the entire corpus of royal administrative documents, ecclesiastical records and narrative sources that survive in a

---

19 For example, Dermot MacIvor, 'The Knights Templar in County Louth', *Seanchas Ardmhacha* 4:1 (1960–1), 72–91; Tom Nolan, 'The order of the Knights Templar in the Waterford area', *Decies* 14 (1980), 52–60. Two contributions of wider scope on the crusading military orders should be mentioned, however: Eric St John Brooks, 'The Irish possessions of the order of St Thomas of Acre', *PRIA* 58C (1956–57), 21–44; Charles Tipton, 'The Irish Hospitallers during the Great Schism', *PRIA* 69C (1970), 33–43.   20 *MRHI*, pp 327–31. The book was the third in a series, with previous volumes covering England and Wales (1953) and Scotland (1957). On its publication it was described as 'one of the most important books of Irish ecclesiastical history to appear in modern times' (*IHS* 18 (1973), 438–40).   21 Browne & Ó Clabaigh, *Soldiers of Christ*, pp 7, 97, 106–7, 188.   22 Björn Weiler, '*Negotium terrae sanctae* in the political discourse of Latin Christendom, 1215–1311', *International History Review* 25 (2003), 1–36, at 5.   23 'Though the number of crusaders was only a small percentage of the population, the effects of crusades were felt in every part of Europe. Crusading was important even for those who never took part, as it had a role to play in domestic life': Hurlock, *Crusades*, p. 1.

Ireland and the crusades: surveying the field

range of different formats, from unpublished manuscripts and transcriptions to calendars and printed editions. Documents issued by the crown and the Anglo-Norman baronage contain information about who went on crusade and how funds were raised for crusading expeditions, as well as revealing how members of the crusading military orders were seconded into royal service in various roles.[24] Papal correspondence and taxation returns shed light on preaching and also financial matters pertaining to crusade.[25] Chronicles and literature in both Latin and Irish give glimpses of the enduring appeal of the Holy Land and crusade in Ireland throughout the Middle Ages.[26] There are three texts — or rather collections of texts — from Ireland that can be specifically associated with the crusades. Two of these relate to the trial of the Templars and its aftermath, comprising a record of the interrogation of Irish Templars and a valuation of the remaining Templar lands and income in Ireland ordered by the king over twenty years later.[27] The third, known as the Register of Kilmainham (*Registrum de Kilmainham*), mentioned above, is an inventory of the rights and possessions of the Knights Hospitaller (1326–39) compiled for the order's chief official in Ireland, Prior Roger Outlaw, which was published by Charles McNeill in 1932.[28]

While it cannot be claimed that the surviving documentary and narrative evidence for Irish participation in the crusades is abundant, by the same token neither is it non-existent. The reason for the neglect of crusade history in an Irish context must therefore also be in part historiographical. Alignment with the traditional view of crusading as a predominantly French movement, the impact of which was mainly felt in the eastern Mediterranean might be relevant in the case of Ireland. As such, crusade could be seen as extraneous to 'national history', insofar as that term is appropriate when referring to the Middle Ages. It is certainly the case that in much of Europe 'national history' and 'crusade history' were for a long time siloed in separate research fields that did not overlap. Yet the impact of ecclesiastical reform in the eleventh century,

---

24 Paul Dryburgh & Brendan Smith (eds), *Handbook of medieval Irish records in the National Archives of the United Kingdom* (Dublin, 2005); Philomena Connolly, *Medieval record sources* (Dublin, 2002).   **25** *CEPR*; *Pontifica Hibernica: medieval papal chancery documents concerning Ireland 640–1261*, ed. Maurice P. Sheehy, 2 vols (Dublin, 1962–5). See also Jean-Michel Picard, chapter 2, this volume.   **26** CELT. Corpus of electronic texts, https://celt.ucc.ie/latlist.html, accessed 22 May 2021; Katharine Simms, *Medieval Gaelic sources* (Dublin, 2009).   **27** *The proceedings against the Templars in the British Isles*, ed. Helen J. Nicholson, 2 vols (Farnham, 2011), i, pp 284–338; 'Documents relating to the suppression of the Templars in Ireland', ed. G. MacNiocaill, *AH* 24 (1967), 183–226.   **28** *RK*. The original manuscript survives (Oxford, Bodleian Library, Rawlinson B501). In an earlier article McNeill made extensive use of the *Registrum de Kilmainham* to reconstruct the layout of the buildings, the organization and the hierarchy of the resident community at Kilmainham (Charles McNeill, 'The Hospitallers of Kilmainham and their guests', *JRSAI* 14 (1924), 15–30). McNeill's interpretation has recently been substantially updated and revised: see Tadhg O'Keeffe & Paolo Virtuani, 'Reconstructing Kilmainham: the topography and architecture of the chief priory of the Knights Hospitaller in Ireland, *c*.1170–1349', *JMH* 46 (2020), 449–77.

24   *Ireland and the crusades*

the spread of new religious orders such as the Cistercians and Augustinians in the twelfth century and the mendicant friars in the thirteenth century (bearing in mind that the crusading military orders too were religious orders) were all developments that affected Christendom as a whole and also found a place in Ireland's national history.[29] It might be argued that historians of medieval Ireland have not been unique in more or less ignoring the crusades; historians of other countries have done likewise. For a long time, this was indeed true. But from as far back as the 1980s there has been a growing recognition elsewhere that the embedding of crusading ideology and practice in the physical and mental landscape of the medieval West was an important development in its own right, and that the 'home front' of crusading was consequently a subject eminently worthy of study. This shift in thinking has led researchers to move away somewhat from the traditional concerns of military campaigns in the East and the politics of the crusader states and towards the impact of crusade within Europe.[30] The investigation of the imprint left by crusade not only in the lands where it originated – broadly speaking, Languedoc, Normandy, the Low Countries and parts of the German empire – but also in areas that had hitherto been considered peripheral to the crusading movement such as Scandinavia and Eastern Europe, has also been a characteristic of this new approach.[31] These developments have been mirrored in crusade research

29 For ecclesiastical reform in Ireland see Marie Therese Flanagan, *The transformation of the Irish Church in the twelfth and thirteenth centuries* (Woodbridge, 2010). For the Cistercians see Roger Stalley, *The Cistercian monasteries of Ireland* (New Haven, 1987). For the canons see Martin Browne & Cólman Ó Clabaigh (eds), *Households of God: the regular canons and canonesses of St Augustine and Prémontré in Ireland* (Dublin, 2019). For the mendicants see Cólman Ó Clabaigh, *The friars in Ireland, 1224–1540* (Dublin, 2012). 30 'The impact of the crusades in the West had long been recognized but the first comprehensive study of it did not appear until 1989': Hurlock, *Crusades,* p. 2, referring to Kenneth Setton (ed.), *The history of the crusades,* vi: *The impact of the crusades on Europe* (Madison, WI, 1989). 31 Some selected examples dealing only with crusades to the East and excluding crusades launched within Europe itself include the following: Kurt Villads Jensen, 'Denmark and the crusading movement: the integration of the Baltic region into medieval Europe' in Allan I. MacInnes, F. Pederesen & Thomas Riis (eds), *Ships, guns and Bibles in the North Sea and Baltic States, c.1350–1700* (East Linton, 2000), pp 185–205; Janus Møller Jensen, 'King Erik Emune (1134–1137) and the crusades: the impact of crusading ideology on early twelfth-century Denmark' in Kurt Villads Jensen (ed.), *Cultural encounters during the crusades* (Odense, 2013), pp 91–104; Pål Berg Svenungsen, 'Norway and the Fifth Crusade: the crusade movement on the outskirts of Europe' in Elizabeth Jane Mylod, Guy J. Perry & Thomas W. Smith (eds), *The Fifth Crusade in context: the crusading movement in the early thirteenth century* (London, 2017), pp 218–29; Janne Malkki, Katja Ritari, Tuomas Lehtonen & Kurt Villads Jensen (eds), *Medieval history writing and crusading ideology* (Helsinki, 2005). Mikołaj Gładysz, *The forgotten crusaders: Poland and the crusader movement in the twelfth and thirteenth centuries* (Leiden, 2012); Darius von Güttner-Sporzyniski, 'Recent issues in Polish historiography of the crusades' in Judith Upton-Ward (ed.), *The military orders,* iv: *On land and by sea* (Aldershot, 2008), pp 13–21; Pavel Soukup, 'Pilgrimage elements in crusades with Czech participation in the twelfth century' in Daniel Doležal & Hartmut Kühne (eds), *Wallfahrten in der europäischen Kultur* (Frankfurt am-Main, 2006), pp 53–64; Attila Bárány, 'Crusades and crusading in Hungarian historiography' in Lévai Csaba (ed.), *Europe and the world in European historiography* (Pisa, 2006), pp 129–48; Weiler, *Negotium terrae sanctae,* 24–7, discusses the kingdoms of Hungary and Norway.

Ireland and the crusades: surveying the field

on England, Wales and Scotland.[32] However, as recently as 2013, one crusade historian observed that Ireland remains 'the least well served of the countries of the British Isles when it comes to crusader studies'.[33]

Another dimension of the historiographical issue, perhaps less obvious at first sight, might be found in the territory of the national grand narrative. In the history of medieval Ireland there can be little doubt that the grand narrative which long held the field was that of the famed 'isle of saints and scholars' (*insula sanctorum*). This vision of Ireland as western Europe's redoubt of Christian civilization goes back to the sixth and seventh centuries, but its afterglow endured long afterwards. It embraced, among others, the intellectuals of the Carolingian Renaissance such as John Scotus Eriugena (815–77), Sedulius Scottus (fl. 840–60), the scholar-monks of the Schottenklöster network of Benedictine monasteries in Germany in the eleventh century and, in the era of the crusades, St Laurence O'Toole (1128–80), archbishop of Dublin, and St Malachy of Armagh (1094–1198), friend and correspondent of St Bernard of Clairvaux.[34] Moreover, it is widely recognized that although the 'isle of saints and scholars' paradigm has its origins in the Middle Ages, it subsequently gained considerable traction in the early seventeenth century and then enjoyed a further heyday in the period *c*.1850–1950.[35] Notwithstanding deconstruction – and some derision – in recent scholarship, the paradigm had a notable influence on historical discourse throughout this time and its power 'in the Christian fairyland of the devout imagination' was even stronger.[36]

Given that a central premise of the 'saints and scholars' narrative was that Ireland carried a torch for Christian culture during the Middle Ages, dispatching pious émigrés to spread light and learning abroad, the discovery that the island also exported the religious intolerance and visceral violence associated with crusades might be discomforting to say the least. The fact that crusading recruitment was overwhelmingly concentrated in the parts of the island controlled by the Anglo-Normans also meant that crusade, viewed through

---

32 Simon Lloyd, *English society and the crusades, 1216–1307* (Oxford, 1988); Christopher Tyerman, *England and the crusades, 1095–1588* (Chicago, 1988); Alan McQuarrie, *Scotland and the crusades, 1095–1560* (Edinburgh, 1985); Kathryn Hurlock, *Wales and the crusades, c.1095–1291* (Cardiff, 2011). 33 Hurlock, *Crusades*, p. 4. 34 For Sedulius Scottus and John Scottus Eriugena see Aidan Breen, 'Sedulius Scottus (the "Irishman")' and Thomas O'Loughlin, 'John Scottus Eriugna', *DIB*; for a crusading connection to Ireland via the *Schottenklöster* see Diarmuid Ó Riain, 'An Irish Jerusalem in Franconia: the abbey of the Holy Cross and Holy Sepulchre in Eichstät', *PRIA* 112C (2012), 219–70; on St Laurence O'Toole and St Malachy see Marie Therese Flanagan, 'Laurence [St Laurence, Lorcán Ua Tuathail, Laurence O'Toole] (*c*.1128–1180)', *ODNB*; Flanagan, 'St Malachy, St Bernard of Clairvaux and the Cistercian order', *Archivium Hibernicum*, 68 (2015), 294–311. Picard, chapter 2, this volume. 35 Donnchadh Ó Corráin, 'Island of saints and scholars: myth or reality?' in Oliver P. Rafferty (ed.), *Irish Catholic identities* (Manchester, 2013), pp 32–61; Seán Duffy, *Ireland, 600–1169: an island of saints and scholars?* (London, 1993). 36 Ó Corráin, 'Island of saints and scholars', p. 50, n.3.

the 'saints and scholars' lens, might have appeared not only as barbaric and uncivilized, but also 'foreign'. For these reasons the story of Irish involvement in the crusades long sat uneasily in the national(ist) grand narrative of Ireland in the Middle Ages and was (consciously or sub-consciously) consigned to the shadows, from where it struggled to emerge, even when this particular historiographical star had begun to wane.[37]

In fact, even in modern standard reference works for the history of medieval Ireland the absence of discussion of the crusades is striking. In the first volume of the *New history of Ireland* covering the Middle Ages, published in 1987, crusade is only mentioned in passing, on a handful of occasions.[38] The *Cambridge history of Ireland*, published in 2018, is scarcely more informative, notwithstanding the appearance of a significant amount of new research on Irish involvement in the crusades in recent years (further discussed below).[39] There is no entry for 'crusade' in the *Medieval Ireland: an encyclopedia*.[40] The aim of all of these works is obviously to provide a comprehensive overview of medieval Ireland, yet an important aspect of medieval life is missing from all of them.

It should be emphasized that this historiographical blind spot (if such it might be called) cuts two ways. General histories of the crusades have consistently ignored Ireland. The well-known 'Wisconsin history of the crusades', published between the 1960s and the 1980s, and widely held at the time to be a definitive monument of crusades scholarship, makes no mention at all of Irish involvement in crusade, not even in the final volume of the series, entitled *The impact of the crusades on medieval Europe*.[41] And more recent exhaustive surveys of crusade history by leading specialists, such as Christopher Tyerman's *God's war*, similarly find no space for discussion of Ireland.[42] In short, a reading of general overviews of either the history of medieval Ireland or the history of the crusades might easily lead to the conclusion that Ireland's involvement with the crusades was negligible. Yet the substantial research outputs of recent years, including the essays contained in the present volume, suggest otherwise.

While it would be an exaggeration to claim that Ireland's engagement with the crusades, *in absolute terms*, was in any way similar in scale to other parts of western Europe that had far larger populations and greater resources, it is now equally apparent that it is a misrepresentation to dismiss it as non-existent.

---

37 For an insightful discussion of nationalist historiography of the Middle Ages see Art Cosgrove, 'The writing of Irish medieval history', *IHS* 27 (1990), 97–111, citing the earlier literature. 38 Art Cosgrove (ed.), *A new history of Ireland*, ii: *Medieval Ireland, 1169–1534* (Oxford, 1987; repr. 1993). 39 Brendan Smith (ed.), *The Cambridge history of Ireland*, iv: 600–1550 (Cambridge, 2018). 40 Ailbhe MacShamhráin, James Moynes, Peter Harbison & Seán Duffy (eds), *Medieval Ireland: an encyclopedia* (London, 2005). The entry on 'crannogs' is followed by the entry on 'cruthni'. 41 Setton, *The history of the crusades*, vi: *The impact of the crusades on Europe* (Madison, WI, 1989). 42 Christopher Tyerman, *God's war: a new history of the crusades* (London, 2006). The work is over 1,000 pages long.

In fact, thanks to recent research, it is now demonstrable that, *in relative terms*, Ireland was as affected as anywhere else by the crusades, and in similar ways. Efforts to bring the crusading message to the general population in Ireland are securely attested: in 1213, for example, Pope Innocent III exhorted the faithful to take the cross, appointing the archbishop of Dublin and abbot of Mellifont as official preachers of crusade.[43] In addition to the rare survival of letters, evidence for papal communication to Ireland is attested to by over sixty lead papal bullae seals, the majority of which date to the time of the crusades (pl. 1.1).[44] Royal missives carrying a similar message are not lacking. In 1250 King Henry III ordered the archbishop of Dublin 'to have the cause of the crusade preached throughout all Ireland'.[45] It is equally clear that such preaching had an effect: recent research has shown that people from Ireland took the cross and travelled to the Holy Land; the crusades exercised influence on the politics and finances of the Anglo-Norman lordship; and the crusading military orders left traces in the Irish landscape. Significantly, it has also been observed that although the military orders were international institutions, very few of the brothers ever left the country where they joined up.[46] In other words it was possible, indeed respectable, to be a 'professional crusader' without ever leaving home – a particularly pertinent consideration in the case of Ireland, which was about as distant from potential Muslim enemies as it was possible to be.[47]

These findings should not really come as a surprise. Ireland might have been located on the western edge of medieval Christendom but it was part of the same world and shared the same cultural and religious values. Crusade was a pan-European phenomenon that became firmly embedded in the mindset of Christian society over a period of more than two centuries. Recognizing this, one of the notable research trends in crusade historiography in recent decades has been towards the examination of the complex matrix of institutions, beliefs, expectations and actions that made up 'crusade'. This 'turn' in historical scholarship has led to the investigation of topics such as piety, preaching, pilgrimage, chivalry, music and – most recently – gender, masculinity, materiality,

---

43 Patrick J. Dunning, 'The letters of Innocent III to Ireland', *Traditio* 18 (1962), 229–53, at 244 nn 48, 49. The letter summarises the famous bull *Quia Maior* which launched the Fifth Crusade.   **44** Ragnall Ó Floinn, 'Papal bullae found in Ireland', *Ulster Journal of Archaeology* 74 (2017–18), 162–74; Matthew Seaver & Maeve Sikora, 'Miscellany', *JRSAI* 149 (2019), 166–70; Muireann Ní Cheallacháin, 'Preliminary report on excavations at Ardee, licence no. 21E0124' (Unpublished report, NMS Archives, 2021).   **45** *CDI* i, p. 457. Arrangements were made for copies of a papal letter recognizing Henry III's crusader vow to be distributed in Dublin, Cashel and Armagh, and for the mendicant friars to preach the crusade that the king intended to lead.   **46** Helen J. Nicholson, 'The changing face of the Templars', *History Compass* 8 (2010), 653–67.   **47** It has been calculated that the journey from Ireland to Jerusalem would have taken between eight and eleven weeks in the thirteenth century (Helen J. Nicholson, 'A long way from Jerusalem: the Templars and Hospitallers in Ireland *c*.1172–1348' in Brown & Ó Clabaigh, *Soldiers of Christ*, pp 1–22, at p. 1).

narrative, memory and othering.[48] The exploration of such issues in the context of Ireland and the crusades is obviously subject to the limitations of the source material that was noted earlier. Nevertheless, a number of new and important studies have begun to shine a light on some of them.

The real upsurge of interest in Ireland and the crusades began in the 1990s. In common with the pioneering research of Wood and Falkiner, more than a century ago, the preponderance of recent published work has been concerned with the military orders. This is understandable as the surviving sources provide more information about the Knights Templar and Knights Hospitaller than about any other aspect of crusading in Ireland. However, although the military orders have attracted the lion's share of scholarly attention, historians have been creative in piecing together fragmentary evidence to shed light on other topics, such as the level of participation in the crusades from Ireland, the motives of crusaders and the perception of crusade in Irish narrative sources. We shall start with a consideration of these aspects before returning, in conclusion, to new work on the military orders.

Kathryn Hurlock's 2013 survey of the crusades in the British Isles, which has already been cited in this essay, touches on all of the issues just mentioned, and now provides an accessible and up-to-date entry point to the study of

---

48 Marcus Bull, *Knightly piety and the lay response to the First Crusade: the Limousin and Gascony, c.970–1130* (Oxford, 1998); Christoph T. Maier, *Crusade propaganda and ideology: model sermons for the preaching of the cross* (Cambridge, 2000); Mikka Tamminen, *Crusade preaching and the ideal crusader* (Turnhout, 2018); William Purkis, *Crusade and pilgrimage spirituality, c.1095–c.1187* (Cambridge, 2007); Kathryn Hurlock & Paul Oldfield (eds), *Crusading and pilgrimage in the Norman world* (Woodbridge, 2015); Stefan Vander Elst, *The knight, the cross and the song: crusade propaganda and chivalric literature, 1100–1400* (Philadelphia, 2017); Linda Patterson, Luca Barbieri & Ruth Harvey (eds), *Singing the crusades: French and Occitan lyric responses to the crusading movements, 1137–1336* (Cambridge, 2018); Christoph T. Maier, 'The roles of women in crusade: a survey', *JMH* 30 (2004), 61–82; Susan Edington & Sarah Lambert (eds), *Gendering the crusades* (Cardiff, 2001); Natasha Hodgson, *Women, crusading and the Holy Land in historical narrative* (Woodbridge, 2007); Natasha Hodgson, Katherine Lewis & Matthew Mesley (eds), *Crusading and masculinities* (London, 2019); William Purkis, 'Introduction: material religion in the crusading world', *Material Religion* 14 (2018), 433–7 and '"Zealous imitation": the materiality of the crusader's marked body', *Material Religion* 14 (2018), 438–53; Marcus Bull & Damien Kempf (eds), *Writing the early crusades: texts, transmission and memory* (Woodbridge, 2014); Marcus Bull, *Eyewitness and crusade narrative: perception and narration in accounts of the Second, Third and Fourth Crusades* (Woodbridge, 2019); Nicholas L. Paul, *To follow in their footsteps: the crusades and family memory in the high Middle Ages* (Ithaca, NY, 2012); Nicholas L. Paul & Suzanne Yeager (eds), *Remembering the crusades: myth, image and identity* (Baltimore, 2012); Megan Cassidy-Welch & Anne E. Lester, 'Memory and interpretation: new approaches to the study of the crusades', *JMH* 40 (2014), 225–36; Megan Cassidy-Welch (ed.), *Remembering the crusades and crusading* (London, 2017); John Tolan, *Saracens: Islam in the medieval European imagination* (New York, 2002); Nicholas E. Morton, *Encountering Islam on the First Crusade* (Cambridge, 2016); Stephen Spencer, 'Emotions and the other: emotional characterizations of Muslim protagonists in narratives of the crusades' in Simon Parsons & Linda Patterson (eds), *Literature of the crusades* (Woodbridge, 2018), pp 41–54. I have here only listed some important works in English published since the late 1990s, but the literature is vast and in many languages.

Ireland and the crusades.[49] Hurlock devotes space to the question of whether the Anglo-Norman conquest itself was considered a crusade or a quasi-crusade in the eyes of contemporaries, judging that on balance it probably was not.[50] She also points to the close connection between the (partial) conquest and settlement of the island by the Anglo-Normans and participation in the crusades that not only linked Ireland into wider aristocratic networks stretching back to England and France, but also led to the establishment of institutional structures such as the shires, chancery and treasury that were integral to the organization of crusade.[51]

The level of Irish participation in the crusades is also examined in Hurlock's book. In Ireland crusaders largely came from the ranks of the Anglo-Noman settlers. Although the numbers seem small, when 'counting' Irish crusaders Hurlock stresses that every named crusader would have been accompanied by a retinue of vassals and retainers.[52] Curiously, royal leadership of crusading expeditions seems sometimes to have acted as a retardant rather than a stimulant to recruitment in Ireland; Henry III and Edward I (when he was lord of Ireland in the 1250s) actively discouraged the Anglo-Norman nobility from taking the cross on account of concern that the resulting exodus would lead to a lack of manpower in Ireland and a weakening of the defences of the lordship; both rulers were, however, happy to collect taxes to finance crusade expeditions even if these never actually departed in the end.[53]

For a slightly earlier period Denis Casey has looked in detail at the evidence for Irish crusaders in the Holy Land at the time of the First and Second Crusades (both of which took place before the Anglo-Norman invasion of Ireland). His findings were essentially negative; he concluded that: 'If Irishmen did join the crusades during the period under discussion, they do not appear to have left their mark on the documentary record of the kingdom of Jerusalem.'[54] However, while still never numerous, crusaders from Ireland are documented intermittently from the time of the Third Crusade (1189–92) onwards. There is even some evidence of a crusading tradition becoming established in Anglo-Norman families in Ireland, with participation spanning generations.[55] Paul Duffy has shown that Irish participation in crusading was

---

49 Hurlock, *Crusades.* The fact that Hurlock's work was not reviewed in any Irish historical journal suggests that the subject still struggles for recognition. **50** Ibid., pp 102–5. See also Maeve Callan, chapter 3, this volume. **51** Hurlock, *Crusades*, p. 21. **52** Ibid., pp 70, 81–2. **53** Ibid., p. 82. **54** Denis Casey, 'Irish involvement in the First and Second Crusades? A reconsideration of the eleventh- and twelfth-century evidence', *Crusades* 13 (2014), 119–42, at 139. **55** For example the de Verdun family: Hurlock, *Crusades*, p. 87; Mark S. Hagger, *The fortunes of a Norman family: the De Verduns in England, Ireland and Wales, 1066–1316* (Dublin, 2001), pp 28, 50 & 96. Similarly the de Geneville family: see Ciarán McDonnell, chapter 6, this volume.

not confined to making war on Islam but included other expeditions such in the infamous Albigensian Crusade (1209–29) directed against Cathar heretics in southern France, in which Hugh de Lacy II, earl of Ulster, took part.[56] The largest recruitment in Ireland for a single expedition was definitely the crusade of Lord Edward (the future Edward I) in 1270. Edward, as well as being the eldest son of Henry III and heir to the throne of England, was also lord of Ireland at this time.[57]

Possibly the most prominent figure who had both crusader and Irish connections in the twelfth and thirteenth centuries was William Marshal, regent of England, earl of Pembroke and lord of Leinster (c.1146–1219). In Ireland Marshal was a figure of great importance through his activities as a political leader, ecclesiastical patron and urban planner, as a recent collection of essays has demonstrated.[58] But his time in Ireland was bookended by episodes that show him to have also been a man deeply influenced by the ideals and practices of crusade in common with others of his social standing and background. In 1184 he had fulfilled the crusading vow of his deceased lord, Henry the Young King, by travelling to Jerusalem. He remained in the East for two years and was thus present in the Holy Land at a profound moment of crisis for the crusader states – the lead-up to the battle of Hattin (4 July 1187) and Saladin's conquest of Jerusalem.[59] Having returned from the East he went on to become a member of the inner circle of the crusader king par excellence, Richard I, and during the Third Crusade, he was entrusted with governmental responsibilities in England during Richard's absence.[60] The Marshal was close to the Templars and seems to have committed himself to joining the order, perhaps when he was in the Holy Land. He did indeed take the Templar habit

---

56 Paul Duffy, '"Ung sage et valent home": Hugh de Lacy and the Albigensian Crusade', *JRSAI* 141 (2011), 66–90; Paul Duffy & Daniel Brown, 'From Carrickfergus to Carcassonne: Hugh de Lacy and the Albigensian Crusade' in Paul Duffy, Tadhg O'Keeffe & Jean-Michel Picard (eds), *From Carrickfergus to Carcassonne: the epic deeds of Hugh de Lacy on the Albigensian Crusade*, pp 9–30. See also Paul Duffy, chapter 5, this volume. The subject of de Lacy's participation in Languedoc has also received thorough treatment in Daniel Brown, *Hugh de Lacy, first earl of Ulster: rising and falling in Angevin Ireland* (Woodbridge, 2016) and in Colin Veach, *Lordship in the four realms: the Lacy family, 1166–1241* (Manchester, 2015). 57 Hurlock, *Crusades*, p. 74; Simon Lloyd, *English society and the crusades 1216–1307* (Oxford, 1988), pp 113–53. 58 John Bradley, Cóilín Ó Drisceoil & Michael Potterton (eds), *William Marshal and Ireland* (Dublin, 2017). See also Ronan Mackay & David Beresford, 'Marshal, William', *DIB*. 59 William's receipt of the cross from Henry the young king and his stay in the East is described in the verse text of his life: *The history of William Marshal*, eds A.J. Holden, S. Gregory & D. Crouch (London, 2002–6), iii, pp 350–1, ll. 6891–905; p. 371, ll. 7275–301. See also Nicholas L. Paul, 'In search of the Marshal's lost crusade. The persistence of memory, the problems of history and the painful birth of crusade romance', *JMH* 40 (2014), 292–310; David Crouch, *William Marshal* (London, 2016), pp 67–8; Thomas Asbridge, *Greatest knight: the remarkable life of William Marshal, the power behind five English thrones* (London, 2015), pp 160–8. 60 David Crouch, 'Marshal, William [called the Marshal], fourth earl of Pembroke (c. 1146–1219), soldier and administrator', *ODNB*.

on his deathbed (1219) and was buried in the Templar church in London, where his tomb effigy survives.[61]

Aside from actual participation in the crusades, the awareness of and perception of the crusades in Ireland has been examined by Kathryn Hurlock on the basis of the evidence of the Irish annals.[62] Examining both Gaelic-Irish and Anglo-Irish annals, which together comprise a substantial body of narrative material, Hurlock observes that while notices concerning crusading are very sparse in the twelfth century, they increase considerably after *c*.1200. The Fifth Crusade, the crusades of King Louis IX, and that of the Lord Edward, were all the subjects of longer entries in the annals.[63] Unsurprisingly, the evidence for crusade participation occurs overwhelmingly in historical narratives produced in the area of Ireland controlled by the Anglo-Normans; the annalists of Gaelic Ireland appear largely uninterested in the crusades. For example, under 1095, the year in which Pope Urban II's proclamation of the First Crusade reverberated around Europe, the *Annals of Inisfallen* record: 'Snow and heavy frost so that the rivers and principal lakes of Ireland were frozen, and a great loss of cattle in this year ... A great mortality of the men of Ireland, so that it is impossible to enumerate all the people that died.'[64] Nevertheless, it has been suggested that other forms of writing in Irish of the twelfth century, notably poetry, might have been influenced by the rhetoric of holy war.[65] Moreover, for a later period, Aisling Byrne has drawn attention to the translation of romances and narratives about the crusades into Irish. She shows how, in the fifteenth century, tales of fictitious crusading knights such as 'Guy of Warwick' and 'Bevis of Hampton' became popular along with the proto-crusading exploits (also largely fictitious) of Charlemagne in Muslim Spain. The context here is probably the revival of crusader enthusiasm following the fall of Constantinople to the Ottoman Turks in 1453, and the vehicle of dissemination the religious orders, most prominently the Franciscan friars.[66]

The era of the so-called 'later crusades' (i.e. post-1291) saw abortive crusades – proposed or planned but never launched – in Ireland itself. Maeve Callan has highlighted the Anglo-Irish petition to the pope requesting a crusade against the 'heretic' Irish in 1331,[67] while Elizabeth Matthew has investigated an invitation sent a century later from the parliament of the lordship to

---

61 *The history of William Marshal*, ii, p. 18, ll. 179–260; Crouch, *William Marshal*, pp 173–6. Robin Griffith-Jones & David Park, *The Temple church in London. History, architecture and art* (Woodbridge, 2010). 62 Kathryn Hurlock, 'The crusades to 1291 in the annals of medieval Ireland', *IHS* 37 (2011), 517–34. 63 Ibid., 525–6. 64 *Annals of Inisfallen*, ed. Seán McAirt (Dublin, 1951): AI1095.2, AI1095.13. 65 Casey, 'Irish involvement', 140–1 and his references. 66 Aisling Byrne, 'Translating the crusades in late medieval Ireland' in Aisling Byrne & Victoria Flood (eds), *Crossing borders in the insular Middle Ages* (Turnhout, 2019), pp 161–77; the essay contains a detailed examination of the manuscript traditions of the texts under discussion. 67 Callan, *Templars*, pp 207–12.

King Henry V (1421) urging him to lead a crusade against the Gaelic-Irish and to seek papal approval for it.[68] Later still, during the Counter-Reformation, the tables were turned and a crusade indulgence was sought from the pope (with more success) for the Irish supporters of the Desmond rebellions (1569–73 and 1579–83), and the uprising of Hugh O'Neill and Red Hugh O'Donnell (1593–1602) against the English crown.[69]

Returning finally to consider the crusading military orders, there can be no doubt that the presence of the Knights Templar and Knights Hospitaller in Ireland would have been a constant reminder of the ongoing crusade effort in the East during the twelfth and thirteenth centuries; the orders were formed, after all, with the specific purpose of coordinating Christian holy war in the Holy Land. The Templars, also known as the Poor Knights of Christ, and the Order of the Hospital of St John, also known as the Knights Hospitaller, both arrived in Ireland in the 1170s at the time of – some have argued possibly even as part of – King Henry II's expedition.[70] Both orders established a network of bases (preceptories) with associated estates mainly in the east of the island in the course of the thirteenth century. The knights became wealthy and prominent members of the Anglo-Norman elite. Their influence and power were no doubt boosted by their closeness to the English crown and leading members of the settler class. The aspects of the history of the orders that have particularly attracted attention are their actions in support of Anglo-Norman rule in the lordship, both as administrators and in a military capacity, their acquisition and management of extensive landholdings, their vigorous defence of their rights in the courts, and finally the material impact they made on the Irish landscape through their construction of preceptories and patronage of churches.

The leading expert on the history or the crusading military orders in the British Isles is undoubtedly Helen Nicholson, whose many publications have thrown light on various aspects of their activities.[71] Her research on the orders in Ireland has investigated their involvement in administrative positions in the lordship,[72] as well as the military campaigns that they led against the

---

68 Elizabeth Matthew, 'Henry V and the proposal for an Irish crusade' in Brendan Smith (ed.), *Ireland and the English world in the late Middle Ages* (Basingstoke, 2009), pp 161–75. 69 See Kathryn Hurlock, chapter 12, this volume. 70 For further consideration of this issue see Maeve Callan, chapter 3, this volume. 71 Helen J. Nicholson, *The Knights Hospitaller* (Woodbridge, 2001); *The Knights Templar: a new history* (Stroud, 2001). Among her articles, see 'The military orders in the towns of the British Isles' in D. Carraz (ed.), *Les ordres militaires dans la ville médiévale (1100–1350)* (Clermont-Ferrand, 2013), pp 113–26; 'The Hospitallers in medieval Britain' in Jurgen Sarnowsky, Krystof Kwiatkowski, Hubert Houben, Laszlo Posan & Attila Barany (eds), *Studies on the military orders, Prussia, and urban history* (Debrecen, 2020), pp 41–55. 72 Helen J. Nicholson, 'Serving king and crusade: the military orders in royal service in Ireland, 1220–1400' in Marcus Bull & Norman Housley (eds), *The experience of crusading*, i: *Western approaches* (Cambridge, 2003), pp 233–52.

Ireland and the crusades: surveying the field

Gaelic-Irish on behalf of the English crown.[73] Most recently she has looked at the knights as religious orders and investigated their relations with the regular clergy.[74] In addition to her edition of the records of the trial of the Irish Templars, mentioned earlier, she has also analysed the Irish trial proceedings in the context of the Europe-wide process that ultimately resulted in the suppression of the order and the execution of Templar Grand Master Jacques de Molay as a heretic in Paris in 1314.[75]

The early 2000s also saw the appearance of a number of other publications on the military orders in Ireland. Eithne Massey provided a biography of one of the best documented priors of the Hospital in Ireland, Roger Outlaw (fl. 1316–41), for whom the *Registrum de Kilmainham* was compiled.[76] Roger Outlaw or Utlagh was clearly a leading figure not only in the Hospitallers but also in the lordship. At various times in the 1320s and 1330s he held the posts of chancellor of Ireland, lieutenant and justiciar.[77] He led a military campaign against Brian Bán O'Brien, lord of Thomond, and imprisoned Maurice fitz Thomas fitz Gerald, first earl of Desmond. He also became involved in the notorious Alice Kyteler witchcraft trial in support of his kinsman William Outlaw, which drew him into a feud with Kyteler's accuser, Richard Ledrede, bishop of Ossory.[78] The history of the Hospitallers in the fifteenth and sixteenth centuries has been meticulously examined by Gregory O'Malley.[79] He concurs with the view that the priors of the Hospitallers were major figures in the later medieval lordship, noting that there were 'ideal soldier-administrators of a type always needed in Ireland'.[80] Otherwise the picture in this period is one of re-organization, retrenchment and decline, exacerbated by interference from the English *langue* and the English crown.[81] Nevertheless, in spite of economic

---

73 Helen J. Nicholson, 'The Knights Hospitaller on the frontiers of the British Isles' in Jürgen Sarnowsky (ed.), *Mendicants, military orders and regionalism in medieval Europe* (Aldershot, 1999), 47–58 and 'The Hospitallers' and Templars' involvement in warfare on the frontiers of the British Isles in the late thirteenth and early fourteenth centuries' in Jürgen Sarnowsky (ed.), *Ordines militaris colloquia Torunensia historica* (Toruń, 2012), 105–19. 74 Helen J. Nicholson, 'Evidence of the Templars' religious practice from the records of the Templars' estates in Britain and Ireland in 1308' in Iris Shagrir, Benjamin Z. Kedar & Michel Balard (eds), *Communicating the Middle Ages*. Subsidia 11 (London, 2018), pp 50–63; 'Negotiation and conflict: the Templars' and Hospitallers' relations with diocesan bishops in Britain and Ireland' in Thomas W. Smith (ed.), *Authority and power in the medieval church, c.1000–1500* (Turnhout, 2020), pp 371–89. 75 Helen J. Nicholson, 'The testimony of Brother Henry Danet and the trial of the Templars in Ireland' in Iris Shagrir, Ronnie Ellenblum & Jonathan Riley-Smith (eds), *Laudem Hieroslymitani*. Subsidia 1 (Aldershot, 2008), pp 411–23; 'The trial of the Templars in Ireland' in Jochen Burgtorf, Paul Fleming Crawford & Helen Nicholson (eds), *The debate on the trial of the Templars, 1307–1314* (Farnham, 2010), pp 225–36. 76 Eithne Massey, *Prior Roger Outlaw of Kilmainham* (Dublin, 2000). 77 Nicholson, 'Serving king and crusade', p. 238. 78 Callan, *Templars*. 79 Gregory O'Malley, *The Knights Hospitaller of the English langue, 1460–1565* (Oxford, 2005), ch. 7. There is a useful list of the priors of Ireland, 1420–1540 (appendix IV). 80 Ibid., pp 228–9. 81 The 'English *langue*' refers to representatives from the priories of England and Ireland based in the Hospitaller convent on Rhodes and, later, Malta.

problems and military threats, the order remained a powerful institution on the island right up until the Dissolution. Niall Byrne traces the history of both Templars and Hospitallers (as well as other orders, such as the Knights of St Thomas of Acre) even further – from their arrival on Ireland in the late twelfth century, through the Middle Ages and beyond, up until the Williamite Wars of the 1680/90s.[82]

In 2013 a landmark conference on the crusading military orders in Ireland was held in Glenstal abbey, Co. Limerick, and the subsequent published volume of essays has added substantially to our knowledge.[83] The contributions span a long period from the arrival of the orders in Ireland in the late 1100s to the seventeenth century, and take in a wide range of topics. Six essays cover the Hospitallers alone while the remainder deal with either the Templars or both orders. Helen Nicholson provides an overview of the orders' histories in Ireland up until the time of the Black Death, by which time the Templars had been suppressed and their properties had been taken over by the Hospitallers.[84] The later medieval and post-medieval history of the Hospitallers is addressed in the essays by Gregory O'Malley and Brendan Scott. O'Malley charts the order's slow decline and subjection to the English *langue*.[85] Scott traces the fate of Hospitaller assets during the Dissolution of the monasteries.[86] Declan Downey shows that even when the Hospitallers had finally disappeared from Ireland's shores altogether following the Dissolution, the titular priors of the Irish order kept its memory alive at the royal court of Spain.[87] Essays by Edward Coleman and Paolo Virtuani explore the litigation in defence of their rights pursued by the Templars and Hospitallers.[88]

---

82 Niall Byrne, *The Irish crusade: a history of the Knights Hospitaller, the Knights Templar, and the Knights of Malta in the south-east of Ireland* (Dublin, 2007). The title is slightly misleading as a considerable part of the book is not focussed on the military orders in Ireland, but on the crusades in the East and events in England and the Irish lordship. Byrne's detailed reconstruction of the estates of the orders in counties Waterford and Wexford is useful. He also provides a new translation of the lengthy section – relating to the south-east of Ireland – of the inventory of Templar possessions drawn up by the Irish exchequer in 1328 after the suppression of the order (appendix B). However, his study must be read with caution. There are some highly speculative statements concerning, for example, Giraldus Cambrensis (pp 52, 84) and Maurice de Prendergast, an early prior of the Irish Hospitallers (pp 51–5, 57, 60), and in places he is rather credulous of local traditions. 83 Brown & Ó Clabaigh, *Soldiers of Christ*. 84 Nicholson, 'A long way from Jerusalem'. 85 Gregory O'Malley, 'Authority and autonomy: relations between Clerkenwell, Kilmainham and the Hospitaller central convent after the Black Death' in Brown & Ó Clabaigh, *Soldiers of Christ*, pp 23–46. 86 Brendan Scott, 'The Knights Hospitaller in Tudor Ireland: their dissolution and attempted revival' in Brown & Ó Clabaigh, *Soldiers of Christ*, pp 47–60. 87 Declan M. Downey, 'Continuity, legitimacy and strategy: the titular priors of Ireland – Romegas, González, Wyse and Brochero – and their relations with the Spanish monarchy, 1576–1625' in Brown & Ó Clabaigh, *Soldiers of Christ*, pp 61–80. 88 Edward Coleman '"Powerful adversaries": the Knights Templar, landholding and litigation in the lordship of Ireland' in Brown & Ó Clabaigh, *Soldiers of Christ*, pp 184–94; Paolo Virtuani, 'Unforgivable trespass: the Irish Hospitallers and the defence of their rights in the mid-thirteenth century' in Brown & Ó Clabaigh, *Soldiers of Christ*, pp 195–205.

Ireland and the crusades: surveying the field

The volume is notable also for the ample space dedicated to economic history and material culture which had hitherto received scant attention in the scholarship on the orders in Ireland. Margaret Murphy looks at the orders' agriculture and estate management, drawing on the informative inventories of preceptories such as Clonoulty, Co. Limerick, the richest Templar house in Ireland, compiled after the order's suppression.[89] Although traces of extant remains are few and unimpressive, three essays by archaeologists reveal that the orders were responsible for a significant amount of building across Ireland. Tadhg O'Keeffe and Pat Grogan discuss architectural aspects of the structures built by the orders, drawing parallels with evidence from England.[90] Kieran O'Conor and Paul Naessens conduct an integrated architectural, historical and landscape analysis of the evocatively named Temple House, Co. Sligo.[91] Eamon Cotter presents the results of excavations and survey work at the sites of Mourneabbey, Co. Cork, and Hospital, Co. Limerick.[92] The order knights were not noted patrons of the arts but there are some hints of an interest in visual culture, which Paul Caffrey surveys in his essay.[93] These consist of sculptural fragments, grave slabs, tomb effigies (possibly including that of Roger Outlaw), as well as some portraits, engravings and heraldic manuscript illustrations. A manuscript is also the subject of Colmán Ó Clabaigh's essay, which closes the volume. This intriguing survival – Cambridge, Corpus Christi College MS 405 – is a compilation of liturgical, legislative, literary and devotional texts associated with the Hospitaller (formerly Templar) preceptory of Kilbarry, Co. Waterford.[94] The contents are eclectic to say the least. In addition to documents illustrating the order's close municipal (Waterford) and royal connections, it includes a significant amount of Irish hagiographical material (on St Patrick, St Brigid and St Finbarr); there is also an Anglo-Norman poem describing the origins of the Hospital of St John, further poetry on Marian and theological themes as well as healing charms, cures and recipes. Ó Clabaigh postulates that the codex was put together at the time of the transfer of Kilbarry from the Templars to the Hospitallers and notes that it gives a 'remarkable insight into the influence, organization and religious

89 Margaret Murphy, 'From swords to ploughshares: evidence for Templar agriculture in medieval Ireland' in Brown & Ó Clabaigh, *Soldiers of Christ*, pp 167–83. 90 Tadhg O'Keeffe & Pat Grogan, 'Building a frontier? The architecture of the military orders in medieval Ireland' in Brown & Ó Clabaigh, *Soldiers of Christ*, pp 81–102. 91 Kieran O'Connor & Paul Naessens, 'Temple House: from Templar castle to New English mansion' in Brown & Ó Clabaigh, *Soldiers of Christ*, pp 124–50. 92 Eamonn Cotter, 'The archaeology of the Irish Hospitaller preceptories of Mourneabbey and Hospital in context' in Brown & Ó Clabaigh, *Soldiers of Christ*, pp 103–12. 93 Paul Caffrey, 'The visual culture of the Hospitaller Knights of the priory of Ireland' in Brown & Ó Clabaigh, *Soldiers of Christ*, pp 151–66. 94 Colmàn Ó Clabaigh, 'Prayers, politics and poetry: Cambridge, Corpus Christi College MS 405 and the Templars and Hospitallers at Kilbarry, Co. Waterford' in Brown & Ó Clabaigh, *Soldiers of Christ*, pp 206–13.

and devotional concerns of the Knights Hospitaller in Ireland from the early fourteenth century onwards'.

Overall this collection of essays makes it abundantly clear that although the ostensible purpose of the military orders throughout their existence was the defence of Christians in the Holy Land and the prosecution of crusade, the day-to-day reality was that the knights became totally immersed in Irish society; their principal concerns were land-owning, farming and commerce; their buildings dotted the landscape; their high social status brought them positions of power and responsibility in the lordship; their elite connections could be used to swing lawsuits in their favour.

Since the *Soldiers of Christ* conference, further works have continued to appear: the career of another Hospitaller Prior, William fitz Roger (fl. 1274–94), has been considered by Edward Coleman.[95] Maeve Callan has looked at the fate of Templars in comparison with others tried for heresy and witchcraft in fourteenth-century Ireland.[96] Tadhg O'Keeffe and Paolo Virtuani have provided a case study reconstructing the layout of the chief Hospitaller preceptory in Ireland at Kilmainham, just west of Dublin, using late medieval and early modern historical and topographical evidence.[97] The authors point to the early fourteenth century as a time of the greatest expansion of Kilmainham due to the acquisition of the properties of the Knights Templar in Ireland and the rise in the number of corrodians, in effect paying guests, who had purchased the right to live in the precinct of the preceptory and share in its privileges.[98] Their architectural reconstruction reveals that Kilmainham was strongly fortified with a *turris*, a ditch and an impressive drawbridge.[99] The interior or castle enclosure was walled and contained a great hall, within which was located the *mensa prioris Hospitalis*, a chapel, a prison and various residential buildings, including the dwellings of the corrodians, which they built at their own expense. An outer enclosure contained ancillary buildings such as stables, a forge, a granary and a dairy, plus further house plots. Despite the lack of upstanding remains, the overall impression is of a sizable and imposing complex, as was befitting of the headquarters of the most important military order in Ireland. It would have dominated the western approaches to the medieval city of Dublin in a similar way to its successor building, the Royal Hospital of Kilmainham in the eighteenth century.[100]

---

95 Edward Coleman, 'The crusader's tale' in Cherie Peters & Sparky Brooker (eds), *Tales of medieval Dublin* (Dublin 2014), pp 92–101.   96 Callan, *Templars*.   97 O'Keeffe & Virtuani, 'Reconstructing Kilmainham'.   98 Ibid., 461.   99 Ibid., 464–6, O'Malley, *The Knights Hospitaller*, pp 233–4, notes that several Hospitaller preceptories appear to have reinforced their defences in the fourteenth, fifteenth and sixteenth centuries.   100 O'Keeffe & Virtuani, 'Reconstructing Kilmainham', 476–7.

Ireland and the crusades: surveying the field

Recent discussion of the military orders takes us back to our starting point – the venerable articles of Wood and Falkiner. Despite the wilderness years that followed, interest in Ireland and the crusades has not only revived but continues to grow apace.[101] Recent publications demonstrate unequivocally that the subject is no longer *terra incognita.* The last two decades have seen notable advances of our understanding both of the participation of people from Ireland in the crusades and the impact of the crusading movement on Ireland. The present volume is therefore a contribution to an expanding body of scholarship that is filling a gap in our understanding of Ireland in the Middle Ages. In 1907 Caesar Litton Falkiner wrote that the history of Kilmainham, the headquarters of the crusading Knights Hospitaller in Ireland, was replete 'with remarkable personages and with interesting events'. He continued: 'it is not ... to be ignored by anyone who cares for historical associations, or feels the attraction that lies in the recovery of lost traditions and in the identification of the scenes of memorable episodes'.[102] The same could be said of the history of Ireland and the crusades as a whole.

---

101 The most recent publication to appear at the time of writing is Rory MacLellan, *Donations to the Knights Hospitaller in Britain and Ireland, 1291–1400* (London, 2021), which looks afresh at the patterns of patronage of the later Hospitallers, their charitable activities and hospitality. **102** Falkiner, 'Hospital', 275.

2 / Inspiring Irish crusaders: St Bernard's writings and Cistercian impact

JEAN-MICHEL PICARD

INTRODUCTION

The establishment of the Latin kingdom of Jerusalem in 1099 after the success of the first crusade provoked a very strong reaction in the Muslim world, with lasting effects. In the conflicts between Muslim and Christian warriors from the seventh and the eleventh centuries, war had mostly been a tool for territorial expansion. After the First Crusade, it acquired a new meaning and purpose, that of holy war ('jihad'). The word 'jihad' occurs several times in the Quran, but mostly in the sense of 'effort' or 'striving' to become a better person and to contribute actively to God's plan for the human race.[1] The more common use of this word today, with the meaning of 'holy war', is a development of the early twelfth century, found in commentaries of the Quran and in treatises written by Middle Eastern scholars.[2] One such text was the *Kitab al Jihad* ('Book of the Jihad'), written by the Syrian scholar Ali ibn Tahir al-Sulami in 1105.[3] His book is a call to all Muslims to get together and organize themselves to fight against the Christians who had invaded the Middle East and taken Jerusalem:

> A number of the enemy pounced on the island of Sicily while the Muslims disputed and competed, and they conquered in the same way one city after another in al-Andalus. When the reports confirmed for them that this country suffered from the disagreement of its masters and its rulers' meddling, with its consequent disorder and disarray, they confirmed their resolution to set out for it, and Jerusalem was their dearest wish. They looked out from al-Sham [a region in what is now modern

---

1 For a clear and succinct presentation of the different meanings of jihad in Islamic tradition, see Douglas E. Streusand, 'What does jihad mean?', *Middle East Quarterly* 4: 3 (1997), 9–17.   2 See Ahmed al-Dawoody, *The Islamic law of war* (New York, 2011), pp 43–70; Suleiman A. Mourad & James E. Lindsay, *The intensification and reorientation of Sunni jihad: ideology in the crusader period: Ibn 'Asākir of Damascus (1105–1176) and his age, with an edition and translation of Ibn'Asākir's 'The forty hadiths for inciting jihad'* (Leiden, 2013), pp 16–62.   3 Niall Christie, *The book of the jihad of 'Ali ibn Tahir al-Sulami (d. 1106): text, translation and commentary* (London, 2016); Nikita Elisséeff, 'The reaction of the Syrian muslims after the foundation of the first Latin kingdom of Jerusalem' in M. Shatzmiller (ed.), *Crusaders and muslims in twelfth-century Syria* (Leiden, 1993), pp 162–72.

Syria] on separated kingdoms, disunited hearts and differing views laced with hidden resentment, and with that, their desires became stronger and extended to whatever their outstretched arms could desire. They did not stop, tireless in fighting the jihad against the Muslims. The Muslims were sluggish, avoiding fighting them and reluctant to engage in combat until the enemy had conquered more of the country than their greatest hopes had conceived and destroyed and humiliated many times the number of people that they had wished.[4]

… In this way it is obligatory on our sultans and whomever God, be He praised, has appointed to rule us, may God make good their peacemaking and guidance, that they emulate those like them who preceded them … Helping them and aiding them all that they can, applying their hands and abilities to the cause, and taking on all this burden and toil in targeting this group [of enemies], is obligatory on all the people, be they soldiers, citizens, peasants or all the rest of the people. Even the smallest contribution will be appreciated. They will perform in their jihad many times what people did in their military expeditions to their lands and the lands of the Rum [the eastern Mediterranean], to drive them from there and efface their traces.[5]

This text did not get a wide circulation outside Syria, but corresponds to a significant development in Muslim thought where jihad doctrine became a subject of debate among scholars, including the great philosopher al-Ghazali (d. 1111). On the Christian side, there was no such text. The concept of just war had been studied by Augustine,[6] but there was no text in the Christian tradition summoning the warrior class and 'all the rest of the people' to a holy war against enemies of their faith. However, the military activity of European warriors in the Middle East that had inspired Al Sulami also provided the context for a new Christian doctrine of the just war. Over a period of twenty years in the 1130s and 1140s, Bernard de Clairvaux, one of the most influential thinkers in the history of the Church, provided a series of texts justifying the waging of war for religious reasons and promoting the ideal the crusade. His treatise, *De laude novae militiae* ('In Praise of the New Knighthood'), written

4 *Kitab al Jihad*, ff 174b-5a (*'Ali ibn Tahir al-Sulami: the Book of the jihad of 'Ali ibn Tahir al-Sulami (d. 1106): text, translation and commentary*, ed. Niall Christie (London, 2016), pp 206–7). 5 *Kitab al Jihad*, f. 189b (*'Ali ibn Tahir al-Sulami*, pp 234–5). 6 For detailed commentaries of texts by St Augustine concerning war, see Robert Regout, *La doctrine de la guerre juste de saint Augustin à nos jours d'après les théologiens et les canonistes Catholiques* (Paris, 1935); Frank Bourgeois, 'La théorie de la guerre juste: un héritage chrétien?', *Études théologiques et religieuses* 81 (2006), 449–74.

between 1128 and 1136 for the Knights Templar, gives a new interpretation of the concept of the *militia Christi*, dear to the founders of early Christian monasticism.[7] While the original context of the *militia Christi* ideal, like that of jihad in Islam, was the fight against sinful and negative tendencies within oneself and against the devil, this fight was transposed to the military realm in the context of physical fighting against the enemies of one's religion. After nearly 800 years of promotion of the 'white martyrdom',[8] the ultimate sacrifice of those who devoted themselves to ascetic life,[9] red martyrdom was back in the forefront. The new martyrs would be those who died in battle in the defence of their faith:

> Go forth confidently then, you knights, and repel the foes of the cross of Christ with a stalwart heart. Know that neither death nor life can separate you from the love of God which is in Jesus Christ, and in every peril repeat, 'Whether we live or whether we die, we are the Lord's'. What a glory to return in victory from such a battle! How blessed to die there as a martyr! Rejoice, brave athlete, if you live and conquer in the Lord; but glory and exult even more if you die and join your Lord. Life indeed is a fruitful thing and victory is glorious, but a holy death is more important than either. If they are blessed who die in the Lord, how much more are they who die for the Lord! To be sure, precious in the eyes of the Lord is the death of his holy ones, whether they die in battle or in bed, but death in battle is more precious as it is the more glorious.[10]

7 See Adolf von Harnack, *Militia Christi: die christliche religion und der soldatenstand in den ersten drei jahrhunderten* (Tübingen, 1905); English translation by David McInnes Gracie, *Militia Christi: the Christian religion and the military in the first three centuries by Adolf von Harnack* (Philadelphia, 1982). 8 Separation from all that one loved, generally through pilgrimage; 'red martyrdom' was achieved through torture or death. 9 See Clare Stancliffe, 'Red, white and blue martyrdom' in Dorothy Whitelock, Rosamund McKitterick & David N. Dumville (eds), *Ireland in early medieval Europe* (Cambridge, 1982), pp 21–46; Jean-Michel Picard, 'The colour purple: cultural cross-fertilisation and translation in early medieval Ireland' in E. Bremer, J. Jarnut, M. Richter & D. Wasserstein (eds), *Language of the people – language of religion: medieval Judaism, Christianity and Islam* (Munich, 2007), pp 241–49. 10 Bernard of Clairvaux, *De laude novae militiae*, eds Jean Leclercq, Charles Talbot & Henri-Marie Rochais, *Sancti Bernardi Opera* (Rome, 1963), iii, pp 212–39, pp 214–15: 'Securi igitur procedite, milites, et intrepido animo inimicos crucis Christi propellite, certi quia neque mors, neque vita poterunt vos separare a charitate Dei, quae est in Christo Jesu; illud sane vobiscum in omni periculo replicantes: "Sive vivimus, sive morimur, Domini sumus". Quam gloriosi revertuntur victores de praelio! quam beati moriuntur martyres in praelio! Gaude, fortis athleta, si vivis et vincis in Domino: sed magis exsulta et gloriare, si moreris et jungeris Domino. Vita quidem fructuosa, et victoria gloriosa: sed utrique mors sacra jure praeponitur. Nam si beati qui in Domino moriuntur, num multo magis qui pro Domino moriuntur? Et quidem sive in lecto, sive in bello quis moritur, pretiosa erit sine dubio in conspectu Domini mors sanctorum ejus. Caeterum in bello tanto profecto pretiosior, quanto et gloriosior.'

In promoting military fighting, St Bernard did not advocate violence for the sake of violence but only as the last resort left to good people when faced with a persistent evil-doer:

> The knight of Christ, I say, may strike with confidence and die yet more confidently, for he serves Christ when he strikes, and serves himself when he falls. Neither does he bear the sword in vain, for he is God's minister for the punishment of evildoers and for the praise of the good. If he kills an evildoer, he is not a man-killer but, if I may say so, a killer of evil. He is evidently the avenger of Christ towards evildoers and he is rightly considered a defender of Christians. Should he be killed himself, we know that he has not perished, but has come safely into port ... I do not mean to say that the pagans are to be slaughtered when there is any other way to prevent them from harassing and persecuting the faithful, but only that it now seems better to destroy them than that the rod of sinners be lifted over the lot of the just, and the righteous perhaps put forth their hands unto iniquity.[11]

The role of St Bernard in the Second Crusade is well known.[12] Between the fall of Edessa to the Turks in late 1144 and Easter 1146 when Louis VII, king of France, convened his vassals at Vezelay to launch the crusade, Bernard had acted as an intermediary between Pope Eugenius III, a former Cistercian monk, and the French king to put together a military campaign to recover Christian lands recently lost in the Middle East. Invested with the authority of the pope, Bernard gave a famous sermon at Vezelay, which galvanized the large crowd gathered there to such an extent that not enough cross insignias could be supplied to satisfy the demand of all those who wanted to join the crusade. The chronicler Odo of Deuil, who reported the event, adds that the crowd started shouting for crosses as soon as they heard St Bernard's voice, which sounded like a heavenly musical instrument (*caelestum organum*).[13]

---

11 Ibid., p. 217: 'Caput III. De Militibus Christi. [...] Miles, inquam, Christi securus interimit, interit securior. Sibi praestat cum interit, Christo cum interimit. Non enim sine causa gladium portat. Dei etenim minister est ad vindictam malefactorum, laudem vero bonorum. Sane cum occidit malefactorem, non homicida, sed, ut ita dixerim, malicida, et plane Christi vindex in his qui male agunt, et defensor Christianorum reputatur. Cum autem occiditur ipse, non periisse, sed pervenisse cognoscitur. [...] Non quidem vel Pagani necandi essent, si quo modo aliter possent a nimia infestatione seu oppressione fidelium cohiberi. Nunc autem melius est ut occidantur, quam certe relinquatur virga peccatorum super sortem justorum: ne forte extendant justi ad iniquitatem manus suas.' 12 Michael Gervers (ed.), *The Second Crusade and the Cistercians* (New York, 1992); John R. Sommerfeldt, 'The Bernardine reform and the crusading spirit', *The Catholic Historical Review* 86 (2000), 567–78. 13 Odo of Deuil: *De profectione Ludovici VII in Orientem*, ed. V.G. Berry (New York, 1948), p. 8.

42   *Ireland and the crusades*

In spite of the success of St Bernard's predication at Vezelay, confirmed by several sources, the text of his sermon does not survive. As Hans-Dietrich Kahl already suggested, the failure of the Second Crusade and the subsequent embarrassment in France might be the reason why Clairvaux might have chosen not to publish copies of this sermon.[14] However, in 1146 and 1147 Bernard wrote several letters in support of the crusades, which were sent to recipients in England, Germany, and Bohemia, and have survived there in a number of manuscripts.[15]

As Dom Jean Leclercq showed,[16] it is worth looking at the different medieval manuscripts of the letters, which were edited in the seventeenth century by Mabillon and again by Leclercq and Rochais in 1974 and 1977.[17] For example, letter 363, generally believed to have been sent to Germany (*ad archiepiscopos Orientalis Franciae et Bavariae*), was also sent to England (*ad gentem Anglorum*) in 1146. In this letter Bernard challenges all brave men to take arms and save Jerusalem and the Holy Land:

> And now, for our sins, the enemies of the Cross have raised blaspheming heads, ravaging with the edge of the sword the land of promise. For they are almost on the point, if there be not one to withstand them, of bursting into the very city of the living God, of overturning the sanctuaries of our redemption, of polluting the holy places of the spotless Lamb with purple blood. Alas! They rage against the very shrine of the Christian Faith with blasphemous mouths, and would enter and trample down the very couch on which for us our Life lay down to sleep in death. What are you doing then, O brave men? What are you doing, O servants of the Cross? Will you give what is holy to the dogs, and cast your pearls to swine?[18]

---

14 Hans-Dietrich Kahl, 'Die kreuzzugseschatologie Bernhards von Clairvaux und ihre missionsgeschichtliche auswirkung' in Dieter R. Bauer & Gotthard Fuchs (eds), *Bernhard von Clairvaux und der beginn der moderne* (Innsbruck, 1996), pp 262–315, at pp 289–93; Hans-Dietrich Kahl, 'Crusade eschatology as seen by St Bernard in the years 1146 to 1148' in Michael Gervers (ed.), *The Second Crusade and the Cistercians* (New York, 1992), pp 35–47.   15 See Jean Leclercq, 'L'encyclique de saint Bernard en faveur de la croisade' in J. Leclercq (ed.), *Recueil d'études sur saint Bernard et ses écrits* (Rome, 1987), iv, pp 227–46; Jean Leclercq, 'Pour l'histoire de l'encyclique de saint Bernard sur la croisade' in J. Leclercq (ed.), *Recueil d'études sur saint Bernard et ses écrits* (Rome, 1987), iv, pp 247–63.   16 Leclercq, 'L'encyclique de saint Bernard', pp 229–43.   17 *Sancti Bernardi Opera*, vii, *Epistolae*, i (Rome, 1974) and viii, *Epistolae*, ii (Rome, 1977).   18 Bernard of Clairvaux, *Epistola CCCLXIII Ad archiepiscopos Orientalis Franciae et Bavariae, Sancti Bernardi Opera*, viii, pp 311–17, pp 312–13: 'Et nunc peccatis nostris exigentibus, crucis adversarii caput extulerunt sacrilegum, depopulantes in ore gladii terram promissionis. Prope enim est, si non fuerit qui resistat, ut in ipsam Dei viventis irruant civitatem, ut officinas nostrae redemptionis evertant, ut polluant loca sancta, Agni immaculati purpurata cruore. Ad ipsum, proh dolor! religionis Christianae sacrarium inhiant ore sacrilego, lectumque ipsum invadere et conculcare conantur, in quo propter nos Vita nostra obdormivit in morte. 2. Quid facitis, viri fortes? quid facitis, servi crucis? Itane dabitis sanctum canibus, et margaritas porcis?'

Inspiring Irish crusaders: St Bernard's writings and Cistercian impact

He sent a similar letter to Duke Wladislas of Bohemia, his vassals and the people of Bohemia, where he reiterates the offer made by Pope Eugenius III in his bull *Quantum praedecessores nostri* (1 December 1145) granting a plenary indulgence to those who would join the crusade:

> Why do you delay, servants of the cross? Why do you hide, you who are in possession of both bodily strength and material wealth? Take up the sign of the Cross and you will be granted a plenary indulgence for all the sins that you will have confessed with a contrite heart, by the supreme Pontiff, the vicar of him to whom it was said: 'Whatever thou shall loose on earth shall be loosed in heaven'. Accept the gift that is offered you, and hasten and vie with each other to avail of this opportunity for indulgence, which will not recur.[19]

In the pope's bull, the offer of a full remission of all sins in case of death in battle went hand in hand with the concept of crusade as a pilgrimage, a holy journey (*iter sanctum*). While greed and the prospect of acquiring new lands has often been put forward as the main motive behind the crusades, religious motives were important and the offer of a plenary indulgence, reiterated by popes throughout the Middle Ages, was a strong and convincing argument in deciding to take up the cross.[20]

The same argument is further developed in a letter Bernard sent after the Diet of Frankfurt in March 1147 to promote the extension of the Second Crusade to eastern Europe against the Slavic-speaking Wends:

> For, since the Lord has entrusted to our humility the task of preaching this word of the cross, we put you on notice, by the direction of the lord king, the bishops and princes who met at Frankfurt, that the strong Christian men must take arms and take up the sign of salvation in order to exterminate or at least to convert those nations. And we promise the same indulgence for their sins as to those who already have set out for

---

19 Bernard of Clairvaux, *Epistola CDLVIII Ad Wladislaum ducem, magnates et populum Bohemiae, Sancti Bernardi Opera*, viii, pp 434–7, p. 436: 'Quid moramini, servi crucis, quid dissimulatis vos, quibus nec robur corporum, nec terrena substantia deest. Suscipite signum crucis, et omnium, de quibus corde contrito confessionem feceritis, plenam indulgentiam delictorum hanc vobis summus pontifex offert, vicarius ejus cui dictum est: Quodcunque solveris super terra, erit solutum et in coelo. Suscipite munus oblatum, et ad irrecuperabilem indulgentiae facultatem alter alterum praevenire festinet'. 20 See Cecilia Gaposchkin, *Invisible weapons: liturgy and the making of crusade ideology* (Ithaca, 2017); Jilana Ordman, 'Was it an embarrassment of rewards?: possible relationships between religious devotion among participants in the Second Crusade, 1145–1149, and their losses in the field' in E. Weber (ed.), *Seduction: the art of persuasion in the medieval world*. Essays in Medieval Studies 30 (2014), pp 113–40.

44

Ireland and the crusades

Jerusalem. Many indeed have taken the sign of the Cross in this land; we have now called on others to take on the same task so that those among Christian men who have not yet taken the cross for the journey to Jerusalem know that they will obtain the same indulgence in joining this expedition, provided that in it they observe the directions of the bishops and princes.[21]

In the years 1146–7, when Bernard was very active in promoting the Second Crusade both in the Near East and in eastern Europe, he was in direct contact with Ireland. Máel Máedóc Ua Morgair (St Malachy), abbot of Bangor and bishop of Armagh, Down and Connor, had visited Clairvaux in 1139 on his way to Rome and had greatly impressed Bernard (pls 2.1 and 2.2). On his way back to Ireland, he stopped again in Clairvaux and left four Irish clerics there to be trained as Cistercian monks. Among these Irish monks was Gilla Críst Ua Conairche, originally from Kerry, who had joined the community of Bangor under Malachy.[22] He trained as a Cistercian monk for three years at Clairvaux between 1139 and 1142. One of his fellow novices there was Bernardo Pignatelli, from the Pisa area, who became abbot of the Cistercian abbey of Tre Fontane in Rome, before being elected pope in 1145. He took the name of Eugenius III, becoming the pope who promoted the Second Crusade and asked St Bernard to lead the preaching and recruiting campaign. Eugenius kept in touch with his fellow novice Gilla Críst and appointed him permanent papal legate for Ireland in 1151. Until 1176, when he retired to the monastery of Abbeydorney, Co. Kerry, Gilla Críst Ua Conairche was a man of influence among men of power, both in ecclesiastical and lay circles. He presided over several synods and took part in the Synod of Kells in 1152, convened to continue the reform of the Church in Ireland. In the world of lay rulers, Gilla Críst was asked to meet Henry II, who stayed with him at his episcopal residence of Lismore for two days in October 1171. Before becoming bishop of Lismore in 1151, Gilla Críst had been the abbot of Mellifont, the first Cistercian abbey in Ireland.

When Mellifont was founded in 1142, Bernard sent to Ireland five French monks to help Malachy and Gilla Críst build their new monastery. Bernard

21 Bernard of Clairvaux, *Epistola CDLVII Ad universos fideles, Sancti Bernardi Opera*, viii, pp 432–3, p. 433: 'Quia enim verbum hoc crucis parvitati nostrae Dominus evangelizandum commisit, consilio domini Regis et episcoporum et principum, qui convenerant Frankonovort, denuntiamus armari christianorum robur adversus illos, et ad delendas penitus, aut certe convertendas nationes illas signum salutare suscipere, eamdem eis promittentes indulgentiam peccatorum quam et his qui versus Ierosolimam sunt profecti. Et multi quidem signati sunt ipso loco, ceteros autem ad opus simul provocavimus, ut qui ex christianis necdum signati sunt ad viam Ierosolimitanam, noverint eamdem sese indulgentiam hac adepturos expeditione, si tamen perstiterint in ea pro consilio episcoporum et principum'.   22 Aidan Breen, 'Ua Conairche, Christian (Gilla-Críst)', *DIB*.

wrote several letters to Malachy (in 1140, 1141 and 1147), and one letter to the Cistercian brothers in Ireland to send his condolences and to give assurance of his support after the death of Malachy in Clairvaux on 2 November 1148.[23] In 1147, he also wrote a letter to Diarmait mac Murrough, king of Leinster, to include him in the Cistercian community of prayer.[24] In fact, Bernard was so busy campaigning for the crusades, including a lengthy tour of public appearances in Germany, that he entrusted his correspondence to a team of redactors in Clairvaux, who wrote formal letters on his behalf.[25] One of them, and possibly their leader for matters concerning the crusade, was Nicolas of Clairvaux, who worked for Bernard between 1145 and 1151. Nicolas was a superb writer, versed in stylish rhetoric, who could develop a set of draft points given to him by Bernard into highly polished letters, sometimes very similar in style to those written by Bernard himself. The authorship of letters attributed to Bernard but originating from Nicolas has been a subject of debate over the last century. In recent years, computational linguistics has been used for tentative identification, but it is still work in progress.[26] Bernard dismissed Nicolas from his team of writers because the latter had grown so confident in his writing skills that he had sent letters using Bernard's seal but without his approval.[27] Nicolas is the secretary who wrote two letters to Ireland on behalf of Bernard some time between 1145 and 1148, possibly in 1147.[28] Both are letters of confraternity (that is, offering a union of prayer) addressed to Malachy of Armagh and to Diarmait mac Murrough, king of Leinster. Both letters express Bernard's admiration for these two men and his gratitude for their hospitality and generosity towards members of the Cistercian order in Ireland.[29] In these letters, as Jean Leclercq pointed out, the writing hand is that of Nicolas, but the short and concise style is that of Bernard, without the flourishes associated with Nicolas' style. In the same years, Nicolas was actively involved in the production of letters promoting the Second Crusade (*negotium crucis*). He certainly was head of the team that produced the copies of the encyclical letter sent to several recipients in England, Germany and Bohemia in 1146 (letter 363).[30] I have mentioned above that he wrote letters acting as Bernard (*in persona domni Clarevallensis*), but independently. Two of these

---

23 Bernard of Clairvaux, *Epistolae* CCCXLI, CCCLVI, CCCLXXIV, *Sancti Bernardi Opera*, viii, pp 282–3, 300 and 335–7.   24 Bernard of Clairvaux, *Epistola* DXLVI, *Epistola confraternitatis ad Dyermetium Hiberniae regem*, *Sancti Bernardi Opera*, viii, pp 513–14.   25 Jean Leclercq, 'Recherches sur la collection des épîtres de saint Bernard', *Les cahiers de civilisation médiévale* 55 (1971), 205–19.   26 Jeroen de Gussem, 'Bernard of Clairvaux and Nicolas of Montiéramey: tracing the secretarial trail with computational stylistics', *Speculum* 92 (2017), 190–225.   27 Giles Constable, *The letters of Peter the Venerable*, 2 vols (Cambridge, MA, 1967), ii, pp 326–30.   28 Jean Leclercq, 'Deux épîtres de saint Bernard et de son secrétaire' in J. Leclercq (ed.), *Recueil d'études sur saint Bernard et ses écrits* 2 (Rome, 1966), pp 313–18.   29 Bernard of Clairvaux, *Epistolae* DXLV, DXLVI, *Sancti Bernardi Opera*, viii, pp 512–14.   30 Leclercq, 'L'encyclique de saint Bernard', p. 243.

are clearly connected to the promotion of the crusade. One is addressed to the emperor of Byzantium, Manuel Commenus, asking him to sponsor the young Henry of Champagne, so that he could fight in the crusade. It is interesting to note that the language in this letter is similar to that used in the letter addressed to Diarmait mac Murrough.[31] The second letter is addressed to the count of Brittany and his vassals, asking them to join the crusade so as not to let down, not only their king, the king of France, but the king of Heaven.[32] We have no evidence that similar letters of request to join the crusade were sent to Ireland, but, given the context of close contacts between Clairvaux, England, Ireland and Brittany in the years 1146–8, it seems unlikely that the Irish were unaware of Bernard's promotion of the Second Crusade.

Within the Cistercian network, Nicolas of Clairvaux was not alone in taking active steps to promote the crusade. While the failure of the Second Crusade in the Near East was a personal blow for Bernard, the success of the second front of the crusade in eastern Europe was followed by a vigorous campaign of Christianization among the neighbouring Slavs, in which the Cistercian network played a significant role.[33] In spite of Bernard's later reservations about holy war, expressed in the last treatise he wrote, the *De consideratione*,[34] the Cistercians were now associated with the crusading spirit and, impressed by their efficiency in liminal areas, the popes would call on their expertise in the decades following the Second Crusade.[35] However, one should not attribute the effort of conquest and Christianization solely to the Cistercians for, as Nicolas Bourgeois has shown in the case of the Livonian crusade, the other orders, including the Benedictines, were equally active.[36] In any case, with the extension of the crusade in eastern Europe, crusading would no longer be just a war against Muslims in the Holy Land but a war against all enemies of the Roman Catholic Church, external or internal.

In the thirteenth century, under popes Innocent III (1198–1216), Honorius III (1216–27), Gregory IX (1227–41) and Innocent IV (1243–4), crusading became an integral part of papal policy and an efficient tool against heretics

---

31 For example 'ut de regno illo ad regnum illius transferamini' in the letter to Manuel Commenus, *PL* clxxxii (Paris, 1854), col. 673 and 'ut de regno terreneo transferamini ad aeternum' in the letter to Diarmait mac Murrough, *Sancti Bernardi Opera*, viii, p. 514.   32 Nicolas of Clairvaux, *Epistola CDLXVII ad comitem et barones Britanniae, in persona domini Clarae-vallensis pro negotio crucis, PL* clxxxii (Paris, 1854), cols 671–72.   33 Iben Fonnesberg-Schmidt, *The popes and the Baltic Crusades, 1147–1254* (Leiden, 2007).   34 Bernard of Clairvaux, *De consideratione ad Eugenium Papam, Sancti Bernardi Opera* (Rome, 1977), iii, pp 393–493.   35 Anti Selart, 'Popes and Livonia in the first half of the thirteenth century: means and chances to shape the periphery', *Catholic Historical Review* 100:3 (2014), 437–58; Marek Tamm, 'The Livonian crusade in Cistercian stories of the early thirteenth century' in T.K. Nielsen & I. Fonnesberg-Schmidt (eds), *Crusading on the edge: ideas and practice of crusading in Iberia and the Baltic Region, 1100–1500* (Turnhout, 2016), pp 365–89.   36 Nicolas Bourgeois, 'Les Cisterciens et la croisade de Livonie', *Revue historique* 635 (2005), 521–60.

Inspiring Irish crusaders: St Bernard's writings and Cistercian impact　　　47

and political rivals in Europe as well as against Muslim rulers in the Middle East.[37] Again, the Cistercians would repeatedly be called upon to play a part in the papal missions. By 1177 the reservations expressed by Bernard in his *De consideratione* twenty-five years earlier were no longer a concern for the new abbot of Clairvaux, Henry de Marcy, who was prominent first in leading the fight against the Cathars and Waldesians and then in preaching the Third Crusade.[38] In his treatise, the *De peregrinante civitate Dei* ('On the City of God in exile'), Henry re-used some of the arguments found in Bernard's *De laude novae militiae* to justify the crusade and exhort all Christians to take an active part in the fight against the enemies of Christ. Like Bernard, Henry de Marcy presented the crusade as a type of martyrdom, which would guarantee the warrior a place in Paradise, but he went further in using the language of the feudal code of honour, which a warrior elite would recognize:

> In fact, faithful soldiers will follow their king and will not hesitate to face the enemy for their king, preferring to die bravely for him than to preserve their own lives by flying like cowards and bring ignominy upon their king. If Christians do behave like this for their mortal king, must they not be much more faithful for their heavenly and immortal king?[39]

Again, it must be pointed out that, while high-profile Cistercians were prominent in promoting the Third and Fourth Crusades, the popes also relied on other orders. For example, in 1198, Pope Innocent III asked Fulk of Neuilly, his chosen preacher for the Fourth Crusade, to recruit not only Cistercians (*monachi albi*) but also Benedictines (*monachi nigri*) and regular canons (*canonici regulari*) to preach the crusade on a larger scale.[40] Also, while the popes and the kings of the major European countries as well as the Holy Roman emperor were the main drivers for the crusades, powerful families of warlords

---

37 See Rebecca Rist, *The papacy and crusading in Europe, 1198–1245* (London, 2009). **38** Yves Congar, 'Henri de Marcy, abbé de Clairvaux, cardinal-évêque d'Albano et légat pontifical', *Analecta Monastica* 5 (1958), 1–90; Beverly M. Kienzle, *Cistercians, heresy and crusade in Occitania, 1145–1229: preaching in the Lord's vineyard* (York, 2001), pp 109–34; P.J. Cole, *The preaching of the crusades to the Holy Land, 1095–1270* (Cambridge, MA, 1991), pp 65–71. **39** Henri de Marcy, *De peregrinante civitate Dei*, Ch. XIII, *PL* cciv (Paris, 1855), col. 355: 'Fideles siquidem milites suum regem sequentur, pro suo se rege hostibus incunctanter objicient, malentes pro eo fortiter occumbere, quam segniter fugiendo vitam sibi conferre, ignominiam suo regi inferre. Si sic pro rege mortali actitant Christiani, quanto fideliores esse debent coelesti et immortali?'. **40** Innocent III, Regesta sive Epistolae, 398, *PL* xxxiv (Paris, 1855), cols 375–6): 'tam de monachis nigris quam albis sive canonicis regularibus aliquot, quos ad praedicandum idoneos esse decreveris'; see also *Die Register Innocenz' III*. Bd. I 1. Pontifikatsjahr, 1198/99 (Graz, 1964–8), and also Chris Schabel, 'The myth of the White Monks' "mission to the orthodox": Innocent III, the Cistercians, and the Greeks', *Traditio* 70 (2015), 237–61.

increasingly became independently involved. Together with their patronage of holy orders and local churches, their participation in the crusades, both in the Middle East and in Europe, became an important element of status building for these families and added legitimacy to their claims as local rulers. Clear examples of this are found both in France and in Spain, where aristocratic families in Anjou, Champagne and Catalonia celebrated the participation of their ancestors in the crusades in order to boost the status of their families among their peers. In exchange for their financial and logistic support, the monastic orders undertook the production of written or iconographic mementos to ensure that the memory of their patrons would be long lasting.[41]

Holy orders were in a position to influence the choice of these European magnates. For example, Gregory Lippiatt has shown in a recent article the extent of the influence of both the Cistercians and the reformers among the theologians in the schools of Paris over Simon de Montfort, earl of Leicester.[42] The Montfort family were generous patrons of the Cistercians and Simon's thinking and decision to take part both in the Fourth Crusade in the Near East in 1202 and in the Albigensian Crusade in 1209 were certainly influenced by Guy des Vaux-de-Cernay, one of the four Cistercian abbots appointed (*Ad mandatum Summi Pontificis*) by Pope Innocent III to promote and take part in the Fourth Crusade, as approved by the general chapter of the Cistercians in 1201.[43] Hugh de Lacy II, earl of Ulster, who joined the Albigensian Crusade in 1210 under Simon de Montfort's leadership, seems to have shared the same religious preoccupations as his mentor. The de Lacy family were generous patrons of the Cistercians in Ireland. Hugh's father, lord of Meath, had already given support to the Cistercian foundations of Mellifont and Bective. Hugh himself also granted land to Mellifont,[44] and his brother Walter, who was a patron of the Cistercian abbey of Beaubec in Normandy, founded a daughter house of this Norman abbey in the townland of Bey More near Drogheda, also called

---

41 See Nicholas L. Paul, *To follow in their footsteps: the crusades and family memory in the high Middle Ages* (Ithaca, 2012); idem, 'The fruits of penitence and the laurel of the cross: the poetics of crusade and conquest in the memorials of Santa Maria de Ripoll' in Nielsen & Fonnesberg-Schmidt (eds), *Crusading on the edge*, pp 245–73; Kathryn Dutton, 'French crusading and political culture under Geoffrey, count of Anjou and duke of Normandy, 1129–51', *History* 29 (2015), 419–44; Anne E. Lester, 'A shared imitation: Cistercian convents and crusader families in thirteenth-century Champagne', *JMH* 35 (2009), 353–70.   42 Gregory E.M. Lippiatt, 'Simon de Montfort, les Cisterciens et les écoles: le contexte intellectuel d'un seigneur croisé (1187–1218)', *Les cahiers de civilisation médiévale* 61 (2018), 269–88; also, Gregory E.M. Lippiatt, *Simon V of Montfort and baronial government, 1195–1218* (Oxford, 2017), pp 79–98. See also Paul Duffy, chapter 5, this volume.   43 See *Statuta capitulorum generalium ordinis Cisterciensis ab anno 1116 ad annum 1786*, ed. Joseph-Marie Canivez (Louvain, 1933), i, p. 270; Andrew W. Jones, 'Fulk of Neuilly, Innocent III, and the preaching of the Fourth Crusade', *Comitatus* 41 (2010), 119–48.   44 A.J. Otway-Ruthven, 'The partition of the de Verdon lands in Ireland in 1332', *PRIA* 66C (1967–8), 401–55, at 405.

Inspiring Irish crusaders: St Bernard's writings and Cistercian impact

Beaubec (*de Bello becco*), for the salvation of his soul and the souls of his wife and of all his ancestors and descendants.[45] Patronage of the Cistercians was not limited to families of Anglo-Norman origin. Irish kings also were generous patrons of the order. We have mentioned above the letter written in 1147 by Bernard to Diarmait mac Murrough, king of Leinster, to thank him for his 'great generosity' (*multa largitate*) towards his poor monks, and to include him into a full union of prayers with the community of Clairvaux.[46] In addition we have the evidence of a significant body of charters known to have been written in favour of the Cistercian order in Ireland.[47] By 1215, out of thirty-four Cistercian monasteries existing in Ireland, ten had been founded by Anglo-Norman families, but the great majority of abbeys were founded by Gaelic-Irish kings.[48] The language used in these charters is similar to that found in the charters of foundation of monasteries on the Continent and the donors' motivations expressed in these texts are also similar. Like their counterparts in France or Spain, Irish donors were concerned with the salvation of their souls and the commemoration of their family.[49] As usual in the language of grants and charters, concern for the everlasting nature of the commemoration is also expressed, as in the grant given to the church of Our Lady in Cîteaux in 1224 by Áed Ua Conchobair, king of Connacht:

> I have given and granted and by my present charter confirmed to God and the church of Blessed Mary of Cîteaux and the brothers serving God there, for the souls of my father and my mother and for myself and my wife and my children, in pure and perpetual alms, five marks of silver every year in perpetuity paid by me and my heirs to the house of Cîteaux.[50]

---

45 *The Coucher book of Furness abbey*, eds J.C Atkinson & J. Brownhill (Manchester, 1919), ii, pp 716–17; see Paul Dryburgh & Brendan Smith, 'Calendar of documents relating to medieval Ireland in the series of ancient deeds in the National Archives of the United Kingdom', *AH* 39 (2006), 1–61, at 23.   **46** Bernard of Clairvaux, *Epistolae* DXLVI, *Sancti Bernardi Opera*, viii, pp 513–14: 'quia pauperes Christi, immo Christum in pauperibus, regia magnificentia suscepistis. Magnum revera apud nos miraculum quod rex in finibus terrae constitutus inter barbaras gentes opera misericordiae multa largitate prosequitur.'   **47** See Marie Therese Flanagan, *Irish royal charters: texts and contexts* (Oxford, 2005).   **48** Marie Therese Flanagan, 'Irish royal charters and the Cistercian order' in M.T. Flanagan & J.A. Green, *Charters and charter scholarship in Britain and Ireland* (New York, 2005), pp 120–39.   **49** See Flanagan, *Irish royal charters*, pp 25–30 and numerous examples in the edited body of charters.   **50** '[...] dedi et concessi et hac presenti carta mea confirmavi Deo et ecclesie Beate Marie Cisterciensis et fratribus ibidem Deo servientibus pro anima patris mei et matris mee et pro me ipso et uxore mea et liberis meis in puram et perpetuam elemosinam quinque marcas argenti perpetuo annuatim a me et ab heredibus meis domui Cistercii [...]', H. d'Arbois de Jubainville (ed.), 'Chartes données en Irlande en faveur de l'ordre de Cîteaux', *Revue Celtique* 7 (1886), 81–6. King Áed Ua Conchobair was correctly identified by Gearóid MacNiocaill, 'À propos du vocabulaire social irlandais du bas Moyen Âge', *Études Celtiques* 12 (1970), 512–46, at 537, no. 3.

Already present at the time of St Bernard and Pope Eugenius III, the link between Church reform and the ideal of crusade became openly stated papal policy under the leadership of Pope Innocent III (1198–1216). In his encyclical letter *Vineam Domini Sabaoth*, dated 19 April 1213, the pope expressed clearly his main aims for calling a general council to be held in Lateran in November 1215:

> Therefore we invoke the testimony of Him, who is a faithful witness in the Heavens, that of all the desires of our heart we long chiefly for two in this life, namely, that we may work successfully to recover the Holy Land and to reform the Universal Church, both of which call for attention so immediate as to preclude further apathy or delay unless at the risk of great and serious danger.[51]

This letter was sent to a large list of Church and secular leaders. Ireland was certainly made aware of the message: the letter was sent to the archbishops of Armagh, Dublin and Cashel, and to no less than four Irish kings (Cork, Limerick, Connacht and Míde) in a list of thirteen European kings that included the kings of France, Aragon, Navarre, León and Castile but not the king of England.[52] Between 19 and 29 April 1213, Innocent III sent two further letters to Ireland. One was the encyclical letter *Quia major*, which contains clear instructions for the preparation of the crusade and renews the offer of 'remission of sins and indulgences' granted for the previous crusades.[53] The other was the circular letter *Pium et sanctum propositum*, appointing papal legates in various parts of Europe, in charge of promoting the crusade in their own area and raising funds for the expedition to the Holy Land.[54] The two men chosen for running the campaign in Ireland were Henry Blund, the Anglo-Norman archbishop of Dublin, and Thomas, the abbot of the Cistercian abbey of Mellifont. As Alberto Forni has shown, the pope's choice for his legates was not dictated only by status and administrative efficiency,

---

51 'Illius ergo testimonium invocamus qui testis est in coelo fidelis quod inter omnia desiderabilia cordis nostri duo in hoc saeculo principaliter affectamus, ut ad recuperationem videlicet terrae sanctae ac reformationem universalis Ecclesiae valeamus intendere cum effectu: quorum utrumque tantam requirit provisionis instantiam ut absque gravi et grandi periculo ultra dissimulari nequeat vel differri.', *PL* ccxvi (Paris, 1855), col. 824.   52 *Register of Innocent III*, 19 Apr. 1213: '[...] In eundem modum regi Corkaiae. In eundem modum regi Lumbricensi. In eundem modum regi Conactie. In eundem modum regi Mídiensi [...]', *Regesta Pontificum Romanorum (AD 1198–1304)*, ed. A. Potthast, 2 vols (Berlin, 1874–), i, p. 408, no. 4706; see also Patrick J. Dunning, 'Pope Innocent III and the Irish kings', *JEH* 8 (1957), 17–32.   53 *Quia Major*, *PL* ccxvi (Paris, 1855), cols 817–22; English translation in Jessalyn Bird, Edwards Peters & J.M. Powell (eds), *Crusade and Christendom: annotated documents in translation from Innocent III to the fall of Acre, 1187–1291* (Philadelphia, 2013), pp 107–12; see *Regesta Pontificum Romanorum*, p. 410, no. 4725.   54 *Pium et sanctum propositum*, *Patrologia Latina*, ccxvi (Paris, 1855), cols 822–3; *Regesta Pontificum Romanorum*, p. 411, no. 4727: 'In eundem modum archiepiscopum Dubliniensem et abbatem Mellifontis [...] per Iberniam'.

but by their reputation as preachers, combining both charisma and learning.[55] In France, besides Pierre des Vaux de Cernay, the abbot we mentioned earlier, Pope Innocent III had chosen among the Cistercians Adam de Perseigne, one of the most influential religious and political thinkers of his generation.[56] Thomas of Mellifont might not have been as learned as Adam de Perseigne, but he belonged to an order where the tradition of St Bernard's eloquence was still very strong and was part of the training of young monks.[57] While the founding texts of crusading ideology were written in Latin, communication with lay people involved the use of vernacular language. The link between the crusades and vernacular literary texts on the Continent has been well studied.[58] For Ireland, modern scholarship has shown that texts such as the epic *Cogadh Gáedhel re Gallaibh*, written to glorify the family of Brian Boru, also reflects an awareness of the crusading spirit.[59]

In the history of the development of the crusading ideology in Europe, Bernard's writings in the 1130s and 1140s were certainly an important turning point and influenced the vocabulary and rhetoric of crusade recruitment for several generations of preachers, Cistercians and others.[60] Far from being isolated from that movement by its geographical location, Ireland was quite close to the centre of the action. From the privileged relationship between Bernard and Malachy, followed by the close contacts between Christian O'Conairche and Pope Eugenius III, and up to the choice of Thomas of Mellifont by Pope Innocent III, Irish Cistercians were in position to play the same role with the warrior elite of Ireland, both Gaelic-Irish and Anglo-Norman, as their counterparts on the Continent.

---

55 A. Forni, 'La "nouvelle prédication" des disciples de Foulques de Neuilly: intentions, techniques et réactions' in A. Vauchez (ed.), *Faire croire: modalités de la diffusion et de la réception des messages religieux du XIIe au XVe siècle* (Rome, 1981), pp 19–37. **56** Laurent Maillet, 'Un maître spirituel de l'Occident chrétien, Adam, abbé de Perseigne', *Revue Historique et Archéologique du Maine* 9 (2009), 97–120; idem, 'Les missions d'Adam de Perseigne, émissaire de Rome et de Cîteaux (1190–1221)', *Annales de Bretagne et des Pays de l'Ouest* 120 (2013), 100–16. **57** William J. Purkis, *Crusading spirituality in the Holy Land and Iberia, c.1095–c.1187* (Woodbridge, 2008), pp 111–19. **58** Pierre Jonin, 'Le climat de croisade des chansons de geste', *Les cahiers de civilisation médiévale* 27 (1964), 279–88; François Suard, 'Chanson de geste traditionnelle et épopée de croisade', *Au carrefour des routes d'Europe: la chanson de geste* (Aix-en-Provence, 1987), i, pp 1033–55; D.A. Trotter, *Medieval French literature and the crusades* (Geneva, 1988). **59** Máire Ní Mhaonaigh, *Brian Boru: Ireland's greatest king?* (Stroud, 2007), pp 85–6. **60** On the Cistercian heritage in the Dominican order see Andrew Jotischky, *The Carmelites and antiquity: mendicants and their pasts in the Middle Ages* (Oxford, 2002), pp 281–6; Beverly M. Kienzle, 'Preaching the cross: liturgy and crusade propaganda', *Medieval Sermon Studies* 53 (2009), 11–32.

3 / Conquest as crusade: Ireland's invasion and a colonial plea to the papacy

MAEVE CALLAN

INTRODUCTION

White supremacist violence fed by 'fantasy' versions of medieval history has increased of late,[1] but distortions of medieval history to serve a racist agenda are nothing new. Rather, they lie at the very foundations of Ireland's colonization by the English,[2] a medieval example of 'fake news' in real time.[3] Though the Irish had been Christian since the fifth century and helped spread Christianity throughout Britain and the Continent since the sixth, when the Norman nobility of England set imperialist eyes upon Ireland in the twelfth century, the papacy blessed its intentions and pronounced the Irish fallen from the faith. The Normans descended from pagan Norse raiders, commonly called Vikings, who had massacred, raped, and enslaved Irish and other Christians, including monks and nuns, since the late eighth century. They converted to Christianity in the tenth century as part of the terms for their settlement of northern France, which became known as Normandy, and integrated so thoroughly into French Christian culture that when William, duke

---

1 'MAA public statement on the assault on the U.S. Capitol', *Medieval Academy blog*, 13 Jan. 2021, http://www.themedievalacademyblog.org/maa-public-statement-on-the-assault-on-the-u-s-capitol/, accessed 16 Feb. 2021; 'Medievalists respond to Charlottesville', *Medieval Academy blog*, 18 Aug. 2017, http://www.theme-dievalacademyblog.org/medievalists-respond-to-charlottesville/, accessed 27 Aug. 2019. See also Dorothy Kim, 'White supremacists have weaponized an imaginary Viking past: it's time to reclaim the real history', *Time*, 12 Apr. 2019, https://time.com/5569399/viking-history-white-nationalists/, accessed 18 Aug. 2019. 2 Ibram Kendi, a leading scholar of race studies, sees racism as emerging only in the fifteenth or sixteenth century, but scholars of earlier periods have traced it through the Middle Ages and into classical antiquity. According to Joshua Greene, the tribalistic instinct that gives rise to racism is older than religion itself and is in fact an impetus for religion, in the dawn of prehistory: Joshua Greene, *Moral tribes: emotion, reason, and the gap between us and them* (New York, 2013), pp 48–101. See also Ibram X. Kendi, *Stamped from the beginning: the definitive history of racist ideas in America* (New York, 2016), and idem, *How to be an antiracist* (New York, 2019); Geraldine Heng, *The invention of race in the European Middle Ages* (Cambridge, 2018); Miriam Eliav-Feldon, Benjamin Isaac & Joseph Ziegler (eds), *The origins of racism in the West* (Cambridge, 2018); and Benjamin Isaac, *The invention of racism in classical antiquity* (Princeton, 2004). 3 Donnchadh Ó Corráin, 'How fake news led pope to bless England's Irish invasion', *Irish Times*, 15 June 2017, https://www.irish-times.com/culture/books/how-fake-news-led-pope-to-bless-england-s-irish-invasion-1.3120786, accessed 19 Aug. 2019; see also Nicole A. Cooke, *Fake news and alternative facts: information literacy in a post-truth era* (Chicago, 2018).

Conquest as crusade: Ireland's invasion and a colonial plea to the papacy 53

of Normandy, invaded England in 1066, he did so with Pope Alexander II's blessing and under his banner.

Roughly a century later, shortly after Henry II, William's great-grand-son, had admitted some responsibility for the murder of Thomas Becket, archbishop of Canterbury, and had gone to Ireland in part to avoid the repercussions for Becket's murder and in part to restrain his subjects who had begun Ireland's conquest without him, Alexander III lauded him as 'so devout a son of the Church ... a most Catholic and Christian prince', who 'stirred by divine inspiration ... has subjected to his dominion that people, a barbarous one uncivilized and ignorant of Divine law'.[4] He wrote this to his own papal legate in Ireland and to its four archbishops, all Irishmen, all solid representatives of the Roman ecclesiastical hierarchy, and all devout Catholic Christians. Indeed, his Latinization of two of their names were Christian (Gilla Chríst Ua Conairche, bishop of Lismore and papal legate) and Catholic (Cadhla Ua Dubthaig, archbishop of Tuam); a third was Lorcán Ua Tuathail (Laurence O'Toole), archbishop of Dublin, soon to be a canonized Catholic saint. Alexander's letter to Henry continues in a similar vein, declaring his joy at how,

> as a pious king and magnificent prince, you have wonderfully and gloriously triumphed over that people of Ireland, who, ignoring the fear of God, in unbridled fashion at random wander through the steeps of vice, and have renounced all reverence for the Christian faith and virtue ... and, by the will of God (as we firmly believe), [you] have extended the power of your majesty over that same people ...

> We hold your purpose good and acceptable in all ways, and therefore render to Him from who all good proceeds, and who disposes the pious deeds of his faithful ones at his good pleasure, all our grateful prayers, beseeching the Almighty Lord with fervent prayer that, even as by your influence those evils which so wickedly are practised in that land begin already to diminish and the seeds of virtue to flourish instead, so also by you with God's aid the said people, with the stains of vice cast away, may receive the whole discipline of the Christian faith, to the glory of an unfading crown for you and the health of their souls.

> And so we exhort and beseech your majesty and enjoin upon you for the remission of your sins that in this work which you have so laudably

---

4 *Irish historical documents, 1172–1922*, eds Edmund Curtis & R.B. McDowell (London, 1943), pp 19–22.

begun you will even more intently and strenuously continue, so that, even as you have to the remission of your sins undertaken so great a task as regards that people, so also for the benefit of their souls you shall be worthy of an eternal crown.

Alexander III presented Henry II's conquest of Ireland as penance for his considerable sins, which included inciting the martyrdom of an archbishop in his own cathedral less than two years earlier. The Irish, on the other hand, he alleged had exchanged Christianity for 'monstrous abuses' too offensive to mention. Yet the only religious failings that Alexander's letters cite – occasionally eating meat in Lent and not paying tithes nor sufficiently respecting the religious – are exceptionally mild, inherently Christian and practically pious compared to the conduct of Henry and his men.[5] In his third letter on the matter, to Irish secular rulers, also written 20 September 1172, Alexander softened his anti-Irish rhetoric somewhat, focusing on his joy at their submission to Henry and warning them not to renounce it, yet similarly proclaiming that 'through the enormity and filthiness of their vices, [the Irish] have fallen away so far from the Divine law, so they shall be all the more surely moulded in it and receive all the more fully the discipline of the Christian faith' through Henry's dominion.[6]

Given such rhetoric, scholars have often likened Ireland's colonization by the English to a crusade.[7] A common focus of such a comparison is *Laudabiliter*, which blessed Henry II's intention to invade Ireland and 'expand the boundaries of the Church, proclaim the truth of the Christian faith to an ignorant and barbarian people, and weed out the new growth of vices from the field of the Lord'.[8] Allegedly issued about 1155 by Adrian IV (pl. 3.1), who, as scholars invariably point out, was the only English pope, it survives solely in *Expugnatio Hibernica*, or *The conquest of Ireland*, by Gerald of Wales, written around 1189. Adrian's ethnic identity fits a convenient narrative: an English pope declared the Irish no longer Christian to provide religious cover for the English colonization of Ireland, which Gerald's work celebrates and which his family helped lead. *Laudabiliter* seems all the more authentic given its parallels with Alexander's letters, and fourteenth-century Irish leaders, who had much

---

5 See Callan, *Templars*, pp 5–11. 6 *Irish historical documents, 1172–1922*, pp 19–22. 7 See for example Maurice Sheehy, 'The Bull "*Laudabiliter*": a problem in medieval diplomatique and history', *Journal of the Galway Archaeological and Historical Society* 29 (1961), 45–70, at 68; John France, *The crusades and the expansion of Catholic christendom, 1000–1714* (London, 2005), p. 144; Anne Duggan, 'The making of a myth: Giraldus Cambrensis, *Laudabiliter*, and Henry II's lordship of Ireland', *Studies in Medieval and Renaissance History* 4 (2007), 107–70, at 158; Donnchadh Ó Corráin, *The Irish church, its reform and the English invasion* (Dublin, 2017), p. 101. 8 Giraldus Cambrensis, *Expugnatio Hibernica*, ed. and trans. A.B. Scott & F.X. Martin (Dublin, 1978), p. 144; my translation.

Conquest as crusade: Ireland's invasion and a colonial plea to the papacy

to gain by rejecting it, accepted it as genuine.[9] Yet, as Anne Duggan has argued, it is at least to some extent a fraud, as discussed below.[10]

A far more credible witness than Gerald of Wales, John of Salisbury similarly testifies to Adrian granting Ireland to Henry II a year or two after pope and king ascended their respective thrones in late 1154. Secretary to the archbishop of Canterbury and friend of Nicholas Breakspear, later Adrian IV, John claimed he had convinced Adrian to grant Ireland to Henry as a hereditary fief on the grounds that all islands of Christendom belonged to the pope by right of the Donation of Constantine.[11] This text, an eighth-century forgery then generally regarded as genuine,[12] purported to be a grant from the Roman emperor Constantine to Pope Sylvester I of various properties and authorities in his domain. Yet Ireland was never part of the Roman empire; thus, even if the Donation had been genuine, it would not authorize Adrian's subsequent granting of Ireland. Much of Britain, including England, *had* belonged to Rome, however, and Giles Constable theorized that the insinuation that Henry's own realm was really under the pope's dominion might have caused John's fall from Henry's favour in 1156.[13] John would have been eager to regain this favour, whatever caused its loss, perhaps prompting him to overstate the grant's nature when he referenced it in 1159. Gerald's credibility is a low bar to clear; John's description does not fit *Laudabiliter*'s contents, although Gerald explicitly claimed it as the grant John obtained. Moreover, Henry never claimed to have papal blessing for Ireland's invasion in advance, nor did he act on it until fifteen years later, after his subjects had started the invasion without him. Henry began considering invading Ireland soon after ascending the English throne, however; roughly contemporary accounts relate that his mother opposed the plan so the invasion was postponed and he redirected his army against the French, but do not suggest papal involvement.[14]

---

9 Maeve Callan, 'Making monsters out of one another in the early fourteenth-century British Isles: the Irish remonstrance, the declaration of Arbroath, and the Anglo-Irish counter-remonstrance', *Eolas* 12 (2019), 43–63. 10 Duggan, 'The making of a myth', 114. 11 J.F. O'Doherty, 'Rome and the Anglo-Norman invasion of Ireland', *Irish Ecclesiastical Record* 42 (1933), 131–45, at 131–2, and F.X. Martin, 'Ireland in the time of St Bernard, St Malachy, St Laurence O'Toole', *Seanchas Ardmhacha* 15 (1992–3), 1–35, at 14. 12 For the Donation, see Henry Bettenson, *Documents of the Christian Church* (Oxford, 1943), pp 135–40. 13 Giles Constable, 'The alleged disgrace of John of Salisbury in 1159', *EHR* 69 (1954), 67–76. 14 *The chronicle of Robert of Torigni*, in *Chronicles of the reigns of Stephen, Henry II, and Richard I*, ed. Richard Howlett (London, 1889), iii, p. 186, s.a. 1155; Marie Therese Flanagan, *Irish society, Anglo-Norman settlers, Angevin kingship: interactions in Ireland in the late twelfth century* (Oxford, 1989), p. 305; Sigebert of Gembloux: *Chronica*, Monumenta Germaniae Historica, Scriptores 6, ed. L.C. Bethmann (Hannover, 1844), pp 268–474, at p. 403, s.a. 1156. This last source, a Flemish addition to Sigebert's *Chronicon*, identifies 'bishops and religious men' as Henry's advisors in the plan, inspiring the theory that the archbishop of Canterbury and other Canterbury clerics (including John of Salisbury) were determined to assert their supremacy over Ireland in retaliation for the papal recognition of the Irish church as a national institution in 1152, prompting *Laudabiliter* in 1155/6.

CLARIFYING TERMS

Constable further theorized that 'Henry may have hoped for the declaration of a crusade, such as his great-grandfather had secured, or simply for the pope's blessing and permission to rule Ireland, which Alexander III later granted'.[15] Constable thus claimed the Norman conquest of England as a crusade, roughly thirty years before Urban II first preached the concept. William did invade England with the pope's blessing, and Normans fought Muslims in Spain and Sicily with the pope symbolically by their side during the eleventh century, 'becoming the self-appointed champions of a new concept of Holy War'.[16] The English, however, were Christian, no matter how much Norman and papal propaganda declared them fallen from the faith and in need of reform under a Norman ruler, just as occurred with the Irish a century later, and indeed as also occurred *against* eleventh-century Normans in Italy, when Leo IX proclaimed them 'more impious than pagans' and led an army against them himself.[17] The meaning of crusade has been vigorously debated,[18] but for the term to retain coherence it should not be applied to events before 1095 without significant qualification.

Crusade is not simply 'holy war', even one in which the papacy put its spiritual thumb – or in the case of Leo IX, his entire body – on the scales. 'Crusades were penitential war pilgrimages',[19] called by the pope with its warriors having made specific penitential vows. At least in theory, they began as an effort to 'reclaim the Holy Land for Christ' from Muslims, who had controlled Jerusalem since the seventh century. Initially, crusaders experienced a degree of military success, conquering Jerusalem (and massacring its Muslim and Jewish inhabitants) in 1099, but losing it again in 1187, prompting 'a series of crusades launched inward against deviants within Christendom'.[20] These internal crusades could be directed against political foes, like Markward of Anweiler in 1198, or heretical sects, like the Cathars of Languedoc starting in 1208, but they postdate the aforementioned actions in Ireland (let alone England) by decades. At times religious rhetoric might blur the distinctions, as in Canon 27 of the Third Lateran Council (1179), which offered plenary indulgences to those who died combatting Cathars and the equivalent of a

---

15 Giles Constable, 'The alleged disgrace of John of Salisbury in 1159', *EHR* 69 (1954), 67–76, at 75.   16 R. Allen Brown, *Normans and the Norman conquest* (2nd ed. Dover, NH, 1985), p. 13, see also pp 28, 128–9.   17 Wibert, 'Vita Leonis IX' in *Pontificum romanorum vitae*, ed. J.M. Watterich (Leipzig, 1872), i, p. 163; Rebecca Rist, *The papacy and crusading in Europe, 1198–1245* (London, 2009), p. 20; Norman Housley, 'Crusades against Christians: their origins and early development, c.1000–1216' in Peter W. Edbury (ed.), *Crusade and settlement* (Cardiff, 1985), pp 17–36, at p. 17.   18 See, for example, Christopher Tyerman, *The invention of the crusades* (Toronto, 1998).   19 Jonathan Riley-Smith, *The crusades, Christianity, and Islam* (New York, 2008), p. 9.   20 Ibid., p. 25.

minimum of two years penance to all who took up arms against them.[21] 'Yet despite the call for military action, at this point there was no suggestion of a *crusade* being authorized against heretics in the south of France. There was no mention of votive obligations, nor any apparatus in place for taking the Cross.'[22] That came nearly forty years after Ireland's invasion by its Anglo-Norman neighbours. Moreover, while Cathars were Christians, they were not Catholics. They had their own doctrine and ecclesiastical hierarchy, among other key differences, whereas the Irish were so Catholic it is hard to detect any authentic heresy among them.[23] Ireland underwent significant ecclesiastical reform during the twelfth century, as did much of western Christendom during what is commonly called the Gregorian Reform, with direct involvement of papal representatives; for example, the Italian Cardinal John Paparo, papal legate, oversaw the Synod of Kells-Mellifont and papal recognition of the Irish Church as a national institution in 1152, just a few years before *Laudabiliter*'s supposed issue (and about seven centuries after Christianity started flourishing in Ireland). Papal propaganda about – and Gerald's rendering of – Ireland's colonization at times evoke crusade imagery, but this is rhetoric, not reality; contemporaries did not confuse the two, as even Gerald's *Expugnatio* makes clear.

The meaning of ethnicity is still more contested and complex than that of crusade, involving imprecise generalities with which people passionately identify and spawning conflicts such as those at the heart of this essay.[24] 'The Irish' refers to Ireland's native people, distinct from the 'Ostmen' or the Hiberno-Norse who had established the towns of Dublin, Wexford, Waterford and Limerick, and also from the colonists who arrived after 1169. Politically organized in multiple kingdoms loosely affiliated under one *ard rí*, or high king, they were ethnically, culturally and linguistically one people, but often fought each other for various reasons, including the tensions that led to the exile of Diarmaid MacMurrough, king of Leinster, in 1166. Diarmaid sought Henry II's help in reclaiming his kingdom, resulting in an alliance with some of Henry's subjects, including Richard de Clare (also known as Strongbow), later earl of Pembroke, who married Diarmaid's daughter Aífe and became lord of Leinster after Diarmaid's death in May of 1171. Henry's concerns that his subjects might establish a rival kingdom in Ireland prompted his own expedition in 1171–2, which the pope would soon portray as penance for his role

---

21 *Decrees of the ecumenical councils*, ed. Norman P. Tanner (London, 1990), i, p. 225. 22 Rist, *The papacy and crusading in Europe*, p. 27. For discussion of 'a series of linked precedents stretching back to the period before the First Crusade' which led to 'the first fully-authenticated crusade against Christians' in 1208, see Housley, 'Crusades against Christians', pp 28 and 31. 23 See Callan, *Templars*, especially the introduction and chapter 5. 24 See Callan, 'Making monsters out of one another', 43–63.

in martyring a saint. According to Gervase of Canterbury, writing about the time Gerald wrote his *Expugnatio*, the Irish asked Henry to come and defend them against Strongbow and his fellow invaders.[25] The 3,457 lines of 'The song of Dermot and the earl', a late twelfth-century Anglo-French poem celebrating the victory of *nos Engleis* ('our English') and especially Strongbow over *les Yrreis* ('the Irish'), 'report more than 4,988 deaths. Fewer than thirty of these were of English as opposed to native warriors'.[26] While these numbers are clearly suspect, such disproportionate slaughter could help explain why the Irish accepted Henry's overlordship when he arrived in 1171.

'The English' is a more ambiguous term, applying to both the Anglo-Saxons and the descendants of the Normans who conquered them; Henry II and his subjects who invaded Ireland starting in 1169 can be referred to as both 'English' and 'Norman', as well as the combination, 'Anglo-Norman'. Though king of England, Henry held even more territory in France and ethnically and culturally might more accurately be called Norman or French, as might most of his nobles, far more than 'English', especially if that is understood as the Anglo-Saxon ethnicity and culture that dominated England prior to 1066.[27] The pre-Norman English were subject to hatred and hostility directed towards them by their Norman invaders and others to justify their conquest in 1066, much as the Irish would be a century later, but Hugh Thomas has argued that the process of Norman and French assimilation into Englishness was essentially complete by Henry II's death in 1189, spurred to a significant degree by fear of 'the Celtic Other' surrounding them, especially the Scots, the Welsh, and the Irish: 'the Celtic Other served not only to draw Normans and English together, and to reinforce Englishness where it already existed, but it also helped to make the former adopt the identity of the latter'.[28] Adding further ethnic intricacies, many of Ireland's late twelfth-century invaders from Henry's domains were Welsh as well as Norman, most notably

---

25 Gervase of Canterbury: *The historical works of Gervase of Canterbury*, ed. William Stubbs (London, 1879), i, pp 234–5; Colin Veach, 'Henry II and the ideological foundation of Angevin rule in Ireland', *IHS* 42 (2018), 1–25, at 9–10.   26 Nicholas Vincent, 'Angevin Ireland' in Brendan Smith (ed.), *The Cambridge history of Ireland*, i: *600–1550* (Cambridge, 2018), pp 185–221, at p. 209–10. *The deeds of the Normans in Ireland/La geste des Engleis en Yrlande: A new edition of the chronicle formerly known as* The song of Dermot and the earl, ed. Evelyn Mullally (Dublin, 2002).   27 The son of Geoffrey, count of Anjou, and Matilda, daughter of Henry I, Henry II was born and raised in France, became duke of Normandy at the age of 17 in 1150, became duke of Aquitaine when he married Eleanor, the former wife of Louis VII of France, in 1152, and became king of England at the end of 1154, as part of the settlement to end the civil war that had consumed England after Henry I died in 1135 and his nephew Stephen of Blois seized the throne.   28 Hugh M. Thomas, *The English and the Normans: ethnic hostility, assimilation, and identity, 1066–c.1220* (Oxford, 2003), p. 315. Gerald of Wales attests to continued contempt of the English ('Anglo-Saxons') and a strong sense of difference between them and Normans at the time of Henry's death and after, however.

Gerald de Barri's kin, known as the Geraldines after Gerald's grandfather, Gerald of Windsor, husband of Nest, daughter of Rhys ap Tawdr. Nest had children with three other men (including Henry I), prompting F.X. Martin to remark that '[m]ore accurately they should be described as Nestines'.[29] Ethnic confusion followed them to Ireland; Gerald tells us that two years into the invasion and only a year after his own arrival in Ireland, his uncle Maurice fitz Gerald exhorted his men to continue their invasion by declaring that they could rely only on themselves, for 'just as we are regarded as English by the Irish, so we are Irish to the English. And the inhabitants of this island and the other pursue us with equal hatred'.[30] Those who settled in Ireland in the wake of this invasion would come to be called Anglo-Irish, or the English colonists of Ireland.

LAUDABILITER ET SATIS AND *SATIS LAUDABILITER*

Maurice fitz Gerald's anecdote surfaces in the work which serves as our sole source for *Laudabiliter*, his nephew Gerald's *Expugnatio Hibernica*, written over thirty years after *Laudabiliter* was allegedly issued.[31] The article most regarded as having settled the matter in favour of its authenticity, Maurice Sheehy's 'The Bull *"Laudabiliter"*: a problem in medieval diplomatique and history', maintains that Gerald made a mistake, claiming he confused a cover letter with the now missing papal grant, in an effort to resolve *Laudabiliter's* divergence from John of Salisbury's description of Adrian's grant. Sheehy glossed over *Laudabiliter's* suspiciously close correlation with another letter from Adrian that is authentic, *Satis laudabiliter* (as opposed to *Laudabiliter et satis*, the titles signifying the documents' first words), written to Louis VII in 1159. Sheehy referred to *Satis laudabiliter* only to claim that 'this resemblance is itself another indication of genuineness', to the delight of counterfeiters and forgers everywhere.[32] That argument is less persuasive than its converse – that *Satis laudabiliter* provided

---

29 F.X. Martin, 'Allies and an overlord, 1169–72' in Art Cosgrove (ed.), *A new history of Ireland*, ii: *Medieval Ireland, 1169–1534* (Oxford, 1993), pp 67–97, at p. 67. 30 *Expugnatio Hibernica*, p. 80. 31 Michael Haren and Anne Duggan offer useful overviews of the debate about its authenticity, but ultimately the matter cannot be definitively determined. My discussion brackets several aspects, focusing primarily on issues relating to colonization and conquest. See Michael Haren, '*Laudabiliter*: text and context' in M.T. Flanagan & J.A. Green (eds), *Charters and charter scholarship in Britain and Ireland* (Basingstoke, 2005), pp 140–63, and Duggan, 'The making of a myth'; see also her '*Totius christianitatis caput*: the pope and the princes' in Brenda Bolton & Anne Duggan (eds), *Adrian IV, the English pope (1154–59): studies and texts* (Aldershot, 2003), pp 138–55, and 'The power of documents: the curious case of *Laudabiliter*' in Brenda Bolton & Christine Meek (eds), *Aspects of power and authority in the Middle Ages* (Turnhout, 2007), pp 251–75. 32 Sheehy, 'The Bull *"Laudabiliter"*', pp 62–3.

the basis from which *Laudabiliter* was forged – especially once *Satis laudabiliter*'s contents are considered beyond surface similarities. Sheehy did not deal with the verified letter in any depth, not even mentioning its suspiciously similar title, thus dodging discussion of its direct opposition to the approach Adrian allegedly advocated in *Laudabiliter*. During a temporary détente, Henry II and Louis VII proposed to jointly wage a crusade in Spain against its Muslim rulers. Adrian praised their desire 'to expand the boundaries of the Christian people, to conquer the barbarism of pagans, to subjugate apostate peoples and those who shun the Catholic faith and refuse to receive the truth to the yoke and authority of Christians', but he discouraged them from this venture unless the Spanish Catholics specifically asked them to do so.[33] Thus even when kings proposed to free formerly Catholic lands from Muslim control, and even though popes had encouraged Spanish crusades since the start,[34] Adrian opposed the plan, unless the Catholic inhabitants invited them to do so.

Given *Satis laudabiliter*'s significant divergence from the approach Gerald would have us believe Adrian took a few years earlier, encouraging Henry to invade an entirely Catholic country for religious reasons, Duggan theorized that Gerald refashioned an actual letter from Adrian that explicitly discouraged Henry from his intentions to invade Ireland and would have conformed in nature and tone to *Satis laudabiliter*.[35] It seems simpler, however, to see the original letter as *Satis laudabiliter*. 'Dependence on *Satis laudabiliter* would explain the curiously mixed language of *Laudabiliter*, which oscillates between crusading rhetoric in its *arenga* and reforming terminology in the body of the letter'.[36] Duggan's main evidence against seeing *Satis laudabiliter* as Gerald's source and in favour of the view that *Laudabiliter* reworked an actual letter about *Hibernia* rather than *Hispania* is 'the fact that Gerald clung to it until his death', whereas he essentially admitted that another alleged papal privilege, *Quoniam ea*, which immediately follows *Laudabiliter* in his *Expugnatio*, was fake, removing it from revised editions.[37] Yet *Quoniam ea* is far from the only probable fake which Gerald included in *Expugnatio*. F.X. Martin showed that of the eight documents Gerald purported to reproduce verbatim, two (*Quoniam ea* and an open letter from Henry II) 'are most probably false'; a letter from Diarmaid MacMurrough begging Strongbow to invade Ireland Martin called 'a concoction'; he suggested three other letters are also fake, while Gerald's text of the decrees of the 1172 Council of Cashel, for which he is again the only source,

---

33 *PL*, clxxxviii, cols 1615–17, at 1615, my translation.   34 Norman J. Housley, 'Jerusalem and the development of the crusade idea, 1099–1128' in B.Z. Kedar (ed.), *The Horns of Hattin* (Jerusalem, 1992), pp 27–40, at pp 32–3.   35 Duggan, 'Power of documents', pp 273–5.   36 Duggan, 'The making of a myth', 133. An identical letter written to Henry II is no longer extant; perhaps that (rather than the version for Louis VII) served as Gerald's source.   37 Duggan, 'The making of a myth', 114.

Conquest as crusade: Ireland's invasion and a colonial plea to the papacy 61

is '[a]t the very most ... authentic but not accurate'. Of the eight documents, Martin regarded *Laudabiliter* as the most reliable, largely because he deferred to certain scholars' arguments, yet still noted his doubts about it.[38] Gerald's determination to depict the Irish as barbarians in need of Norman civilization also needs to be considered, as does the context in which he constructed his *Expugnatio*.

CONDEMNATION FOR CHOOSING COLONY OVER CRUSADE

Gerald travelled to Ireland twice in the 1180s in the company of colonists, including Henry's son John, lord of Ireland, in 1185. He finished his first work on Ireland, the *Topographia Hibernica*, by March of 1188 and his second, the *Expugnatio*, around the time of Henry's death in July 1189. He toured Wales in 1188, preaching a crusade to reclaim Jerusalem, lost to Muslims in 1187, and taking the cross himself.[39] Crusade fervour intensified in the wake of Jerusalem's loss, including a sense of general Christian guilt for this failure, and Gerald especially blamed Henry, whom he served for several years. Henry's own family ruled Jerusalem,[40] though these family ties might have meant even less to Henry than his own personal crusade commitments apparently did. He made serial pledges to go on crusade: in 1170, 'in 1172 as part of his penance for the murder of his archbishop', in 1177 and then a fourth time in 1187, just before the West learned of Jerusalem's fall.[41] Heraclius, the patriarch of Jerusalem, came to England to try to convince Henry to honour his vows in 1185; Henry refused, pleading his vulnerability to the French, and John, then preparing to visit his new lordship, 'begged to be sent to Jerusalem instead'. Still Henry refused, and Heraclius prophesied that Henry's glory would soon turn to grief: 'you will be abandoned by the Lord whom you now abandon, and altogether deprived of his favour'. Heraclius' prophecies prompted Gerald to step outside of his chronology and report that John's Irish expedition would be disastrous and Henry would lose much of his

---

38 F.X. Martin, 'Gerald as historian' in *Expugnatio Hibernica: the conquest of Ireland*, ed. and trans. A.B. Scott & F.X. Martin (Dublin, 1978), pp 278–82. Duggan is well aware of these texts' dubious nature.   39 Gerald was released from his crusading vows a year and a half later, 'but retained a strong emotional commitment to the crusading ideal': Robert Bartlett, *Gerald of Wales: a voice of the Middle Ages* (Stroud, 2006), p. 68.   40 His grandfather, Fulk of Anjou, abdicated as count of Anjou in favour of Henry's father and became king of Jerusalem from 1131 until his death in 1143; Fulk's sons and Henry's uncles, Baldwin and Amalric, ruled until 1163 and 1174, respectively; Amalric's son, Baldwin IV, succeeded him until 1184, and Baldwin's sister Sibyl was acting as regent when Saladin so decisively defeated the crusaders in 1187.   41 Christopher Tyerman, *England and the crusades, 1095–1588* (Chicago, 1988), p. 40.

62   *Ireland and the crusades*

French territory, with his own son against him.[42] Perhaps these prophecies combined with his own misfortunes and the fall of Jerusalem had an effect: in January 1188 Henry at long last took the cross, but still never made it to the Holy Land. He died battling his two remaining 'legitimate' sons, who had joined the French to fight him.

Gerald thus faulted Henry for choosing colony over crusade, fighting fellow Christians in Ireland and France when he should have been saving Jerusalem from Saladin and his Saracens. He also repeatedly if implicitly admitted the emptiness of claims that the colonizers came as reformers or were needed as such. His *Topographia* tells of a Dublin synod in 1186, when the Irish Cistercian abbot of Baltinglass, Ailbe Ua Máel Muaid, castigated the Welsh and English clergy who had arrived with the invaders for infecting the Irish with rampant religious abuses, as that synod's constitutions substantiate.[43] Gerald conceded that the Irish clergy were exemplary but faulted them for acting too much like monastics, then denounced the Irish generally for their rudeness and failure to produce martyrs. The archbishop of Cashel, Muirges O'Heney, responded that Gerald spoke truly, for the Irish were a rude and ignorant people, yet they had ever honoured the Church, the religious and the saints; though they had not yet produced martyrs, Muirges continued, 'now a people has come to the kingdom which knows how, and is accustomed, to make martyrs. From now on Ireland will have its martyrs, just as other countries.'[44] Gerald thus preserved an echo of Irish scorn for his propaganda and the suggestion that the martyr-making Henry could be anyone's spiritual saviour. Tellingly, Gerald refused to put his money where his mouth was; he declined an offer of an Irish bishopric, having seen for himself 'that the state of Ireland was every day the worse for [the colonists'] coming'.[45]

Yet Gerald primarily portrayed the Irish as so deviant as to seem no longer Christian and thus their island's invasion as akin to a crusade, a concept that consumed him following Jerusalem's fall. *Laudabiliter* reflects these

---

42 *Expugnatio Hibernica*, p. 203. In a later retelling, Gerald claimed Heraclius invoked Becket's example in this exchange, saying to Henry, 'Do to me what you did to the blessed Thomas! I would as well have my head cut off by you in England than in Palestine by the Saracens; without a doubt you are worse than any Saracen' (quoted in Bartlett, *Gerald of Wales*, p. 73).   43 Giraldus Cambrensis, *Opera* (ed.), J.S. Brewer, J.F. Dimock & G.F. Warner, *Rolls series* 21. 8 vols (London, 1861–91), i, pp 66–72; Aubrey Gwynn, *The Irish church in the eleventh and twelfth centuries* (Dublin, 1992), p. 273. This synod's constitutions officially praise Irish clergy for their chastity and recognize that the colonial clergy may well corrupt them with their own crimes; see 'Provincial and diocesan decrees of the diocese of Dublin during the Anglo-Norman period', ed. Aubrey Gwynn, *Archivium Hibernicum* 11 (1944), 31–117, at 42.   44 *The history and topography of Ireland: topographia Hibernica*, ed. and trans. John J. O'Meara (Mountrath, 1982), pp 112–16, at p. 116.   45 *Autobiography of Gerald of Wales*, ed. and trans. H.E. Butler (Woodbridge, 2005), p. 90; Giraldus, *Opera*, i, p. 65. Gerald pointed the finger specifically at John, not the colonists in general, but he repeatedly criticizes colonists who came to Ireland after his family.

Conquest as crusade: Ireland's invasion and a colonial plea to the papacy

dynamics, but nothing more than Gerald's word supports his claim that it reflects Adrian's perspective or the grant John of Salisbury claimed he got from Adrian, a claim for which Gerald, writing thirty years later and after many momentous developments, provides John's only corroboration. Alexander's three authentic letters from 1172 take a similar stance to the one Gerald ascribed to Adrian almost twenty years after Alexander's letters, but Alexander wrote after the Irish had already accepted Henry's dominion and after he had agreed to significant concessions to the Church to compensate for his role in Becket's murder; furthermore, Alexander needed Henry's help against the anti-pope Calixtus III, who was supported by the Holy Roman emperor, Frederic Barbarossa. Alexander's letters echo *Laudabiliter* at points,[46] but perhaps more accurately *Laudabiliter* echoes them or they echo *Satis laudabiliter*, just as Henry seemed to do what *Satis laudabiliter* prescribed: act only with the inhabitants' approval.[47] Neither Henry nor Alexander ever mentioned *Laudabiliter* or any grant of Ireland to Henry by Adrian. As Duggan noted, 'Normally, the argument *ex silencio* is considered the weakest of all; but there are not one but five silences where one would expect some kind of reference' if it were authentic: Henry, contemporary chroniclers, Alexander III, the Black Book of the exchequer (a list of royal rights and precedents carefully compiled during John's reign) and 'the hundred-year long absence of *Laudabiliter* from official debate'.[48]

FOURTEENTH-CENTURY REFRAINS AMID A FALTERING COLONY

The English periodically returned to *Laudabiliter* to bolster their claims in Ireland in the second half of the thirteenth century as the colony started to shrink, but no pope referenced it until John XXII in 1318, writing in response to Irish complaints that the English had failed to uphold *Laudabiliter*'s terms. John hardly endorsed its authenticity; his letters to Edward II and papal ambassadors in England enclosed a copy but noted that Adrian only 'is said (*dicitur*) to have granted' it.[49] John also included the letter detailing English and Anglo-Irish abuses of the Irish, which historians have named the Irish Remonstrance and which raised no questions about *Laudabiliter*'s authenticity; instead, it used its terms to condemn the English, specifically Henry and his heirs, and especially

---

46 Duggan calls these echoes '*Laudabiliter* ghosts' ('The making of a myth', 136). Alexander was Adrian's chancellor as well as his immediate successor.   47 Curiously, Gerald did not refer to Alexander's letters, however.   48 Duggan, 'The making of a myth', 134–7.   49 *Vetera monumenta Hibernorum et Scotorum historiam illustrantia qae ex Vaticani, Neapolis ac Florentiae tablularis deprompsit, 1216–1547*, ed. Augustinus Theiner (Rome, 1864), p. 201, nn. 422–3; Duggan, 'The making of a myth', p. 154.

64 *Ireland and the crusades*

colonists in Ireland. Written by Northern Uí Neill leaders in 1317, they portrayed *Laudabiliter* as the result of the papacy's close relationship with English rulers whose 'snarling and viperous slanders' and 'unfair and false charges' had poisoned the papacy against the Irish, who had been devout Christians loyal to Rome since the fifth century.[50] Henry, the Remonstrance argued, should have lost his own kingdom for Becket's murder rather than being rewarded with lordship over another land; instead, he manipulated Adrian, 'tragically blinded by his affection for the English', into *Laudabiliter*.[51] The letter describes how English colonists terrorized the Irish, murdering them at will and receiving rewards for their crimes, as happened with Peter de Bermingham's massacre of his guests the O'Connors at the final course of a feast at his home;[52] Thomas de Clare's sudden, savage murder of Brian Ruad O'Briain, his co-godfather, following a religious celebration at de Clare's Bunratty Castle, after which de Clare hung O'Briain's headless body upside-down from a beam;[53] Geoffrey de Pencoyt's murder of the MacMurrough brothers as they slept in his home,[54] and so on.

The Remonstrance especially excoriated the English for perverting religion for imperialist ends rather than furthering the faith, as *Laudabiliter* required of them. English persecution, regularly given a religious veneer, had made the Irish like hunted animals, endangering not only their bodies but also their souls. Moreover, the letter maintained:

> Not only [English] laity and secular clergy but also some of their religious preach the heresy that it is no more a sin to kill an Irish person than to kill a dog or any other brute beast. And in the assertion of this heretical argument, some of their monastics fearlessly declare that if they should happen to kill an Irish person (as often does happen), they would not abstain from celebrating mass for even a single day on account of the murder.[55]

---

50 *Scotichronicon by Walter Bower in Latin and English*, ed. D.E.R. Watt (Aberdeen, 1990), iv, p. 384.   51 Ibid., p. 386, see also p. 388. Chronology is not the Remonstrance's strong suit.   52 See *Calendar of the justiciary rolls or proceedings in the court of the justiciar of Ireland, preserved in the Public Record Office of Ireland*, ed. James Mills, 3 vols (Dublin, 1905–14), ii, p. 82; John Clyn, *The Annals of Ireland by Friar John Clyn*, ed. and trans. Bernadette Williams (Dublin, 2007), pp 95–6, 101 and *CSMA* ii, p. 332.   53 See Sean MacRuaidhrí Mac Craith, *Caithréim Thoirdhealbhaigh*, ed. and trans. Standish Hayes O'Grady (London, 1929), ii, p. 10; *Annála Connacht: the Annals of Connacht (A.D. 1224–1544)*, ed. Alexander Martin Freeman (Dublin, 1944), pp 166–7; *The annals of Clonmacnoise, being the annals of Ireland from the earliest period to A.D. 1408*, trans. Conell Mageoghan (1627), ed. Denis Murphy (Dublin, 1896), p. 271; Aoife Nic Ghiollamhaith, 'Dynastic warfare and historical writing in north Munster, 1276–1350', *Cambridge Medieval Celtic Studies* 2 (1981), 73–89, at 83–5.   54 Robin Frame, 'The justiciar and the murder of the MacMurroughs', *IHS* 18 (1972), 223–30.   55 Bower, *Scotichronicon*, vi, pp 394–6.

As with crimes committed by secular colonists, the letter names religious who practiced what they preached — the Cistercians of Granard in Ardagh and of Inch in Down, as well as a Franciscan, Simon le Mercer, the bishop of Connor's brother. This view persisted among colonists; Richard fitz Ralph, archbishop of Armagh, reminded the Anglo-Irish in the 1350s 'that killing native Irish people might not be a felony in English law, but was nevertheless a sin in the eyes of God'.[56]

The Remonstrance admitted that the Irish were not blameless, acknowledging that 50,000 people 'of each nation' have been killed in warfare since *Laudabiliter's* time, a situation which only drastic steps could change.[57] Since Edward II would not redress the situation, Dónal O'Neill, whom the Remonstrance calls 'king of Ulster', renounced his own rights to Ireland's high kingship in favour of Robert Bruce's brother Edward,[58] who had already been inaugurated as high king through O'Neill's support two years previously amid ongoing battles against colonists. The letter emphasized the connections between Ireland (*Major Scotia*) and Scotland (*Minor Scotia*) through language, culture and blood, whereas the Irish and the English 'have a natural enmity for each other' arising from centuries of mutual slaughter and could not differ more from each other 'in their way of life, speech, and other customs', ignoring the fact that the Bruces were more than half-Norman themselves, in blood, language and culture.[59]

John was sufficiently moved by this plea to forward it to Edward II and papal representatives in England, where it got little response. The Anglo-Irish, on the other hand, apparently stewed on it for over a decade; around 1330, they wrote their own appeal to the pope, repeating these accusations but with colonists as the victims and the Irish as the perpetrators. This 'Counter-Remonstrance' also reflected more recent developments in the colony, especially the hunt for heretics by Richard Ledrede, bishop of Ossory, which resulted in Ireland's first death at the stake in 1324 and alerted Ledrede's fellow colonists to the lethal potential of heresy accusations. They sent an Irishman to the stake in 1328, shortly after defeating his kin in battle amid ongoing war, alleging that he had renounced Christianity as if he were the claims of *Laudabiliter* incarnate and using his death as a pretext to plead with the pope to call a crusade to help complete the conquest of Ireland, an increasingly losing battle in the fourteenth century.

After attributing the letter to England's justiciar in Ireland, his council and the dean and chapter of St Patrick's Dublin, the letter paraphrased

---

56 Quoted in Robin Frame, 'Exporting state and nation: being English in medieval Ireland' in Len Scales & Oliver Zimmer (eds), *Power and the nation in European history* (Cambridge, 2005), pp 143–65, at p. 151. 57 Bower, *Scotichronicon*, vi, p. 388. 58 Ibid., p. 400. 59 Ibid., pp 398–403.

Laudabiliter, reminding John that Adrian gave Ireland to Henry II to expand Christendom. Recently, however, 'in that same land of Ireland, heresy and dissension have arisen and are spreading among the Irish, a sacrilegious and savage people, hostile to God and humanity'.[60] It offered generalized assertions of Irish immorality, proclaimed that they attacked Christians and renounced their faith, and said that it is no sin to kill an Englishman. It proclaimed its sole named offender, 'Aduk Duff Octohyl', a heresiarch who endangered Irish and Anglo-Irish alike by his perverse teachings, which amounted to a systematic denial of the basics of Christian doctrine. Thus, the letter entreated the pope, 'may your glorious clemency deign to call a crusade (*crucesignationem*) for the well-being of your soul and the souls of countless others who are fighting a just war against those evildoers', and thereby strengthen powerless colonists.[61]

John de Pembridge, a Dublin Dominican and contemporary chronicler, provides more context. The Irish started winning back their land in the mid-thirteenth century and in early 1328 the O'Tooles, O'Byrnes and MacMurroughs, who had been waging war against Dublin colonists from the Wicklow hills for more than fifty years, united behind Dónal, son of Art MacMurrough, one of the sleeping brothers murdered by their host, Geoffrey de Pencoyt, remembered in the Remonstrance. After his inauguration, Dónal had his standard placed two miles from Dublin, 'and afterwards carried throughout all the lands of Ireland'.[62] Such acts by a new king of Leinster, who led clans who had been attacking Dublin for decades, probably caused colonists to fear that his ultimate goal was kingship of Ireland itself.[63] They remembered all too keenly the depredation brought by Edward Bruce's attempts to become Ireland's king in 1315–18 and were determined to prevent Dónal from becoming a similar threat. He was quickly captured and imprisoned in Dublin Castle, after which, according to Pembridge, 'many misfortunes befell the Leinster Irish … and many Irish were killed'.[64] Among them was Adducc Dubh O'Toole's execution for heresy on 11 April 1328, Ireland's second such death, sentenced by men who had been directly involved with Ledrede's claims a few years earlier.[65]

Pembridge presented Adducc's alleged heresy as a denial of basic Catholicism: 'contrary to the Catholic faith he denied the Incarnation of Jesus Christ, said that there could not be three Persons and one God,

---

60 J.A. Watt, 'Negotiations between Edward II and John XXII concerning Ireland', *IHS* 10 (1956), 1–20, at 19. 61 Ibid., p. 20. 62 *CSMA* ii, pp 365–6. 63 James Lydon, 'Medieval Wicklow: "a land of war"' in Ken Hannigan & William Nolan (eds), *Wicklow: history and society* (Dublin, 1994), pp 151–89, at p. 172. 64 *CSMA* ii, p. 366. 65 For discussion of Ledrede's heresy prosecutions and allegations as well as the case against Adducc Dubh O'Toole, see Callan, *Templars*, especially chapters 2–3 and 5.

declared that the Most Blessed Mary, Mother of the Lord, was a whore, denied the resurrection of the dead, declared that the Holy Scriptures were nothing more than fables, and rejected the authority of the sacred Apostolic See'.[66] The Counter-Remonstrance added that Adducc's teachings corrupted colonists, a claim arising from colonial fear of Irish/Anglo-Irish alliances and Anglo-Irish assimilation into Irish culture. Some Anglo-Irish joined Irish attacks on colonists, while even otherwise loyal Anglo-Irish adopted native customs and the Irish language, a 'degeneration' against which colonial authorities had legislated since 1297.[67] The Counter-Remonstrance suggested that Irishness itself was heresy, proclaiming the Irish a sacrilegious people against whom a crusade had to be called to eliminate the contagion. The allegations made against Adducc echoed the claims made against the Irish in *Laudabiliter*, which the Counter-Remonstrance cited. As the colony constricted, Dublin leaders tried to persuade the papacy to help them complete the conquest which it had endorsed almost two centuries earlier, claiming themselves impotent without this outside support,[68] and using tactics that Ledrede, bishop of Ossory, had recently proven effective against enemies: heresy accusations.

Pope John did not heed this call for crusade, but in 1332 he excommunicated the Leinster Irish and put their lands under interdict.[69] Yet he also advised Edward III on 1 July 1331, that, since Ireland has 'two sorts of people, pure Irish, and those of a mixed race, care should be taken to have governors and officers of the same respectively'.[70] Such a response was not the Counter-Remonstrance's aim, but at the start of his pontificate, John had received the Remonstrance's far more detailed account of Anglo-Irish abuses of the Irish. Moreover, Ledrede's own heresy allegations against Anglo-Irish colonists had forced him to flee Ireland and seek refuge with John in Avignon, where he stayed in 1329–31, when the Counter-Remonstrance was likely written and received. Ethnically English and hand-picked by John as bishop of Ossory in 1317 when he lived in Avignon, Ledrede levelled multiple heresy accusations against colonists and even raised questions concerning the queen's chamber, yet his ongoing efforts against heresy in Ireland did not include allegations against the Gaelic-Irish.

---

66 *CSMA* ii, p. 366; emended by Gilbert. 67 *Statutes and ordinances and acts of the parliament of Ireland: King John to Henry V*, ed. H.F. Berry (Dublin, 1907), pp 210–11; Seán Duffy, 'The problem of degeneracy' in James Lydon (ed.), *Law and disorder in thirteenth-century Ireland: the Dublin parliament of 1297* (Dublin, 1997), pp 87–106. 68 Norman Housley rightly pointed out that the text does not state that the crusade would be preached outside Ireland, however ('An English proposal for a crusade against the Irish, *c*.1329–31' (Unpublished paper, 2017); I thank Dr Housley for sharing his paper with me). 69 *CSMA* ii, pp 376–7. 70 *CEPR* ii, p. 500.

CONCLUSION

The Counter-Remonstrance made explicit the connection between colonization and crusade lurking behind *Laudabiliter* and Alexander's letters, but with a fourteenth-century twist: identifying the Irish as heretics, whereas *Laudabiliter* and its like claimed the Irish had lost their Christian identity, primarily by papal pronouncement, over 700 years after they first adopted it. Forty years after Ireland's invasion, in a work written for Emperor Otto IV, Henry II's grandson, Gervase of Tilbury even claimed that Ireland 'was the last country to adopt the true religion, and then only under compulsion'; in an apparent homage to Alexander III, among the 'filthy vices' Gervase attributed to the Irish before the coming of 'true religion' is 'ignoring the Lenten fast', which would have relevance only for Christians.[71] Yet not until after the Templar trial in 1310, which Ireland was obligated to participate in along with the rest of western Christendom, was heresy invoked. In a petition to Edward II around 1317, Anglo-Irish colonists called the fifth-century pre-Christian Irish 'ere-tiks',[72] even though a non-Christian, especially one who has never heard of Christianity, cannot be a heretic. This same confusion surfaced with Adducc Dubh, proclaimed a heretic when, by his accusers' own definition, he would more accurately be an apostate (someone who had renounced the faith; a heretic keeps the faith but deviates doctrinally). Heresy's meaning mattered less to colonial leaders than its accusation's force, and on that, Ledrede had taught them well. He exiled a powerful, politically connected woman and sent another to the stake on allegations that were outlandish even by the standards of the day, thereby initiating 'the dawn of the devil-worshipping witch'.[73]

Considering how well 'alternative facts' had worked against the Irish in the twelfth century, colonial leaders had reason to believe they might enlist the papacy once again in their cause, especially given what Ledrede had accomplished a few years earlier with his own 'fake news'. *Laudabiliter*, the text most cited as justification for the English colonization of Ireland, was likely literally fake news, forged by Gerald from *Satis laudabiliter*, taking Adrian's words about Muslims and apostate Christians who had converted to Islam under Muslim rule in Spain and applying them to Irish Catholics. Over fifteen years after *Laudabiliter*'s supposed issue but seventeen years before its first appearance in the record, Alexander III espoused similar sentiments, claiming the Irish fallen from the faith in some indeterminate way, building upon bigotry directed at an ever-rotating list of fellow Catholics who were deemed barbarian and no

71 Gervase of Tilbury, *Otia Imperialia: recreation for an emperor*, ed. and trans. S.E. Banks & J.W. Binns (Oxford, 2002), p. 309.   72 *Documents of the affairs of Ireland before the king's council*, ed. G.O. Sayles (Dublin, 1979), pp 99–100.   73 See Callan, *Templars*, especially chapter 2.

longer Christian for political purposes, with opposition to them often likened to crusades. Significantly, however, Alexander did so after learning that Henry had done what he had planned since his accession and invaded Ireland, then had his vaguely defined dominion accepted by the country's Catholic people and princes, as *Satis laudabiliter* stipulated about Spain. Over 150 years later, as the colony experienced significant setbacks and after its first heresy execution, colonial leaders applied *Laudabiliter* to their own context and made its crusade connections concrete, presenting Adducc Dubh O'Toole as Irish apostasy incarnate but calling it heresy, 'heretic' being the new 'barbarian'. John XXII was not persuaded by their plea for a crusade to complete the conquest, and a proposal by colonial leaders to have Henry V ask the pope for a crusade against the Irish in 1421 gained even less traction.[74] The papacy called multiple crusades against Christians starting in the late twelfth century, often for political reasons. The Irish escaped that particular fate but endured something similar in their ongoing colonization, which prefigured similar colonizations in the Americas, Africa, Asia and Australia. These later colonizations are sometimes characterized as crusades as well, but by then the English were no longer Catholic.[75]

---

74 Elizabeth Matthew, 'Henry V and the proposal for an Irish crusade' in Brendan Smith (ed.), *Ireland and the English world in the late Middle Ages* (Basingstoke, 2009), pp 161–75.　**75** See, for example, Nicholas P. Canny, 'The ideology of English colonization: from Ireland to America', *William and Mary Quarterly* 30 (1973), 575–98, at 598.

4 / 'Palmers' as ex-crusaders in Irish urban environments? The evidence of the *Dublin Guild Merchant Roll*

CATHERINE SWIFT

In discussing the military orders, Helen Nicholson has written 'The Templars and Hospitallers came to Ireland because the invaders gave them lands there' before going on to discuss land-owners who have featured very largely in discussion on Irish involvement in crusading.[1] In this short note, I look at a source describing a hither-to unstudied group of possible crusaders, namely the travelling merchant class of early thirteenth-century Dublin. The descriptive epithet 'palmer', which is the most common description of career experience incorporated into the early section of the *Dublin Guild Merchant Roll*, requires a historical explanation and it is argued here that it could indicate the presence of many who returned from the Holy Land to become urban colonists and merchants in Ireland after the Third Crusade.

The *Dublin Guild Merchant Roll* has long been used by scholars as a guide to the first Anglo-Norman settlers in Dublin.[2] Its editors state that 'the origins of the Dublin guild almost certainly lie in the pre-Conquest settlement' but the roll itself is acephalous and the earliest dated figures appear to belong 'to the middle and later years of King John's reign'.[3] It is not thought to be a list of the entirety of Dublin's citizens, but given the difficulty of evaluating the importance of craft and mercantile activities in early Irish towns, the exact percentage of the city's citizenry that the *Roll* might represent is unclear. It is also uncertain what percentage of the entire population of the city were classified as citizens but it seems generally assumed that many, if not most, Dublin households included people of lower status who did not qualify for citizenship, let alone for membership of the guild.

For these reasons, the *Roll* is perhaps most useful as an indicator of the use of by-names and other epithets within what it depicts as a highly internationalized community that was resident, at least sporadically, on Irish soil.

---

1 Nicholson, 'A long way from Jerusalem', pp 6–7. 2 Robin Frame, *Colonial Ireland, 1169–1369* (Dublin, 1981), pp 88–90; Patricia Becker, 'An analysis of the *Dublin Guild Merchant Roll, c.1190–1265*' (MPhil, TCD, 1996). 3 *The* Dublin Guild Merchant Roll, *c.1190–1265*, eds Philomena Connolly & Geoffrey Martin (Dublin, 1992), pp xviii, xiii.

'Palmers' as ex-crusaders in Irish urban environments? 71

It is in such a context it is examined here. By far the most common type of names within the *Roll* are those with the preposition *de* followed by a town or district name. There are also names marked by locational adjectives such as *Cornubiensis* (thirty-one examples), *Walensis* (twenty-two examples), *Flandrensis* (twenty), *Norensis* (fourteen) and *Francigena* (fourteen). There is a very large group of X *filius* Y names that might or might not be a Latin translation of Norman *fitz*, English/Norse *son/sonr*, Welsh *map*, or Irish *mac*, and considerably smaller numbers of names referring to other family relationships such as *nepos* or *frater*.

To indicate the relative strength of the different formulae in the section of the roll pre-1223 (the first year for which absolute dates are provided), there are 765 names incorporating *de*, 264 occupational names, 205 names with a patronymic (X *filius* Y), and seventy-four that incorporate both patronymic and a place of origin (X *filius* Y *de* Z). In a text where occupational names form roughly a quarter of the overall count, the inference must be that each occupation is under-represented. Be that as it may, it is of interest to examine the numbers of people identified with specific occupations relative to one another if only to ponder the picture of the town's activities thus represented. Concentrating on the most popular occupations within this earlier (pre-1223) section on the roll, therefore, one finds nine men termed *parmentarius*, twelve identified as *carpentarius*, eighteen different spellings of *taillor*, thirty-six as *pistor*. There are also forty-six examples of *palmer*, thirty-one of *palmerus* (five in the genitive) and five as *palmerius*, the Latin equivalent of Middle English and Anglo-Norman *palmer* (pl. 4.1). In other words, palmers are by far the biggest group among those whose occupations are attested to in this earlier section of the roll.

The word 'palmer' is defined in the *Anglo-Norman dictionary* as 'pilgrim'.[4] According to William of Tyre, writing in 1188, the palm of Jericho was worn by pilgrims as the formal sign that their pilgrim's vow to travel to Jerusalem had been completed and that they had undergone, at least symbolically, baptism in the river Jordan. As such the palm was akin to but distinct from the scallop shell worn by visitors to Santiago, and a palmer, at least initially, was someone who had specifically travelled to the Holy Land rather than on other pilgrimages.[5] An alternative definition of 'palmer' in the *Dictionary* (supported by citations from the twelfth to the fourteenth centuries) identifies the word as 'palm-tree, date-palm'. By the fourteenth century the word 'palmer' had lost its initial meaning and could be seen more generally as a pilgrim or simply as

---

4 *Anglo-Norman dictionary*, https://anglo-norman.net/entry/palmer_1, accessed 24 Aug. 2020. 5 Jonathan Sumption, *The age of pilgrimage: the medieval journey to God* (Mahwah, NJ, 2003), pp 247–50.

a family surname, but, given the early date of this section of the *Merchant Guild Roll*, this seems an unlikely explanation here.[6]

Overlapping in date with the *Dublin Guild Merchant Roll*, the *Register of the Hospital of St John the Baptist* contains names of men who presumably were residents if not necessarily citizens of Dublin. The editor, Eric St John Brooks, attempted to date the separate texts within the *Register* by reference to the individuals named. In each decade from 1190 to 1229, people with the sobriquet 'palmer' figure in these *Register* texts as indeed do bakers, shoe-makers, gold-workers, money-changers, mercers and glovers among others. The most important of the palmers in the *Register* was Aldredus Palmerus, *magister hospitalis*, who, with his wife, founded the Hospital before 1188 as a religious house for both men and women (pl. 4.2). Other early palmers in the *Register* include a Roger *Palmerus/ Palmer/ le Palmer* who acted as a witness c.1200 and gave land to the Hospital; Radulf and Robert *Palmer*, c.1210, who witnessed a grant of land by the then prior of the Hospital; a Peter *Palmerus* of c.1210 who witnessed a donation of land inside the walls of Dublin by Elias son of Siward the goldsmith, and an Edwardus *Palmerius* who held land in the parish of St Patricks, c.1215.[7] At least some of these might have been members of the religious community founded by Aldred and the sobriquet of 'palmer' might, in this instance, be a reflection of the fact that they were known for their religious piety and affiliation to the Hospital. On the other hand, it is hard to believe that men distinguished for their piety alone could represent the biggest group within a merchant guild. To be a pilgrim, after all, is not a commercial occupation and palmers thus occupied a very different position from the other popular occupation names in the *Merchant Roll*, such as bakers, tailors, wood-workers and cloth merchants.

Given that long distance travel in the medieval period required one to be tough, savvy, alive to danger and good at negotiating, a palmer's life experience might well be seen to overlap with the commercial interests of a merchant guild. By virtue of the fact that Ireland and Britain are both islands, all travellers to the Holy Land must have had access to sea transport and at least some knowledge of European ports both along the Atlantic coasts and within the Mediterranean. Whether such men travelled in small groups or within the broader regulatory framework of a medieval army, they must have had substantial experience of huckstering on an almost daily basis simply in order to eat, find shelter and survive. Given the frequency of references to brigands in sources from throughout Europe, they must also have had considerable exposure to the arts of self-defence.

---

6 *Anglo-Norman dictionary*, http://www.anglo-norman.net, accessed 24 Aug. 2020.　7 *Register of the hospital of St John the Baptist without the New Gate, Dublin*, ed. Eric St John Brooks (Dublin, 1936), pp 114, n. 158; 8, n. 13; 62, n. 92; 92, n. 127.

The logistics of transport for Dublin merchants or indeed crusaders have not been the subject of much consideration in an Irish context. A reference in the *Close Rolls* under the year 1224 refers to the ship of Stephen de Bleden, merchant of Dublin, and tells the bailiffs of Sandwich to let him depart if his vessel was incapable of carrying ten horses. This implies that at least some merchant shipping in and out of Dublin was of relatively limited capacity.[8] This was also true of the ships used by armies. Gerald of Wales speaks of Raymond le Gros carrying thirty knights, one hundred horse-soldiers and three hundred archers in thirty ships around the Irish coast from Leinster to Waterford, and this implies that each ship held, on average, something under twenty men.[9] If such small capacity represents a thirteenth-century norm, it follows that an expedition bearing crusaders to the Holy Land of any scale must have included a substantial number of professional seamen and their boats. Any of these men, whether they were classified as camp-followers or crusading soldiers, could have qualified for the title of palmer once they returned home, provided they had accompanied the army to their ultimate destination.

The names of thirty-one palmers in the early section of the *Dublin Guild Merchant Roll* have a place-name qualifier, of which all but two have been identified by the editors. Eighteen are from England, with the biggest group from Bristol and its environs (six), followed by three from London and its hinterland, three from northern England, two from Sussex, two from the area of Winchester and two from the Cotswolds. The second largest group, perhaps surprisingly, is from Ireland, with at least five examples: *Clunard*, Limerick, Cork, *Ultonia*, Kilmainham and possibly *Villa Laprihd* (Leopardstown?). Four are from Wales (with two from Haverfordwest) and one each from Scotland and Cornwall. This pattern is broadly consistent with the general trends of the *Roll*, although, as the editors have pointed out, the most frequent town mentioned is Cardiff[10] (not associated with any palmers) and the Irish element above is stronger than in the early section of the *Roll* as a whole. Only one is identified with a specific occupation: Radulphus *Palmerus le Tannur*.

Of the personal names of the *Roll* palmers, the most popular is William (sixteen examples), followed by Ricardus with five, Robert and Roger with four, Ade/Adam, Galfrid and Elias with three and Osbert, Walter, Hugo, Jordan, Eilward, and Ernald with two each. Again, this fits with the trends of the *Roll*: all these names, with the exception of Eilward and Ernald, occur among the *Roll's* fifteen most frequent personal names in the early section.[11]

---

8 *CDI* i, no. 1192. 9 Giraldus, *Opera*, v, p. 312. 10 *Dublin Guild Merchant Roll*, p. xix. 11 Anglo-Saxon Alward and Arnold are both relatively common in Domesday Book (J. McNeal Dodgson & J.J.N. Palmer, *Domesday Book: index of persons* (Chichester, 1992), pp 29, 37).

74   *Ireland and the crusades*

The evidence for sons and fathers in England suggests the rapid spread of names such as William after the Norman conquest and an example of such processes in the *Roll* is perhaps Willelmus *palmerius filius* Torkil or Nicholaus *palmerius filius* Aillardi, while Turstinus *palmer* might have been either Anglo-Scandinavian or a Norman of Norse descent.[12] Reiner *palmer* looks as if he might be of Germanic background, possibly from Flanders (although one has to remember the many Flemings who settled in England and Wales after 1066). There is also Galgethel *palmer filius* Reinaldi, the etymology of whose name remains obscure.

By far the most common membership fee of the *Dublin Guild Merchant Roll* is 9*s*. The Dublin palmers are typical of other Guild merchants with thirty-one paying 9*s*.; seventeen paying 9½*s*., six on 8½*s*. and ten on 8*s*.

Those paying lower fees might have been local residents; one of the best parallels for the *Dublin Guild Merchant Roll* are the borough records for Leicester and there the evidence is rather different. The first *Leicester Guild Roll*, running from 1196 to 1233, shows a greater variety of payments in entrance fee, together with hanse money and bull-fees. The exact meaning behind the term bull-fee is not clear; it might originally have involved the actual purchase of bulls, but by the time of the borough rolls it had been converted to a money payment. Similarly, hanse money might have been a monetary contribution to one of the town's burdens in taxes, possibly one levied by the earl. The descendant of a guildsman in Leicester could inherit a seat free of these charges while men native to Leicester paid 3*s*. only; those who were not native paid 6*s*. 8*d*.[13] Four of the five Leicester 'palmer' references are to relatives rather than to men who are palmers in their own right and none pay membership fees. William *palmerius de* Beuerle (Beverley in Yorkshire) is the exception and, notably, his fee was at the high rate (for Leicester) of 9*s*., indicating the probability that he was a recent incomer.[14]

The Leicester pattern is very different from that of Dublin; in the latter, only five men are identified as relatives of palmers: *nepos* Walteri *palmeri*, *cognatus* Willelmi *palmeri* and three *filius Palmeri* (with no personal name). It is possible that these five might represent the second generation of their families in Dublin though the fees paid were apparently all non-native with the exception of Walter *filius Palmeri* who paid 6*s*. At the lower end, there are single examples of men paying 5 ½*s*., 5*s*. and 4*s*., which might also represent second-generation inhabitants; interestingly, the man paying least is Reiner *palmer*. Overall, however, the fees paid by the Dublin palmers, as with the general membership of

12 Gillian Fellows Jensen, *Scandinavian personal names in Lincolnshire and Yorkshire* (Copenhagen, 1968), pp 236–9, 313–16. 13 *Records of the borough of Leicester, 1196–1327*, ed. M.E. Bateson (London, 1899), pp xxviii–xxix. 14 *Records of the borough of Leicester*, pp 15–17, 24, 28 30.

the *Dublin Guild Merchant Roll*,[15] indicate that most were probably newcomers to Dublin while their personal names suggest that most originated in the wider Anglo-Norman world.

It is suggested here that a plausible explanation for this large influx of palmers into the Dublin merchant guild in the earliest years of the thirteenth century is that they represent veterans of the armies that had fought on the Third Crusade. The most common Latin term at this period for crusading combatants was *crucesignatus*, of which only one example is found in the *Dublin Guild Merchant Roll*: Willelmus *crucesignatus* who paid the incomer's fee of 9s. This title bestowed important legal privileges on those who bore it and not everybody involved in the wider crusading environment was necessarily entitled to it.[16] Another term, used for participants in the Albigensian Crusade, was the less specific *peregrinatus* (wanderer or pilgrim); this word is not found in the *Merchant Guild Roll*.[17] The contemporary vernacular word in Middle English for all such men, however, especially for those belonging to the lower social orders, was 'palmer' and even Richard the Lionheart could be so described.[18] The key element in the definition, as it is used in Middle English, is the state of being travel-worn and a stranger and it thus presumably also covers the wider group of camp followers, servants and seamen who accompanied the armies to the East.

The Dublin palmers were located in a city that was, at the time, involved in building a strong royal castle and was the administrative head of a colony in which an extensive programme of castle building was taking place. It does not seem strange that such an environment would have attracted many ex-military men, or, as they grew older and less able for army life, that such seasoned travellers might have turned to making their money in transport. The early thirteenth-century *Tristams saga ok Ísöndar*, with its relatively extensive treatment of Dublin, describes how men-at-arms (*riddara*) operating on Europe's north Atlantic coasts could easily be mistaken for *kaupmenn* or merchants, and that such men were among the merchants who visited Dublin harbour and sought permission to trade.[19] There is also explicit reference to the existence of fighting men among the guild members of Dublin with names such as Johannes Flandrensis le Riddire, Gillibertus Se[...] *militis*, Rogerus Cniht, Willelmus

---

15 *Dublin Guild Merchant Roll*, p. xix.   16 Giraldus, *Opera*, iv, p. 151; Jessalyn Bird, 'Crusaders rights revisited: the use and abuse of crusader privileges in early thirteenth-century France' in Ruth Mazo Karras, Joel Kaye & E. Ann Matter (eds), *Law and the illicit in medieval Europe* (Philadelphia, 2008), pp 133–46.   17 Laurence W. Marvin, *The Occitan war, a military and political history of the Albigensian Crusade, 1208–1219* (Cambridge, 2008), p. 16. My thanks to Paul Duffy for this reference.   18 *Middle English dictionary*, https://quod.lib. umich.edu/m/middle-english-dictionary/dictionary/MED32260/track?counter=2&search_id=4176784 and linked quotations, accessed 20 Aug. 2020.   19 Marianne E. Kalinke (ed.), *Norse romance I: the Tristan legend* (Cambridge, 1999), pp 94–7.

filius Herberti *militus* and Patricius *miles*.[20] Tough men with experience of travel and warfare were presumably not only common but valued members of the guild, capable not only of transporting goods to and from foreign lands but also of defending themselves and their wealth from attack.

Finally, it is worth considering Duvenaldus *palmerius de* Limeric, the only palmer in the *Roll* with an Irish name (although see Patrick *miles* above). The Ostman town of Limerick had been briefly occupied by Anglo-Norman troops in 1175/6 but had then reverted to independent rule under Domnall Mór Ua Briain until 1194. Duvenaldus *palmerius* (otherwise Domnall) presumably originated in an Irish-speaking environment, but where and when he might have decided to travel to the Holy Land is unclear. He might, of course, have been encouraged by clerical recruiters in the same way that three thousand Welshmen 'highly skilled in the use of the spear and the arrow' had been enlisted by Archbishop Baldwin.[21] The Norse *Tristams saga* offers us a description of a contemporary Irish merchant: *grimmr ok drjúgr at afli ok í vápnaskipti, djarfr í atreiðum, mikill at vexti* ('a harsh man, fierce in using his power and adroit in battle, bold in fighting on horseback and huge in size').[22] One can imagine Domnall as one such, arriving back into Ireland, swarthy after his journey to Jerusalem and swaggering down the streets of Dublin and Limerick, a man well able to hold his own among his English and French-speaking peers in the thriving environment of the rapidly expanding colony that King Richard's brother John was creating in Ireland.

20 *Dublin Guild Merchant Roll*, pp 1 [f. 1/a], 33 [9d/a], 36 [f. 10/a], 39 [10d/b].   21 *The journey through Wales: the description of Wales*, trans. Lewis Thorpe (London, 1978), p. 204 (II 13).   22 Kalinke, *Norse romance* I, pp 74–5.

5 / Curtailing kings: Ireland, the Cathar Crusade and the cult of Simon de Montfort

PAUL DUFFY

CATHARS AND DOMINICANS

In 1162, a small group of preachers led by a man named Gerard landed in England promulgating an extreme and unorthodox version of the Christian faith.[1] These people are believed to have been what modern scholars term 'Cathars', dissident Christians who subscribed to varying degrees of dualist beliefs and who flourished in areas of Europe in the twelfth and thirteenth centuries.[2] The 1160s in particular appear to have been a period of significant increase in such proselytizing activity, with preaching heretics reported by various chronicles across the south of France, and in Catalonia, northern France, Flanders and Germany.[3] It appears, however, that Gerard and his confreres met with little success among the English and were soon driven off the island.

William of Newburgh, who recorded this event, claimed that Gerard's group came from Gascony, an area within the domain of Henry II of England.[4] Given the extensive importation of wine into Ireland from the western seaboard of France through the later twelfth century, it is interesting to speculate on whether a group such as Gerard's might have visited Ireland around this time.[5] Hundreds of thousands of sherds of ceramic from the region of Saintonge, immediately north of Bordeaux in western France, have been excavated in urban contexts from the medieval Irish port towns. The volume of ceramic from this area is not paralleled in English sites, where ceramic imports from Normandy and Flanders proliferate, and this serves to highlight

---

1 See Peter Biller, 'William of Newburgh and the Cathar mission to England', *Studies in Church History*. Subsidia 12 (1999), 11–30. 2 The Cathar faith offered a very personal spirituality and revolved around the administering of a single sacrament: the *consolamentum*. The much-debated nature and origin of Catharism has seen extensive scholarly research published in recent decades and a full treatment of such falls far beyond the scope of this paper. For full discussion see Michel Roquebert, *La religion cathare le bien, le mal et le salut dans l'hérésie médiévale* (Paris, 2001); Malcolm Barber, *The Cathars: dualist heretics in Languedoc in the high Middle Ages* (London, 2000); Mark Pegg, *A most holy war: the Albigensian Crusade and the battle for Christendom* (Oxford, 2008). 3 Heinrich Fichtenau, *Heretics and scholars in the high Middle Ages, 1000–1200* (University Park, PA, 1998), pp 83–5. 4 Though some commentators suggest Flanders as a more likely point of departure: see Fichtenau, *Heretics and scholars*, p. 84. 5 Jean-Michel Picard, 'Aquitaine et Irlande dans le haut moyen age', in Jean-Michel Picard (ed.), *Aquitaine and Ireland in the Middle Ages* (Dublin, 1994), pp 17–30.

78   *Ireland and the crusades*

the significant trade in wine coming to Ireland from western France throughout this period.[6] While Gascony and the Saintonge region are not strongly
associated with the spread of Catharism, there are some indications of the
heresy in this area. Of Catharism, William of Tudela, writing *c.*1213, stated that
'all the way from Beziers to Bordeaux many, or indeed, most people believed
in or supported it.'[7] Clare Taylor has drawn attention to a cleric working for
the archbishop of Bordeaux in 1214 who was forced to flee following accusations of heresy, and to a *diachonum haereticorum* (heretical deacon) of Saintonge,
recorded in the Languedoc in 1237.[8] These examples illustrate that the region
with which Ireland was carrying out frequent and substantial maritime trade
was no stranger to Catharism.

What is clear, however, is that if Cathar beliefs or doctrine were ever
whispered around the quays of Dublin, Galway or Limerick by Continental
travellers or merchants, or indeed proclaimed more confidently in front of
the market cross at Cork, New Ross or Waterford by proselytizing groups, no
mentions of such activities survive in the documents. The well-known heresy
trials of Adam Duff O'Toole and Philip Braydock in the fourteenth century
cannot be said to contain any accusation against those involved that could be
aligned with Catharism, and they have been shown quite unambiguously to
have had political or racial motivations.[9] It is fair to say, therefore, that, as with
England, Cathar beliefs never significantly impacted upon either colonial or
Gaelic-Irish populations in Ireland.

Some sixty-two years after Gerard's visit, a small group led by the Dominican
friar Gilbert de Freynet landed in England to spread Dominican preaching,
which had evolved in direct opposition to, and in some respects had appropri-
ated, the methods of the Cathars. The group travelled to Canterbury in 1221,
where archbishop Stephen Langton was presiding. Langton was apparently so
taken with their preaching that he instantly granted them permission to set
up chapters in London and Oxford. The fact that the Dominicans were the
preaching arm of the anti-Cathar crusaders must have helped their cause, given
that the archbishop had himself preached against heresiarchs in Italy in the
early thirteenth century.[10] The archbishop's brother, Walter Langton, had also
spent at least seven years on the crusade against the Cathars in southern France.

---

6 Clare McCutcheon, *Medieval pottery from Wood Quay, Dublin* (Dublin, 2006), pp 87–8.   7 Janet Shirley,
The song of the Cathar wars: a history of the Albigensian Crusade (Farnham, 1996), p. 12.   8 Clare Taylor, 'Heresy
in medieval France: dualism in Aquitaine and the Agenais, 1000–1249' (PhD, University of Nottingham,
1999), p. 143; *Matthaei Parisiensis, monachi Sancti Albani chronica maiora, 1200–1259*, ed. H.R. Luard (London,
1877), iv, pp 270–2.   9 See Bernadette Williams, 'Heresy in Ireland in the thirteenth and fourteenth centuries' in Seán Duffy (ed.), *Princes, prelates and poets in medieval Ireland* (Dublin, 2016), pp 339–51.   10 Jessalyn
Bird, 'Paris masters and the justification of the Albigensian Crusade', *Crusades* 6 (2007), 117–55, at 117.

Curtailing kings: Ireland, the Cathar Crusade and the cult of Simon de Montfort

Within three years of this audience at Canterbury, Dominican foundations had been established in Dublin and Drogheda, and the order was to spread across both the English colony in Ireland as well as Gaelic-Irish-controlled lands over the coming century. Over the following centuries, the Dominicans were to leave a significant mark on the religious and cultural life of the island. As shall be seen, St Dominic was materially assisted and supported in the south of France by Hugh de Lacy II, earl of Ulster.[11]

TAKING THE CROSS

The event known to history as the Albigensian (or more popularly Cathar) Crusade raged from 1209 to 1229 across the southern portion of France, comprising modern departments of Languedoc and Midi-Pyrenees, a cultural zone often termed 'Occitania' by modern historians.[12] The conflict was characterized by years of siege warfare in which crusaders, comprised largely of northern French knights, besieged and consolidated towns and villages across the region, establishing themselves and their captains as overlords. The two principal nodes within this vacillating current of conflict were the large urban centres of Carcassonne, which was occupied early on by the crusaders under Simon de Montfort, and Toulouse, a bulkhead of resistance for the southern nobility led by the counts of Toulouse, Raymond VI, brother in-law to King John, and subsequently his son Raymond VII.

While there is no evidence to support large-scale Irish participation in the crusade, surviving papal documents show that Innocent III dispatched letters to instruct the preaching of crusade to the Holy Land among the Irish. Innocent III issued a letter promoting the anti-heretical crusade in 1208. However, no papal letters survive for Ireland between 1207 and 1210. It remains unclear if such a letter was sent as far as Ireland. The survival of other letters relating to crusade provide some indication that the pope did not hesitate to target Ireland as a recruiting ground. In April 1213, the pope issued the letter *Quia major* across Christendom, including copies to Mellifont and Dublin, to exhort the Irish to take part in what would ultimately become the Fifth Crusade, launched in 1217.[13] An accompanying letter read: 'To the executors of the above letter: to preach the cross and to collect the Holy Land subsidy; in *eudem modum* to the archbishop of Dublin and the abbot of Mellifont for Ireland.'[14]

---

11 Paul Duffy, 'The exiled earl and soon to be saint', *HI* 24: 5 (2016), 16–19.   12 Also referred to as the Midi or Languedoc in writings on the period.   13 Patrick J. Dunning, 'The letters of Innocent III to Ireland', *Traditio* 18 (1962), 229–53, at 244.   14 Ibid.

In sending this letter to Mellifont, there is an implicit expectation that the Cistercians would play an active role the dissemination of crusader ideology in Ireland. While such a preaching role is at variance with the cloistered rule of the Cistercians, Beverly Mayne Kienzle wrote that:

> Led by the example of Bernard of Clairvaux, Cistercian monks turned their attention to the world outside the monastery walls in response to the threat posed by heretical Christians, in particular the Cathars. The white monks, with other intellectuals, turned to pen, pulpit and popular preaching to counteract heresy, some accepting posts as bishops and papal legates, helping and even directing the Albigensian Crusade, and contributing to the formulation of procedures for inquisition.[15]

While the papal letters in this instance clearly refer to a crusade to the Holy Land, preaching crusade to the Levant, and not against the Cathars, the two movements were not mutually exclusive. Robert Courson, the Paris-educated Englishman and French legate during this period, was actively preaching the Fifth Crusade as well as continuing in his role promoting the crusade in southern France.[16] Indeed, it has been noted that the widespread call to 'preach the cross' issued by Innocent in 1213 was due, in part, to the preoccupation of the French crusading classes with the Cathars and the opportunities to be had in their lands.

Given that the Fifth Crusade was preached in 1213 with papal instruction to collect the 'Holy Land subsidy', although the crusade did not eventuate until four years later, there might have been a number of Irish men sufficiently inflamed by the Cistercian rhetoric to embark upon the Cathar Crusade, which was then in full force and had the advantage of being much closer to home. For those traveling from western Europe, the Cathar enterprise called for less expense, less risk and less commitment of travel time, while also offering a full plenary indulgence.

CONSPIRACY AND CRUSADE

The most tangible and significant link between Ireland and the Cathar Crusade comes in the form of Hugh de Lacy II's participation in Occitania and his subsequent administration of a crusader lordship there for over a decade. This

---

15 Beverly M. Kienzle, *Cistercians, heresy, and crusade in Occitania, 1145–1229: preaching in the Lord's vineyard* (York, 2001), p. 2.   16 John W. Baldwin, *Paris, 1200* (Stanford, 2010), p. 10.

previously overlooked element of Irish history has been extensively examined in recent years.[17] In 1211, Hugh played a crucial part in the victory of the crusaders over the army of Raymond VI at Castelnaudary. As a result, he paved the way for de Montfort's army to triumph over Peter II of Aragon in 1213 at Muret. De Lacy was granted a lordship of critical importance, commanding the route between Toulouse and Carcassonne, over which he presided until 1221. During this time, he made several grants to the nascent Dominican order, established a Hospitaller commandery that would endure until the French Revolution, and participated in the major sieges and battles of the period, in the process leaving an enduring mark upon the literary heritage of the crusade.

In the context of this study, several elements of this story bear revisiting, in particular the events leading to Hugh's exile from Ireland in 1210, which resulted in him joining the first rank of the crusaders under Simon de Montfort. It has been established that Hugh de Lacy II, earl of Ulster, was intriguing with the French king in 1210, along with his brother Walter, lord of Meath, his half-brother William, William de Braose, lord of Limerick and of Bramber, and John de Lacy, constable of Chester.[18] The great Welsh prince Lwellyn ab Iorwerth, and the Scottish king William, were also involved to some degree.[19] While the exact nature of this conspiracy has remained obscure, the objective was clearly to remove John from the English throne.

The justification for deposing John in 1210 was simply constructed: John had refused to admit Stephen Langton, the pope's candidate, to the see of Canterbury, leading to an interdict placed upon England in 1208. Further, John's willingness to take the part of his brother-in law Raymond VI of Toulouse at the outset of the crusade opened the king up to exaggerated claims of sympathy for heretics. The pope, Innocent III, the man who had appointed Langton to the see of Canterbury in the first instance, would go so far as to offer the English crown to Phillip Augustus in 1213.[20]

These factors are significant considering Stephen Langton was, for periods, in Paris during his exile and was no stranger to the Capetian court. Indeed, a connection with the conspirators is clearly indicated in that Gilbert de Braose, brother to William, was in Langton's entourage in the years immediately following the interdict. Langton was certainly involved in the later

---

17 Paul Duffy, '"Ung sage et valent home": Hugh de Lacy and the Albigensian Crusade', *JRSAI* 141 (2011), 66–90; Daniel Brown, *Hugh de Lacy, first earl of Ulster: rising and falling in Angevin Ireland* (Woodbridge, 2016), pp 115–64; Colin Veach, *Lordship in the four realms: the Lacy family, 1166–1241* (Manchester, 2014), pp 147–52; Duffy et al., *From Carrickfergus to Carcassonne*. **18** Brown, *Hugh de Lacy*, pp 106–7; Veach, *Lordship in the four realms*, pp 138–41. **19** Brown, *Hugh de Lacy*, pp 108–9. **20** John W. Baldwin, 'Master Stephen Langton, future archbishop of Canterbury: the Paris Schools and Magna Carta', *EHR* 123 (2008), 811–46, at 842–3; Stephen Church, *King John: England Magna Carta and the making of a tyrant* (London, 2015), p. 179.

82   *Ireland and the crusades*

conspiracy of 1216 during the First Barons' War.[21] The objective of that plot was to de-throne King John, and supplant him with Prince Louis of France. While Prince Louis would have been too young to be installed on the English throne in 1210, the Dunstable annalist claimed that John was to be replaced by Simon de Montfort, leader of the Cathar Crusade.[22]

This claim, which at first seems unlikely, is given credence by the events that followed. In the wake of comprehensive defeat by John in Ulster, Hugh de Lacy II and William de Braose regrouped in Paris. Evidence would suggest that they were in the company of Langton or at least his entourage during this time. De Lacy departed to Occitania on crusade early in 1211 in the company of Langton's brother Walter. De Lacy was instantly installed as a captain of the crusade while William de Braose was to die a few months later and was buried by Langton in the abbey of St Victor.

Associations between de Montfort and the de Braose and de Lacy families have been teased out by Colin Veach, illustrating several generations of significant connections in Normandy.[23] The men who attempted to represent Hugh de Lacy II's interests to the minority government in 1213, Ranulf of Chester and his nephew William Ferrers, count of Derby, were also both closely related to the Montforts of Evreux.[24] Colin Veach has also uncovered evidence that there was a familial relationship between the de Lacys and Ranulf of Chester.[25]

The congregation of exiles in Paris fleeing the regime of King John in 1211 was therefore far from coincidental. All of these men, in casting around for a substitute for King John, had settled upon the charismatic, driven and pious Simon de Montfort as a candidate. Montfort had claims to an English title – that of the count of Leicester – through his mother Amicia de Beaumont, and he had already visited England in 1207 with a view to claiming these lands. John ultimately denied his appeal, remaining inflexible in his decision, despite the fact that de Montfort was shown to be in favour with the pope. Innocent III even went so far as to command John to restore the title to de Montfort, although this command was ignored. The plausibility of this conspiracy is firmly strengthened by the attempt to overthrow John in 1216 and replace him with Prince Louis of France, a scheme that had the backing of the pope and of Stephen Langton.

The above detail illustrates that de Lacy's participation in the Cathar Crusade was far from opportunistic and that his immediate promotion within

---

21 Simon Langton, Stephen's brother and probable chancellor, was sighted on the flotilla of ships comprising Louis' invasion force. See Baldwin, 'Master Stephen Langton,' 844–6.   22 Veach, *Lordship in the four realms*, p. 139.   23 Ibid., 24–5.   24 Ranulf's mother was Bertrade de Montfort, countess of Evreux, making him a first cousin to Simon de Montfort.   25 Veach, *Lordship in the four realms*, p. 193.

Curtailing kings: Ireland, the Cathar Crusade and the cult of Simon de Montfort   83

the ranks of the crusaders was most likely owing to the fact that he had conspired with de Montfort, building upon a longstanding family obligation and connection. What has gone unexplored in the literature is the potential role of Stephen Langton in this conspiracy.[26] In addition to his public dispute with John, Langton was well known for his preaching and theological treatments, which advocated for a constraint of absolute royal power over subjects. Baldwin outlined one of the archbishop's principal positions: 'Langton formulated political propositions of which the most striking included the necessity of written law to protect the people from the king and, in particular, the people's right to resist a decision which was rendered without a judgment of the king's court.'[27]

This ideology appears to have guided de Lacy and his fellow conspirators in 1210 and might have also influenced Simon de Montfort's Statutes of Pamiers, issued in 1212. Langton and his fellow Paris confreres, chiefly Robert Courson, advocated for a curtailment of the king's power throughout the early thirteenth century. This kind of ideology incubated far from the purview of royal intervention is sure to have found favour among the kind of warrior confraternity exemplified by the crusaders in Occitania. In some of its aspects, the Statutes of Pamiers prefigured Magna Carta, first issued in 1215, a document that Langton was instrumental in drafting.[28] Both Jessalyn Bird and Gregory Lippiatt made the case that the input of the Paris masters can be clearly read in the language of de Montfort's statutes.[29] Hugh de Lacy II was almost certainly present at the parliament that gave rise to the statutes and such an assembly, with its promise of a receptive, blank canvas upon which his political reforms could be exercised, might have attracted Stephen Langton from his place of exile in Pontigny abbey in Burgundy.[30]

THE CULT OF SIMON DE MONTFORT

Following Hugh de Lacy II's return to Ireland and his unleashing of war there in 1224, it would be Stephen Langton who would secure the lifting of excommunication from the exiled earl. In 1229, two years after Hugh's

26 Though Gregory Lippiatt skirts the possibility. See G.E.M. Lippiatt, *Simon V of Montfort and baronial government, 1195–1218* (Oxford, 2017), p. 80.   27 Baldwin, 'Master Stephen Langton', 823.   28 Nicholas Vincent, *Magna Carta: a very short introduction* (Oxford, 2012), pp 62–4.   29 Bird, 'The Paris masters', 129; Lippiatt, *Simon V of Montfort*, pp 90–6.   30 Langton is not named in the short list of ecclesiasts at the opening of the statutes; however, the document also makes mention of many unnamed 'wise men and barons and chiefs amongst my followers'. See Peter of les Vaux-de-Cernay: *The history of the Albigensian Crusade*, ed. and trans. W.A. Silby & M.D. Silby (Woodbridge, 1998), p. 321.

restoration to Ulster, the earldom of Leicester, denied to Simon de Montfort on account of his French loyalties, was conferred on Ranulf, earl of Chester. In 1231 this earldom was unexpectedly ceded to the young Simon de Montfort, who, exhibiting many of his father's qualities, was to have an enormous impact upon the English kingdom.[31] Simon, as a child, had lived with his mother in the crusaders' camp and would have been well acquainted with Hugh de Lacy II in Occitania.[32] He was present at the siege of Tolouse in 1218 where Hugh was a celebrated captain and they both would have witnessed the violent death of Simon the elder (pl. 5.1). Hugh remained loyal to the Montfort family during the following years in Languedoc, despite the unfurling of the crusade, and participated in the Battle of Baziège (pl. 5.2). In 1237 he witnessed a grant by de Lacy to the church of St Andrew, confirming that de Lacy had met the son of his former captain on at least one further occasion.[33] In fact, the connection between the two men is likely to have been much more significant than that hinted at in the sources.

The ceding of the vast and wealthy county of Leicester to Simon the younger by Ranulf of Chester has been explained in the context of Ranulf's lack of an heir and an ill-defined avuncular feeling towards the young de Montfort.[34] The conspiracy of 1210, outlined above, provides a broader perspective for this event. As we have seen, Ranulf was a cousin of the young Simon and also a consistent supporter of (and relation of) Hugh de Lacy. Given Hugh's close association with Ranulf, it is plausible that some kind of interest was exerted by Hugh in favour of the son of his former captain.

Over the following decades, Simon de Montfort the younger was to champion the political ideology of Langton (who had died in 1228) and reintroduce shades of the failed conspiracy involving his father in 1210, almost bringing both aspirations to fruition. Known popularly as the 'first parliamentarian', Montfort was the central figure in the Second Barons' War and almost succeeded in supplanting the Angevin throne and wresting power for himself and his followers. His parliamentary credentials rest upon his relentless insistence upon the implementation of Magna Carta and the very 'Langtonian' ideals upon which it was founded. Following his defeat and death in 1265 at Evesham, Simon de Montfort the younger became the centre of a saint's cult that was to persist for the following generations despite prohibition from both the crown and papacy.

---

31 John R. Maddicott, *Simon de Montfort* (Cambridge, 1994), p. 8. 32 Ibid., p. 4. 33 *Liber cartarum prioratus Sancti Andree in Scotia*, ed. Thomas Thompson (Edinburgh, 1841), p. 119. For a discussion of the context of this grant see Daniel Brown, 'Power and patronage across the north channel: Hugh de Lacy, St Andrews and the Anglo-Scottish crisis of 1209 [Part 1]', *Scottish Historical Review* 94 (2015), 1–23. 34 Sophie Thérese Ambler, *The song of Simon de Montfort: England's first revolutionary and the death of chivalry* (London, 2019), pp 38–41.

Curtailing kings: Ireland, the Cathar Crusade and the cult of Simon de Montfort

While Hugh de Lacy II had died before Simon de Montfort's rebellion, it is tantalizing to speculate whether the earl would have been among the ranks of the Irish barons who fought against Simon at Evesham, or whether he would have supported the rebel cause.[35] Two fascinating fragments of evidence for a cult of Simon de Montfort existing among de Lacy's milieu in Ireland might suggest the latter. The first, a poem lamenting Simon's death at Evesham, has recently been discussed by Jean-Michel Picard.[36] The poem is preserved in a Franciscan codex containing, among other documents, the so-called *Annals of Multyfarnham* written by Stephen de Exonia (of Exeter).[37] It is one of two extant copies of the poem. The second, quite a famous document, is preserved in the British Museum.

Hugh Shields described the text as 'a poem in rough style marked neither by the stirrings of genius nor by the exercise of careful craft, and yet a moving record of something like personal indignation at a tragic and unexpected turn in history'.[38] The sincerity of the poet is hard to doubt in the following heartfelt lines:

> All in tears,
> I wrote the song
> about our valiant lord
> who for the sake of peace
> so far removed
> let himself be tortured
> in order to save
> the people of England.[39]

Shields illustrated how, due to some discreet changes to the text, the TCD version of the lament was drafted in Ireland, and Picard argues that the poem was constructed to be sung as a lament.[40] The poem has been dated to the early 1270s and falls within the time frame when Stephen of Exeter was drafting his annals.[41] Stephen of Exeter has long been associated with Strade priory, Co. Mayo, founded by Jordan of Exeter, and prevailing opinion has followed

---

35 *Annales Monastici: Annales Monasterii de Waverleia*, ed. H.R. Luard (London, 1865), ii, p. 365; for discussion of the context of this participaton, see Robin Frame, *Ireland and Britain, 1170–1450* (London, 1998), pp 59–69. 36 Jean-Michel Picard, 'Transmission and circulation of French texts in medieval Ireland: the other Simon de Montfort', in Duffy et al., *From Carrickfergus to Carcassonne*, pp 129–50, at pp 148–50. 37 TCD MS 347 [C.5.8]. 38 Hugh Shields, 'The "Lament for Simon de Montfort": an unnoticed text of the French poem', *Medium Ævum* 41 (1972), 202–7, at 202. 39 Picard, 'Transmission of French texts', pp 148–9. 40 Shields, 'The "Lament for Simon de Montfort"', 203–4; Picard, 'Transmission of French texts', p. 149. 41 Ibid., p. 205.

86 *Ireland and the crusades*

the view that the annals were written in this house.[42] However, Bernadette Williams has shown, through meticulous research, that Stephen of Exeter, while probably of the Exeter family of Meath, was writing in Roscommon.[43]

Though not immediately apparent, Strade priory owes its foundation to Hugh de Lacy, earl of Ulster. The southern half of the cantred of Luighne, including the greater part of the barony of Gallen (Gailenga), was given by Hugh de Lacy II to Jordan of Exeter immediately following the conquest of Connacht in 1235. This conquest was achieved by a military campaign involving a confederation of Anglo-Norman barons and Gaelic-Irish supporters, led by Richard de Burgo and including Hugh de Lacy as a principal captain. During the campaign, the island fortress of Lough Cé was besieged and the specifics of the attack – covered fighting galleries mounted on rafts, the use of perriers and mangonels – represent a first in an Irish context. These tactics must have come from Hugh's decade of participating in siege warfare in Occitania, where covered galleries and other siege engines were used extensively.

If indeed, as appears likely, Stephen de Exeter was in the entourage of Richard of Exeter during his time in Roscommon, there is also a clear connection with the de Lacys. Richard of Exeter, constable of Roscommon Castle during the years that the annals were being drafted, was also a baron in Uriel (Louth) and was connected to the de Lacys by marriage.[44]

While it is by no means certain that the lament was drafted by Stephen of Exeter, the poem appears on a quire that is probably contemporary with the annals and Stephen is therefore the closest name with whom we can associate the poem.[45] It is notable that, through his marriage to the widow of William Marshal the younger, Simon de Montfort inherited significant estates in Leinster, yet it is not from his own lands or feudatories in Ireland that evidence for his cult derive but, rather, from families connected to the de Lacys.

The second indication of an Irish cult to de Montfort is contained within *The liber miraculorum Simonis de Montfort*[46] and can be more closely linked to the de Lacys. The *liber* is a collection of miracle stories attributed to Simon that was produced in the years after his death at Evesham, and John St Lawrence pointed to this manuscript as an illustration of how Montfort partisans

---

42 A.B. Scott, 'Latin learning and literature in Ireland, 1169–1500' in Dáibhí Ó Cróinín (ed.), *A new history of Ireland*, i: *Prehistoric and early Ireland* (Oxford, 2005), pp 934–5, at p. 990. 43 *The 'Annals of Multyfarnham': Roscommon and Connacht provenance*, ed. and trans. Bernadette Williams (Dublin, 2012), pp 92–3. 44 Brendan Smith, 'The medieval border; Anglo-Irish and Gaelic Irish in late thirteenth and early fourteenth century Uriel' in Raymond Gillespie & Harold O'Sullivan (eds), *The borderlands: essays on the history of the Ulster-Leinster border* (Belfast, 1989), pp 41–54, at p. 45. 45 *The 'Annals of Multyfarnham'*, p. 22. 46 *The chronicle of William de Rishanger, of the barons' wars: the miracles of Simon de Montfort*, ed. James Orchard Halliwell-Phillipps (London, 1840).

Curtailing kings: Ireland, the Cathar Crusade and the cult of Simon de Montfort   87

managed 'covertly to transmit stories about the new St Simon to the keepers of his shrine'.[47] Simon's tomb at Evesham and a nearby spring that was found after the battle, according to the *liber*, 'in the place where the holy martyrs fell',[48] appear to have formed the focus of the pilgrimages (pl. 5.3). In his doctoral study of the *liber*, St Lawrence concluded that scribes belonging to Evesham abbey compiled the *miracula* by recording the stories relayed by pilgrims visiting the tomb and holy well there in the later thirteenth century. The pilgrims' central aim was to give or convey thanks for a miracle already performed and there are hundreds of such miracles recorded in the *Liber*. Of these, two are associated with Ireland and the de Feypo family, who were household knights of the de Lacys in Herefordshire and subsequently grantees of the important barony of Skryne in Meath. As these miracles have not, as far as I can ascertain, been discussed in an Irish context, they bear reproduction here. The miracle of primary interest was presumably related to the scribe of Evesham sometime in the later 1260s or 1270s runs as follows:

> Richard Seypo [Feypo], an Irish knight, had a wife pregnant and feverish, and, because of suffering and pain, she lost the power of speech; the doctors despaired and said, 'either the child will die or the mother'. A little later she turned and vomited, and bore a beautiful boy, but stillborn. The aforementioned Richard bent a penny to our martyr [de Montfort], over the mother and the boy, and the boy returned to life and the mother was well; and they gave the name, Simon de Montfort. Also, the aforementioned Richard, having chest pains for a year, in a similar fashion recovered. The witnesses to this thing, the said Richard, along with his entire household.[49]

This remarkable vignette of medieval pilgrimage from Ireland can be corroborated by the de Feypo family tree and is consistent with the main branch of the Skryne de Feypos, who held their barony from Walter de Lacy. Adam de Feypo was a household knight to the de Lacy family in Herefordshire and he accompanied his lord Hugh de Lay (the elder) to Ireland in the 1170s. Adam was the only household knight of de Lacy's retinue who was granted a substantial holding in Meath. Adam was succeeded by his son Richard (d. 1232), who was in turn succeeded by his son Richard (d. 1284). Richard the younger had two sons, another Richard who died young, and a second

---

47 John Edward St Lawrence, 'The liber miraculorum of Simon de Montfort: contested sanctity and contesting authority in late thirteenth-century England' (PhD, University of Texas, 2005), pp vi–vii.   48 *Rishanger, the barons' wars*, p. 68.   49 Ibid., pp 72–3; St Lawrence, 'Liber miraculorum', pp 203–4.

88   *Ireland and the crusades*

son who succeeded to the barony who was indeed named Simon de Feypo who served against the Scots (1296), was summoned to parliament (1297) and proved a successful 'old English' baron throughout the tumults of the fourteenth century.[50] Two entries previous to that of Richard de Feypo, we see the following:

> Christiana from Ireland, in the first year after the battle [1265], having had the gout for five years, dreamt that she should go to the tomb of St Wulfsige and should take some of the dust and carry it away with her. And she did so and recovered. And before she had reached home the dust was changed into salt. Her husband Roger and son Richard, and many others, are the witnesses of this.[51]

St Lawrence concluded that Christiana, wife of Roger and mother of Richard, was the mother of the Richard de Feypo from the miracle first cited. The *miles Hiberniae*,[52] Richard de Feypo, active in the 1270s was, however, son of Richard the elder. We have seen above that this Richard had died some forty years previously and it must be concluded that Roger was not Christiana's first husband. Wulfsige was a local saint whose tomb lay in the choir of the abbey church at Evesham, near to that of Simon de Montfort. St Lawrence interpreted the inclusion of this story in the *miracula* as a preamble to the later de Feypo entry that was interrupted in the telling by the arrival of another pilgrim only to be taken up afterwards by another interlocutor from the 'entire household' assembled before the scribe. A large, familial procession appears to be suggested. It is a very visual and boisterous image that these miracle tales conjure, perhaps not something that immediately gives off the ring of truth. However, all of the individuals named can be accounted for and those names we do know from the de Feypo family at this time match with historical persons.

By embarking upon a pilgrimage from Skyrne to Evesham in the years following the Second Barons' War, the de Feypos might have attracted negative royal attention to themselves. However, a visit to the de Feypo relations in the Herefordshire baronies of Pipe and Lyde, some fifty miles west of Evesham, might have afforded a less ostentatious opportunity to visit the tomb of their fallen 'martyr'. A handful of earth from the tomb of the uncontroversial St Wulfsige may have provided further cover. In any event, it is clear from these

50 Elizabeth Hickey, *Skyrne and the early Normans* (Drogheda, 1994), p. 10.   51 BL Cotton MS Vespasian A VI, f. 165v. I am very much indebted to David Cox for this translation (*The miracles of Simon de Montfort*, ed. and trans. David C. Cox, in prep.) and for his generous and helpful comments on the text. See also *The chronicle of William de Rishanger*, p. 73.   52 St Lawrence, 'Liber miraculorum', p. 204 n.

entries in the *liber miracula* that a dedicated cult to Simon de Montfort was flourishing in Meath in the later thirteenth century.

CONCLUSION

We have seen that there was no large-scale Irish involvement in the Cathar Crusade, with no evidence for any Gaelic-Irish princes taking the cross. Neither have we evidence for proselytizing groups of heretics arriving in the Irish port towns. However, Ireland was affected both directly and indirectly by the papal and martial currents at work in Occitania. In a broad sense, the end result of the Cathar Crusade – the annexation of Occitania to the kingdom of France, did much to counterbalance the exorbitant Angevin gains made during Henry II's reign and paved the way for the Hundred Years War – a conflict of singular impact upon the development of the colony in Ireland and to the resulting Gaelic-Irish resurgence.

More specifically, a Capetian-backed plot to depose or undermine King John and replace him with the crusade's leader, Simon de Montfort, saw its largest martial expression in Ireland, spilling over soon afterwards into Wales. The plot involved many nobles with important stakes in Ireland including Ireland's first earl, Hugh de Lacy II, William de Braose, lord of Limerick and founder of Fethard, Co. Tipperary, Walter de Lacy, lord of Meath, and William Gorm de Lacy.

At a time of high tension between Rome and England over the matter of the accession of the archbishop of Canterbury, Stephen Langton, who had the immunity of papal backing, as well as de Braose's brother Gilbert in his retinue, appears to have played a role in the conspiracy. As archbishop of Canterbury, Langton would later lift excommunication from Hugh de Lacy in 1224, and act as a touchstone for the Second Barons' War and nursemaid to Magna Carta. Langton worked to curtail the absolute right of kings, an ideology that can be seen at work in the crusader's camp in Occitania, expressed in the Statute of Pamiers, a charter drafted by Montfort, quite possibly with the input of Langton or his Victorine adherents.

Following defeat in Ireland, Hugh de Lacy hastened to de Montfort's side in the company of the archbishop's brother, Walter Langton. He spent twelve years in the region and played a pivotal role in the early success of the crusade.

Perhaps armed with Langton's doctrine, de Lacy and his milieu in Ireland contested royal authority in open rebellion in 1210 and again in 1224. While no direct evidence exists for close partnership between Hugh de Lacy and Simon de Montfort the younger following his accession in England, evidence of a cult to de Montfort among de Lacy adherents would seem to suggest the families were closely aligned in the mid-thirteenth century.

It seems, therefore, that from the conspiracy of 1210 to the Statute of Pamiers to Magna Carta and the Second Barons' War an evolution can be traced, threaded through with the three constants of Langton, de Lacy and Montfort.

6 / From the Boyne valley to the Holy Land: the crusading tradition of Geoffrey de Geneville and Jean de Joinville

CIARÁN McDONNELL

INTRODUCTION

For many of the knightly families of medieval Europe, crusading was a deeply held tradition. Not only did this tradition span generations but also countries, as many of these families held estates and titles in various kingdoms and semi-independent states. Taking the cross offered the chance for advancement, increased wealth and influence, as well as salvation of the soul. The experiences of one particularly ambitious knight, Geoffrey de Geneville (*c.*1226–1314), perfectly illustrate both the power of a family tradition and the great opportunities that came with taking the cross.

This chapter will examine the deep-rooted tradition of crusading that surrounded Geoffrey's family, many of whom served in the major crusades of the thirteenth century. Geoffrey's own brother, Jean de Joinville, became one of France's most celebrated crusade chroniclers thanks to his personal account of serving with King (and later Saint) Louis IX of France on his first crusade. While Jean pledged allegiance to France, Geoffrey chose to go to England to seek his fortune. From there he made his way to Ireland, thanks to an advantageous marriage, and became lord of Trim, taking control of a vast estate that included the largest castle in Ireland. Geoffrey's decision to follow Prince Edward of Wales (the future Edward I) and King Louis of France on Louis' second attempt at a crusade will be explored. What made Geoffrey take the cross, and why would he risk his new fortune on such a dangerous venture? Geoffrey would eventually return from the crusade and continue to rise, occupying senior positions in the Irish administration and also undertaking foreign assignments for the king. Was this thanks to his service on crusade, his ability as a commander or his loyalty to the crown?

By examining the experiences of Geoffrey, his brother Jean and their family, a better understanding might be gained of how the knightly classes of

92   *Ireland and the crusades*

medieval Europe expressed their power, their faith and their loyalty, linking kingdoms and lordships such as France, England and Ireland with the far-off lands of Outremer.

THE BOYNE VALLEY, HUGH DE LACY AND THE HOLY LAND

The river Boyne is fringed with many famous prehistoric monuments and provides the focus for most of the major towns of counties Meath and Louth. In the medieval period two of the most important towns of the English lordship were located along this river: Drogheda stood at the mouth of the Boyne, perfectly positioned to trade across the sea to England and France, while the largest Anglo-Norman castle in Ireland was built by Hugh de Lacy (d. 1186) at Trim. De Lacy had been appointed lord of Meath by Henry II of England, to counter the rising power of Richard de Clare (Strongbow) in the south of the colony.[1]

De Lacy already held substantial territories in the Marches between England and Wales and brought not only Anglo-Norman ways and customs to the Boyne valley but also a connection to the crusades. Members of the de Lacy family had either taken the cross themselves or given land grants to the military orders. Hugh's father, Gilbert de Lacy, even became a member of the Order of the Temple in later life,[2] while Margaret de Lacy, great-granddaughter of Hugh, granted land in Louth at Cooley and Kilsaran to the Templars.[3] One of Hugh's sons, Hugh II (c.1176–1242), took part in the Albigensian Crusade (1209–29) under Count Simon de Montfort (d. 1218) against the Cathar Christians of southern France, after he had been forced into exile following his defiance of King John.[4]

The Knights of the Hospital of St John of Jerusalem owned a number of properties in Meath in the vicinity of Kells and Nobber. The order established a preceptory at Kilmainhamwood near Nobber, the place name referring to the order's main priory at Kilmainham in Dublin.[5] Income was also generated from land in and around Kells.[6] Some slight ruins of a manorial farm

---

1 *The deeds of the Normans in Ireland/ La geste des Engleis en Yrlande: A new edition of the chronicle formerly known as* The song of Dermot and the earl, ed. Evelyn Mullally (Dublin, 2002), pp 112–13. 2 C.P. Lewis, 'Lacy, Gilbert de (fl. 1133–1163)', *ODNB*. 3 Nicholson, 'A long way from Jerusalem', pp 1–22, at p. 7. 4 Paul Duffy, '"Ung sage et valent home": Hugh de Lacy and the Albigensian Crusade', *JRSAI* 141 (2011), 66–90. See also Paul Duffy, chapter 5, this volume. The count's son (also Simon) would later lead an attempted revolution against Henry III and autocratic royal power. 5 SMR, NMS , ME005–028, accessed 25 Jan. 2021. 6 Philip O'Connell, 'Kells, early and medieval: part II', *Ríocht na Midhe* 2 (1960), 8–22, at 18.

From the Boyne valley to the Holy Land

still exist at Kilmainhambeg, just outside Kells, now on the grounds of the Headfort Golf Club.[7] Even on the Hill of Tara, the ancient ceremonial royal site of Meath, the knights made their mark. The original medieval church on the hill, of which small fragments remain beside the present 1822 church, was granted to the Hospitallers, perhaps by the elder son of Hugh I, Walter de Lacy (*c.*1170–1241), who had granted Kilmainhambeg to the order in the 1190s.[8] It was not only the Anglo-Normans who knew of the crusades; Irish awareness of the endeavours grew over the centuries, to the extent that even the Gaelic-Irish annals began to record crusade events.[9]

GEOFFREY DE GENEVILLE

Walter de Lacy succeeded his father Hugh to the lordship of Meath but when he died in 1241 he had no surviving male heirs and his estate was divided between his two granddaughters, Margaret and Matilda. While the Irish lands were now divided, they still constituted substantial amounts of territory and both women were very eligible heiresses. Margaret married John de Verdon while Matilda married a knight from Champagne, Geoffrey de Geneville. Geoffrey would bring with him a deep family tradition of crusading and this would be reflected in his transnational career in Ireland, England, France and the Holy Land. It is important to not simply see him as an individual but also as part of a complex network of aristocratic personalities that spanned Europe in this period.[10]

Geoffrey was the second son of a relatively important aristocratic family from Champagne, known as Joinville in France (Anglicized as Geneville when referring to Geoffrey) (pl. 6.1). Geoffrey's elder brother, Jean de Joinville, wrote a celebrated biography of King Louis IX of France, having served alongside the king on the Seventh Crusade.[11] Michael Prestwich, in his biography of Edward I (alongside whom Geoffrey crusaded on the Eighth Crusade), has lamented that Geoffrey never wrote a biography of the English king, like his brother had of King Louis.[12] The Joinville family had important connections

7 SMR, NMS, ME017–023; Tadhg O'Keeffe & Pat Grogan, 'Building a frontier? The architecture of the military orders in medieval Ireland' in Browne & Ó Clabaigh, *Soldiers of Christ*, pp 81–102, at p. 90. **8** Michael Potterton & Margaret Murphy, 'Agriculture in the Tara/Skreen region, *c.*AD 1179–1660' in Muiris O'Sullivan, Christopher Scarre & Maureen Doyle (eds), *Tara: from the past to the future* (Dublin, 2013), pp 391–400, at p. 392. **9** Hurlock, 'The crusades to 1291', 517–34. **10** H.F. Delaborde, 'Un frère de Joinville au service de l'Angleterre, Geoffroy, sire de Vaucouleurs', *Bibliothèque de l'école des chartes* 54 (1893), 334–43, at 335. **11** Jean de Joinville, 'The life of St Louis' in *Jean de Joinville and Geoffrey de Villehardouin: chronicles of the crusades*, trans. Caroline Smith (London, 2008). **12** Michael Prestwich, *Edward I* (New Haven, 1988), p. 108.

among the European kingdoms and states; Geoffrey and Jean's father, Simon de Geneville, had married Béatrice d'Auxonne of Burgundy, great grand-daughter of Frederick Barbarossa (1122–90), one of the greatest of Holy Roman emperors.[13] The heads of the Joinville family, including Jean, were traditionally the seneschals to the counts of Champagne. Geoffrey was granted the town of Vaucouleurs, though it is worth noting that until 1301 parts of the territory of Vaucouleurs fell within the Holy Roman empire, rather than forming part of the kingdom of France. From their vantage at such a crossroads between such political powers, it is fair to say that Geoffrey de Geneville and his sons looked both east and west.[14]

Looking for advancement Geoffrey made his way to Paris. In addition to their connections to the Holy Roman empire, his family were also related by marriage to Peter, duke of Savoy, nicknamed 'Le Petit Charlemagne'.[15] The duke was very influential at the French royal court and his supporters became known as the Savoyards. Geoffrey and his brother Simon joined this circle and accompanied other Savoyards who went with Eleanor of Provence, niece of the duke, on her journey to England to marry Henry III of England. Geoffrey met with the king, who knighted him in 1247.[16] Henry tended to favour the Savoyards and other foreigners who would owe their loyalty to him alone, rather than existing English lords.[17] This practice was understandable given the experience of John, Henry's father, with troublesome noblemen, but it would also breed resentment that would culminate in the Second Barons' War.

Geoffrey's standing continued to rise when Henry permitted him to marry Matilda (also known as Maud) de Lacy in 1252.[18] As mentioned previously, the de Lacy sisters were very eligible heiresses and Geoffrey was now lord of Trim, owning significant lands in the east of Meath as well as the mighty castle[19] (pl. 6.2). The territory was a 'liberty', with added rights and benefits, and on 8 August 1252 Henry granted these to both Matilda and Geoffrey, the same rights that had been enjoyed by Walter de Lacy.[20] This special favour aroused the ire of royal officials in Dublin Castle, and Geoffrey and Matilda spent considerable time in the courts defending their Irish possessions and rights. It has been argued that the king used this process to keep Geoffrey from getting

13 Aine Bonnefoy, 'The role of Vaucouleurs in the careers of Geoffrey de Geneville and his sons', p. 2. https://www.academia.edu/29384540/The_role_of_Vaucouleurs_in_the_careers_of_Geoffrey_de_ Geneville_and_his_sons. Unpublished paper, accessed 11 Sept. 2019.   14 Ibid.   15 Delaborde, 'Un frère de Joinville au service de l'Angleterre', 336.   16 Beth Hartland, 'Vaucouleurs, Ludlow and Trim: the role of Ireland in the career of Geoffrey de Geneville (c.1226–1314)', *IHS* 32 (2001), 457–77, at 460.   17 Hartland, 'Vaucouleurs, Ludlow and Trim', 457.   18 The duke of Savoy had first arranged Matilda's marriage to Pierre de Genève, another Savoyard who had died in 1249.   19 Michael Potterton, 'French connections in late medieval Ireland: the case of Geoffrey de Geneville (c.1226–1314)', *Explorations in Renaissance Culture* 39 (2013), 59–81, at 66.   20 *CDI* ii, no. 69.

From the Boyne valley to the Holy Land

too powerful, reminding him that he owed his position to continuing royal favour.[21] Possession of the liberty, and as well the town and castle, would pass back and forth as Geoffrey fell in and out of this royal favour.

Like the de Lacys before him, Geoffrey invested significant money in Trim and Meath. It is likely that he was responsible for the new great hall built beside the main keep, as well as the first phase of town walls.[22] Like most medieval noblemen, he donated money to the Church as a way to ensure passage into heaven and this included the foundation in 1263 of a Dominican friary at the north side of Trim, outside the town wall.[23] The Dominicans had become very popular in Ireland in the wake of the Anglo-Norman conquest. Their organizational ability, structured hierarchy and papal connections also made the mendicant friars ideally suited for preaching and assisting in preparing for a crusade.[24] The Dominicans played a key role in preaching the benefits of taking the cross; Humbert of Romans wrote a manual on crusade preaching, while in 1252 Henry III had requested friars be sent to London who were experienced in crusade preaching.[25] During the Albigensian Crusade Hugh de Lacy II had even encountered and supported the order's founder, Dominic de Guzmán.[26]

As with the castle, Geoffrey invested a significant amount of money in the friary. The size and splendour of the complex can still be seen today, albeit below the ground. Recent archaeological excavations have uncovered much of the friary's footprint as well as numerous artefacts and building remains. These include stained-glass windows, painted plaster and medieval floor tiles, while large amounts of expensive Purbeck marble were imported from Dorset for the columns of the cloister (pl. 6.3).[27] The Geneville crest can be seen on a depiction of the Blackfriary's seal; the crest has on it horse brays, or barnacles, instruments associated with cavalry and the crusades.[28]

Geoffrey was evidently held in high regard, even taking on the role of acting justiciar in December 1264.[29] It was during this period that the king and

---

21 Hartland, 'Vaucouleurs, Ludlow and Trim', 461.   **22** Alan R. Hayden, *Trim Castle, Co. Meath: excavations, 1995–8* (Dublin, 2000), p. 196; Denis Shine, Ashley Green, Finola O'Carroll, Stephen Mandal & Bairbre Mullee, 'What lies beneath: chasing the Trim town wall circuit', *AI* 30: 1 (2016), 34–8, at 34.   **23** The Blackfriary (SMR, NMS: ME038–048023), dissolved in 1540 and demolished in the mid-eighteenth century, is currently undergoing archaeological excavation. For more see Finola O'Carroll, Denis Shine, Mark McConnon & Laura Corrway, 'The Blackfriary button', *Ríocht na Midhe* 27 (2016), 30–6; Finola O'Carroll, 'The blackfriars preachers, Trim, Co. Meath and the legacy of Geoffrey de Geneville' in M. Krasnodebska-D'Aughton, E. Bhreathnach & K. Smith (eds), *Monastic Europe: medieval communities, landscapes, and settlements* (Turnhout, 2019), pp 121–53.   **24** Christopher Tyerman, *How to plan a crusade* (London, 2015), p. 72.   **25** Ibid., p. 73.   **26** Paul Duffy, 'The exiled earl and the soon-to-be saint', *HI* 24: 5 (2016), 16–19, at 18.   **27** Finola O'Carroll, Ian Kinch & Laura Corrway, 'Digging the past, growing the future: the Blackfriary project', *Ríocht na Midhe* 29 (2018), 27–38.   **28** Potterton, 'French connections in late medieval Ireland', 72–3.   **29** Ronan Mackay, 'Geneville (Joinville), Geoffrey de', *DIB*.

indeed the monarchy in general came under a bold challenge, when Simon de Montfort, son of the crusader Count Simon de Montfort (d. 1218), rose up against Henry and even ousted him from power for a period. Prince Edward was captured but escaped to lead a counterattack that eventually defeated de Montfort at Evesham in 1265. When Prince Edward had escaped captivity, it was at Ludlow Castle, one of Geoffrey's properties in Shropshire, that he had sought sanctuary.[30] While he was not present at Evesham, Geoffrey was at the siege of Kenilworth Castle in 1265.[31] These actions likely further reinforced Geoffrey's ties with the royal household, but the ties were reciprocal. Just as much as Geoffrey needed Henry, so too did Henry (and Edward) need every loyal baron that they could muster.

JEAN DE JOINVILLE, KING LOUIS AND THE SEVENTH CRUSADE

The Joinville family boasted a deep and 'impeccable' connection with the crusades.[32] Geoffrey III de Joinville (1137–c.1188) took the cross in the Second Crusade while Geoffrey IV, Geoffrey and Jean's grandfather, took part in the Third Crusade, dying in Acre in 1190. Geoffrey V also took part in the Third and Fourth Crusades, while Geoffrey and Jean's father, Simon de Joinville, had taken part in the Albigensian Crusade and the Fifth Crusade.[33] Others had joined the military orders or took part in tournaments across Europe.[34]

It is Geoffrey's older brother Jean who has emerged as the most famous crusader of the family. Jean was born c.1224 and like his forefathers he became seneschal to the count of Champagne, after his father died in 1233. He was only around nineteen years of age when he decided to take the cross.[35] Jean wrote about his time on crusade, and his account might be seen in two lights: the personal account of taking part in the king's crusade and a later representation of the newly canonized saint.[36] By examining Jean's account, insights might be gained into why a knight would take on what could be quite a perilous (and expensive) venture. It might also demonstrate how an aristocratic family's crusader tradition 'clearly served as important markers of belonging and social status' in the medieval period.[37]

---

30 Hartland, 'Vaucouleurs, Ludlow and Trim', p. 466.   31 Mackay, 'Geneville (Joinville), Geoffrey de'.   32 Christopher Tyerman, *God's war: a new history of the crusades* (London, 2006), p. 782.   33 Simon Lloyd, *English society and the crusade, 1216–1307* (Oxford, 1988), p. 101.   34 Potterton, 'French connections in late medieval Ireland', 61.   35 Caroline Smith, 'Introduction' in Jean de Joinville, 'The life of Saint Louis', p. xxxiii.   36 Cecilia Gaposchkin, *The making of Saint Louis: kingship, sanctity, and crusade in the later Middle Ages* (Ithaca, 2008), p. 19.   37 Andrew D. Buck, 'Settlement, identity, and memory in the Latin East: an examination of the term "crusader states"', *EHR* 135 (2020), 271–302, at 273.

From the Boyne valley to the Holy Land

In December 1244, following a near fatal illness, Louis took the cross, along with his three brothers, Robert, count of Artois, Alphonse, count of Poitiers, and Charles, count of Anjou (and later king of Sicily).[38] In doing so, Louis was following in the tradition of earlier French kings who had used the crusades (and the prestige of a crusading tradition) as a means of strengthening their own positions domestically.[39] While Louis was more secure in his position than earlier French monarchs, he did not hesitate in taking the cross; for him being a king and going on crusade went hand-in-hand.[40] He was also following in the footsteps of his father, who had partaken in the Albigensian Crusade. The aim of the Seventh Crusade was to attack the Ayyubid caliphate of Egypt, which controlled Jerusalem at this time. Jean de Joinville made the decision to take part in this crusade when it was announced, but he did so by himself, rather than out of loyalty to Louis. In 1248 the king summoned his barons to Paris in order to swear an oath of loyalty to his children, lest he not return. Jean refused: 'I was unwilling to swear an oath because I was not his man.'[41] Jean was not officially a vassal of France (and Louis) in 1248, although he would soon become one during the crusade.

At Easter in 1248 Jean made preparations to leave, which included a week of feasting. Geoffrey, whom Jean referred to as the 'Lord of Vaucouleurs', was present for the celebrations and provided the meal on one of the evenings.[42] Jean does not appear to have had land or riches in mind as he was preparing to leave; he settled all disputes before he left, admitting 'I am going away overseas and I do not know if I will return.'[43] Jean appears to have genuinely believed in the piety of taking the cross and going on an (armed) pilgrimage to the East; he even wrote a Credo while there.[44] The abbot of Cheminion, said by Jean to be one of the wisest of all Cistercians, gave to him his pilgrim's staff and purse. Jean left his home 'on foot, bare-legged and wearing a hair shirt'.[45] He visited a number of local shrines, and in a remarkable admission of sentiment he related how 'I did not want to cast my eyes back towards Joinville at all, fearful that my heart would melt for the fine castle and two children I was leaving behind.'[46] Jean was not the only nobleman from his region to take the cross; while Count Theobald of Champagne had declined to join, there was a significant Champenois contribution who did: about 175 knights and other men, totalling around 1,000.[47] Louis was also making his own preparations, including the dedication of the magnificent Sainte-Chapelle in Paris, which

38 Joinville, 'The life of Saint Louis', § 107–8.   39 James Naus, *Constructing kingship: the Capetian monarchs of France and the early crusades* (Manchester, 2016).   40 Naus, *Constructing kingship*, p. 2.   41 Ibid., § 114.   42 Ibid., p. 110.   43 Ibid., p. 111.   44 Gaposchkin, *The making of Saint Louis*, p. 181.   45 Joinville, 'The life of Saint Louis', § 122.   46 Ibid., § 122.   47 Tyerman, *God's war*, p. 775.

98   *Ireland and the crusades*

was built to house the holy relics of the Passion that Louis had purchased in 1238.[48]

In August 1248 Jean and his entaurage, which included nine knights and two knights-banneret (who could display their own banners and have their own followers), embarked at Marseilles and set sail for Cyprus. Louis was already in Cyprus when Jean arrived, amassing supplies for the expedition to Egypt. Jean had almost run out of money by this point, illustrating how expensive it was to raise even a small force of knights and retainers.[49] Louis came to Jean's aid, giving him money and taking him into his service.[50] This was a common practice for kings and other crusade leaders; they would use their wealth to contract the services of knights, often directly into their own retinue or 'familia'.[51] Yet even for a king like Louis a crusade was extremely expensive.

In March 1249 Louis' fleet of 1,800 ships set sail for Egypt. Louis had brought 2,800 knights with him but bad weather scattered the fleet and only 700 were able to land with him initially. The sultan's army awaited them at the coastal town of Damietta, and as the crusaders landed Jean admiringly described the king's bravery as he jumped into the sea, 'with his shield at his neck, his helmet on his head and his lance in his hand, to join his men who were on the shore'.[52] While Jean clearly admired the king for his bravery and piety, he did not always agree with his decisions during the crusade.[53] His account highlights the 'secular, chivalric, and aristocratic values' that he himself personified 'as a member of the high aristocracy, a knight, a crusader himself, a descendant of a long noble lineage, and a member of the royal entourage'.[54]

The Muslim army retreated, allowing the crusaders to occupy Damietta. Louis' barons advised an attack to seize the port of Alexandria but the count of Artois argued for a direct attack on Cairo.[55] Command and control was a serious challenge for crusader strategy, especially as crusades often had multiple competing leaders.[56] After waiting several months, the king eventually decided to listen to his brother and the army began a long and arduous march up the Nile towards Cairo. Despite the high level of organization for this crusade, conditions on the ground took a heavy toll on the army, a toll which increased the further they got from their supply base at Damietta.

---

48 Norman Housley, 'The thirteenth-century crusades in the Mediterranean' in David Abulafia (ed.), *The new Cambridge medieval history* (Cambridge, 1999), v, pp 569–89, at p. 580. 49 Steve Tibble, *The crusader armies* (New Haven, 2018), p. 101. 50 Joinville, 'The life of Saint Louis', § 109. 51 Tyerman, *How to plan a crusade*, p. 156. 52 Joinville, 'The life of Saint Louis', § 162. 53 Gaposchkin, *The making of Saint Louis*, p. 181. 54 Ibid., p. 185. 55 Xavier Hélary, 'Les rois de France et la Terre Sainte de la Croisade de Tunis à la chute d'Acre (1270–1291)', *Annuaire-Bulletin de la Société de l'histoire de France* 118 (2005), 21–104, at 35. 56 John France, 'Crusading warfare' in Helen J. Nicholson (ed.), *Palgrave advances in the crusades* (Basingstoke, 2005), pp 58–80, at p. 71.

From the Boyne valley to the Holy Land

99

Meanwhile, the Ayyubid army mustered a fierce counterattack outside the town of al-Mansourah on 8 February 1250. The crusaders emerged victorious, but at a heavy cost; many were killed, including the count of Artois, and the town remained in Muslim hands.[57]

The road to Cairo remained blocked and Louis took the difficult decision to turn back. However, the retreat quickly turned into a rout as the army suffered from heat and disease, in particular dysentery, which even struck down the king himself. The Muslim pursuit was led by the elite Mamluk regiment of slave soldiers known as the Bahriyyas.[58] Eventually Louis, Jean and the rest of the army were forced to surrender and found themselves captives of the Ayyubids. However, Louis was still a king and still had the ability to negotiate a ransom for himself and his men.

Events took yet another turn however, as the Bahriyya regiment decided to take this moment to seize power themselves and killed the Ayyubid sultan – their emir becoming Sultan Baibars – and presented the old sultan's heart to Louis, before agreeing to honour the ransom.[59] Louis and his army were permitted to leave, returning Damietta to Muslim hands. Louis decided to set sail for Acre and Jean followed the king to the Holy Land. There Louis remained for four years but achieved little beyond occasional raiding and alliance making. He even engaged in diplomatic talks with representatives from the Old Man of the Mountain, the leader of the sect of Assassins.[60] Coastal defences were improved and a permanent garrison was established in Acre at Louis' expense.[61] In the end the king did not succeed in returning Jerusalem to Christian hands and he eventually returned to France.

GEOFFREY AND LORD EDWARD'S CRUSADE

King Louis might have suffered a severe setback in his crusading ambition but he was not to be deterred. It was testament to both his wealth and organizational ability that ten years later he was able to launch yet another crusade to defeat Muslim Egypt. It also shows the drive to succeed on crusade that was embedded in the Capetian dynasty of French kings.[62] The initial target of the Eighth Crusade was Tunisia, which was also in Muslim hands and could be used as a staging post for future attacks on Egypt.[63] Despite his friendship

---

57 Tyerman, *God's war*, pp 792–3. 58 Ibid., p. 795. 59 Ibid., p. 797. 60 Joinville, 'The life of Saint Louis', § 452–62. 61 Peter Edbury, 'The crusader states' in David Abulafia (ed.), *The new Cambridge medieval history* (Cambridge, 1999), v, pp 590–606, at p. 602. 62 Sean Field & Cecilia Gaposchkin, 'Questioning the Capetians, 1180–1328', *History Compass* 12 (2014), 567–85, at 573. 63 Thomas Ashbridge, *The crusades: the war for the Holy Land* (London, 2012), p. 640.

with Louis, Jean declined to follow his liege lord, arguing that his responsibilities now lay with the people of Joinville.[64] Jean had evidentially matured from the young man who had taken the cross over a decade previously. While he decided to stay at home, his brother Geoffrey took the decision to join the crusade. It is likely that Geoffrey made this decision not out of loyalty to the king of France, but rather because he saw that Prince Edward of England (later Edward I) had pledged in 1268 to join Louis on his second attempt.

Edward was lord of Ireland, as well as a tall and energetic prince, and it is unsurprising that he might have wished to go on crusade. His spiritual motivations might have stemmed from his very pious father, who had never managed to go on crusade, despite declarations that he intended to.[65] Equally, a sense of military adventure might have played a part, especially as the French royal princes were also accompanying their father on the expedition.[66] It must also be remembered that Louis was Edward's uncle by marriage; Edward's aunt, Margaret of Provence, was married to the French king. His paternal uncle, Richard of Cornwall, had also taken part in the Barons' Crusade.

Edward raised for the crusade a substantial force of 225 knights, other troops and retainers.[67] Even though Louis advanced him the sum of 70,000 *livres tournois* Edward still had to borrow money from the Riccardi bankers of Lucca, Tuscany, as well as securing support from the Templars.[68] Yet even so, the amount spent on Edward's crusade was much less that what he spent on later wars in Wales and Scotland.[69] Geoffrey was one of the many Anglo-Irish nobles who took part in this crusade, 'more than at any previous time, due in large part to Edward's lordship in Ireland'.[70] Previously, in 1252, Henry had attempted to induce the magnates of Ireland to accompany him on crusade.[71] The fact that Henry's son was actually taking part would have encouraged the lords this time around.

Why did Geoffrey and other English lords in Ireland (insofar as we can call Geoffrey 'English') take the cross? Religion would have played a role, just as it had in Geoffrey's decision to found the Blackfriary in Trim several years previously. He could serve God the best way he knew how, by knightly warfare.[72] Geoffrey prepared for the crusade of 1270 by building religious houses – the Dominican friars were actively preaching the crusade in the Sligo and Roscommon area in 1266 – and he also enabled the building of a church college in Vaucouleurs.[73] It is likely that the Dominicans and Franciscans in Trim

---

64 Joinville, 'The life of Saint Louis', § 735.   65 *CDI* ii, no. 25.   66 Prestwich, *Edward I*, p. 68.   67 Ibid., p. 72.   68 Tyreman, *How to plan a crusade*, pp 210–12.   69 Ibid., p. 203.   70 Hurlock, 'The crusades to 1291', 94.   71 *CDI* ii, no. 25.   72 Jean Flori, 'Ideology and motivations in the First Crusade' in Helen J. Nicholson (ed.), *Palgrave advances in the crusades* (Basingstoke, 2005), pp 15–36 at p. 27.   73 Hartland, 'Vaucouleurs, Ludlow and Trim', p. 467.

From the Boyne valley to the Holy Land   101

were also preaching the crusade, as orders had been made by Henry in 1252 for the crusade to be 'assiduously preached by Dominicans and other fit preachers'.[74] Preaching led to donations, a vital source of income for the crusade. In Ireland, as in England, a tenth of ecclesiastical tax went to the crusades; in 1254 the archbishop of Dublin was appointed to oversee the collection of this tax.[75] Certain groups were exempt, including the Templars and Hospitallers.[76] We cannot get the same insight into Geoffrey's reasoning as we do with his brother, given that Geoffrey did not write about his experiences, but it might be argued that Geoffrey's decision was more to do with ambition than it was to do with piety. As seen already, Geoffrey owed his position of power in Ireland (and England) to royal favour and a crusade with the future king would have helped reinforce that bond.

Despite the determination of the French king, the Eighth Crusade achieved even less than his previous attempt. Louis and his army made landfall at Tunis on 18 July 1270 but disease once again struck the camp. Matters reached a nadir when both Louis and his son Prince Jean Tristan died, bringing the crusade to an effective end.[77] The sudden death of Louis happened before the entire army even had time to assemble; Edward and his English contingent were only able to arrive in November, having been delayed due to the death of the archbishop of Canterbury and the subsequent politicking. With the death of Louis the crusade had lost its most zealous promotor.[78] The other crusade leaders, including Louis' brother, the count of Anjou, had little appetite for prolonging the crusade and decided to return home.[79] Edward decided to push on to the Holy Land, setting off in spring 1271, and this is usually known as the Ninth Crusade.

However, Edward, accompanied by Geoffrey and an estimated force of 1,000 men, arrived in Acre in May 1271. Like Louis during the previous crusade, he remained there for a time as the temporal ruler of the kingdom of Jerusalem.[80] He sought an unsuccessful alliance with the Mongols against the Mamluks and defended Acre from an attack by Sultan Baibars in December. The sultan was wary of having Edward in Acre while the Mongol threat was growing to the north, and eventually concluded a truce with the kingdom of Jerusalem in April 1272.[81] The following June, Edward barely survived an attempt on his life, when an assassin managed to gain entry to his private chambers, attacking him with a dagger. Edward successfully fought off the attack, killing his assailant, but soon fell ill, possibly from the poison of the assassin's blade. He eventually recovered, although the romantic tale of his

74 *CDI* ii, no. 25. 75 Ibid., no. 375. 76 Ibid., no. 516. 77 Tyerman, *God's war*, pp 811–12. 78 Hélary, 'Les rois de France et la Terre Sainte', 21. 79 Prestwich, *Edward I*, p. 74. 80 Hélary, 'Les rois de France et la Terre Sainte', 25. 81 Ashbridge, *The crusades*, p. 644.

wife, Eleanor of Castille, who had accompanied him on crusade, sucking the poison from the wound, is likely to be apocryphal.[82] The crusade might have been unsuccessful but Edward's reputation was certainly enhanced, not least as he was the only European monarch to make it to the Holy Land during this crusade.[83] As Edward was making his way home he learned that his father had died in November 1272, and that he was now king.[84] It appears that Geoffrey had left Acre prior to this, as he had been summoned (as a vassal of the French king) to fight for Philip III and was not one of the witnesses to Edward's will which was made in Acre in 1272.[85]

GEOFFREY RETURNS TO IRELAND

When Geoffrey returned to Ireland in 1273 he was appointed justiciar, one of the chief administrative positions in the colony. It is likely that this appointment to high office was in recognition of his loyal service during the crusade; Edward bestowed rewards on many of the knights who had followed him, his 'cluster of loyal dependents'.[86] Thomas de Clare, another of the lords in Ireland who had accompanied Edward on crusade, was created earl of Thomond in 1276, following an appeal for aid from warring factions in the Gaelic-Irish kingdom in the south-west.[87] Another crusade veteran, William de Vescy, lord of Kildare, was later appointed justiciar too.[88] Edward employed a network of household knights in Ireland during his reign, both as lord and later king, in order to strengthen links between Dublin and Westminster.[89]

Geoffrey held the justiciarship for three years to 1276. The role was both a military and a political one, and he led punitive expeditions each year into Glenmalure, Wicklow, in response to raiding from the mountains by the MacMurroughs. The first expedition went particularly badly and the Hospitaller prior of Kilmainham was among the nobles captured by the Irish, while many others were killed.[90] Some have dismissed Geoffrey's military ability, but subsequent justiciars also struggled to deal with the Gaelic-Irish insurgency.[91] It was not just the Gaelic-Irish who could cause trouble either; Geoffrey also had to deal with competing Anglo-Irish lords.[92] However, Geoffrey pacified Ireland and its warring barons, thereby enabling him to raise

---

82 Prestwich, *Edward I*, p. 78. 83 Tyerman, *God's war*, p. 813. 84 Prestwich, *Edward I*, p. 83. 85 Hartland, 'Vaucouleurs, Ludlow and Trim', 461. 86 Robin Frame, *Colonial Ireland, 1169–1369* (Dublin, 1981), p. 35. 87 Ibid., p. 36. 88 Ibid., p. 66. 89 Beth Hartland, 'The household knights of Edward I in Ireland', *Historical Research* 77 (2004), 161–77. 90 G.H. Orpen, *Ireland under the Normans, 1169–1333*, 4 vols (Oxford, 1911–20; repr. Dublin, 2005), iv, p. 15. 91 Hartland, 'Vaucouleurs, Ludlow and Trim', 462. 92 Ibid., 466.

From the Boyne valley to the Holy Land

troops for Edward against rebellious barons in England.[93] He placed his Irish resources and manpower at the disposal of the king, likely in gratitude for his appointment as justiciar.[94]

Geoffrey also strengthened the borders of the colony, refortifying and upgrading the castles at Roscommon and Rindown.[95] When Geoffrey resigned the office in 1276 it did not mean a quiet retirement. His position in the estimation of Edward is evident by the number of diplomatic missions he was sent on by the king. He had previously been sent as an envoy to Prince Llewelyn of Wales in 1267, and, after his term as justiciar, he was again a royal envoy in numerous European peace negotiations between 1280 and 1301.[96] He signed the Treaty of Montreuil with France, on Edward's behalf, in 1299.[97] His military appointments continued too; Edward appointed Geoffrey as marshal of his army, which he sent to Flanders in 1297.[98] He raised money to secure men to fight in Edward's Scottish campaign in 1301–2, and was also sent on a diplomatic mission to the Vatican.[99] The shrewd Edward would not have assigned these tasks to someone he did not trust.

While his focus was undoubtedly his relationship with the English king, Geoffrey still attended to duties in his homeland of Vaucouleurs, settling legal disputes and other matters.[100] In this he was not alone as many knights active in Ireland held lands in multiple kingdoms. His lands in Champagne became more of a liability when Vaucouleurs became part of France in 1301 and Anglo-French relations broke down. Perhaps in order to avert potential embarrassment he shared the lordship of Vaucouleurs with his son Walter.[101] His other son, Simon, served with Edward in 1303 in his Scottish campaigns.[102] Geoffrey was not constantly in favour with Edward, and gained and lost rights and privileges on Trim and his other lands depending on his willingness to serve the king, pay the correct taxes and so on.[103] Likewise, he went in and out of favour with the Church; the rough behaviour of his bailiffs had previously provoked complaints by the monks of Mellifont abbey, and the archbishop of Cashel even excommunicated him for a number of offences, including building a prison on Church land, yet he was also praised by the Dominicans of Roscommon.[104]

---

93 Prestwich, *Edward I*, p. 52. 94 Hartland, 'The household knights of Edward I in Ireland', 163. 95 Hartland, 'Vaucouleurs, Ludlow and Trim', 462. 96 *CPR, Henry III*, vi, pp 95–124. 97 Potterton, 'French connections in late medieval Ireland', 70. 98 *CDI* iv, no. 447. 99 Hartland, 'Vaucouleurs, Ludlow and Trim', 464–7; *CDI* ii, no. 797. 100 Bonnefoy, 'The role of Vaucouleurs', p. 4. 101 Ibid., p. 5. 102 *CIRCLE* Edward I *Patent Roll* 31, §22, https://chancery.tcd.ie/document/close/18-edward-i/2, accessed 27 Sept. 2020. 103 *CIRCLE*, Edward I, *Close Roll* 18, §2, https://chancery.tcd.ie/document/close/18-edward-i/2, accessed 27 Sept. 2020; Bonnefoy, 'The role of Vaucouleurs', p. 7. 104 Potterton, 'French connections in late medieval Ireland', 67–8. This praise may have been due to large donations to the order.

Geoffrey's wife Matilda died in 1304 and three years later Geoffrey eventually retired from a busy career. It might be significant that 1307 was the same year that his patron and brother-in-arms, King Edward, died. Perhaps he did not expect the same favour from the new king, Edward II? Geoffrey joined the friary in Trim, which he had helped found, becoming a friar himself, before dying and being buried there in 1314 at the remarkable age of 93. His sons had chosen to seek their own careers in England and later, on the Continent, so the de Geneville lands in Ireland were passed to the hands of his granddaughter Joan, and her husband, the infamous Roger Mortimer (1287–1330), who ruled England through the dowager Queen Isabella of France and the teenage King Edward III.[105] Trim and its lands would remain in Mortimer hands until 1425, and thereafter became a royal possession.

CONCLUSIONS

The careers of Jean and Geoffrey demonstrate the varied motivations and varied experiences of knights who took the cross in the medieval period. It is likely that the strong crusading tradition in the Joinville family would have motivated both brothers to take the cross, as was the case in many knightly families in Europe.[106] A crusading ancestry was something to be 'proudly cherished'.[107] In some cases this could lead in unexpected directions; the crusading tradition in the de Montfort family might have inspired Simon de Montfort (d. 1265) to rise up against up Henry III.[108] In the case of Jean we have the added value of having his own chosen words, his personal account of what it was like to go on crusade, and his family's crusading tradition. This account has made Jean a 'landmark figure in discussion of family crusading traditions'.[109] It is clear that faith was a major factor in the decision for Jean to take the cross and his account frequently makes reference to religious matters and the piety of Louis and others, in particular in the framing sections that start and end the account.[110] Jean was aware of the perils of the crusades. He was a young man leaving behind a wife and children and this separation evidentially weighed on him. He displayed the typical bravado of a young crusader upon arrival but gradually matured as he spent more time with the king, becoming

105 Hartland, 'Vaucouleurs, Ludlow and Trim', 471; Bonnefoy, 'The role of Vaucouleurs', p. 10; Potterton, 'French connections in late medieval Ireland', 70.   106 Nicholas L. Paul, *To follow in their footsteps: the crusades and family memory in the high Middle Ages* (Ithaca, 2012).   107 Lloyd, *English society and the crusade, 1216–1307*, p. 102.   108 Sophie Thérèse Ambler, *The song of Simon de Montfort: England's first revolutionary and the death of chivalry* (London, 2019), p. 1; Paul Duffy, chapter 5, this volume.   109 Paul, *To follow in their footsteps*, p. 9.   110 Gaposchkin, *The making of Saint Louis*, p. 183.

From the Boyne valley to the Holy Land 105

a close friend. This maturity had developed even more by the time of Louis' second attempt; Jean now saw that his responsibility lay with his people and their welfare. Many others over the centuries also declined to take the cross, despite a family tradition.[111]

In the actions of Geoffrey we can see perhaps more earthly reasons for taking the cross. Since we do not have his own words we must extrapolate from his decisions and when we compare them to the rest of his career a pattern emerges. Geoffrey was determined to advance his career and climb the social ladder. As the younger son, he was not going to be seneschal like his brother Jean, so he sought advancement elsewhere, first at the French court and then the English court. He did not need to seek his fortune as his family were not impoverished and his own holdings sufficient.[112] Yet he still chose to set out, and his family ties to Peter of Savoy were a key part of his rapid rise.[113] Joining the Savoyard circle was an astute move and his standing with Henry III is evident in his marriage to Matilda de Lacy. As lord of Trim he acted as expected, improving his holdings, fortifying his properties, donating money to the Church and founding a friary in Trim as well as others in his French lands. When Prince Edward decided to join King Louis on crusade Geoffrey no doubt saw an opportunity to reinforce his position in Ireland (and England) by demonstrating his loyalty to the crown, while also continuing the crusading tradition of his family. This loyalty was well-rewarded, and Geoffrey continued to serve the now King Edward as justiciar. He might not have been a great success on the battlefield but fighting an insurgency was never an easy task for a government army in Ireland, then or in the centuries to come. His repeated selection as a diplomat and emissary shows not only his skills but also the trust and esteem in which he was held by Edward. Two of his younger brothers also benefited from English royal patronage, Simon as a lord, and William as a churchman.[114]

The choice of a liminal location for where Geoffrey sought his fortune might be significant too. Having grown up in an area between two powerful kingdoms (France and the Holy Roman empire), Geoffrey might have seen the potential these border regions offered to ambitious knights.[115] When he travelled to France and then on to England he was rewarded, via his marriage, with border lands in the Welsh Marches and then in Ireland too. The 'frontier' (itself a debated term) has become a strong image in the historiography of medieval Ireland as well as in crusader historiography.[116] The

---

111 Paul, *To follow in their footsteps*, p. 203.   112 Robert Bartlett, *The making of Europe: conquest, colonization and cultural change, 950–1350* (London, 1993), p. 47.   113 Ibid., p. 26.   114 Ibid., p. 27.   115 Bonneyfoy, 'The role of Vaucouleurs', p. 11.   116 O'Keeffe & Grogan, 'Building a frontier?', pp 81–2; Nora Berend, 'Frontiers' in Helen J. Nicholson (ed.), *Palgrave advances in the crusades* (Basingstoke, 2005), pp 148–71; Ronnie Ellenblum, *Crusader castles and modern histories* (Cambridge, 2007). See Tadhg O'Keeffe, chapter 14, this volume.

relative independence offered in Ireland, and specifically in Meath as a frontier zone, far from the centre of royal power, might have been quite attractive to Geoffrey.[117] His sons continued this upwardly mobile path, carving out careers across Europe, including serving Charles d'Anjou, king of Naples and brother of Louis IX.[118]

Lydon described Geoffrey as 'a man of piety, a true knight' due to his military actions and his decision to join the Blackfriary.[119] Can we say he was a true knight? Or was he simply interested in advancing his career? In the final analysis, the decision to go on crusade, or take positions on frontier lands, was quite a normal one for the knightly classes of medieval Europe. Many took the cross, even if it proved vastly expensive for themselves and their families.[120] Jean and Geoffrey might have taken the cross for a variety of reasons but they had at least three motivations in common. First, they had a deep-rooted family tradition in crusading. Family tradition is a complex thing and Paul has argued that while it was never guaranteed that the tradition would be continued, those who took the cross did so 'in the context of powerful discourses and an elaborate cultural system which at least conditioned their creative acts to make them more predictable'.[121] Second, a sense of piety would have compelled them; we see in Jean's writings or Geoffrey's religious foundations the piety (and perhaps fear for one's soul) that influenced many crusaders, and was part of the wider faith of daily life in medieval Europe.[122] Third, both engaged in this dangerous venture in the retinue of a powerful leader, whether for advancement or from a sense of duty or perhaps both.[123] This crusading tradition also infused the French monarchy; Louis' decision to take the cross was 'preconditioned by nearly a century's worth of image making'.[124] The rising power of the French and English monarchies needed loyal supporters, and likewise ambitious knights needed the favour of powerful kings. By considering these two brothers we might begin to see the complex and multifaceted nature of crusading in this period, and how members of the knightly Christian elite of medieval Europe were able to forge transnational careers across the known world, from the Boyne valley in the west to the Holy Land in the east.[125]

---

117 Hartland, 'Vaucouleurs, Ludlow and Trim', 473, 477. 118 Bonneyfoy, 'The role of Vaucouleurs', p. 11. 119 James Lydon, *The lordship of Ireland in the Middle Ages* (Dublin, 1972), p. 96. 120 Flori, 'Ideology and motivations', p. 29. 121 Paul, *To follow in their footsteps*, p. 201. 122 Flori, 'Ideology and motivations', pp 23–5. 123 Ibid., p. 30. 124 Naus, *Constructing kingship*, p. 4. 125 I would like to thank the editors and reviewers of this volume for their comments, my former colleagues at the Blackfriary Archaeology Field School for their support during the initial phase of my research and Dr Paolo Virtuani, for his helpful advice on the later stage of research.

7 / The military-religious orders in Ireland: their patrons and their purpose

HELEN J. NICHOLSON

The military-religious orders were Latin Christian institutions that developed in the city of Jerusalem in the first half of the twelfth century, in the wake of the First Crusade.[1] Their members took lifetime monastic vows of poverty, chastity and obedience, and promised to help defend Christians and Christian territory. Although they were connected to monastic orders in their early years – the Hospitallers were initially connected to the Benedictines, while the Templars were supported by the Cistercian Abbot Bernard of Clairvaux – they were closer to the orders of regular canons in their active works of charity and in following a canonical liturgy.[2] They won great admiration from both Christians and Muslims for their military discipline and effectiveness, but in the eastern Mediterranean they were eventually unsuccessful in holding off Muslim resurgence. In the Iberian peninsula, military-religious orders played an important role in the so-called 'reconquest' and in the Baltic states and Prussia they brought about by one means or another the conversion of the native pagan peoples to Christianity. In the seventeenth and eighteenth centuries these orders' military role declined, and although some still survive today, they are no longer military institutions.[3]

The Templars and the Hospitallers were the earliest of these religious orders to take up military roles and quickly acquired privileges and property in Latin Christian Europe. The papacy exempted them from episcopal oversight and payment of ecclesiastical dues, and allowed their travelling alms collectors to open churches under interdict to preach to the laity and collect gifts to aid the Holy Land. Secular rulers exempted them from secular exactions and duties. The Hospitallers received lands in France and Italy in the

---

1 Some of the material in this article appeared in my chapter 'A long way from Jerusalem: the Templars and Hospitallers in Ireland, *c.1172–c.1348*' in Browne & Ó Clabaigh, *Soldiers of Christ*, pp 1–22.   2 Jonathan Riley-Smith, *The Knights Hospitaller in the Levant, c.1070–1309* (Basingstoke, 2012), pp 17–18, 114; Malcolm Barber, *The new knighthood: a history of the Order of the Temple* (Cambridge, 1993), pp 12–18, 44–9; Helen J. Nicholson, *The everyday life of the Templars: the Knights Templar at home* (Stroud, 2017), pp 40, 125–6.   3 General scholarly histories include: Alain Demurger, *Chevaliers du Christ: les ordres religieux-militaires au moyen âge, XIe–XVIe siècle* (Paris, 2002); Alan Forey, *The military orders: from the twelfth to the early fourteenth centuries* (Basingstoke, 1993); Nicholas E. Morton, *The medieval military orders, 1120–1314* (Harlow, 2013).

first two decades of the twelfth century and the Templars followed in the 1120s, when both orders were also given land and fortifications in the Iberian peninsula. The Templars received their first gifts of land and privileges in England and Scotland in 1128. The Hospitallers arrived in England around the same time, possibly a little later in Scotland, and obtained their first properties in Wales in the 1130s and 1140s, where their patrons were from Norman families who had settled in the south and south-west.[4] In contrast, the Templars did not arrive in Wales and the Welsh Marches until the 1150s, possibly because their close ties to the king of England made them unattractive to local donors.[5] These orders' royal and national connections might account for their late arrival in Ireland, where the Hospitallers came with the invaders from England and Wales and the Templars apparently arrived with King Henry II of England.

A third military-religious order also came to hold land in Ireland. The order of St Thomas of Acre, which was founded by English crusaders during the Third Crusade and was patronized by the king of England, received two hospitals in Ireland during the thirteenth century, one in Kilkenny and the other in Carrick-on-Suir. These were pre-existing institutions entrusted to the English brothers' care.[6]

The military-religious orders came to Ireland because the invaders and their successors gave them lands there, but they did not form part of the invading force. Admittedly, among the invaders was a Maurice de Prendergast, who by 1203 was prior of Kilmainham, the Hospitallers' chief house in Ireland. However, as the contemporary sources for the invasion do not call him 'Brother' or mention the Hospitallers, it appears that Maurice was not a Hospitaller at the time of the invasion.[7] Presumably he joined the military order later in life, as a generation earlier Gilbert de Lacy had joined the Templars after a successful career as a baron in the Welsh Marches.[8] The first

---

4 Michael Gervers, 'Donations to the Hospitallers in England in the wake of the Second Crusade' in Michael Gervers (ed.), *The Second Crusade and the Cistercians* (New York, 1992), pp 155–61; Ian B. Cowan, P.H.R. Mackay & Alan Macquarrie (eds), *The Knights of St John of Jerusalem in Scotland* (Edinburgh, 1983), pp xviii, xxvi; William Rees, *A history of the order of St John of Jerusalem in Wales and on the Welsh border, including an account of the Templars* (Cardiff, 1947), pp 105–6.   5 Rees, *History of the order of St John*, pp 124, 126; David Knowles & R. Neville Hadcock, *Medieval religious houses: England and Wales* (2nd ed. London, 1971), p. 294; Helen J. Nicholson, 'The military orders in Wales and the Welsh March in the Middle Ages' in Peter W. Edbury (ed.), *The military orders*, v: *Politics and power* (Farnham, 2012), pp 189–207, at p. 202.   6 *MRHI*, p. 343; Eric St John Brooks, 'Irish possessions of St Thomas of Acre', *PRIA* 58C (1956), 21–44, at 23; Hurlock, *Crusades*, p. 152.   7 Paolo Virtuani, 'The Knights of St John of Jerusalem in medieval Ireland (c.1169–1378)' (PhD, UCD, 2014), pp 15–21, 36; G. Lennox Barrow, 'The Knights Hospitaller of St John of Jerusalem at Kilmainham', *Dublin Historical Record* 38 (1985), 108–12, at 112.   8 Barber, *New knighthood*, p. 106; C.P. Lewis, 'Lacy, Gilbert de (fl. 1133–1163)', *ODNB*.

clear mention of the Templars and Hospitallers in Ireland dates from around 1177, after both the initial invasion and King Henry II's intervention.[9]

The question of how far the invasion of Ireland was a crusade is examined in detail elsewhere in this volume by Maeve Callan, but should be noted here in the context of possible motivations for the first donations to the military-religious orders in Ireland. If the invasion was a crusade, then the military-religious orders could have been endowed to assist that crusade. However, although Pope Adrian IV's bull *Laudabiliter* could be interpreted to indicate that the invasion was a crusade, Anne Duggan has argued that the *Laudabiliter* that has come down to us was effectively a forgery by Gerald of Wales and that in fact Pope Adrian's original letter probably urged King Henry II to consult the Irish before taking troops to Ireland.[10] If the expedition was not a crusade, the military-religious orders were not introduced to fight a crusade against the Irish. Rather, Kathryn Hurlock has suggested that the initial donations to the Templars and Hospitallers were a 'thank-offering' for the success of the invasion.[11] In the same way, the invaders also founded many new monasteries for religious orders already established in Ireland and introduced additional orders of canons.[12]

The scholarly consensus is that all grants to the Templars came from the crown or Anglo-Norman patrons, although the dates when they received or acquired many of their properties are unclear. Likewise, it appears that all the Hospitallers' patrons in Ireland were Anglo-Cymro-Norman incomers rather than Irish, although many of the donors and precise dates of donation are uncertain. The donors to the Order of St Thomas of Acre were also from Anglo-Norman families settled in Ireland.[13] In addition to the property they received, the king of England granted the Templars and Hospitallers the right to have one *hospes* or guest in each borough in England and Ireland, who was exempt from tallage and other exactions.[14] The bulk of these institutions' Irish possessions lay in the south and east of Ireland, the area dominated by the invaders. The Templars received an estate in Co. Sligo and the Hospitallers

---

9 Virtuani, 'The Knights of St John of Jerusalem in medieval Ireland', p. 28.   10 Anne Duggan, 'The power of documents: the curious case of *Laudabiliter*' in Brenda Bolton & Christine E. Meek (eds), *Aspects of power and authority in the Middle Ages* (Turnhout, 2007), pp 251–75.   11 Hurlock, *Crusades*, p. 146.   12 *MRHI*, pp 5–6.   13 Ibid., pp 329–31, 334–42; Billy Colfer, *The Hook Peninsula, County Wexford* (Cork, 2004), pp 48, 50; O'Conor & Naessens, 'Temple House', p. 128; St John Brooks, 'Irish possessions'. For a debate over the identification of Templar properties see, for example, Eamonn Cotter, Paul MacCotter & Tadhg O'Keeffe, 'A blow to the temple: the "monastic castle" at Rincrew (Co. Waterford) reinterpreted', *JIA* 24 (2015), 163–78.   14 Helen J. Nicholson, 'The military-religious orders in the towns of the British Isles' in Damien Carraz (ed.), *Les ordres militaires dans la ville médiévale (1100–1350)* (Clermont-Ferrand, 2013), pp 113–26; Clarence Perkins, 'The Knights Templar in the British Isles', *EHR* 25 (1910), 209–30 at 215.

held property on the Ards peninsula in Ulster, donated by the de Lacys, but these were exceptions to the general pattern.

Donors to these orders would have hoped to mitigate their sins in return for their generosity to these institutions that served Christ in the Holy Land. As already mentioned, a donation could be a thank-offering to God for the successful invasion. Some of the donor families were already established patrons of the military-religious orders. For example, the de Lacys, who patronized both Hospitallers and Templars in Ireland, were already patrons of the Templars in Yorkshire and Gloucestershire and went on to patronize the Hospitallers in Gloucestershire and Herefordshire.[15] The de Lacys also took part in the holy wars of Latin Christendom. As mentioned above, Gilbert de Lacy had become a Templar brother and in 1163 was serving in the Holy Land. After fleeing from Ireland in 1210 following an unsuccessful revolt against King John, Hugh de Lacy II, earl of Ulster, took part in the Albigensian Crusade in the service of Simon de Montfort, received the title of lord of Castelnaudary and Laurac, and requested the Hospitaller habit from the prior of St John of Jerusalem of Toulouse in return for a gift of the town of Renneville, part of his gains from the crusade.[16] Hugh would have been applying to become an associate of the order rather than a full brother, but in seeking this closer relationship with the Hospitallers he was developing a previously established family connection.

The de Lacys were not the only donor family with a previous connection to the Holy Land or crusading. King Henry II had donated generously to the defence of the Holy Land and took the cross in 1188.[17] William Marshal, who married Richard fitz Gilbert's (Strongbow's) daughter Isabel, gave the Hospitallers property at Ballyhoge in Co. Wexford, and he and Isabel might have been involved in the original donation of the Hospital of St John the Baptist at Kilkenny to the order of St Thomas of Acre. William went on pilgrimage to the Holy Land in around 1183–5 and was also a patron of the Templars, taking their habit on his deathbed.[18] For such powerful families, supporting the military-religious orders underlined their commitment to crusading.

---

15 Edward Coleman, '"Powerful adversaries": the Knights Templar, landholding and litigation in the lordship of Ireland' in Browne & Ó Clabaigh, *Soldiers of Christ*, pp 184–94, at p. 189; 'Margaret de Lacy and the Hospital of Saint John at Aconbury, Herefordshire' in Anthony Luttrell & Helen J. Nicholson (eds), *Hospitaller women in the Middle Ages* (Aldershot, 2006), pp 153–77, at pp 160–1.   16 Paul Duffy & Daniel J.F. Brown, 'From Carrickfergus to Carcassonne: Hugh de Lacy and the Albigensian Crusade' in Duffy et al., *From Carrickfergus to Carcassonne*, pp 9–30, at p. 27; Paul Duffy, 'The exiled earl and the soon-to-be saint', *HI* 24: 5 (2016), 16–19, at 19.   17 Hans E. Mayer, 'Henry II of England and the Holy Land', *EHR* 97 (1982), 721–39.   18 St John Brooks, 'Irish possessions'; Colfer, *Hook Peninsula*, p. 50; Hurlock, *Crusades*, p. 152; David Crouch, 'Marshal, William [called the Marshal], fourth earl of Pembroke (*c.*1146–1219), soldier and administrator', *ODNB*.

The military-religious orders in Ireland: their patrons and their purpose

Although it is not always possible to see a direct link between a donor and crusading, there is enough evidence of Irish or Anglo-Irish connections with and interest in the Latin East to suggest that the military-religious orders' connections with the crusade could have been a general motivation for donations. Pilgrims travelled to the Latin East, Anglo-Irish lords joined crusades to the Latin East or (as in the case of Hugh de Lacy II) crusades elsewhere in Europe and poets, contemporary commentators and compilers of histories mentioned crusades and crusaders. The presence among the witnesses against the Templars in Ireland in 1310 of three men who had been in the eastern Mediterranean suggests that travel between Ireland and the eastern Mediterranean was not uncommon. Donors would have been aware of the military-religious orders' deeds in the eastern Mediterranean and could have hoped to support their work in God's service.[19]

Donors also hoped for some worldly gain. Scholars have suggested that the grants given to the military-religious orders in Ireland were intended to control ports and waterways. Edward Coleman has pointed out that Henry II's donations to the Templars in Wexford and Waterford gave the Templars control over 'the key arteries of transport to the interior of south-east Ireland as well as a major Anglo-Norman landing point on the island' (pl. 7.1). Kieran O'Conor and Paul Naessens suggested that Richard de Burgh I (d. 1243), as lord of Connacht, or his successors, granted the Templars the property in Co. Sligo that became Temple House to ensure that the 'strategic location was under the firm control of an order they could trust, rather than a fickle baron': the estate controlled a crossing over the Owenmore river, a navigable waterway on the boundary between two cantreds. West of Dublin, the Hospitallers held extensive property on both sides of the Liffey, donated by two of the original Anglo-Cymro-Norman invaders, Richard fitz Gilbert and Hugh Tyrrell. The military-religious orders could represent their patrons' authority in these localities, even though their members' role was primarily to pray rather than fight.[20] Patrons also expected to influence the orders' activities and benefit directly from them, for example, by renting estates cheaply, receiving money for their support, or seeing their family members promoted within the order.[21]

---

19 See Paul Duffy, chapter 5, and Ciarán McDonnell, chapter 6, this volume, and Hurlock, 'The crusades to 1291', 517–34; Hurlock, *Crusades*, pp 128–9, 133–4.   20 Coleman, '"Powerful adversaries"', p. 187; O'Conor & Naessens, 'Temple House', pp 129–30, at p. 130, citing Billy Colfer, *Arrogant trespass: Anglo-Norman Wexford, 1169–1400* (Dublin, 2002), p. 196; Paolo Virtuani, 'Unforgiveable trespasses: the Irish Hospitallers and the defence of their rights in the mid-thirteenth century' in Browne & Ó Clabaigh, *Soldiers of Christ*, pp 195–205, at pp 195, 199.   21 For example, see Gregory O'Malley, *The Knights Hospitaller of the English langue 1460–1565* (Oxford, 2005), pp 235, 247, 253–5.

In frontier regions and areas of underdeveloped land across Latin Christendom it was common for landowners to give disputed or undeveloped land to religious orders for them to invest in and develop. Through such gifts patrons could retain some claim over the land, while reducing the risk that it would be seized by rival claimants. Religious orders could invest capital and labour in developing land, which would benefit the local economy and thus the original donor.[22] The bulk of the land given to the military-religious orders in Ireland was not on a frontier with the Irish, so it appears that donors were not using them as a buffer as at Baldongan, Co. Dublin (pl. 7.2).[23] However, they might have donated land that needed investment. The military-religious orders put resources into developing their property, because their intention was to make a profit from it.

The function of the military-religious orders' properties in Europe, away from the frontiers of Latin Christendom, was to generate resources to support their activities in the defence of Christendom, principally an annual render called the 'responsion'. The collection of the responsion was organized by the chief official in each province or grand priory, through an annual provincial chapter meeting. Although the contribution that the Templars and Hospitallers in Ireland owed to their orders' headquarters in the eastern Mediterranean was perhaps only a quarter of that made by the English houses of these orders, in the Hospitallers' case at least it was comparable to that made by other smaller provinces, such as Portugal, and was certainly not the smallest. That said, the sum due was not always paid.[24] The orders' commitments within Ireland would have swallowed up much of the resources generated there. For instance, the estates of St Thomas of Acre at Kilkenny and Carrick-on-Suir were probably absorbed by the expenses of the hospitals these estates were intended to support.

Within each province, these orders' lands and other properties were grouped together for administrative purposes into units called *preceptoriae* (in Latin) or *commanderies* (in French), each centred on a larger manor, which might have smaller farms, churches and parcels of land associated to it. Within the organizational structure of their order, the Irish Hospitallers were part of the English *langue* but had their own prior, although the English priory was always seeking to expand its authority over Ireland and also Scotland.[25] In

---

22 Hurlock, *Crusades*, pp 154–5.   23 Tadhg O'Keeffe & Pat Grogan, 'Building a frontier? The architecture of the military orders in medieval Ireland' in Browne & Ó Clabaigh (eds), *Soldiers of Christ*, pp 81–102, at p. 82.   24 Nicholson, 'A long way from Jerusalem', pp 21–2; Gregory O'Malley, 'Authority and autonomy: relations between Clerkenwell, Kilmainham and the Hospitaller central convent after the Black Death' in Browne & Ó Clabaigh, *Soldiers of Christ*, pp 23–46, at pp 37–9, 45.   25 O'Malley, 'Authority and autonomy', pp 23–46.

The military-religious orders in Ireland: their patrons and their purpose

contrast, the Templars' commander of Ireland was subordinate to the grand commander of England, although in practice they operated under different secular administrations.[26]

What evidence survives of the orders' membership indicates that they included a wide social range, both full members and associates. It is unclear whether members of the orders in Ireland whose toponymic family names indicate British origin were born in Britain or came from British families who had settled in Ireland, but it is clear that initially members of these orders were drawn from the so-called Anglo-Irish community and not the Irish.[27] As estate owners, the orders would have employed household workers, estate officials and specialized craftspeople, and male and female farm labourers. Just one man who had 'formerly served the Templars' gave evidence against them during the trial in Ireland; he had been on Cyprus, evidence of active links between Ireland and the eastern Mediterranean, but his family name, Broghton, was Anglo-Irish or British.[28] What evidence exists indicates that initially the Hospitallers also recruited their workforce from the local Anglo-Irish community: none of the servants noted in the *Registrum de Kilmainham*, a list of contracts made by the Hospitallers between 1321 and 1350, had Gaelic-Irish names.[29] However, by the late fourteenth century, as the Hospitallers in Ireland came to regard themselves as distinct from the Hospitallers in England, these internal divisions became less significant. By the early sixteenth century brothers of Gaelic-Irish descent were holding office within the Hospital in Ireland.[30]

The members of the military-religious orders in Ireland had to fulfil their liturgical duties and farm the estates they had been granted, collecting the ecclesiastical dues from their churches, pleas and perquisites of court and any other income they had been granted to form their *responsion* to the Holy Land. Evidence from the trial of the Templars in Ireland suggests that timber and grain were this order's main cash crops.[31] The 1308 inventories of the Templars' Irish estates reveal, as Margaret Murphy has shown, that 'their lands were well managed and productive' and that 'they embraced some innovations and were commercially oriented'. However, their estate management was not in any way out of the ordinary: although 'they occupied the more productive and diversified ends of the spectrum', 'their activities fell within the parameters of manorial agricultural practice across the Anglo-Norman colony'. The

26 Nicholson, *Proceedings*, i, pp 28, 379; ii, pp 30, 433. 27 Nicholson, 'A long way from Jerusalem', pp 12–13. 28 Nicholson, *Proceedings*, i, pp 335–6; ii, pp 377–8. 29 Eithne Massey, *Prior Roger Outlaw of Kilmainham, 1314–1341* (Dublin, 2000), p. 12; *RK*, p. 9. 30 O'Malley, 'Authority and autonomy', pp 40–1. 31 Nicholson, *Proceedings*, i, p. 313; ii, p. 349.

Templars' estates in England and north-eastern France seem to have been managed in a similar way.[32]

In addition to running their estates, the Hospitallers and Templars were involved in royal service. The two leading military-religious orders' earliest surviving appearance in the English government records for Ireland occurred in September 1220, when King Henry III's government instructed the justiciar of Ireland to deposit the proceeds of an aid with the Templars and Hospitallers under their seals.[33] The two orders were then responsible for transporting the money to England. This type of operation was familiar to both orders, which were regularly given responsibility for secure storage of cash for the English and the French royal treasuries.

The orders' administrative service in Ireland developed along similar lines as elsewhere in Europe, as envoys and as financial officers. In 1234 two Templars acted as intermediaries between royal officials in Ireland and the rebel Richard Marshal; in the same year Henry III appointed the archbishop of Dublin, Maurice fitzGerald, the justiciar of Ireland, and the master of the Knights Templar in Ireland as auditors of the annual accounts produced by the treasurer and barons of the exchequer. The Templars continued in this role and the Hospitallers joined them from 1270. They were also involved in collecting taxes.[34]

It was the Hospitallers who provided the more prominent members of the English king's government in Ireland. The Hospitaller Brother Stephen de Fulbourn (d. 1288) became treasurer of Ireland in 1274, rose to be justiciar in 1281 and ran the administration in the interests of himself and his family until his death in 1288. The post of lieutenant justiciar went on to be held by two priors of the Hospital in Ireland, William fitzRoger and William de Ros. Roger Utlagh or Outlaw, prior of the Hospital in Ireland c.1314–41, was appointed by Edward II as chancellor of Ireland in January 1322, was reappointed by Edward III in 1327 and also acted as lieutenant justiciar of Ireland as well as chancellor throughout the 1330s. After his death in 1341 his successor, the English Brother John Larcher (1342–9) became chancellor of Ireland and held the post on and off throughout his priorship. For the remainder of the fourteenth century successful priors of Ireland held the post of chief justice, chancellor of Ireland and treasurer of Ireland. The pattern was broken briefly with the appointment of Brother Peter Holt as prior of Ireland (before

32 Margaret Murphy, 'From swords to ploughshares: evidence for Templar agriculture in medieval Ireland' in Browne & Ó Clabaigh, *Soldiers of Christ*, pp 167–83, at p. 183; Nicholson, *Everyday life of the Templars*, pp 80–96, 101. 33 Helen J. Nicholson, 'Serving king and crusade: the military orders in royal service in Ireland, 1220–1400' in Marcus Bull & Norman Housley (eds), *The experience of crusading*, i: *Western approaches* (Cambridge, 2003), pp 233–52, at p. 236. 34 Idem, 'Serving king and crusade', pp 233–52, at pp 236–7.

1396), as he was hardly if ever resident in Ireland, but recommenced after the grand master and convent on Rhodes acknowledged Brother Thomas Butler as prior in Ireland in 1410: in 1412 Butler appeared as deputy of Thomas, duke of Lancaster, Henry IV's deputy in Ireland. Disputes within the Irish priory between Anglo-Irish and English-born brothers during the fourteenth century do not appear to have had any impact on the Hospitallers' service for the king.[35]

As leading members of the English king's administration in Ireland, from the 1270s onwards the priors of the Hospital in Ireland also took part in active military service against the Irish. At various times they were also involved in fighting between the Anglo-Irish and rebels against the king.[36] Like other religious orders in Ireland, the Hospitallers had many fortified buildings and were also entrusted with royal fortresses to defend. Kilmainham was more thoroughly enclosed than any of the Hospitallers' houses in England and Wales: even its bridge over the river Liffey was fortified.[37] The Hospitallers claimed the king's special favour on the basis that they played a leading military role in Ireland, in addition to their holy war in the eastern Mediterranean. In June 1360 King Edward III noted that the Hospitallers in Ireland maintained war against the enemies of the Christian faith on Rhodes, while in Ireland they 'bonum locum ibidem nobis tenent ad repulsionem hibernicorum hostium nostrorum guerram super fidelem populum nostrum in dies machmantum' ('hold a good position for us there for the repulse of our Irish enemies, who daily maintain war upon our liege people').[38]

Both Irish and Anglo-Irish claimed to be fighting a just war against the other, as Maeve Callan and Kathryn Hurlock discuss elsewhere in this volume. Even after the dissolution of the Hospitallers in 1540, leading members of the Anglo-Irish establishment suggested re-forming the order in Ireland to fight the Irish.[39] Yet the Hospitallers did not try to justify their involvement in warfare against the Irish on the basis of holy war; they were involved in warfare because they were the faithful servants of the king of England.

---

35 Nicholson, 'Serving king and crusade', pp 238–9; O'Malley, 'Authority and autonomy', pp 23–7; Charles Tipton, 'Peter Holt: turcopolier of Rhodes and prior of Ireland', *Annales de l'Ordre Souverain Militaire de Malte* 22 (1964), 82–5.   36 Hurlock, *Crusades*, p. 150; Helen J. Nicholson, 'The Hospitallers' and Templars' involvement in warfare on the frontiers of the British Isles in the late thirteenth and early fourteenth centuries' in Jürgen Sarnowsky (ed.), *Ordines militaris colloquia Torunensia historica* (Toruń, 2012), 105–19, at 114–17; idem, 'Holy warriors, worldly war: military-religious orders and secular conflict', *Journal of Medieval Military History* 17 (2019), 61–79; O'Malley, *The Knights Hospitaller*, pp 234–6, 239–41, 244, 250, 256–7.   37 O'Malley, *The Knights Hospitaller*, pp 233–4.   38 Kew, National Archives of the UK: C 54/198, mem. 27 (*Close Rolls*, 34 Edw. III); *CCR Edw. III* xi p. 39.   39 O'Malley, *The Knights Hospitaller*, p. 256; Brendan Scott, 'The Knights Hospitaller in Tudor Ireland: their dissolution and attempted revival' in Browne & Ó Clabaigh, *Soldiers of Christ*, pp 47–60.

All those involved in the royal administration in Ireland had to lead armies on behalf of the government. The archbishop of Dublin and other churchmen who played leading roles in the English royal administration in Ireland fought in the field as part of their duties of office.[40] In 1364, on the appointment of a new chancellor of Ireland, a layman, it was recorded that the chancellor must often ride to war and therefore could retain in his service six men-at-arms and twelve mounted archers at the rate of pay usually given to royal troops in Ireland.[41] As Hospitaller prior of Ireland, Roger Outlaw maintained close relations with many of the senior officials in the English administration in Ireland, many of whom were corrody-holders at the Hospital's house at Kilmainham. He used these connections to protect and advance his order's interests in the political and military turmoil of Ireland.[42] As a central figure in Anglo-Irish society, he could not have avoided involvement in war, which was a part of everyday life. The Hospitallers, therefore, were engaged in military activities in Ireland because of their involvement in royal administration and political life, not because they were a military religious order.

As elsewhere in Europe, the Hospitallers' connections to leading families and their service for kings drew them into secular politics and led them to participate in civil conflicts and revolts, with some catastrophic results for individuals. In the fourteenth and fifteenth centuries Hospitaller priors and Hospitallers in Castile, England, Hungary and Navarre played active roles in revolts against these kingdoms' governments and in civil wars, leading in some cases to their deposition and, in England, execution.[43] In Ireland in 1461 the Hospitaller prior Thomas Talbot was removed from his office because of his anti-Yorkist views. His replacement James Keating seemed acceptable to the king of England, the Irish Hospitallers and the order because he was Irish-born, he had served for some years at the Hospitallers' central convent on Rhodes, and as a supporter of the earl of Desmond he would be loyal to the Yorkist King Edward IV of England. But when Desmond was seized and executed in 1468 Keating was also imprisoned and fined. After this, Keating sided with the Anglo-Irish aristocracy, who resisted royal authority. As constable of Dublin castle in 1478 he broke the castle's drawbridge to prevent the

---

40 James Lydon, 'The years of crisis, 1254–1315' in Art Cosgrove (ed.), *A new history of Ireland*, ii: *Medieval Ireland, 1169–1534* (Oxford, 1993), pp 179–204, at pp 183–4; J.A. Watt, 'The Anglo-Irish colony under strain, 1327–99' in ibid., pp 352–96, at pp 362–3.   41 *CPR Edw. III* xiii, p. 25.   42 Massey, *Prior Roger Outlaw*, pp 24–42.   43 Philippe Josserand, *Église et pouvoir dans la péninsule Ibérique: les ordres militaires dans le royaume de Castille (1252–1369)* (Madrid, 2004), pp 501–22; R.A. Griffiths, 'Langstrother [Longstrother], Sir John (d. 1471), administrator and prior of the hospital of St John of Jerusalem in England', *ODNB*; Zsolt Hunyadi, *The Hospitallers in the medieval kingdom of Hungary, c.1150–1387* (Budapest, 2010), pp 62–4; Carlos Barquero Goñi, 'The Hospitallers and the kings of Navarre in the fourteenth and fifteenth centuries' in Helen Nicholson (ed.), *The military orders*, ii: *Welfare and warfare* (Aldershot, 1998), pp 348–54, at pp 353–4.

royal deputy, Henry, Lord Grey of Ruthin, from entering. After the change of regime in England in 1485, with the victory of the Lancastrian faction and the accession of Henry Tudor to the English throne, Keating supported the king's enemies. He played a leading role in Lambert Simnel's rebellion of 1487. He received a royal pardon, but in 1494 he went on to support Perkin Warbeck's rebellion. He was deposed from office and convicted for treason by the English parliament.[44] Following Keating's actions the English government commanded that in future the prior of the Hospital in Ireland should be English by descent and birth. This ensured that subsequent priors were faithful servants of the king of England – Prior John Rawson supported the king during the revolt of Thomas fitz Gerald in 1534 and played an important role in putting it down – but did not change the views of individual Hospitallers, who were among the rebels in 1534.[45]

The military-religious orders also played other, more traditional religious roles in society, supporting parish churches and providing hospitality. The privileges that successive popes bestowed on them to support their military activity against the enemies of Christendom allowed them to offer attractive indulgences to the laity, such as the general remission of sins which in 1467 drew crowds from Munster, Leinster and Connacht to hear a sermon at the Hospitallers' house at Limerick.[46] Although little evidence survives to cast light on these orders' spirituality in Ireland, the inventories of the Templars' Irish houses indicate that their chapels were well equipped with the necessary devotional furnishings: clerical vestments, liturgical and other books and liturgical plate, suggesting that the Templars took their liturgical duties seriously.[47] Cambridge Corpus Christi MS 405, a Hospitaller codex probably assembled at Kilbarry in the fourteenth century, offers some insights to Hospitaller spirituality, as Colmán Ó Clabaigh has discussed. The codex includes copies of papal exemptions and rights granted to the Hospitallers by the king of England, liturgical texts including a liturgical calendar, a version of the Hospitallers' origins and earliest regulations in Anglo-Norman French, devotional poetry and some works of theology including some apocalyptic texts. It combines material of English and Irish interest, reflecting the background of the Hospitallers in Ireland. Much of the material is in the vernacular, and is 'theologically unsophisticated and moralizing in tone',

---

44 O'Malley, 'Authority and autonomy', pp 32, 39; O'Malley, *The Knights Hospitaller*, pp 241–6. **45** Scott, 'Knights Hospitaller in Tudor Ireland', pp 47–9; O'Malley, *The Knights Hospitaller*, pp 246–53. **46** O'Malley, 'Authority and autonomy', p. 46, citing Brian Ó Cuív (ed.), 'A fragment of Irish annals', *Celtica* 14 (1981), 83–104, at 86, 93, 97 (paragraph 17). **47** Helen J. Nicholson, 'Evidence of the Templars' religious practice from the records of the Templars' estates in Britain and Ireland in 1308' in Iris Shagrir, Benjamin Z. Kedar & Michel Balard (eds), *Communicating the Middle Ages*. Subsidia 11 (London, 2018), pp 50–63.

118   *Ireland and the crusades*

indicating that the Hospitallers lacked theological learning but were personally pious.[48]

The fact that parish churches were given to the military-religious orders to ensure that divine service was maintained indicates that contemporaries believed that these orders were spiritually fit to have care of souls. These orders willingly took on responsibility for parish churches, which could generate considerable income as the accounts for the Templar estates in Ireland in the years 1308–15 show.[49] But the orders also used their own buildings to provide the laity with devotional space: although at the Templars' house of Kilcloggan the brothers' chapel and the parish church were separate buildings, at many sites it appears that the commandery church doubled as a parish church.[50] All that is left of many former Templar and Hospitaller houses is the ruins of the commandery church, evidence that these continued in use as parish churches long after the dissolution. This is the case, for example, at Killure, Kilbarry and Crooke in Co. Waterford. Crooke was in good repair as a parish church in 1613, Kilbarry likewise in 1615, while Killure was in ruins in 1615 but had previously been the parish church. The fact that these were parish churches at least in the late sixteenth century suggests that they had already been parish churches under the Hospitallers and Templars.[51]

The Hospitallers held several churches at Wexford in south-east Ireland, including the parish church of St John's and possibly a hospice.[52] They might have received this property from Richard fitz Gilbert, alias Strongbow, before they received the site at Kilmainham. In 1212 Pope Innocent III confirmed their possession of five churches in Wexford, but the Hospitallers apparently gave away or sold three of these. By the time of the dissolution in Ireland the Hospitallers held only two churches at Wexford and a house or hospital.[53]

Scholars have struggled to find specific evidence that the Hospitallers had any hospitals that actively cared for the sick in Ireland, although there might have been such a hospital at Ainy in Co. Limerick.[54] Thomas Ivory discusses

---

48 Colmán Ó Clabaigh, 'Prayer, politics and poetry: Cambridge, Corpus Christi College MS 405 and the Templars and Hospitallers at Kilbarry, Co. Waterford' in Browne & Ó Clabaigh, *Soldiers of Christ*, pp 206–17, at p. 215.   49 'Documents relating to the suppression of the Templars in Ireland', ed. G. MacNiocaill, *AH* 24 (1967), 183–226, at 220–6.   50 O'Keeffe & Grogan, 'Building a frontier?', pp 85–6, 90–1, 95–100; 'Documents', ed. MacNiocaill, 200, 202. See Tadhg O'Keeffe, chapter 14, this volume.   51 Michael Moore, *Archaeological inventory of County Waterford* (Dublin, 1999), pp 171, 177, 179.   52 *MRHI*, p. 339.   53 'S. Michaelis de Wesefort, S. Joannis, S. Patricii, S. Brigide, S. Marie Magdalene Wesfort': *Cart. Gen. Hosp.* ii, p. 148, no. 1394; Virtuani, 'The Knights of St John of Jerusalem', pp 39–42, 228–9; *MRHI*, p. 339; Michael Moore, *Archaeological inventory of County Wexford* (Dublin, 1996), p. 163.   54 Virtuani, 'The Knights of St John of Jerusalem', pp 193–4; on this house, see: O'Keeffe & Grogan, 'Building a frontier?', pp 91–5; Eamonn Cotter, 'The archaeology of the Irish Hospitaller preceptories of Mourneabbey and Hospital in context' in Browne & Ó Clabaigh, *Soldiers of Christ*, pp 103–23, at pp 117–20.

elsewhere in this volume the military-religious orders' possible influence on hospitals in Ireland. There is some evidence that they supported pilgrims and the poor: Alexander de Bykenore, archbishop of Dublin 1317–49, gave the Hospitallers the parish church of Rathmore with its chapels, tithes and obventions for the support of pilgrims and the necessities of the poor.[55] Although no specific evidence survives of hospitality for the poor at Rathmore, this is not surprising; routine hospitality to the poor required few records to be kept.

In contrast, hospitality for the wealthy and powerful involved the order in large investments in resources and could bring large returns, so records were needed. The *Registrum de Kilmainham* shows that by the first half of the fourteenth century the Hospitallers of Kilmainham had forty-nine corrodians, many of whom lived within the precinct of the house.[56] They received different levels of support, depending on their status: nobility could receive fine clothes and food, lodging for servants and horses and other privileges, while servants received only simple clothing and food. These corrodians were treated as the Hospitallers' guests and allowed to build and extend their own accommodation within the enclosure of the house. As many of the corrody-holders were powerful men involved in legal service or the government, Kilmainham could have provided them with a temporary refuge at times of political or personal crisis.[57] The Hospitallers at Kilmainham also received other prominent guests: in 1354 Prior John Frowyck received there the Hungarian nobleman George Grissaphan, a pilgrim to the cave shrine known as St Patrick's Purgatory in north-west Ireland.[58] In contrast, there is no evidence that the Hospitallers at Kilmainham made any provision for caring for the sick and it is unclear whether they welcomed non-noble travellers beyond the customary social duty to give all travellers hospitality as required.

CONCLUSION

The histories of the military-religious orders in Ireland reflected their connection with the invaders and particularly with the king of England, who was largely responsible for introducing the Templars to Ireland. Yet the Templars'

55 Charles McNeill, 'The Hospitallers at Kilmainham and their guests', *JRSAI* 54 (1924), 15–30, at 20. 56 For what follows see also Nicholson, 'Military-religious orders in the towns', pp 117–18. 57 Massey, *Prior Roger Outlaw*, pp 10–20, 24–8, 31; G. Lennox Barrow, 'The Knights Hospitaller of St John of Jerusalem at Kilmainham', *Dublin Historical Record* 38 (1985), 108–12; McNeill, 'Hospitallers at Kilmainham and their guests', 15–30. 58 Michael Haren, 'Two Hungarian pilgrims' in Michael Haren & Yolande de Pontfarcy (eds), *The medieval pilgrimage to St Patrick's Purgatory: Lough Derg and the European tradition* (Enniskillen, 1988), pp 129–68, at 120–4; *Il purgatorio di San Patrizio, documenti letterari e testimonianze (secc. XII–XVI)*, ed. G.P. Maggioni, R. Tinti & P. Taviani (Florence, 2018), pp 190, 191, 206.

loyal service for the king of England could not prevent their dissolution. Following the papal bull of 22 November 1307 the Templars in Ireland were arrested on 3 February 1308 by royal command on charges of heresy. After an investigation in spring 1310, involving the interrogation of Templars and collection of third-party evidence, the Templars in Ireland were dissolved and the bulk of their properties passed to the Hospitallers.[59]

Although initially the Hospitallers were not generously endowed by the king, they came to serve the government in Dublin even more extensively than did the Templars. The Hospitallers and the order of St Thomas of Acre continued to hold property in Ireland until the dissolution of the monasteries by King Henry VIII of England. The Hospitallers were suppressed in 1540; the order of St Thomas of Acre was probably suppressed before August 1536, although patrons were still expressing the wish to be buried within the order's church at Kilkenny after that date.[60] But the military-religious orders were so valuable to the royal administration in Ireland that almost at once there were attempts to resuscitate them. Immediately after the Hospitallers' dissolution in 1540 the king's council proposed using the former Hospitaller assets to set up what Rory MacLellan has termed 'a police force'. The king and his royal council in England turned down the scheme. The Hospitallers in Britain and Ireland were resuscitated under Mary and Philip in 1557 and the Irish brothers held at least one provincial chapter; but after Mary's death in the following year her successor Elizabeth, allowed the order to disappear, although it was never formally dissolved.[61]

In many ways the Hospitallers, Templars and Order of St Thomas of Acre were like any other religious orders in Ireland, holding estates, maintaining churches and their spiritual lives, and playing a political role within the local area and the country. Yet they had an additional dimension because the focus of their orders was on Jerusalem and care for pilgrims to the Holy Land. Their exemptions from ecclesiastical taxes and secular dues, granted by popes and kings to enable them to focus their resources on helping the Holy Land, made them more attractive landlords. Their connection to crusading made them particularly prestigious objects of religious patronage and, possibly, more trusted royal servants. In any case, they were a visible reminder of the crusade within Anglo-Irish society.

---

59 Callan, *Templars*, pp 48–70, at p. 49; Helen J. Nicholson, *The Knights Templar on trial: the trial of the Templars in the British Isles, 1308–1311* (Stroud, 2009), pp 145–69, at p. 146; Wood, 'Templars', 348. 60 St John Brooks, 'Irish possessions', 27–8. 61 Rory MacLellan, 'Abandoning piety and pugnacity? New military orders in the sixteenth and seventeenth centuries' in Nicholas Morton (ed.), *The military orders, vii: Piety, pugnacity and property* (London, 2019), pp 208–17, at p. 209; O'Malley, *The Knights Hospitaller*, pp 256–7, 331–2; Scott, 'Knights Hospitaller in Tudor Ireland'.

8 / *Tuitio fidei?* The Irish Hospitallers at war

PAOLO VIRTUANI

The defence of the Faith (*tuitio fidei*) is often mentioned as one of the two pillars upon which the mission of the Hospitaller Order of St John of Jerusalem was eventually built, the other – and antecedent one – being *obsequium pauperum* (the care for the poor and sick).[1] Understandably, scholarly research on the military activities of the Hospitallers has largely focused on their endeavours in the Latin East and, after 1291, in the Mediterranean. However, on a few occasions, Knights Hospitaller based in Europe took up arms. This has not gone unnoticed by scholars. In recent years, for example, an overview from Helen Nicholson scoured the 'frontiers' of the British Isles (Scotland, Wales, Ireland) looking at this aspect, for both Hospitallers and Templars.[2] The present contribution builds on that work, focusing on the Hospitaller order's military activities in Ireland, where a wealth of evidence allows for substantial conclusions.

MILITARY-RELIGIOUS ORDERS AND WARFARE IN EUROPE

In 1989 historian Alan Forey touched on this subject – more specifically, on warfare 'against Christians' – in a comprehensive article.[3] Excluding from the analysis crusading activity in Spain, and allowing for *distinguos* and exceptions, he concluded that the main military-religious orders largely strived to remain faithful to their core mission of fighting the 'infidel' and resisted secular and religious attempts at utilizing their military expertise for other goals. These conclusions he confirmed and summarized three years later: 'although in the thirteenth century military orders were being used against Christians, little record has survived of their military undertakings in this sphere: their contribution was presumably too limited to merit much comment in narrative sources'.[4]

---

1 According to Jonathan Riley-Smith the militarization of the order may have begun as early as the 1120s (*The Knights Hospitaller in the Levant, c.1070–1309* (Basingstoke, 2012), pp 27–8).   2 Helen J. Nicholson, 'The Hospitallers and Templars' involvement in warfare on the frontiers of the British Isles in the late thirteenth and early fourteenth centuries' in Jürgen Sarnowsky (ed.), *Ordines militaris colloquia Torunensia historica* (Toruń, 2012), 105–19.   3 A.J. Forey, 'The military orders and holy war against Christians in the thirteenth century', *EHR* 104 (1989), 1–24.   4 Idem, *The military orders from the twelfth to the early thirteenth centuries* (Basingstoke, 1992), p. 44.

This view is reinforced by the consideration that the enormous military and economic undertakings in the Holy Land would not leave room for distracting fronts.[5] This eminently practical reason, though, would have to deal with the uncomfortable (for the Hospitallers) clash of priorities between their mission and their religious and geo-political loyalties in Europe, or in other words between popes and rulers. In Jonathan Riley-Smith's words, 'the custom of the Hospital was that the violence was to be employed only against Muslims, but, as James of Vitry pointed out early in the thirteenth century, the military orders had the obligation to obey the papacy if called upon to fight against schismatics or heretics'.[6] Two examples followed this quote, which Riley-Smith used to typify the aforementioned challenges: the Franco-papal crusade against Aragon (1283) and the Angevin campaign against Conradin of Hohenstaufen (1266). In these cases, the Hospitallers were either forced to disappear 'diplomatically' into the shadows, or to participate in the fray, with disastrous political and economic consequences.

This general introduction to the subject rings all the truer when we apply its conclusions to the situation in the British Isles, as Nicholson did.[7] In Britain and Ireland, the biggest player was the king; although the pope's ultimate authority over the order was never questioned, here 'the Templars, and particularly the Hospitallers, were increasingly secularised institutions, serving the king of England and playing important roles in royal government'.[8]

IRISH HOSPITALLERS AND THE CRUSADES

The Knights of St John of Jerusalem's presence in Ireland dates to the very first years after the Anglo-Norman invasion of 1169, although the formalization of the Irish priory within the order's provincial framework can be dated to c.1206–12.[9] It is interesting to note that the priory of Ireland did not depend from its English counterpart based in Clerkenwell, but it reported directly to the Master and Convent. It might be counterintuitive to think that such a remote priory would maintain close links with the headquarters in the Latin East, but there is solid evidence of the fact that the Irish priory was not forgotten, nor did it forget its duties.[10] Such duties, in short, were the

---

5 Nicholson, *Knights Hospitaller*, p. 42. For a case study, see also Zsolt Hunyadi, 'The military activity of the Hospitallers in the medieval kingdom of Hungary (thirteenth to fourteenth centuries)' in K. Borchardt, N. Jaspert & H.J. Nicholson (eds), *The Hospitallers, the Mediterranean and Europe* (Aldershot, 2007), pp 193–203.   6 Riley-Smith, *The Knights Hospitaller in the Levant*, p. 187.   7 Nicholson, 'The Hospitallers' and Templars' involvement in warfare'.   8 Ibid., p. 107.   9 Probably as a direct result of the Statutes of Margat, 1206. See Virtuani, 'The Knights of St John of Jerusalem in medieval Ireland', pp 43–8.   10 Ibid., pp 217–18.

Tuitio fidei? The Irish Hospitallers at war   123

same as every other priory, castellany, or capitular commandery in Europe: to raise revenue and send it to the East in the form of *responsiones*, together with equipment and occasionally manpower. This occasional contribution of manpower might have happened for Ireland, too, although its distance from the theatre of operations made it less likely. The famous excerpt from Matthew Paris' *Chronica Majora* depicting thirty Hospitallers in arms departing from Clerkenwell in 1237 bound for the Holy Land paints a likely scenario involving any brethren summoned from Ireland.[11] The first solid evidence of a summons, however, would occur much later, in the early 1270s: as a consequence of the sudden and violent reverses suffered by the crusader states on account of the onslaught of Baibars, the Hospitaller Master Hugh Revel mustered soldiers and resources from all corners of Christendom. Prior William fitz Roger, who had had an active military record in Ireland (see below), received the summons probably in 1275 or shortly before, but was abruptly stopped by King Edward I, with the threat of the loss of his (and his order's) lands, and had to revert back to Ireland, performing royal duty.[12] This episode is strikingly exemplary, as the direct clash of priorities resulted in Edward overruling a direct command of Hugh Revel, a very assertive master of the Hospital, in a situation of dire need. This event seems to have been a template for later occurrences: one hundred years later, in 1375, a small *passagium* was being organized, with the aim of countering Ottoman expansion in Epirus. The summons was issued for thirty-eight knights from the English *langue*, which included Ireland, to join the expedition, and then-Prior William Tany was addressed personally:

> The pope has planned, as contained in his letters to the prior of England, a certain crusade (*passagium*) of 500 brethren and as many esquires; and the prior of Ireland is to take order that at the time to be fixed for him by the prior of England the knights and esquires of his priory may be ready simultaneously with those of England.[13]

The expedition set out in 1378 and ended in abject failure, but William Tany does not appear to have moved from Ireland: he is documented as having been asked to contribute soldiers to fight off Murrough O'Brien's foray into Leinster in April, and filed a claim to recover his expenses from previous expeditions in October of the same year.[14] However, we must allow for the

---

11 Matthew Paris, *Chronica maiora, 1216–1239*, ed. Henry R. Luard, 7 vols (London, 1872–83), iii, pp 404–6. 12 Edward Coleman, 'The crusader's tale' in Cherie Peters & Sparky Brooker (eds), *Tales of medieval Dublin* (Dublin, 2014), pp 92–101. 13 *CEPR* iv, p. 141. 14 *CIRCLE*, Irish Chancery *Close Roll* 1, Richard II, nn. 92, 93 (24 Apr. 1378) and *Close Roll* 2, Richard II, no. 11 (21 Oct. 1378), accessed 17 Oct. 2020. This relatively recent online resource proved instrumental in establishing the Prior's movements.

124   *Ireland and the crusades*

possibility that a handful of Irish knights might have joined that expedition,
as requested.

IRISH HOSPITALLERS AND THE SCOTS

Another front that saw some involvement on part of the Irish Hospitallers was
the troublesome relationship between the English crown and Scotland. It has
been well proven that the military-religious orders in England and Scotland
were staunch allies of Edward I throughout the crisis of 1297–8 and suffered
losses as a result of that loyalty:[15] the Hospitaller house of Torphichen was
temporarily lost to William Wallace and visited by him in 1298,[16] while the
subsequent battle of Falkirk claimed the lives of the Templar Master Brian le
Jay and – possibly – of the Hospitaller preceptor of Torphichen.[17]

Ireland was dramatically drawn into the fray a few years later (1301–4),
when Edward harnessed the military and economic resources of the realm to
try and settle the score with the Scottish rebellion once and for all. As the
king demanded the participation of a strong Irish contingent, the justiciar,
John Wogan, had to leave the island and lead the troops there, leaving the
administration of the lordship in the hands of the Hospitaller prior, William
de Ros, as lieutenant justiciar. De Ros' effort included waging war against the
Irish in Wicklow (see below), but also contributing to the Scottish effort by
paying the wages of recruited Welshmen.[18]

Of more direct impact on the Hospital's warring activities was the invasion of Ireland by Edward and Robert Bruce (1315–18).[19] Fearing an assault
on Dublin, the justiciar appointed the Hospitaller prior Walter del Aqua
to 'direct the defence of the City of Dublin', without much success.[20] After
rampaging south from Ulster to Dublin, with possible but unevidenced consequences for the extensive Hospitaller properties situated in modern-day
counties Louth and Meath, the Scottish army encamped at Castleknock, Co.
Dublin. Perhaps in the grip of panic, or probably to deprive the Scots of a
chance to sneak up to the walls, the Dubliners set fire to their western suburbs,

---

15 Nicholson, 'The Hospitallers' and Templars' involvement in warfare', pp 109–14.   **16** Ian B. Cowan,
P.H.R. Mackay & Alan Macquarrie (eds), *The Knights of St John of Jerusalem in Scotland* (Edinburgh, 1983), p.
xxix.   **17** *Willelmi Rishanger, quondam monachi S.Albani et quorundam anonymorum, chronica et annales regnantibus Henrico
tertio et Edwardo primo, AD 1259–1307*, ed. H.T. Riley, *Rolls series* 28 (London, 1865), p. 415.   **18** *CIRCLE*, Irish
Chancery *Close Roll*, 29 Edw. I (3 Nov. 1301), accessed 17 Oct. 2020.   **19** For a general study, see James
Lydon, 'The impact of the Bruce Invasion, 1315–27' in Art Cosgrove (ed.), *A new history of Ireland*, ii: *Medieval
Ireland, 1169–1534* (Oxford, 1993), pp 275–302. For a more recent study, see Seán Duffy (ed.), *Robert the
Bruce's Irish wars: the invasion of Ireland, 1306–1329* (Stroud, 2002).   **20** Philomena Connolly (ed.), *Irish excheq-
uer payments 1270–1446* (Dublin, 1998), p. 234.

Tuitio fidei? The Irish Hospitallers at war

causing extensive damage, but the Bruces decided against besieging the city and moved away to the west.[21] A hint to the fact that the Hospitallers had been heavily involved in the defence comes from another two documents, evidencing the contribution of the future prior, Roger Outlaw, to the effort and King Edward II's gratitude to him.[22]

WARFARE IN IRELAND: WITHIN THE LORDSHIP

In Ireland, violence was not limited to engagements against the Scots or the Gaelic-Irish. The Anglo-Irish lordship was often in political turmoil within itself, either by mirroring political strife in England or because of homegrown dissent. It is rare to find instances of violence involving Irish Hospitallers against fellow citizens of the lordship, but two cases stand out, and have been analysed elsewhere by the present author.[23]

The first case is the well-known dispute (*c.*1259–61) between the Irish Hospitallers and the mayor and citizens of Dublin over the fisheries of the Liffey, which saw the order build a 'dam' close to the river mouth, thus monopolizing the catch of salmon to the exclusion of others, and the citizens responding by laying nets further to the east in order to thwart the Hospitallers. The legalities of the case are dealt with elsewhere, but it is interesting to note that the first reaction of the knights to the instalment of the nets was to simply destroy them.[24] Strictly speaking, this was hardly an act of war, but it might account for a certain readiness to solve issues *manu militari*.

The second, almost contemporary, case (1262–9) saw an attempt by the archbishop of Dublin, Fulk de Sandford, to exert his control over Stachfythenan, an obscure church situated in modern-day Co. Kildare, owned by the Hospitallers, thus potentially bringing into question the entire set of prerogatives and exemptions the order enjoyed within his diocese. Once again, this case was ultimately resolved in the courts, but the initial contact was potentially violent: the archbishop's envoy was blocked by two Hospitaller knights in coat of arms, 'wearing the cross' and leading an 'armed multitude'.[25] No physical confrontation ensued, as the threat was enough to temporarily convince the Dublin party to postpone the issue, but this document once

21 *CSMA* ii, pp 299, 353. 22 *CCR, Edw. II* ii, pp 464–5. See also Nicholson, 'The Hospitallers' and Templars' involvement in warfare', p 114. 23 P. Virtuani, 'Unforgivable trespasses: the Irish Hospitallers and the defence of their rights in the mid-thirteenth century' in Browne & Ó Clabaigh, *Soldiers of Christ*, pp 195–205. 24 Ibid., p. 199. Needless to say, the citizens retaliated in similar fashion. 25 Ibid., p. 201. The primary source is to be found in *Calendar of Archbishop Alen's register, c.1172–1534*, ed. Charles McNeill (Dublin, 1950), n. 207.

126   *Ireland and the crusades*

again shows a fairly determined attitude from the order when it came to confrontation. Interestingly, it is also the first appearance of the Hospitallers' habit in documentary evidence relating to Ireland.

No other events are to be found before the end of the fourteenth century to show the Hospitallers' exertion – or threat – of violence against fellow Anglo-Irish.[26] When it came to dealing with the Gaelic-Irish, however, things would be drastically different.

WARFARE IN IRELAND: THE ORDER AND THE GAELIC-IRISH

The lion's share of the evidence for Hospitaller involvement in warfare concerns their attitude towards the Gaelic-Irish, which was in line with the lordship's policy. The Hospitallers in Ireland often acted as royal servants, taking over high-ranking posts, be they administrative, financial or military.[27] This meant that they were exposed to any friction or clashes that might have pitted the local Gaelic-Irish communities against the Anglo-Irish.

These engagements could be active or passive, depending on whether the lordship would take the fight to separate elements of rebellion (or chieftains outside the crown's area of control) or be forced into a defensive position. The mountains of Wicklow proved to be a hotbed for rebellion throughout the Middle Ages (and beyond) and it is here that in 1274 William fitz Roger, shortly before his summons to go to the Holy Land (see above), led an ill-fated expedition against the O'Tooles and McMurroughs, which resulted in his capture by the rebels and subsequent ransom (pl. 8.1).[28] Contemporary to fitz Roger was Stephen de Fulburn, a cleric of the order, who was entrusted by Edward I with several high-ranking positions within the lordship. There is evidence of his direct involvement in the organization of at least one expedition into Connacht, staged from the royal castle of Rindown in 1285, in the company of William fitz Roger.[29] If this can be categorized as an almost 'neutral' duty for a justiciar of Ireland, de Fulburn was likely involved in another violent act which required more conviction: in 1282 he seems to have masterminded the murder of two Irish rebels, Art and Murchertach McMurrough, in Arklow, Co. Wicklow, thereby pacifying the Wicklow rebellion for a while.[30] This service was certainly appreciated

26 This would not be the case for the fifteenth century, particularly during the priorship of James Keating, see Gregory O'Malley, *The Knights Hospitaller of the English langue, 1460–1565* (Oxford, 2005), pp 226–66.   27 A full list can be found in Virtuani, 'The Knights of St John of Jerusalem', pp 213–15.   28 Falkiner, 'Hospital', 275–317, at 316.   29 *CDI* i, no. 814.   30 Robin Frame, 'The justiciar and the murder of the MacMurroughs in 1282', *IHS* 18 (1972), 223–30.

Tuitio fidei? The Irish Hospitallers at war

by Edward, as de Fulburn's temporary justiciarship was made permanent shortly afterwards.[31]

Returning to more traditional forms of warfare, in 1301–2 Prior William de Ros was once again leading contingents in Wicklow, around Newcastle McKinegan, with 'mounted and foot soldiers'.[32] The highly volatile situation in Dublin and Wicklow was also reflected in the nature of the Hospitaller built environment: Hospitaller houses such as Kilteel and Killergi (modern day Killerrig, Co. Carlow) were exposed to raids and,[33] in the first case, the remains still speak of a fortified preceptory (pl. 8.2). This preoccupation with defence was evident in the physical layout of the headquarters of the Knights of St John in Ireland, the manor of Kilmainham, which has been the subject of a very recent study.[34] There is no doubt that the manor was a heavily fortified complex, probably since its foundation, and certainly after the Bruce invasion, featuring strong towers, a drawbridge and an outer court, protected by a curtain wall.

The fourteenth century saw a series of priors involved in diplomatic and military exchanges with the Gaelic-Irish. Documents tend to yield more detail on the nature of their armed retinues. In 1347, Prior John Larcher, then deputy justiciar, travelled to Connacht with mounted archers and armed men.[35] It is important to stress that these retinues are not to be imagined as small contingents of Hospitaller knights and sergeants. They are likely to have been royal soldiers/militia, as the priors were not acting as Hospitallers, but as royal officers. One particular prior, Thomas de Burley, seems to have seen a lot of active duty during his stint at the helm of the order in Ireland (1359–69). In 1359, he took arms against the Irish rebel Art Kavanagh, once again in the Wicklow/Carlow region, with 'twenty armed hobelars, twenty-four mounted archers and twenty-four foot soldiers'.[36] The end of the campaign saw him stationed in Athy, Co. Kildare, 'after the killing of Irish enemies and rebels'.[37]

A final violent episode sums up the difficult position in which the Hospitallers often found themselves. In September 1367, a member of the le Poer family, Richard More, entered into a dispute with the city of Waterford. This soon turned violent, and Richard gathered an army of both English 'rebels' and native Irish and made for the city. A force was gathered to oppose

---

31 *CDI* ii, no. 1972.   32 Connolly, *Irish exchequer payments*, p. 163 and *CDI* v, no. 3.   33 Connolly, *Irish exchequer payments*, p. 435 and *CIRCLE*, Irish Chancery Patent Roll, 29 Edw. III, nn 30, 31, 62, accessed 23 Oct. 2020. The documents are dated 19 May, 5 June and 8 July 1355.   34 Tadhg O'Keeffe & Paolo Virtuani, 'Reconstructing Kilmainham: the topography and architecture of the chief priory of the Knights Hospitaller in Ireland, *c*.1170–1349', *JMH* (2020), 449–77.   35 Connolly, *Irish exchequer payments*, pp 426–7.   36 Ibid., p. 498. The mention of 'hobelars' (Irish light cavalry) is interesting, as he may have recruited local troops to fight the rebels.   37 Ibid., p. 505.

them, which included the mayor, the sheriff of the city and the Hospitaller preceptor of Kilbarry, Brother John Walsh, explicitly described as 'Guardian of the Peace [*sic*] of the lord King in the aforesaid county'. These soldiers were ambushed and killed (and presumably John Walsh, too), together with thirty-six other armed men. Le Poer then assaulted the city itself and killed another sixty defenders.[38] In this case, the ethnic lines were blurred, but the Hospitallers were seen once again fulfilling their role as royal servants.

CONCLUSIONS

This brief overview leads to rather straightforward conclusions. Irish Hospitallers shared the same duties as their European brethren: they were expected to provide *responsiones*, but occasionally also manpower to be sent to the Holy Land. When it came to local warfare, though, the Irish priory seems to have been a troublesome one, compared to others.[39] Holy war itself was a given, when it came to their commitment to their order's cause in the East, but there is no evidence for this ever to have been a motive in their dealings with the Gaelic-Irish.[40] The priory of Ireland was not a quiet place for service and the Irish Hospitallers' activities were heavily marked by loyalty to the English crown and royal service. This was both a distraction and a necessity, as it ensured the maintenance of their properties, prerogatives and royal protection, thus enabling them to contribute to their brethren's cause.

The original question of whether the order in Ireland was true to its mission to defend the faith can perhaps still be answered positively: it did so indirectly, not by physically fighting enemies of the faith, but by maintaining a high degree of adaptability and responsiveness within a very difficult environment, even though this sometimes meant raising arms against fellow Christians.

---

38 *The great parchment book of Waterford*, ed. Niall Byrne (Dublin, 2007), pp 18–19.   39 With the obvious exception of Spain.   40 Nicholson, 'The Hospitallers' and Templars' involvement in warfare', p. 116. The author here seems to leave the door open to this aspect, albeit hypothetically.

1.1 Papal bulla lead seal, John XXI (1276–7), found recently at Moorehall Ardee. (Photo Muireann Ní Cheallacháin)

2.1 Fifteenth-century carving believed to represent St Malachy from the cloister of Bective abbey, currently at Johnstown church, Navan, Co. Meath. (Photo Paul Duffy)

2.2 Fifteenth-century carving of an abbot believed to represent St Bernard from the cloister of Bective abbey. (Photo Paul Duffy)

3.1 Pope Adrian IV from Johannes Berardi, *Chartularium monasterii Casauriensis, ordinis S. Benedicti*. Bibliothèque nationale de France Latin, MS 5411, f. 253r. (Redrawn by Matthew Ryan)

4.1 *Dublin Guild Merchant Roll*, f. 12d. (Dublin City Library & Archive)

4.2 Medieval burial under excavation in the graveyard of the Hospital of St John, John's Lane West, Dublin. (Photo Rubicon Heritage Services)

5.1 Fragment of Simon de Montfort's tomb at Carcassonne showing the great siege of Toulouse, 1218. (Photo Carol Duffy)

5.2 The Battle of Baziège (1219) from the manuscript of the Canzo de lo Crozada BNF, fr. 25425, f. 228. (Redrawn by Matthew Ryan)

5.3 The Battle Well at Evesham, Worcestershire. (Photo David Cox)

6.1 Geoffrey de Geneville, as justiciar on the fourteenth-century *Waterford Charter Roll*. (Courtesy of Waterford Treasures – Three Museums in the Viking Triangle)

6.2 Trim Castle and the Sheep Gate, the last remaining medieval gate of the town. (Photo Ciarán McDonnell)

6.3 East range of the Blackfriary, Trim, established by Geoffrey de Geneville in 1263. The Purbeck marble columns would have stood on the cloister wall in the left of the image. The remains of the night stairs to the dormitory can be seen in the background. (Photo Blackfriary Archaeology Field School)

7.1 The late medieval stone tower on the commandery site at Crooke, Co. Waterford. (Photo Tadhg O'Keeffe)

7.2 Baldongan church, Co. Dublin. (Photo Christine Baker)

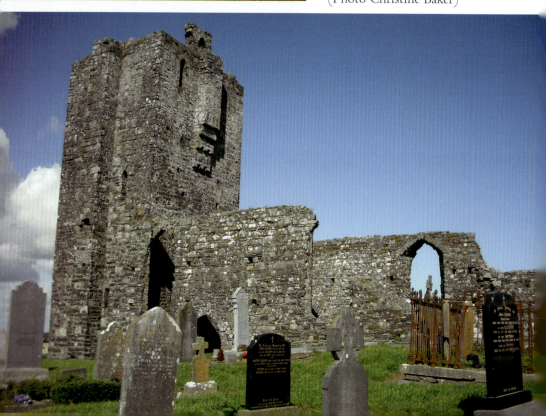

8.1 Glenmalure, Co. Wicklow, where fitz Roger was defeated. (Photo by Shever & Kimmrs, used under CC BY 2.0 licence)

8.2 Remains of Kilteel preceptory, Co. Kildare. (Photo Paolo Virtuani)

9.1 St John's priory, Newtown Trim, Co. Meath. (Photo Paul Duffy)

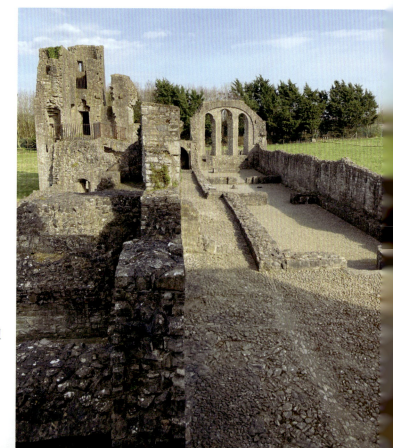

9.2 View along the nave of St John's priory church, Newtown Trim, Co. Meath. (Photo Paul Duffy)

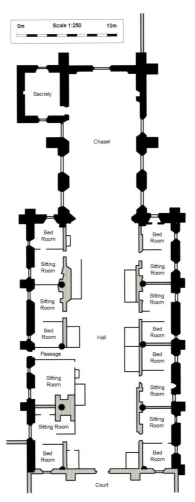

9.3 Plan of St Mary's Chichester showing nave as possible hospital. (After Dollman 1858, pl. 51, redrawn by Bob Burns)

10.1 Ballyman church, Co. Dublin. (Photo David McIlreavy)

10.2 CUCAP Archive No. BDP024 with possible double-ditched enclosure visible to the north (left) of Ballyman Road, Co. Dublin.

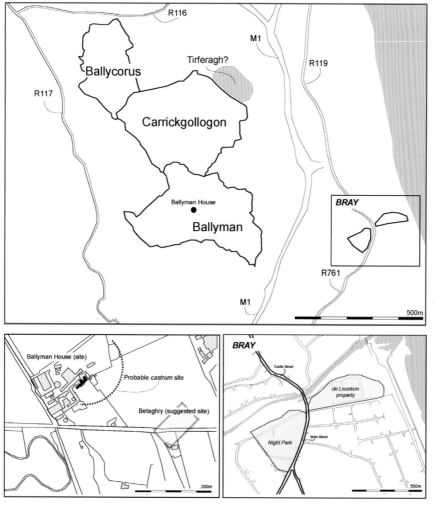

10.3 Map showing suggested reconstruction of the manor of Ballyman and associated lands, Cos Dublin and Wicklow. (By David McIlreavy and Tadhg O'Keeffe)

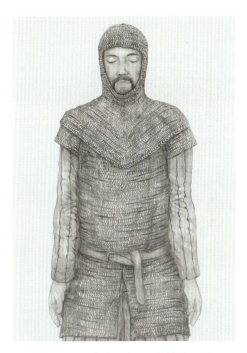

11.1 Conjectural drawing of St Peter's graveyard armoured burial. (By Matthew Ryan)

11.2 Knight in relief at Hospital church, Co. Limerick. (Photo Dave Swift)

11.3 Detail of rowel spur on the knight effigy at Christ Church cathedral, Dublin. (Photo Dave Swift)

11.4 'The Brethren' double effigy at Jerpoint Abbey, Co. Kilkenny. (Photo Tadhg O'Keeffe)

11.5 Knights from Athassel tomb surround – currently housed at Cashel – showing cross-legged pose. (Photo National Monuments Service)

11.7 King receiving keys of the city *Waterford Charter Roll*. (After du Noyer, redrawn by Matthew Ryan)

11.6 King Edward III from *Waterford Charter Roll* reclining against throne in cross-legged pose. (Photo Colm Moriarty)

 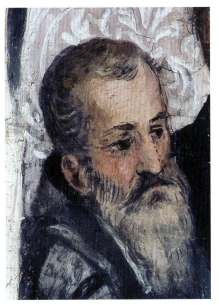

12.1 Portrait of Thomas fitz Gerald (1513–37), Lord Offaly, 10th earl of Kildare, from *Memoirs of the Court of Queen Elizabeth*, published in 1825 (Wikimedia Commons).

12.2 Hugh O'Neill, earl of Tyrone, at a ceremony in the Vatican, from a contemporary fresco in the Vatican (Wikimedia Commons).

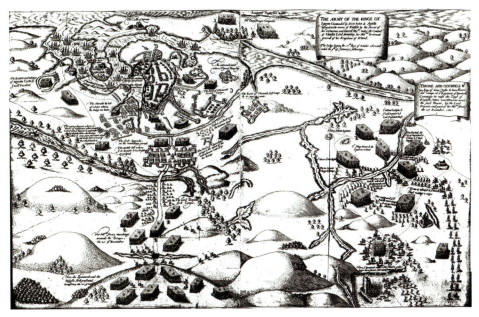

12.3 Siege and Battle of Kinsale, 1601, from *Pacata Hibernia*, 1633 (Wikimedia Commons).

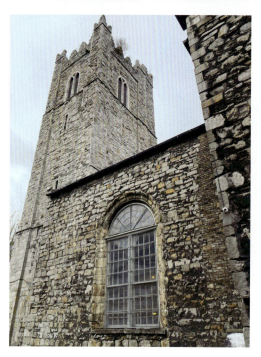

13.1 St Michan's church, Dublin, nave and tower. (Photo Paul Duffy)

13.2 Steps descending into the crypt at St Michan's church. (Photo Ed O'Donovan)

13.3 The St Michan crusader, centre. (Photo Ed O'Donovan)

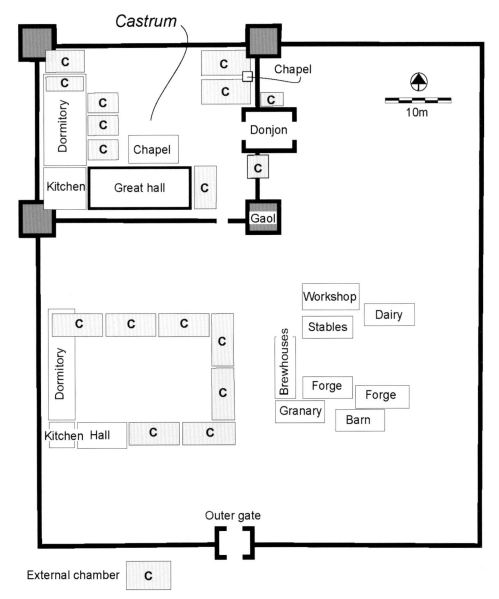

14.1 Conjectural plan of Hospitaller commandery of Kilmainham, Co. Dublin. (By Tadhg O'Keeffe)

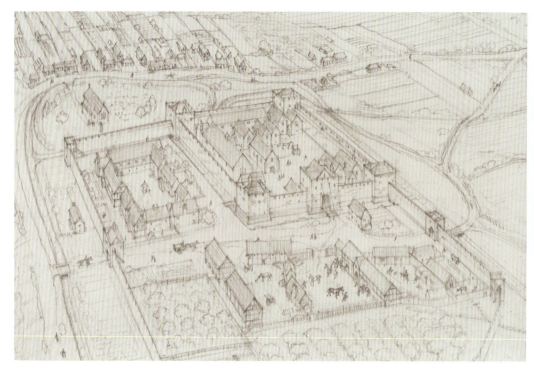

14.2 Conjectural reconstruction drawing of Hospitaller commandery, Kilmainham by Stephen Conlin. (Reproduced with kind permission of Dublin City Council Archaeology)

14.3 Hospital church, Co. Limerick. (Photo by Tadhg O'Keeffe)

9 / The medieval hospital in Ireland: a comment on the crusader connection

THOMAS IVORY

INTRODUCTION

One of the two great military monastic orders of the Middle Ages, the Knights Hospitaller originated in the Holy Land as a community of monastics that ran a hospital for the physical care and repair of pilgrims to the sites of Christ's Passion. That mission was not pursued as a *raison d'être* among the Hospitaller communities established in western Europe, although the Knights had some involvement with 'medical' hospitals. The association of the Hospitallers with places, sites or monuments identified historically as 'hospitals' has created some confusion, which this contribution addresses. It also includes a brief comment of hospital-foundation by another monastic order with reputed links to the Holy Land, the Fratres Cruciferi or Crutched Friars.

THE MEDIEVAL HOSPITAL

In 1023, merchants from Amalfi and Salerno in Italy were permitted to re-establish in Jerusalem the hospital that had been founded in the seventh century but destroyed in 1005. Built on the site of a monastery dedicated to St John the Baptist, it was served by Benedictine monks. In the aftermath of the First Crusade, the hospitaller community attainted the status of an order, the Order of St John. Like the Knights of the Order of the Temple – the Templars – the Hospitallers adopted military practices in response to the needs of pilgrims to be protected, and indeed the greatest castle of the crusader lands, Crac des Chevaliers, was their property, but they retained a focus on the sick, and were therefore more recognizably monastic than the Templars.[1] The Jerusalem hospital was a fairly conventional hospital as we would understand it today. It offered care and, insofar as it was possible, cure.

---

1 The literature is extensive. See, for example, A.J. Forey, *The military orders from the twelfth to the early thirteenth centuries* (Basingstoke, 1993); Nicholson, *Knights Hospitaller*.

But the term 'hospital' connoted many things in medieval culture. It could connote 'a house or hostel for the reception and entertainment of pilgrims, travellers, and strangers', or 'a charitable institution for the housing and maintenance of the needy', or 'an institution or establishment for the care of the sick or wounded, or of those who require medical treatment'.[2] So, the institutions in the medieval West that are understood from the sources to have been hospitals served multiple functions, ranging from those which offered medical care, to those which provided overnight refuge to travellers. Some were effectively retirement homes. Some had quite specialized functions, such as the *leprosaria*. In one sense, they offered much more than modern hospitals; in another sense, rarely being places with personnel trained in any form of medicine, where they offered far less. Common to almost all was some compassionate custodial care, dispensed by religious communities and following routines modelled on the monastic.[3] Care of the body was also care of the soul in the Middle Ages.[4]

Identifying the function of any one place described in the sources as a medieval hospital is clearly difficult. That might be the key. Rarely, perhaps, were hospitals just one thing, even at the one moment in time, and it is difficult to discern which hospitals provided medical care and which hospitals were places of hospitality, of refuge. In Ireland, where many original documentary sources from the Middle Ages have been lost, there is the additional problem of knowing whether indicative references pertain to actual institutions or to lands held by religious communities that ran hospitals. Aubrey Gwynn and Neville Hadcock enumerated 211 possible hospitals in Ireland, and that figure is not entirely unbelievable, but the identification of no less than 45 in Co. Cavan (making it the county with the most 'hospitals') raises the problem of knowing what the sources are referring to.[5] One can imagine a hospital of some description at an important site like Drumlane, but not in the many rural townlands they list. These might simply be lands owned by a hospital, or more precisely by a monastic community that had a hospital. The study of medieval hospitals in Ireland is also hampered by a paucity of physical evidence. With few exceptions, such as Kilbixy, Co. Westmeath, for example, where a free-standing building is identified as a hospital,[6] all that survives at most at

---

2 *Oxford English dictionary.* The range of functions is discussed in all the major studies of English medieval hospitals: R.M. Clay, *The medieval hospitals of England* (London, 1909); M. Carlin, 'Medieval English hospitals' in L. Granshaw & R. Porter (eds), *The hospital in history* (London, 1989), pp 21–41; Elizabeth Prescott, *The English medieval hospital, 1050–1640* (London, 1992); Nicholas Orme & M. Webster, *The English hospital, 1070–1570* (New Haven & London, 1995). 3 Carole Rawcliffe, *Medicine for the soul* (Stroud, 1999). 4 D.W. Amundsen, *Medicine, society, and faith in the ancient and Medieval Worlds* (Baltimore, 1996), pp 175–222. 5 *MRHI,* pp 346–57. 6 Tadhg O'Keeffe, *Tristernagh priory, Co. Westmeath: colonial monasticism in medieval Ireland* (Dublin, 2018), pp 20–2.

the places where hospitals are documented are churches (and, even then, there are relatively few of these). Knowing the range of hospital types in medieval England,[7] one can suggest, for example, that space inside some churches was devoted to care of the sick, or that hospital buildings were attached to the sides of churches, but the evidence in Ireland is difficult to read.

FROM EAST TO WEST?

The Knights Hospitaller of Jerusalem are likely to have had some familiarity in the twelfth century with the Muslim hospital, the *bīmāristān*, that word meaning 'location of disease'.[8] The *bīmāristān* was a carefully designed medical institution. Its parts were arranged spatially to maximize their access to running water and natural light, and wards were set aside for specific ailments.[9] Medical practices within *bīmāristāns* were advanced. For example, the physicians in the hospital in Damascus, established by Sultan Nūr al-Dīn in 1156, had access to a medical library and were accustomed to filling in patient charts.[10] Operations in *bīmāristāns* included amputations and cataract removal, and were free and available to all.[11] *Bīmāristāns* were secular institutions, unlike most, probably all, comparable hospitals of the Christian world.

One cannot be sure that knowledge of hospitals in the Muslim world and their medical practices shaped the great hospital in Jerusalem in any way, because firm evidence on that matter is lacking, but the Hospitallers must at the very least have been aware of the culture of the *bīmāristāns*. It is known that the grand masters of the Hospitallers referred to themselves as 'guardians of Christ's poor', and that they referred to their charges as 'our lords the sick'.[12] The care they offered was, first and foremost, spiritual; a sick person's confession was to be heard first, followed by communion, and the provision of a bed.[13]

Had the Hospitallers adopted Muslim practices in the Holy Land, there were two means by which aspects of the culture of the *bīmāristān* could have diffused to the West in the twelfth century, and informed the culture of

---

7 See, for example, Prescott, *The English medieval hospital*; Orme & Webster, *The English hospital*. 8 A.C. Miller, 'Jundi-Shapur, bimaristans, and the rise of academic medical centres', *Journal of the Royal Society of Medicine*, 99 (2006), 615–17; Sharif Kaf al-Ghazal, 'The origin of bimaristans (hospitals) in Islamic medical history', Foundation for Science, Technology and Civilisation (2007). 9 A. Alansari & K. Hirao, 'The impact of bimaristans design on design factors of therapeutic buildings', *International Design Journal* 7 (2017), 59–66. 10 S. Hamarneh, 'Development of hospitals in Islam', *Journal of the History of Medicine and Allied Sciences* 17 (1962), 366–84. 11 C. Toll, 'Arabic medicine and hospitals in the Middle Ages: a probable model for the military order's care of the sick' in Helen Nicholson (ed.), *The military orders*, ii: *Welfare and warfare* (Aldershot, 1998), pp 35–43. 12 Jonathan Riley-Smith, *The Knights Hospitaller in the Levant, c.1070–1309* (Basingstoke, 2012). 13 Miri Rubin, *Charity and community in medieval Cambridge* (Cambridge, 1987), p. 151.

care there. First, the agents of such diffusion might, in such a scenario, have been those who experienced some Muslim-influenced hospital care from the Hospitallers while on pilgrimage and they might have brought that knowledge back, and informed those religious communities of western Europe that ran hospitals. Second, the Order of the Hospital itself might have transmitted such knowledge. This is not entirely unlikely. Hospitaller foundations across western Europe existed to ensure a supply of revenue to the order's operations in the Holy Land, not to provide the West with hospital care. But the Knights sometimes engaged in running actual hospitals in the West, offering medical services much as Islamic hospitals were doing further east. They did not do much of it, but they did it.

In England, the Hospitallers were involved in running about twelve 'public' hospitals (in the manner of the Jerusalem hospital) and one hospital for members of their own order, and this amounts about 3 per cent of hospitals for which there are records in England in the late fourteenth century.[14] That percentage statistic is important, because it underscores how relatively unimportant hospital-running was among the knights: the other monastic orders, none of them renowned today for their hospitaller activities, were far more active as hospitallers. In fact, the Templars, the more military of the two main military orders, were only a little less active in England as hospitallers than the Hospitallers, with only four hospitals, two for themselves and two for non-community members, while the Order of St Lazerus of Jerusalem, an unarmed hospitaller order of crusader-land origin, had twelve or thirteen hospitals for lepers in England by the fourteenth century.[15]

In Ireland, there is no evidence to suggest that any of the establishments of the Hospitallers (or Templars) were, or had, hospitals providing medical care.[16] One needs to be careful, though, because community members might have had access to on-site infirmaries. The priory at Kilmainham, the headquarters of the Hospitallers in Ireland, certainly offered accommodation and hospitality, its early fourteenth-century register recording the presence of corrodians, but there is no evidence that it provided any specialized medical care. In fact, food consumption was permitted in private rooms when members of the priory community were unable to eat in the hall for reasons of infirmity or poor health, suggesting that there was no infirmary.[17] The institution that replaced the Kilmainham priory in the late seventeenth century, almost on the same site, was the Royal Hospital, and it was not a conventional hospital either; it

---

14 Orme & Webster, *The English hospital*, p. 72.   15 Ibid.   16 For a general survey, see Nicholson, 'A long way from Jerusalem', pp 1–22.   17 Tadhg O'Keeffe & Paolo Virtuani, 'Reconstructing Kilmainham: the topography and architecture of the chief priory of the Knights Hospitaller in Ireland, *c*.1170–1349', *JMH* 46 (2020), 449–77.

is conceivable that the Hospitaller priory was perceived as a hospital in the Middle Ages, despite the lack of medical facilities, and that there is therefore some continuity between the Middle Ages and the early modern period, but this merely underscores the range of meaning of 'hospital'. The hospital of Ainy, Co. Limerick, is very likely to have been a place that was known to have offered refuge, because the site is now in the village of Hospital, but we can say no more about it. The fact that it is a rural location does not militate against the possibility that it was also a place of medical care, as the Hospitaller 'public' hospitals in England were mainly rural too.[18]

In thinking comparatively about the association of medical hospitals with military orders in England and Ireland, one difference to note is the chronology of the arrival of the Hospitallers relative to the respective Norman and Anglo-Norman invasions. In England, the order probably arrived in the reign of Stephen, or possibly Henry I, so six or seven decades had passed since the battle of Hastings, by which stage the character of the Norman kingdom was established. Sethina Watson has convincingly argued that the idea of the hospital was refined in England with the coming of the Normans, and that by 1130 the term *hospitalis* was being used 'alongside and in lieu of other terminology'.[19] In Ireland, however, the Hospitallers arrived in the immediate aftermath of the invasion, so they potentially had an active role in shaping the lordship from the outset. Indeed, the Kilmainham priory was probably one of the first fortified complexes in Ireland.[20] But there is no evidence that their arrival in Ireland had any specific impact on the culture of the hospital.

THE CRUTCHED FRIARS AND THE HOSPITAL OF NEWTOWN TRIM

The discussion above reveals how, in the absence of good evidence, it is difficult to identify a direct link between crusading and the medieval hospital in Ireland, but it also shows that one cannot rule out the possibility that the Knights Hospitaller were involved in hospital care in Ireland, nor that lessons about such care had been learned in the crusader lands and were put into practice in Ireland.

One order which was present in Ireland and had both a hospitaller mission and a supposed link to the Holy Land was that of the Fratres Cruciferi, the Crutched Friars. These were not actually friars but canons regular.[21] Their

18 Orme & Webster, *The English hospital*, p. 72. 19 Sethina Watson, 'The origins of the English hospital', *TRHS* 16 (2006), 75–94, at 80. 20 O'Keeffe & Virtuani, 'Reconstructing Kilmainham'. 21 The key work is J. Michael Hayden, *Crutched friars and croisiers: the canons regular of the order of the Holy Cross in England and France* (Rome, 2013).

origins are somewhat clouded, thanks to the destruction of records but also to the conflicting origin-stories of the different communities across north-west Europe that identified with the order. The order traced its own history back to the Holy Land, to the aftermath of Third Crusade (1210–40), but also, ultimately, to the papacy of Anacletus (died AD 92), but it was not a crusading order, and it had little involvement in the Holy Land. The Fratres Cruciferi of Ireland were, Hadcock asserted, 'of the same pattern as those in the Italian Congregation'. Those Italian canons, who had a hospital at Acre in 1159, traced their origins to Jerusalem, and to the discovery of the True Cross by St Helena, the mother of Constantine.[22] Had the Fratres Cruciferi of Ireland any familiarity with eastern Mediterranean hospital culture, they would presumably have acquired it from Acre, but a direct acquisition from the Holy Land seems unlikely. In any case, they did not acquire it through crusading.

The Fratres Cruciferi are first attested to in Ireland in Dublin, in the period 1185–1216, when they were running the hospital of St John the Baptist at Newgate. This hospital was founded 1188, with Ailred Palmer recognized by Pope Clement III as its master.[23] Known as Palmer's hospital, it was described by Archbishop John Alen towards the end of the Middle Ages as 'a charitable hospital', unlike the priory of Kilmainham, which he described as 'a guest house'.[24] The early date of the Newgate foundation might be a hint that these canons were encouraged to come to Ireland because they were hospitallers.

The hospital of St John the Baptist at Newgate is long gone, but there remains a hospital of the same dedication and the same order at Newtown Trim, Co. Meath (pl. 9.1). Although not associated with a military order, there is merit in a brief description of it here, as it gives the reader a sense of what a medieval hospital was like in Ireland.[25]

Its date of foundation is not recorded, but Hadcock dates it to before 1225.[26] If so, it was built when Simon de Rochfort was bishop of Meath, and was built simultaneous with the building of the great cathedral a little upriver.[27] Horden has argued that hospitals in the medieval Christian world were under the patronage of their local bishops.[28] It is not really conceivable that the

22 R. Neville Hadcock, 'The Order of the Holy Cross in Ireland' in J.A. Watt, J.B. Morrall & F.X. Martin (eds), *Medieval studies: presented to Aubrey Gwynn, S.J.* (Dublin, 1961), 44–54. 23 Grace O'Keeffe, 'The hospital of St John the Baptist in medieval Dublin: functions and maintenance' in Seán Duffy (ed.), *Medieval Dublin IX*, pp 166–82; see Catherine Swift, chapter 4, this volume. 24 *Extents of Irish monastic possessions 1540–1541: from the manuscripts in the Public Records Office, London*, ed. Newport B. White (Dublin, 1941), pp 184–5. 25 P. David Sweetman, 'Archaeological excavations at St John's priory, Newtown Trim, Co. Meath', *Ríocht na Mídhe* 8 (1990/1), 89–104. 26 Hadcock, 'The Order of the Holy Cross in Ireland', 51. 27 Tadhg O'Keeffe & Rhiannon Carey Bates, 'Colonial monasticism, the politics of patronage, and the beginnings of Gothic in Ireland: the Victorine cathedral priory of Newtown Trim, Co. Meath', *Journal of Medieval Monastic Studies* 6 (2017), 51–76. 28 P. Horden, 'The earliest hospitals in Byzantium, western Europe, and Islam', *Journal of Interdisciplinary History* 35 (2005), 361–8.

hospital at Newtown Trim had a patron other than Bishop de Rochfort. There was a possible link with Newgate: there was a grant in 1281 from one Walter, son of Alured (and therefore a descendent of Ailred of Newgate?), of an annual rent of 40s. 'in pure and perpetual alms'.[29]

The buildings on the site comprise a rectangular church of the early thirteenth century (pl. 9.2), divided in the fifteenth century by a rood screen. There is an east-west range of rooms to the north-west of the church, and this is largely of the thirteenth century. There was originally a courtyard in front of it and the west wall of the church, but that was partly filled-in at an unknown date by a long rectangular extension to the front of the church. The range on the north side of the complex was conceivably a space for those cared for, but an alternative view identifies this as a domestic range, and identifies the nave of the church as an infirmary hall, and the extension to the nave as an extension of the hospital space. A parallel for a nave functioning as a hospital is St Mary in Chichester, founded in 1172 (pl. 9.3).

CONCLUDING COMMENT

This brief comment has served to highlight the problem of understanding the term 'hospital' when used in medieval sources. It is a cliché, but archaeological excavation is needed to advance the study significantly. Sites of the Hospitallers merit such investigation anyway, but one might hope to find at sites like Kilteel, Co. Kildare, where the site of the preceptory has not been touched since the buildings were demolished, actual buildings associated with care. The question: how might be they identified?

---

29 R.D. Butler, *Some notices of the castle and of the eccesiastical buildings of Trim* (Naas, 1978), p. 242.

10 / Reconstructing the manor of Ballyman: the Poor Knights of Christ and the Temple of Solomon in the southern marches of Dublin

DAVID McILREAVY

INTRODUCTION

Approximately 2.7km east of the modern town of Bray, on the northern ridge of the Glenmunder river valley, remnants of a church, a castle site and several associated features are believed to represent the manor of Ballyman, understood to have been a preceptory of the Knights Templar.[1] Drawing upon overlooked historical sources and employing fresh interpretations of the extant archaeology, this paper attempts to reconstruct the constituent elements of the manor and its adjoining holdings at Carrickgollogan and Ballymacorus.[2] The various patterns of landholding exercised by the Knights Templar over the different components of their estates both in Ireland and abroad are used as a framework to examine the possible trajectory of Ballyman's development through the thirteenth century. Finally, an explanation is offered as to how such a significant estate could have slid into relative historical anonymity.

THE KNIGHTS TEMPLAR IN IRELAND

In 2002 Christopher Gerrard noted the recent re-invigoration of the profile of the Knights Templar within the public consciousness.[3] This was driven by a range of historical discussions on the topic that advanced a more thorough and nuanced understanding of the order in Britain.[4] Today, we are fortunate that exploration of the Templars has progressed even further, not least with published translations of the trials within the British Isles and comparisons of their suppression in different parts of Europe.[5] Shining a particular light on

---

1 SMRs DU026-063; DU026-064 and DU028-002001-11.   2 Cognate with the modern townland of Ballycorus.   3 Philip Mayes (ed.), *Excavations at a Templar preceptory, South Witham, Lincolnshire, 1965–67* (Leeds, 2002), p. xii.   4 Malcolm Barber, *The new knighthood: a history of the Order of the Temple* (Cambridge, 1993); Helen J. Nicholson, *The Knights Templar: a new history* (Stroud, 2001).   5 Nicholson, *Proceedings*; Burgtorf et al., *Debate*.

Ireland, the publication of *Soldiers of Christ: the Knights Hospitaller and the Knights Templar in medieval Ireland* represented something of a ground-breaking examination of the subject within this country.[6] However, as Edward Coleman pointed out, examination of the Templars in Ireland remains 'fraught with difficulties'.[7] There are two distinct problems in such research: untangling the distinctive organization of the Irish order, and understanding the extent of, and the management systems employed at, their possessions. In terms of unravelling the particular organization of the Irish order, it is important to realize that it remained somewhat separate from its nominal superiors in the English grand commandery. This separation was clearly demonstrated when Pope Clement V was obliged to send separate inquisitors to Ireland to assist with the suppression in 1309. Evidence suggests that the Irish order demonstrated an unusual institutional fluidity, most clearly epitomized by the lack of a permanent fixed headquarters on the island. The degree to which the opacity of the Irish organizational system could be exploited can be seen in the case of Thomas de Lindsey and Stephen de Stapelbrugge. It was only in later inquisitions of the Irish order that these two former English Templars had claimed Irish pensions, despite being wanted in England.[8]

Tracing the extent and management of the Irish order's holdings is almost a more difficult proposition than following the peculiarities of their organization. A natural starting point for many researchers is the round of arrests and property seizures that signalled the beginning of the suppression in 1309. However, the practicalities of supporting members of the order by royal council during their investigation saw the estates of Kilcloggan, Crooke and Kilbarry remain under Knights Templar control until Michaelmas 1311.[9] In the interim, between the active suppression of the order in 1309 and the papal bull *Vox in excelso* issued 22 March 1312, formally disbanding the Knights Templar 'by an inviolable and perpetual order', control over significant portions of the former order's property evaporated.[10] The papal edict had declared that the Knights Hospitallers were to inherit all former Templar property, but in some cases competing monastic institutions and even original donors made significant gains. It was only in 1325 that the Irish exchequer was requested to provide the inventories of the various estates to the English exchequer. However, these records were deemed so inadequate that they were rejected by the English authorities and a more substantial set of inventories was provided by the Irish exchequer in 1328.[11]

---

6 Browne & Ó Clabaigh (eds), *Soldiers of Christ.*   7 Coleman, '"Powerful adversaries"', pp 184–94, at p. 188.   8 Nicholson, 'A long way from Jerusalem', pp 1–21, at p. 10.   9 Ibid.   10 Malcolm Barber, *The new knighthood: a history of the Order of the Temple* (Cambridge, 1993), p. 280.   11 Murphy, '"From swords to ploughshares"', p. 170, no. 21.

The process of defining these estates has been further complicated by later misidentification of former Knights Templar property. An example of such a process has been recently discussed in a study relating to Rincrew, Co. Waterford.[12] The study concluded that the erroneous association of Rincrew Castle with a military order is but one of numerous examples of such similar misidentifications that are a common feature in Irish historiography. Crucially, the paper identifies the problematic 'emergence and descent of mistakes which prove extremely difficult to eradicate from the body historic'.[13] Taking full cognizance of these pitfalls, my paper aims to illustrate that there is much that can still be inferred from the existing historical sources, while comparative analysis of Templar estates in Ireland and Britain can help to further inform an approach to a site such as Ballyman.

That the Ballyman estate was not one of the order's most valuable estates, and yet possessed manorial rights over a substantial landholding in the foothills of the Wicklow mountains, makes it an interesting case study. As Nicholson states, 'the military orders were Christian institutions which first appeared in the city of Jerusalem in the early twelfth century. Their members took lifetime monastic vows of poverty chastity and obedience and promised to help defend Christians and Christian territory.'[14] The maintenance of such a force proved to be a constant war of attrition, with mounting loses of men and materiel in the Holy Land, especially through the thirteenth century, 'resulting in a constant demand for money to replace equipment and train new recruits'.[15]

The envelopment of the lordship of Ireland within the Angevin 'empire' in 1171 might well have been regarded as a much-needed socio-economic boost by the Knights Templar hierarchy. Henry II, as part of his reparation for his complicity in the murder of Archbishop Thomas Beckett, had already pledged the maintenance of 200 Knights Templar in the Holy Land. Byrne calculates that this force would have cost in the region of 10,000 marks annually to maintain.[16] Had it not been for Henry's acquisition of lands in Ireland at this time, the provision of estates to maintain such forces would have been a considerably more demanding prospect. It was the acquisition and effective management of such estates that would remain at the centre of the Templar's involvement with Ireland. The reputation that the Knights Templar established as estate managers was formidable, and Margaret Murphy notes several contemporary references to good management practices.[17]

---

12 Cotter et al., 'A blow to the Temple', 163–78. 13 Ibid., 177. 14 Helen Nicholson, 'A long way from Jerusalem', p. 2. 15 Murphy, 'From swords to ploughshares', p. 169. 16 Niall Byrne, *The Irish crusade: a history of the Knights Hospitaller, the Knights Templar, and the Knights of Malta, in the south-east of Ireland* (Dublin, 2007), p. 64. 17 Murphy, 'From swords to ploughshares', p. 169.

The range of privileges and exemptions granted to the order in Ireland were substantial. Lennon lists both freedom from customs levies and relief from feudal and military services,[18] while Murphy notes the grant issued in 1213 allowing the master of the order to convey wheat free of tolls to wherever he wished in Ireland.[19] In addition to their capacity as estate managers, the Templars also collected 'ecclesiastical dues from their churches, pleas and perquisites of court', and other incomes they had been granted to form their 'reponsion[20] to the Holy Land'.[21]

Barber provides probably the most accurate portrayal of the those who manned such estates across Europe.[22] He contrasts 'the modern stereotype of the bloodstained Templar Knight, dressed in a white surcoat with its red cross, heavily armoured, and mounted on a powerful warhorse ... his function the relentless war against the Saracens', with one Brother Odo of Wirmis, a master carpenter aged sixty who had never left France, or indeed his wider locality, during his life as a Templar. For Barber, Brother Odo represents the administrators, craftsmen and agricultural workers who manned the order's estates in the West, and comprised the majority of the order's manpower in western Europe.

The successes of the Templars' land-management practices led to further endowments, and this is hinted at in the surviving evidence for the estate of Ballyman and adjacent holdings, where the history of such endowments seems to have stretched further than with most.

THE EVIDENCE FOR THE MANOR OF BALLYMAN

The manor of Ballyman[23] is just one example of a Knights Templar estate that has been recorded by several commentators, but without a serious engagement with the physical extent and tenurial complexity of what the estate actually comprised.[24] Establishing the physical footprint of the manor of Ballyman is undoubtedly complicated at a remove of 700 years. Elements of a medieval

---

18 Colm Lennon, 'The medieval manor of Clontarf, 1171–1540' in Seán Duffy (ed.), Medieval Dublin XII (Dublin, 2012), pp 189–205, at p. 195.   19 Murphy, 'From swords to ploughshares', p. 169.   20 The reponsie is defined as an annual levy (on the incomes received above) paid by the military orders to their headquarters.   21 Helen Nicholson, 'A long way from Jerusalem', p. 14.   22 Barber, The new knighthood, p. 229.   23 Ballyman has been interpreted variously as Baile na Manach, see Eugene Curry Ordnance Survey letters relating to Co. Dublin (Dublin, 1837) or Baile na munire – see p. 143 below for discussion.   24 Helen J. Nicholson, 'A long way from Jerusalem', fig. 1.1, p. 5.

manorial centre survive in the modern landscape at Ballyman. These include a church site and a castle site, and evidence for at least one substantial enclosure arranged on either side of a historic routeway (pls 10.1 and 10.2).

Direct historical evidence for the Ballyman estate comes almost exclusively from Herbert Wood's 1907 paper.[25] He recorded that the estate held 100 acres of arable land, 60 acres of pasture, 12 acres of *subbosci* (scrub wood), and 2 acres of *prati* (fresh-water meadow). He also recorded that the Knights Templar held lands at the adjacent townland of Ballymacorus, but that they were probably only tenants there. The information presented by Wood comes from the translation of a document contained within the manuscript collection of Archbishop William King (1650–1729).[26] While this record has been viewed with some caution in the past, the information presented has much to offer when properly contextualized, and modern scholarship in this area has tended to accept its veracity.[27]

At first glance, the 174 total acres accounted for in the King manuscript differs markedly from the 423 acres comprising the modern townland of Ballyman. However, as Otway-Ruthven established, a ratio of 1:2.5 should be applied when considering medieval 'Irish' versus modern acres, especially in the Dublin region.[28] Applying this ratio to the King manuscript would mean that the Knights Templar at Ballyman possessed 250 acres of arable land, 150 acres of pasture, 5 acres of *prati* and 30 acres of *subbosci*, giving a combined area of 435 acres. This is much closer in size to the 423 acres of the modern townland. That the modern townland boundary is still defined by snaking hedgerows to the north, east and west that all follow natural topographical features, and to the south by the river Glenmunder, which is a townland, parish and county boundary, suggests that the limits of the townland have changed little in the intervening centuries.

The remainder of the relevant historical sources are concerned with holdings in the immediate surrounds of Ballyman. The principal primary sources for the 1328 suppression of the Templars in Ireland were published by Gearoid MacNiocaill in 1967.[29] Contained within these documents is a record of the

---

25 Wood, 'Templars', 365.   26 Compiled by the Anglican Archbishop of Dublin William King (1650–1729), who researched ecclesiastical orders and their possessions in Ireland. It contains information about both the Templars and the Hospitallers that in some but not all cases can be corroborated by surviving medieval manuscript sources or calendared documents. The original manuscript is in the diocesan library of Cashel. It was transcribed by the antiquarian Walter Harris (1686–1761), whose transcription is in the National Library of Ireland (NLI MS 13).   27 Wood was followed by Gwynn and Hadcock in *MRHI*, p. 174, and also by Margaret Murphy & Michael Potterton, *The Dublin region in the Middle Ages* (Dublin, 2010), pp 257 and 447; see also Browne & Ó Clabaigh 2016, p. 5, fig. 1.1.   28 A.J. Otway-Ruthven, 'The organisation of Anglo-Irish agriculture in the Middle Ages', *JRSAI* 81 (1951), 1–13.   29 'Documents relating to the suppression of the Templars in Ireland', ed. G. MacNiocaill, *AH* 24 (1967), 183–226.

Reconstructing the manor of Ballyman: the Poor Knights of Christ

sale of produce from lands at Ballymacorus during the liquidation of Templar assets in 1326. This suggests that the Templars possessed land there at the time of the suppression in 1312, and continued to farm it up until 1326, at which point produce (mainly grain) was sold off by the royal bailiffs liquidating the order's remaining Irish assets.[30] The produce was sold for 84s. 8d., and the bailiffs executing the liquidation are named in the document as Jordano Banagh and Aluredo. A separate sale of 80s. 9d. worth of crops and other concerns is listed immediately under that of Ballymacorus. This sale was similarly effected by Jordano and Aluredo, and it could potentially refer to produce from Ballyman.[31] No further records survive relating to the extended possessions pertaining to the manor, and no further reference to Templars in this area can be found in either the translated trial documents for the British Isles or in commentaries on the trial.[32]

During the suppression of the Templars, members of the order were often subjected to interrogation in response to charges of heresy and diabolical worship, although, perhaps more importantly in the eyes of the Church, these interviews served to inventory Templar properties and goods. That any actual Templar brothers present at the manor of Ballyman escaped mention, or even actual interrogation, is perhaps not surprising for, as Maeve Callan noted, 'the records documenting the arrests pay closer attention to Templar goods than the brothers themselves [...] mentioning only eleven Templars, three of them solely in connection with the worth of their beds'.[33]

Another important secondary historic source surviving in the *Liber niger* of Archbishop John Alen (1476–1534)[34] appears to be a copy of an original grant of territories at Carrickgollogan – adjacent to Ballyman – to the Knights Templar.[35] This transfer illustrates how fluid land holding could be for the order, given that the donation to the Templars by a William de Lissebon *c.*1260

---

30 'Documents', ed. MacNiocaill, 221, mentions a Templar manor at 'Ballymacorus' in Co. Dublin. 31 Ibid. 32 For detail, Nicholson, *Proceedings*; Jochen Burgtorf, Paul Crawford & Helen J. Nicholson (eds), *The debate on the trial of the Templars (1307–1314)* (Farnham, 2010). 33 Callan, *Templars*, p. 49. 34 The *Liber niger*, also known as the *Liber niger Alani*, is a register documenting the properties and prerogatives of the archbishopric of Dublin, compiled by Archbishop John Alen (1476–1534). The manuscript which Wood cited as being in Trinity College is a copy, the original being in the Dublin Diocesan Archives catalogued under the title *Liber niger Alani: A chartulary of the dioceses of Dublin and Glendalough, 12th–16th cent., compiled under the direction of archbishop John Allen, c.1530*. The published edition is *Calendar of Archbishop Alen's register c.1172–1534*, ed. Charles McNeill (Dublin, 1950). 35 The grant relating to the Templars was summarized by G.T. Stokes as follows: '"William son of John of Clonmour, grants to the knights of the Temple of Solomon the undermentioned lands" including one carucate of land called Le Dalgin near Shankhill'. (G.T. Stokes, 'Calendar of the "Liber niger Alani" (Continued)', *JRSAI* 7 (1897), 404–22, at 404). However, this does not accurately represent the original Latin text, as reproduced by Wood ('Templars', 364), which reads that the grantor William was son of John 'de Lisbone' not 'of Clonmour' although the first piece of land he granted to the Templars was in Clonmore; *Liber niger*, TCD MS 1061.

142   *Ireland and the crusades*

was transferred in the same year to a Fromund le Brun, who granted the order
4 marks in free alms from the rents of the property.[36] The location of these
lands is important to understanding the interplay between the Templar holdings in the area, since Carrickgollogan adjoins the townlands of Ballyman to
the south and Ballycorus to the north (pl. 9.3), illustrating that the Templars
were landowners with varied interests in the area.

Though admittedly slight when considered individually, the pieces of documentary evidence presented above begin to coalesce into a more solid picture
of the probable land tenure of the Templars in this area of south Dublin when
viewed collectively and in association with the geographic context. Ballyman,
with a known castle and church, and evidence for at least one enclosure, presents the most convincing location for the manorial centre, with associated
lands in Ballymacorus given over at least in part to grain production.

PLACE-NAME EVIDENCE

More ephemeral traces within the many place-names associated with the area
can broaden the perspective, offering a potential chronology for the establishment of the Templar estate. Both Glenmunder and Ballyman have been used in
reference to the area throughout historical sources. Other names that appear in
historical documents include Glenmunare, Glenmondyr, Clumore, Clonmore,
Ballemunder or Ballimany.[37]

The church of Glinne Munire has a long and quite distinguished history,
which partly explains the retention of that place name to the present day. The
church is strongly associated with the *Familia Coemgeni* of Glendalough in the
Litany of Irish Saints,[38] while the Martyrology of Tallaght[39] suggests a specific association with a saint Sillán.[40] The association of Glinne Munire with
Glendalough is further stressed by the dedication of a holy well adjacent to
the church to St Kevin.

Importantly, the church of Glennmuneri was included in the grant of
Earl Richard 'Strongbow' fitz Gilbert de Clare to Thomas, his clerk, of
Glendalough and all of its lands between 1172–6.[41] The church is also men-
tioned in a confirmation charter issued to Abbot Thomas by John, count of

---

36 *Calendar of Archbishop Alen's register*, p. 91.   37 Kathleen Turner, *If you seek monuments: a guide to the antiquities
of the barony of Rathdown* (Dublin, 1983), no. 23.   38 Ailbhe MacShamhráin, *Church and polity in pre-Norman
Ireland: the case of Glendalough* (Maynooth, 1996), pp 174–6.   39 R.I. Best & H.J. Lawlor (eds), *The martyrology of Tallaght* (London, 1931).   40 Elizabeth O'Brien, 'Churches of south-east County Dublin', in G.
MacNiocaill & P.F. Wallace (eds), *Keimelia* (Galway, 1988), pp 504–24.   41 *Calendar of Archbishop Alen's
register*, p. 2.

Mortain and lord of Ireland on 11 May 1192, confirmed by a papal charter of Innocent III in 1198 as Glenmunare.[42] O'Brien noted that following the unification of the ecclesiastical sees of Glendalough and Dublin in 1216, the name Glenmunder is not mentioned in Dublin church documents or grants, which, she argued, implies a transfer of the land to the Knights Templar around this time. This would tie in with the archaeological evidence for a rebuild of the church in the thirteenth century.

It appears that, in addition to the names Glenmunder and Ballyman, the area was also known as Clonmore/Clumore.[43] O'Brien proposed that Glinne Munire derives from either the Gaelic-Irish *immaire* (ridge/division) or *mainder* (enclosure).[44] When the surrounding toponyms are considered, the former seems more likely. The adjoining townland Barnasligan (*barr na slinnéan*, the top of the ridge[45]) makes it clear that this 'shoulder' or 'ridge' immediately northwest of Ballyman was a notable landscape feature for which *glen immaire* ('glen of the ridge') and *cluan immaire* ('meadow of the ridge'), giving Clonmore/Clumore, might well be named.

The place-name root 'more' [mór] is further evidenced in very early references to the area compiled by Elizabeth O'Brien.[46] The entries in the Martyrology of Donegal and the Martyrology of Tallaght refer variously to 'Sillan of Glinn Munire, or of Dún More' and 'Sillan of Dúine Móine'.[47] This last name is crucially important to understanding when the Templar estate might have been established. Returning to the Lisbone charter preserved in the *Liber niger*, the principal element of this grant relates to 'all of the lands of Clonmore' (*totam terram de Clonmore*).[48] Dating to *c*.1260, this grant might well represent the foundational document for the Templars' tenure in the area of Ballyman.[49] It follows that the place-names of Ballyman (*Baile ne Manach*) and the adjacent townland of Monastery derive from this period, a time when the church of Glenmunder was rebuilt and there were associated

---

42 Ibid., p. 21. 43 *CDI* v, p. 241 (Ecclesiastical Taxation of Ireland, *c*.1302), Deanery of Bray, 'The church of Kyllegre [Killatheger] with the chapel of Clumore, 10l 13s. 4d.') See also George Digby Scott, *Stones of Bray* (Dublin, 1913), p. 195. 44 Elizbeth O'Brien, 'Final report on excavations at Ballyman, E182 (1979–86)' (Unpublished report, NMS Archives, 2000), p. 5, quoting M. Joynt, *Contributions to a dictionary of the Irish language* (Dublin, 1976), pp 37 and 120. 45 Literally top of the 'shoulder blade'. 46 Elizabeth O'Brien, 'Pre-Norman ecclesiastical sites in the half barony of Rathdown' (MA, UCD, 1980), p. 4; Padraig Ó Riain, *Dictionary of Irish saints* (Dublin, 2011), p. 500. 47 O'Brien, *Pre-Norman ecclesiastical sites*, p. 9, and idem, 'Churches of south-east County Dublin', p. 520. 48 'Williemus filius Johannis Lisbone dedit Deo et Beate Marie et Fratribus Militie templ Salomonis Jerusalimitani in Hibernia totam terram de Clonmore fermoffyn Maghrenlyn et Termagarran et villam de Carriklydam [Carrickgollogan] cum omnibus suis pertinentiis et sexa crs propinquiores lande de Tirferagh et quandum carrucatam terre juxta terram Domini Archiepiscopi de Shenkyll que vocatur Le Dalgin cum omnibus suis pertinentiis Habendum et tenendum.' *Liber niger*, TCD MS 1061; *Calendar of Archbishop Alen's register*, p. 91; see also Wood, 'Templars', 364. 49 See *Calendar of Archbishop Alen's register*, p. 91.

144   *Ireland and the crusades*

industrial processes of ore processing and woodworking (as identified through excavation).[50]

TEMPLAR HOLDINGS IN THE WIDER AREA

The earliest establishment of the Knights Templar in this area south of Dublin might be traced to the first half of the thirteenth century, during the initial stages of the development of the *vill* of Bray at the time of Walter de Ridelesford the younger (1180–1240).[51] Walter had been granted the *vill* of Bray by Strongbow, and the description of half a carucate (60 acres) of land held by Templars there in an inquisition dated to 1284 could suggest that the donation was made by either Walter himself or by one of those with significant holdings in the area.[52] The statement in this document that the master of the Temple 'claims to hold [the land] by charter' indicates that the original donation charter was already lost by this date.[53] Another contender for such a donation would be Richard de Cogan, brother-in-law of Walter de Ridelesford the younger, who received and subsequently redistributed large tracts of land to religious orders in the area.[54]

While no direct evidence survives of a de Ridelesford grant to the Templars at this time, a reinterpretation of the place-name evidence contained within the grant of lands by Strongbow to de Ridelesford in 1173 could potentially shed some light on the matter. The original grant contains a reference to Tachehemeder and Climethedta, reckoned at two carucates (240 acres).[55] Between this 1173 grant and a charter issued by Prince John as count of Mortain 1188–9 concerning the same geographical area, these place-names disappear.[56] It is therefore considered likely that de Ridelesford disposed of these between 1173 and 1188–9.

Various locations have been proposed for both Tachehemeder and Climethedta, although these are not conclusive.[57] However, both names

---

50 See O'Brien, 'Final report on excavations at Ballyman' and Elizabeth O'Brien, 'Ballyman', *Medieval Archaeology*, 29 (1985), 214.   51 As discussed above, see Eric St John Brooks, 'The de Ridelesfords', *JRSAI* 82 (1952), 45–61, at 51.   52 In January 1284 an inquisition was made into the full extent of Christina de Marisco's lands in Ireland by the justiciar. Christina was the granddaughter of Walter de Ridelesford, and had petitioned Edward I in 1280 to exchange those Irish lands for comparable estates in England. The inquisition was part of Edward's inquiries into establishing the extent of those estates, see Brooks, 'The de Ridelesfords' [1952], 50. For Strongbow's grant to Walter de Ridelesford see idem, 'The de Ridelesfords', *JRSAI* 81 (1951), 115–38, at 117–18, Orpen, *Ireland under the Normans*, iv, p. 140.   53 *CDI* ii, p. 560, no. 2340; Brooks, 'The de Ridelesfords' [1952], 51.   54 Brooks, 'The de Ridelesfords' [1951], 132.   55 Ibid., 118.   56 Charles, McNeill, 'Harris: Collectanea de rebus Hibernicis', *Analectica Hibernica* 6 (1934), 248–450, at 253; Brooks, 'The de Ridelesfords' [1951], 122. This grant has been recently digitised – *CIRCLE, Antiquissime Roll* no. 53, accessed 8 Oct. 2021.   57 For discussion, see Brooks, 'The De Ridelesfords' [1951], 119.

could contain elements of the 'munire' term discussed above. In this context, Tachehemeder could give Teach Munire, the settlement/manorial centre of 'munire', with Climethedta giving Coill Munire, woodland of 'munire'. This is far from conclusive but it bears consideration in the context of a possible grant of land from de Ridelesford to the master of the Temple in the later twelfth century.

The location of this land holding is not mentioned within the 1284 inquisition, but there is an indication of such in a later partition deed of the manor. This deed, compiled in 1666 to confirm the partition of the manor between the earls of Meath and Tyrconnell, mentions a large field west of the present Main Street in Bray, known as the 'mill' or 'night park', which might be a corruption relating to the former Knights Templar tenure.[58] Mary Davies located this field to the west of the present Main Street in Bray, in the area of Parnell Road, Davitt Road and St Kevin's Square.[59] As the earliest record of land grants within the *vill* of Bray is recorded in 1207, and Walter de Ridelesford the younger died *c*.1240,[60] it is suggested that the charter to the master of the Templars was granted within this time frame.[61]

In the wider context of the crusades, it is tempting to speculate that any donation Walter might have made could have been motivated to some degree by the memory that a member of the extended de Rideleseford family, Gerald 'de Ridefort', rose to the position of Grand Master of the Knights Templar in 1185. Such a dramatic rise to power must have been communicated throughout the wider de Ridelsesford *familia*, extending to their Irish baronial relations. Certainly, the order would not have been beyond reminding the Irish baron of his connection to, and his need to provide for those fighting in the East.

Two other rental possessions within the *vill* of Bray, not held by charter, are also mentioned in the 1284 inquisition. The first of these is a tenement held by John de Lissebon, a member of the local prominent family that owned lands in Dublin (town and county), whose son William, as we have seen, was probably responsible for the foundational grant to the Templars at Ballyman.[62] In the late 1250s, John Lissebon was a juror at an inquisition concerning cases in the Shankill, Rathmichael and Dalkey area.[63] It is probable that John de Lissebon bequeathed his tenement to the Templars as part of his will. The

---

58 *Partition of the manor of great Bray, 1 April 1666.* Meath Estate Deed, bundle 162, Kilruddery House, Bray. **59** Mary Davies, *Bray,* Irish Historic Towns Atlas, no. 9 (Dublin, 1998), p. 3; Mary Davies, *That favourite resort: the story of Bray, Co. Wicklow* (Bray, 2007), p. 55. **60** David McIlreavy, 'Walter de Ridelesford', *DIB.* **61** Mark Clinton, *Carrickmines Castle: the rise and fall* (Bray, 2019); also Malcolm Barber, 'The reputation of Gerard de Ridefort' in Judith Upton-Ward (ed.), *The military orders,* iv: *On land and sea* (Aldershot, 2008), pp 111–19. **62** See Clinton, *Carrickmines Castle,* pp 18–19, for discussion of Lissebon holdings in Dublin city and Co. Dublin. **63** *CDI* i, p. 443, no. 2970.

location of the Lissebon tenement cannot be at present accurately plotted, but the value of 1 mark recorded in the inquisition would suggest a substantial holding. The half-carucate that the Knights Templar held by charter was also valued at 1 mark in rent, suggesting that the de Lissebon tenement might have been of similar size. One possible location for the Lissebon tenement is in the *vill* of Bray, though this remains unlocated at present.

The final rental property noted in the 1284 inquisition is a tenement formerly held by one 'J[ohn] of Howth'. The rental value of this property is noted as 11s. 3d., which suggests the holding was slightly smaller than that the Knights Templar held by charter, or the former John de Lissebon holding, and was possibly in the region of 40–50 acres. Unfortunately, no further information on John de Howth that might shed light on a date of donation is currently available.

It was the involvement of the Knights Templar with the de Lissebon family which was to secure further donations in this area of the southern marches of Dublin. The first stage of these new donations came from William de Lissebon, who would seem to have inherited a significant rental holding consisting of Clonmore/Ballyman, the area of Carriklydan (Carrickgollogan), as well as some acreage in the neighbouring Tirferagh (unlocated). Both Tirferagh and Carrickgollogan were part of the archbishop of Dublin's estate of Shankill.[64] Tirferagh was noted in the grant by William as lying between Carrickgollogan and the carucates known as Le Dalgin in the archbishop's estate of Shankill.

William's inheritance might well have come from his uncle, one Aunger de Lissebon, who held tenure of Carrickmines during the thirteenth century.[65] The grant totalled about 230 acres. However, the Knights Templar might have disposed of this holding almost immediately, as the lands are noted to have passed to one Fromund le Brun the elder in 1260. Fromund is recorded as confirming a *frankalmoigne* grant of 4 marks to the Knights Templar (£2 13s. 4d.) for these lands.[66]

Another carucate was granted by William de Lissebon to the Knights Templar around Dalkey.[67] Unfortunately, no later documentation is extant referring to the subsequent use of this holding by the order, but given the disposal of the Carrickgollogan grant, that at Dalkey might also have passed to a secular holding.

In the context of these extensive grants to the Templars in the wider locality, the argument that a manorial centre was established by the Templars around

---

64 Clinton, *Carrickmines Castle*, p. 20.   65 Ibid., 20.   66 *Calendar of Archbishop Alen's register*, p. 91. The term *frankalmoigne* derives from Norman French *fraunch aumoyne* as 'free alms'. In this case the grant was probably free of all other secular services owed to the grantor, and was usually reserved from royal legal jurisdiction.   67 *Calendar of Archbishop Alen's register*, p. 91.

RECONSTRUCTING BALLYMAN

1260 on land granted by a member of the Lissebon family at Clonmore/ Glenmunder fits into the wider context of land tenure. The Lissebon grant is therefore believed to be the 435 modern acres that would become the townland of Ballyman, *baile na manach*, centred upon the nucleus of church site and castle.

Drawing upon the evidence presented above, certain elements of the Templar estate can be imagined through the lens of studies that have been undertaken into Templar estates elsewhere. As has been illustrated, the most comprehensive estate breakdown of the Templar lands at Ballyman is described as comprising '1 *castrum*, 3 *messugia*, 4 *cottagia*, 100 *arabiles*, 60 pasture, 2 *prati*, 12 *subbosci*'.[68] The breakdown of these units would have been determined by the topography of the Ballyman landholding, with the narrow Glenmunder valley accounting for the 5 (modern) acres of meadow grassland (2 acres *prati*), while the gradually inclining plain towards Carrickgollogan provided for the arable (100 acres *arabilis*) and pasture holdings (60 acres), totalling 400 modern acres. The remaining 30 modern acres of scrub woodland (12 *subbosci*) is likely to have covered river margins, steep slopes and uplands.

In accounting for those inhabitants bound to the estate, the three *messuagia* (likely relating to *betagh* holdings) probably represented free farmers with a defined area of land they often cultivated in common. Margaret Murphy and Michael Potterton have noted that this class of manorial tenant should not be presumed to represent the bottom of the social hierarchy, despite the fact that most would have been classified as Irish. In fact, an inquisition of one *betagh* on a royal estate in Dublin would seem to have been in possession of produce that would have necessitated access to 25 modern acres.[69] If indeed the *betaghs* of the estate at Ballyman farmed in common, then their lands would have been known as a 'betaghry'.[70]

An enclosure site located less than 250m from the main Knights Templar centre at Ballyman, described below, might well have been the centre for such a 'betaghry'. This feature, identified during the Cambridge aerial photography survey,[71] has been truncated by the modern Ballyman Road, but is recorded within the NMS Sites and Monuments Record as 'two contiguous ditches', *c*.85m in width, which are part of a much larger enclosure.[72] Revisiting the

---

68 Wood, 'Templars', 365. 69 Murphy & Potterton, *The Dublin region*, p. 187. 70 Ibid., p. 187. 71 Cambridge University Collection of Aerial Photography (CUCAP), BDP 24. 72 SMR, NMS, DU026–064, accessed via the Historic Environment Viewer, www.archaeology.ie, 25 Oct. 2020.

148

information, it is clear that the enclosure is rectangular in shape and measures about 136m by about 66m, with at least one rounded corner. A distinctive kink on the northern length of the enclosure is consistent with a possible entrance feature. The identification of a moated site with a *betagh* settlement of thirteenth century date has been made by James Eogan for a site at Attyflynn in Limerick.[73] Closer to Ballyman, at Baldoyle, north Dublin, evidence for a moated site possibly associated with *betaghs* connected to a Grange Farm of All Hallows priory has also been described.[74]

In addition, the 4 *cottagia* (more properly cottars) noted in the description would suggest unfree manorial workers with landholdings of less than 1 (modern) acre each. Although technically free, the small scale of their holdings placed cottars in a position of substantial dependence on the manorial lord.[75] It is entirely possible that these cottars occupied the same 'betaghry' as that described above. Therefore, out of the Knights Templar holdings at Ballyman, about 75 acres[76] could have been given over to the *betaghs* and *cottagia* mentioned above.

By far the largest area of land at Ballyman was given over to arable production. Wheat and oats dominated on Knights Templar estate farms, with many estates in the Leinster region devoting their whole sown acreages to these two crops.[77] Carbonized wheat, barley and oats were retrieved from thirteenth-century horizons during excavations adjacent to the church at Ballyman, which might suggest that all three were cultivated on the estate.[78]

As the number of acres under potential arable cultivation can now be calculated for the Ballyman estate, this can be compared against the bailiff's report for 1328. Margaret Murphy's study of the Knights Templar estate at Cooley has shown that the price of a crannock of wheat was valued at 40*d*. The common rule was that one (medieval) acre produced a crannock of grain,[79] and under the operation of a three-field system (as at Clontarf[80]), it would appear that Ballyman had the potential for arable production worth almost £4. This is interesting given the sale of £4 9*d*. of 'corn and other produce', recorded at an unnamed location by the bailiffs liquidating the Templars' assets in 1328 but almost certainly relating to either Ballyman or Ballymacorus.[81]

---

73 James Eogan, 'A betagh settlement at Attyflin, Co. Limerick' in Christiaan Corlett & Michael Potterton (eds), *Rural settlement in medieval Ireland in the light of recent archaeological excavations* (Bray, 2009), pp 67–78, at p. 76.   74 Paul Duffy, 'The church of Bearach, the grange of Baldoyle and the town of the dark stranger' in Seán Duffy (ed.), *Medieval Dublin XV* (Dublin, 2015), pp 89–118, at p. 115.   75 Murphy & Potterton, *The Dublin region*, p. 189.   76 If the estate at Ballyman had three *messuagia*, likely *betaghs*, and one *betagh* had access to about 25 acres, then the Ballyman betaghs may have had access to about 75 acres.   77 Nicholson, 'A long way from Jerusalem', p. 172.   78 O'Brien, 'Final report on excavations at Ballyman', p. 45.   79 Murphy, 'From swords to ploughshares', p. 173.   80 Ibid., p. 172.   81 See above p. 141.

It is unfortunate that the bailiff's report is not more detailed regarding the nature of the arable production, or indeed the 'other produce' for which the Knights Templar received revenue. Carroll suggested 'vegetable gardens' as part of the estate, and the order certainly had a reputation for such production, with the justiciar John Wogan ordering some 200 quarters of beans and peas from Knights Templar lands to supply the royal army in Scotland.[82] While the principal leguminous crops were beans and peas,[83] Murphy noted almost 4 acres of land dedicated to leek production, suggestive of almost commercial production, at the Knights Templar estate of Kilsaran.[84]

Arable land was not the only basis of production at Ballyman. Murphy categorized Templar agriculture as 'sheep-corn husbandry', with the former important for milk and wool production, while their manure improved soil fertility.[85] Statistics generated by Newman regarding the interaction between sheep manure and grain production suggests that almost two animals were required to fertilize one acre. An optimum number of 160 sheep would therefore have been required to fertilize the full arable acreage at Ballyman.[86]

Other livestock included draught animals and of course horses associated with the Knights Templar as a military order. In relation to the former, Murphy stated that the usual practice on Templar manors was to use a mixed plough team of oxen and affers (work-horses).[87] Down noted that the order's manors in Louth, Waterford and Wexford ran six oxen alongside two work horses.[88] Horses, which would have been more expensive to equip than oxen, would have lent speed to a plough team, which would have been particularly important given the unpredictability of the Irish climate.

Such animals and the equipment they utilized would have required specialist housing within the demesne complex of the Knights Templar at Ballyman, and this is where one of the most interesting parts of the Ballyman preceptory is encountered: the *castrum*, though this does not need to imply that a large fortified structure lay at the heart of the manor. The historic root of the word *castrum* has been shown to refer to a plot of land larger than that designed to offer protection to an aristocratic *familia*.[89] The present Ballyman House farm complex stands on the site of, and might partially incorporate part of a former

---

82 M.J. Carroll, *The Knights Templar in Ireland* (Bantry, 2006), p. 118. 83 Kevin Down, 'Colonial society and economy' in Art Cosgrove (ed.), *A new history of Ireland*, ii: *Medieval Ireland, 1169–1534* (Oxford, 1993), pp 439–91, at p. 471. 84 Murphy, 'From swords to ploughshares', p. 174. 85 Ibid., p. 182. 86 E.L. Newman, 'Medieval sheep-corn farming: how much grain yield can each sheep support?', *Agricultural History Review* 50 (2002), 164–80, at 179. 87 Murphy, 'From swords to ploughshares', p. 175. 88 Down, 'Colonial society and economy', p. 474. 89 Charles Coulson, *Castles in medieval society: fortresses in England, France, and Ireland in the central Middle Ages* (Oxford, 2003), pp 29–49; for a full and up-to-date treatment of the subject see Tadhg O'Keeffe, *Ireland encastellated: Insular castle-building in its European context* (Dublin, 2021), pp 28–33. 90 John D'Alton, *The history of County Dublin* (Cork, 1838), p. 459. 91 R.C. Simington (ed.), *The Civil*

towerhouse structure (DU026–063) first recorded in 1590[90] and described as a 'thatched castle' in the mid-seventeenth-century Civil Survey of the townland.[91] This might be the modified heart of the original Knights Templar complex, possibly even the *camera* accommodation for members of the order. To the north-east of the site of this former castle, a distinctive curved field boundary and trackway, visible on the first edition OS map, might be part of the '*castrum*' enclosure. Extrapolated out, the curved boundary might form the south-eastern quadrant of a large sub-circular enclosure, with a maximum diameter of about 150m.

Such a complex, dedicated to members of the order, would have formed a discrete cluster consisting of a hall, chapel and accommodation, although it is unlikely that such an arrangement would have included any recognizable cloistered area.[92] In terms of what such buildings could have looked like, an example might be the two-storey rectangular building at Temple House in Sligo.[93] This building is described as a typical chamber tower or *camera* of the thirteenth century, and it might well have been the only masonry building in the early Templar complex.[94] Separate accommodation might also have been provided for visitors, both from within and without the order. The necessity of this accommodation was revealed by a Brother Bradley, who, during interrogation in 1310, revealed that 'the visitor' would arrive periodically to co-ordinate the sale of timber and grain for the order.[95] The *castrum* enclosure would also have functioned as a large haggard, containing not only a barn for the important cereal produce of the estate described above but accommodation for the livestock and their equipment and produce as part of the demesne. Additional buildings associated with the ancillary activities such as bee-keeping, brewing, cheese-making and poultry production were also common elements of the Knights Templar agricultural estates.[96]

The 12 acres of *subbosci* recorded at Ballyman would certainly have been exploited in numerous ways. Given Ballyman's proximity to the lucrative oak forestry in the Glencree valley and to other Templar holdings that might have supplied timber for sale,[97] it is likely that Ballyman had some form of timber industry. The term 'underwood' refers to coppiced wood as well as firewood; rods from coppicing were used as timber for houses, pathways and waterfronts and the raw material for an array of domestic and industrial crafts.[98] Records

Survey AD 1654–56, 10 vols (Dublin, 1931–61), vii, p. 279.   92 O'Keeffe & Grogan, 'Building a frontier?', p. 89.   93 Ibid., p. 83.   94 O'Conor & Naessens, 'Temple House', p. 147.   95 Nicholson, 'A long way from Jerusalem', p. 14.   96 Murphy, 'From swords to ploughshares', p. 182.   97 Such as the *c*.60 acres rented by the order at Bray: see Fiona Beglane, *Anglo-Norman parks in medieval Ireland* (Dublin, 2015), pp 78–83.   98 Aidan O'Sullivan, 'Wood in archaeology', *AI* 4: 2 (1990), 69–73.
99 James Mills (ed.), *Account Roll of the priory of the Holy Trinity, Dublin 1337–46* (Dublin, 1891), p.

Reconstructing the manor of Ballyman: the Poor Knights of Christ

from the priory of Holy Trinity in Dublin show that underwood was cut at the nearby Clonkeen manor (Kill of the Grange), in the autumn and was used for 'brewing and baking for the abbey'.[99]

That more substantial timber was available at Ballyman is hinted at in the retrieval of 'several iron spikes of a type used in heavy woodworking' from the archaeological excavations close to the church.[100] Another record relating to Clonkeen might provide evidence that more substantial timber was being harvested at Ballyman. Timber to the value of 3s. and 6d. was bought in Glenwhery by the carpenter Richard Taloun to build a new cow house at Clonkeen.[101] The cost for transporting the timber from Glenwhery to Clonkeen was 4d., which suggests (on the basis of 1d. per diem for a labourer recorded elsewhere in the roll) that the distance was not great. Mills suggests that Glenwhery is probably Glencree due to the long tradition of sourcing timber from this area.[102] However Glen munire is a closer phonetical match, particularly if 'munire' was treated as a possesive descriptor and subjected to lenition (which would give Glenmhunire).

Direct evidence for the exploitation and processing of iron in the thirteenth/fourteenth centuries was retrieved from the excavations close to the church. The source of the iron was located nearby at St Kevin's Well, where limonite, an iron-bearing rock, was identified. The excavated evidence strongly suggests that this stone was crushed, heated, smelted and smithied in one spot. Though a smelting site was not identified, slag retrieved from contexts was likely the result of smelting in small bowl-type furnaces. Two anvil stones were discovered, wedged upright in a stone setting, and a stone maul or hammerstone was likely used in the crushing process. O'Brien suggested that this iron-working was associated with the Templar rebuild of the church of Glenmunder.[103] The operation of such a forge, albeit small in scale, would have provided a significant advantage to the estate, especially with the identification of a suitable ore load at the St Kevin's Well site to the immediate west.[104]

CONCLUSIONS

The case has been made that the combined surviving evidence, on balance, warrants an acceptance that the Templars did in fact possess lands at Ballyman

64. 100 O'Brien, 'Ballyman', 214. 101 *Account Roll of the priory of the Holy Trinity*, p. 61. 102 Ibid., p. 175. 103 Elizabeth O'Brien, 'Excavations at Ballyman Co. Dublin, E182 (1979–1986)' (Unpublished report, NMS Archives, 2000), p. 22; O'Brien, 'Ballyman'; see also Murphy & Potterton, *The Dublin region*, p. 447. 104 Murphy & Potterton, *The Dublin region*, p. 447.
105 That Ballyman and Ballymacorus survived as the cores of the estate passed to the Knights Hospitallers

and Ballymacorus, and that these lands probably constituted a manorial tenure. Through examination of the various grants in association with rein-terpretation of the place-name evidence, two potential foundational grants are suggested for the establishment of a manorial estate at Ballyman. These are, first, a grant of land in the area of Bray known to have been held by the Templars in the thirteenth century and potentially granted in the later twelfth century by Walter de Ridelesford, and second, a grant of land by John de Lissebon that included the entirety of Clonmore (shown to be cognate with Glenmunder/Ballyman) sometime in the final quarter of the thirteenth century. This second scenario carriers the greater weight with respect to the documentary sources.

Either way, at the fullest extent of their holdings in the area, it seems that the Knights Templar held around 695 acres *in capite*, across the adjoining lands of Ballyman and Ballymacorus,[105] while renting another 160 acres or so within the nearby *vill* of Bray,[106] and receiving *frankmaloigne* payments for a further tenement at Carrickgollogan. Something of the nature of the activities carried out at Ballyman and Ballymacorus has been sketched here, with particular focus on the types of agricultural output possible using methods known to have been employed by the Templars in Ireland, in conjunction with the type of land listed under the order's holdings in the thirteenth century.

As this paper has demonstrated, significant discoveries within the footprint of the Knights Templar holdings remain to be made through a combination of historical research and interrogation of the archaeological record. The exploration of the mechanisms by which estates such as Ballyman developed is important to our wider historical understanding of territories like the southern marches of Dublin. Perhaps more intriguing is the apparent disintegration of most of the extended holdings at Ballyman, not only in the years following suppression of the order but also in the years preceding it.

The speed with which the Knights Templar lands at Carrickgollogan, and probably Dalkey, were transferred from direct management to rental properties indicates the often overlooked but continued importance that the *responsion*[107] retained in the organization of the order. The acquisition of landed estates can be seen to be a secondary consideration if a guaranteed monetary income could be secured. Even in those properties which the Knights Templar continued to hold in rental until 1308, their degree of investment might have been deliberately insubstantial to the point that, upon seizure of Templar lands,

---

suggests that they were owned outright.   **106** These lands were held within the manor of Bray as per the inquisition of 1284, which notes monies paid from the master of the Templars to Christina de Marisco for these properties.   **107** Nicholson, 'A long way from Jerusalem', p. 21.

holdings without a Templar presence would have been easily re-absorbed into the local secular environment, either by unofficial reclamation by original grantees, or via the type of fraud that Archbishop Alexander de Bicknor (treasurer of Ireland in 1308) was accused of by the barons of the exchequer in October 1325.

11 / Regal poise: the 'cross-legged' phenomenon on Irish effigy tombs during the age of the crusades

DAVE SWIFT

INTRODUCTION

The stone effigial monuments of the thirteenth and fourteenth century in Ireland represent in artistic terms the most martial survivals from the age of the crusades. In the popular imagination, these detailed representations of individuals provide tangible links to medieval Ireland and invite, through their seemingly undeniable 'personhood', associations with famous individuals or links to that other medieval experience that is so evocative to the modern mind: that of crusade. Several of the effigies have traditional associations with known individuals, and an enduring and commonly held belief with respect to the effigy tombs is that the phenomenon of knights depicted with crossed legs is an iconographic device intended to convey that the individual had been on crusade.[1] The following short paper seeks to examine the small corpus of thirteenth- and fourteenth-century effigy tombs depicting armoured knights, with a view to discussing the frequency of the cross-legged phenomenon and its likely connotations. Associations with individuals and their crusading links are also explored.

THE MATERIAL CULTURE

The archaeological record in Ireland is sparse when it comes to the armour and garniture of the armed warrior during the age of the crusades. Weapons and armour are rare survivors from a culture where such items were of high symbolic and practical value. The opportunity for reworking iron into new objects once a weapon or element of armour had become defunct is another major factor in the lack of survival, while the more esoteric elements of armour

---

1 James Graves, 'On the cross-legged effigies of the county of Kilkenny', *Transactions of the Kilkenny Archaeological Society* 2 (1852), 63–4, 67–70, at 64. For a more up-to-date consideration of knightly tomb effigies, see Rachel Dressler, 'Cross-legged knights and the signification of English medieval tomb sculpture', *Studies in Iconography* 21 (2000), 91–121, esp. 94. For possible contexts for Irish tomb sculpture see Philip J. Lankester, 'The thirteenth-century military effigies in the Temple church' in Robin Griffith-Jones & David Park (eds), *The Temple church in London: history, architecture, art* (Woodbridge, 2010), pp 93–134.

Regal poise: the 'cross-legged' phenomenon on Irish effigy tombs

and garniture might be misclassified if recovered as un-contexted artefacts from archaeological investigations. It is possible that future discoveries might help to expand upon current knowledge, and the scope for retrieving elements of armour from medieval burials has been recently illustrated during excavations in Dublin city where an individual interred in some kind of mail or banded armour was uncovered (pl. 11.1). This individual was buried in the graveyard of St Peter's church, about 150m to the south of Dublin Castle, sometime between 1440 and 1515, and a heavily corroded iron-rich garment covered the torso and upper arms, and extended over the neck and part of the head. A distinct iron object around the neck might have formed part of a bevoir or similar, while iron clasps at the shoulders were also suggested in CT and X-ray scans.[2] Ongoing post-excavation analysis has identified two further adjacent burials that exhibit similar areas of corroded iron on their torsos. At present, no parallels for this type of armoured burial are known in an Irish context. The finds from St Peter's graveyard – though slightly later than our study period – illustrate the rarity of such findings and highlight the limitations of interpreting such denuded remains in the context of the complex armour of the period.[3]

Scholars in this field must therefore rely heavily upon figurative representations. A few notable manuscript illustrations can assist in this regard, chief among these being Gerald of Wales' *Expugnatio Hibernica*, the famous illustrations adorning Jean Créton's account of Richard II in Ireland, and the book of the de Burgos.[4] However, it is the stone funereal monuments of the period with, in many cases, three-dimensional representations of figures in full armour, which provide the richest repository for the study of the military material culture of the age. The holistic treatment of the arms and armour and the detail necessary to complete a near life-sized representation of a given individual result in finished objects that lend themselves to close study. It has to be imagined that such works were commissioned by the individuals depicted, who would have doubtless had opportunities to comment and direct the sculptors during the process. That a patron would have been intimately acquainted with each component of his armour is not in question. However, what is less clear is the attention to such detail paid by the sculptor and the amount of artistic licence allowed. Nonetheless, these representations of long-dead individuals capture the imagination and

---

2 Paul Duffy, 'Preliminary excavation report for 6–13 Stephen Street Upper, 7–19 Longford Street & 71–75 Aungier Street, Dublin 2, Licence Ref. 17E0212' (Unpublished report, NMS Archives, 2019), pp 19–20. 3 The rarity of such finds was highlighted by the media attention surrounding a recent claim that a medieval mail shirt was found in a drain at Longford. This object has since been shown to be a modern replica through, detailed analysis by the current author in conjunction with the National Museum of Ireland. 4 See, respectively, NLI MS 700; James Lydon, 'Richard II's expeditions to Ireland,' *JRSAI* 93 (1963), 135–49; TCD MS 1440.

156   *Ireland and the crusades*

embody the physicality of the fighting man of the period like no other material relics.

THE THIRTEENTH- AND FOURTEENTH-CENTURY EFFIGY TOMBS

The earliest survivals of effigy tombs date to the first quarter of the thirteenth century in Ireland, a time when crusades to the Holy Land were already over one hundred years underway. The fashion for effigy tombs continued until a comparative lull in Ireland and Britain around the middle of the fourteenth century, not long after the loss of the last crusader state in the Holy Land in 1291. The effigy tombs therefore provide us with an insight into the knightly panoply from Ireland during the time that the crusading ideal was being promoted across western Europe, Ireland included. By the mid-fourteenth century, effigy tomb-making entered into an era of relative hiatus. This diminished productivity in sculptural work can partially be explained by the Black Death which appears to have caused stagnation from *c.*1350 in the making of these monuments. Furthermore, in Ireland the Bruce Wars earlier in the fourteenth century and mounting Gaelic-Irish resistance and resurgence must have played their roles in retarding the making of these elaborate tombs. There was a second flourishing of the tradition in Ireland towards the later part of the fifteenth century, with distinct schools of sculptural styles developing in different parts of the island. In the words of Edwin Rae, whose work on this later period of effigy tombs remains authoritative, 'Gothic Ireland shared fully in that remarkable flowering of the visual arts which took place in Europe during the fifteenth century and the first half of the sixteenth century.'[5]

As a natural consequence of the great expense involved in commissioning such a sepulchral monument, and the influence required to have it sited in some appropriate place and to have it maintained, the arms and armour represented are invariably not those of the lowly foot soldier but rather of the fully fledged man-at-arms or the landholding knight. Whatever the motivations in the commissioning of such elaborate funerary monuments by the deceased and their kin, this barrier in social stratigraphy precludes the depiction of rank-and-file types such as levied archers, crossbowmen, javelin-armed infantry and other lightly armed and armoured soldiers. Practicality in terms of the physical constraints of the monuments limited the type of weapon which could be displayed. The stone slabs selected for carving, for example, were not

---

5 Edwin C. Rae, 'Irish sepulchral monuments of the later Middle Ages: part I: the Ormond Group', *JRSAI* 100 (1970), 1–38; idem, 'Irish sepulchral monuments of the later Middle Ages: part II: the O'Tunney atelier', *JRSAI* 101 (1971), 1–39; Peter Harbison, 'In memoria', *Irish Arts Review* 28: 4, 110–13.

large enough to showcase, to scale, the longer weapons, such as the military lance wielded by the heavy cavalry of the age. Mounts are not represented on the surviving effigies either and so details of any possible caparisons[6] or other equine armour as well as horse harness parts and saddlery are not recorded either.

With this first flowering of tomb effigies, racial and cultural barriers also existed insofar as those who were portrayed were members of the colonial elite, descendants of those who led the Anglo-Norman invasion of Ireland in 1169, as opposed to individuals of status from the Gaelic-Irish world.[7] Consequently, as Hunt pointed out, the main concentration of the effigies occurs in the south and east of Ireland where the invaders generally held strongest sway.[8] However, for the man-at-arms of Anglo-Norman descent, there is much detail to be gleaned from these funereal effigies; the mail-clad warrior's panoply, including helmets, surcoats, shields, spurs, swords and their suspension systems, are well attested to.

THE EFFIGIES – WHO ARE THEY?

Just over a dozen of these military monuments survive intact from the period 1200–1350 with perhaps a little over half of these displaying detail enough to be of substantial value to this study.

Few effigies can be definitively identified with a historical individual, but a most accomplished and well-proportioned limestone effigy of a lean and austere looking mail-coifed knight at Kilfane church in Co. Kilkenny was certainly a member of the Cantwell family as the clearly defined heraldic charges on his triangular heater shield proclaim.[9] He is known variously as 'Cantwell Fada', 'Long Cantwell', or simply 'The Long Man', and at a height of 2.4m it could be said that his monikers are well earned.[10] The Cantwell or de Canteville family were among the earliest Anglo-Norman families to settle in the counties of Kilkenny and Tipperary, with Thomas de Kentewall appearing as one of the witnesses to a charter granted by Theobald Walter to his town of Gowran in the reign of Henry II.[11] Roger Stalley assigned a date of *c*.1240–50 to the effigy

---

6 A type of horse armour – usually cloth, though it can refer to other horse trapping also. 7 This was to change in later centuries, see Rae, 'Irish sepulchral monuments: part II'. 8 John Hunt, *Irish medieval figure sculpture, 1200–1600*, 2 vols (Dublin, 1974), i, p. 21. 9 Gerald Crotty, 'Heraldry in medieval Ireland I: prolegomena', *Peritia* 24–5 (2013–14), 313–47, at 318. 10 Jacqueline O'Brien & Peter Harbison, *Ancient Ireland: from prehistory to the Middle Ages* (London, 1996), p. 136. 11 Graves, 'On the cross-legged effigies', 68. Graves states in a footnote that the charter of Hubert Walter witnessed by Thomas de Kentewell was 'preserved in the record room, Kilkenny Castle, amongst the Ormond MSS'. This collection was subsequently edited by Edmund Curtis as *The calendar of Ormond deeds, 1172–1350 AD*, Irish Manuscripts Commission.

158   *Ireland and the crusades*

and drew parallels with English examples, notably with the Longespée effigy at Salisbury,[12] although Hunt had earlier proposed a date significantly later – *c*.1330 – based on the depiction of rowel spurs.[13]

The somewhat bulbous-headed knight at the Church of Ireland church in Timolin, Co. Kildare, has long been associated with Robert fitz Richard, lord of Norragh, an ancestor of the modern Wall family.[14] Hunt ascribed an early thirteenth-century date to this effigy. In fact, this sculpture might represent the earliest surviving example in Ireland. In this regard, it is plausible that the person represented is Robert fitz Richard, who founded a convent of Arroasian nuns here around the beginning of John's reign (*c*.1199).[15]

The early fourteenth-century 'Strongbow' tomb in Christ Church cathedral in Dublin – which in fact dates to 150 years after the death of Richard 'Strongbow' de Clare – was of the fitz Osbert line, judging from the effigy's still discernable arms.[16] Other effigies are less certain, such as the finely rendered *c*.1260 knight in high relief at Hospital, Co. Limerick, which has been associated with Geoffrey de Marisco, lord of Ainy and one-time justiciar (pl. 11.2). While a spurious image depicting this effigy associated with heraldic arms linking it to de Marisco has long been mistrusted and recently debunked by Con Manning,[17] Eamon Cotter had made the following case for the link with de Marisco:

> a photograph in Trinity College Dublin's online Edwin Rae collection shows the effigy lying in a niche in the north wall, near the north-eastern corner of the church, a common location for a founder's memorial. This may have been its original position and it is likely that it does indeed represent Geoffrey de Marisco, who died in France in 1245.[18]

There are another two roughly contemporary incised portrayals of men-at-arms on slabs at Hospital – one of them a double effigy with a lady – but

6 vols (Dublin, 1932–43). In Curtis' edition, only a charter of Theobald Walter witnessed by Thomas de Kentewell (p. 18, n. 34), dated 'before 1206', concerns lands and rights in Co. Tipperary granted to Gilbert de Kentewell. Unless Graves was mistaken – which seems unlikely – Theobald Walter's charter to Gowran is therefore lost.   12 Roger Stalley, 'A misunderstood gothic masterpiece: the Cantwell effigy at Kilfane, Co. Kilkenny' in Etienne Rynne (ed.), *Figures from the past* (Dún Laoghaire, 1987), pp 209–22, at p. 216.   13 Hunt, *Irish medieval figure sculpture*, i, p. 136.   14 Albert Hartstone, 'Notes on a recumbent effigy in Timolin churchyard', *Journal of the County Kildare Archaeological Society*, 1 (1892), 131–4; Walter Fitzgerald, 'Timolin', *Journal of the County Kildare Archaeological Society* 2 (1899), 413–25, at 420–2; Hunt, *Irish medieval figure sculpture*, i, p. 164.   15 Tracy Collins, 'Timolin: a case study of a nunnery estate in later medieval Ireland', *Anuario de estudios medievales* 44: 1 (2014), 51–80, at 63.   16 Hunt, *Irish medieval figure sculpture*, i, p. 136; Crotty, 'Heraldry', 319.   17 Conleth Manning, 'Hervey Morres and the "Montmorency imposture"', *HI* 28: 2 (2020), 22–5, at 24.   18 Eamonn Cotter, 'The archaeology of the Irish Hospitaller preceptories of Mourneabbey and Hospital in context,' in Browne & Ó Clabaigh (eds), *Soldiers of Christ*, p. 119.

Regal poise: the 'cross-legged' phenomenon on Irish effigy tombs

they are not as decipherable as the 'de Marisco knight'. One of these might have been made for Roger Outlaw (d. 1341), prior of Kilmainham (1317–41), who died at the hospital and was buried there.[19] It is likely that the knight on the double effigy and the 'de Marisco' effigy represent benefactors of the church rather than actual Hospitaller knights.

Several intriguing effigies survive from Cashel, where they are currently positioned upright within niches constructed specifically for the purpose within the boundary wall of the Church of Ireland cathedral of St John the Baptist. The effigies are of a knight in chain mail and surcoat, and three women in robes. These effigies were reputedly taken from the Hackett chapel of the now-lost Franciscan friary of Cashel. Sir William de Hacket founded the friary c.1265 and it is locally believed that the effigies represent William, his wife and two daughters. Hunt followed the dating of the Kilfane effigy and ascribed a date of c.1320 based upon the similarities in the armour and the rowel spur in particular (pl. 11.3).[20] George du Noyer described these effigies in detail in 1845, remarking in particular upon the female tombs and noting that the head-dress common to all three finds parallels in many thirteenth-century depictions, notably at Romsey and the famous chapterhouse at Southwell. He wrote:

> The rest of the costume of these figures is equally characteristic of the thirteenth-century; the loose robe confined at the waist by a narrow strap and buckle, and falling so low as to envelope the feet entirely in its folds, the mantle kept in its place by a narrow strap crossing the breast and held in the left hand, the square cushion under the head, are all fashions observable in the monuments of that period. The fashion of closing, by means of a circular brooch, the vent or fente, which was made in the upper part of the robe, in order that it might fit more closely around the throat, may be seen in several monumental effigies, especially those of Berengaria the queen of Richard I, and Isabel d'Angoulesme, the queen of John.[21]

Du Noyer believed, drawing on local knowledge of the circumstance of the retrieval of the effigies, that they might represent Sir William, his wife and two daughters, although the late date ascribed to them by Hunt, if correct, would probably preclude this possibility. The knight exhibits many points of similarity with the Cantwell effigy at Kilfane. In view of the earlier date

19 Paul Caffery, 'Visual culture of Hospitaller knights of the priory of Ireland' in Browne & Ó Clabaigh (eds), *Soldiers of Christ*, p. 155. 20 Hunt, *Irish medieval figure sculpture*, i, p. 136. 21 George du Noyer, 'Notice of the cross-legged sepulchral effigies existing at Cashel', *Archaeological Journal* 2 (1846), 121–31.

160 *Ireland and the crusades*

now proposed for the Cantwell effigy by Roger Stalley, it seems reasonable to revert to du Noyer's reading of the Cashel effigy, ascribing to it a thirteenth-century date. The shorter shield and separated coif would push for a date later in the century, presenting a revised date for the effigies which would allow their identification with William and his family, however no heraldic evidence survives on the knight's shield that could confirm this.[22]

The identity of other knightly effigies remains entirely unknown, such as the beautifully incised pair of 'brethren' at Jerpoint abbey, Co. Kilkenny (pl. 11.4), or, in the same county, the fine sword-grasping knight at Duiske abbey, Graiguenamanagh. But despite their anonymity, these hewn sculptures evoke the age of the crusading knight like no other extant monuments.

CROSSED LEGS

Of the Irish military effigies, several have their legs crossed, that posture being in vogue from the middle of the thirteenth century and enduring for some hundred years. Therefore, fittingly, the early thirteenth-century Timolin knight's legs are extended straight. Where the legs are crossed on Irish effigies it is more common to see the right leg crossed – usually high on the thigh – over the left, the knights at Hospital, Christ Church, Kilfane and Cashel all being examples of this. The Graiguenamanagh knight, however, has his left leg crossed atop the right leg and the evidence from fragments of an effigy at Tralee, Co. Kerry, indicate a similar posture where the left leg is 'crossed over and free of the right'.[23] Not all renderings of recumbents on Irish monuments of this period conform to a cross-legged posture, a case in point being the late thirteenth-century double effigy of the Jerpoint 'brethren' on which both knights are portrayed with their legs laid straight and their toes all pointing towards the sinister.

The Irish material therefore reflects the pattern in Britain where, from the mid-thirteenth centry to the mid-fourteenth century, the great majority of military effigies had the cross-legged pose. This applies to both three-dimensional effigies in stone and wood and to two-dimensional representations in incised stone and brass.[24]

The cross-legged pose is often associated in the modern mind as the quintessential mark of the veteran man-at-arms of Christendom lately returned

22 Crotty, 'Heraldry', p. 325.   23 Laurence Dunne, 'Murder, pillage and destruction: archaeological finds from medieval Tralee' in Griffin Murray (ed.), *Medieval treasures of Co. Kerry* (Tralee, 2010), pp 61–72, at p. 67.   24 Oliver Harris, 'Antiquarian attitudes: crossed legs, crusaders and the evolution of an idea', *Antiquaries Journal*, 90 (2010), 401–40, at p. 401.

from crusade in the Holy Land. The traditional thinking for this interpretation dates as far back as the sixteenth century, but there is no direct link with this association that goes back to the crusading period itself. In writing of this phenomenon in 2010, Oliver Harris stated that 'no other instance of what has been dubbed "monument lore", however, has achieved the ubiquity, the longevity or the resilience of the myth of the cross-legged crusader, in which the weight of tradition and the appeal of romantic legend continue to defy the challenges of scholarship'.[25]

The evolution of this idea resulted in knights represented with crossed legs being regarded as either crusaders or Templars. Arguments against this line have been made by researchers since the nineteenth century.[26] Some alternative interpretations that have been circulated include that the crossed legs denoted authority, or strength of mind and body, or promoted greater naturalism to the figure, or conveyed virility and sheer physicality.[27] Dressler ascertained that the cross-legged posture 'presents the lower limbs as especially powerful and active' and discussed the motif as a counter to charges of effeminacy laid against the knightly class by clerics and chroniclers of the day.[28] This logic encounters problems when the examples of the cross-legged pose of the female effigies at Cashel are considered. An additional example of a female with crossed legs has been identified on a double effigy from St Mary's church, Kilkenny further undermining Dressler's interpretation.[29]

It is clear that a different explanation must be sought for the pose. Again, sculptural detail from an Irish tomb might prove crucial here. The tomb surrounds from Athassel, Co. Tipperary, which both Leask and Manning dated to the late thirteenth century, exhibit a row of knights in an arcade of pointed-trefoil niches. The knights are portrayed as individuals. Each knight is mail-clad and wears a long surcoat. These are cinched at the waist by a narrow belt. All four figures carry heater shields and two of the four figures are depicted standing in a cross-legged pose (pl. 11.5).[30] All four figures are beautifully carved and convey a sense of being braced and solidly upright. In other words, these figures are not recumbent as with all depictions discussed so far. It would seem therefore that the cross-legged pose was a common posture adopted by knights at ease. This posture might indeed have had the effect of expressing vitality and dexterity as suggested by Dressler, but in a courtly setting it is clearly something that was adopted by civilians, including women.

25 Harris, 'Antiquarian attitudes', 430–1. 26 For a thorough treatment of the historiography of this idea see ibid. 27 Rachel Dressler, 'Cross-legged knights', 115. 28 Ibid., 112–14. 29 Brian Gittos & Moira Gittos, *Interpreting medieval effigies: the evidence from Yorkshire, to 1400* (Oxford, 2019), pp 13, 112. 30 Harold Leask, 'An altar tomb at Athassel abbey, Co. Tipperary,' *JRSAI* 76 (1946), 215–18; Conleth Manning, 'The Athassel tomb,' *Irish Arts Review* 22: 4 (2005), 132–5.

162   *Ireland and the crusades*

A courtly, even royal, origin for this posture is suggested by another piece of evidence preserved in Ireland: the *Waterford Charter Roll*.[31] The roll, which dates to *c*.1373, contains the earliest contemporary portrait of a medieval English monarch: Edward III on his throne with full kingly regalia. Significantly, Edward is not fully seated on the throne but, rather, he is depicted leaning back on the edge of the throne with his left leg crossed over his right just above his right knee (pl. 11.6). A second image in the roll shows an unidentified monarch in the same posture receiving the key to the city from the mayor and bailiffs (pl. 11.7). These images, broadly contemporary with the phenomenon of the cross-legged posture on the recumbent effigies, illustrate unambiguously that the posture was used during this period to convey authority, power and strength.

CONCLUSIONS

In considering the phenomenon of the cross-legged motif in Irish funerary sculpture, this short study illustrates what has been accepted in academic writings for quite some time, namely that the antiquated yet persistent belief of a link with the crusades is spurious, and that there is no evidence from the Irish examples for links with the Templars. This has not stopped the perpetuation of this tradition in guidebooks, interpretive panels and other sources of popular history. Further, of the Irish branches of the families and individuals purportedly linked to the effigies discussed above, namely the Cantwells, the fitz Osberts, Geoffrey de Marisco, William de Hacket and Robert fitz Richard, none appear to have participated in the crusades. Only the unsubstantiated suggestion of a connection between one of the effigies at Hospital and the one-time prior of the Hospitaller commandery of Kilmainham, Roger Outlaw, could be said to provide any link to the crusading orders. As if to highlight the remoteness of this link, this effigy, in an act of defiance, has refused to cross its legs.

In examining the Irish effigy tombs, two important new pieces of evidence bring a further perspective to the cross-legged pose. The knights on the Athassel tomb are represented very much in the quick. They are full of life, suggesting that movement and a certain bravado could be read into their postures. It is probable therefore that the cross-legged pose was something commonly struck by military men at ease. The cross-legged pose would therefore seem to represent an affectation that likely originated as a military gesture

31 Julian Walton, *The royal charters of Waterford* (Waterford, 1992).

exhibiting strength and confidence. From the evidence of the *Waterford Charter Roll*, which, at the close of the fourteenth century is at the later end of our study period, it is clear that this pose was taken up as a royal gesture used by kings in majesty. A military over a regal origin can therefore be tentatively proposed as the seed which led to the adoption of the cross-legged pose more widely among both men and women in courtly society. The depiction of Edward III in the *Waterford Charter Roll* is therefore in keeping with what we know of Edward, who was, by his own estimation as well as his peers', a notable warrior king.

12 / Crusading rhetoric and Anglo-Irish relations, *c.*1300–1600

KATHRYN HURLOCK

Although the twelfth-century conquest of Ireland was couched in the language of crusade, and the Anglo-Irish continued to use this language in their disputes with the Irish into the fifteenth century, no crusade was ever launched against the Irish. Instead, in the sixteenth century the Irish themselves took up the language of holy war – at times for political convenience, and at times from genuine devotion – and succeeded in gaining the critical papal support and spiritual indulgence needed to turn rebellion into crusade. This chapter looks at how and why this shift occurred, how the Irish tried to use crusading in the era when the English Church broke with Rome, which rebellions could genuinely be considered crusades and what that meant for holy war in Ireland. In doing so, it challenges general assumptions about crusades and crusaders in sixteenth-century Ireland, and highlights the dangers and problems of launching a papally backed holy war at home.

Though there are numerous works on Irish rebellion, and on Tudor rebellions more widely, they do not consider the development of the use of crusading over a long historical perspective in order to understand the employment of crusading language in these conflicts, and the elements needed to make a rebellion into a crusade.[1] Indeed, many refer to the rebellions as crusades and their participants as crusaders, with little or no consideration of whether they were or not, and if so, who recognized them as such.[2] This article reassesses the language used in calls for crusades and in Irish rebellions, the attitudes of the papacy and foreign powers to religiously motivated rebellion and the applicability of crusading ideas in Anglo-Irish relations.

The use of crusading language in Anglo-Irish relations was born in the twelfth century, when the Anglo-Norman invasion of Ireland was linked to

---

1 Hiram Morgan, *Tyrone's rebellion: the outbreak of the Nine Years War in Tudor Ireland* (Woodbridge, 1993); James O'Neill, *The Nine Years War, 1593–1603: O'Neill, Mountjoy and the military revolution* (Dublin, 2018); Ruth A. Canning, *The Old English in early modern Ireland: the Palesmen and the Nine Years War, 1594–1603* (Woodbridge, 2019); Cyril Falls, *Elizabeth's Irish wars* (Syracuse, 1997).   2 See, for example: Henry A. Jefferies, 'The early Tudor Reformation in the Irish Pale', *JEH* 52 (2001), 34–62, at 45; Steven G. Ellis, 'Centre and periphery in the Tudor State' in Norman L. Jones & Robert Tittler (eds), *A companion to Tudor Britain* (Oxford, 2008), pp 133–50, at p. 147; D. George Boyce, *Nationalism in Ireland* (London, 1995), p. 63.

religious reform, and portrayed by Gerald of Wales in a manner similar to crusade narratives.[3] Gervase of Tilbury, writing in the early thirteenth century, justified Henry II's rule in Ireland by stating that the Irish had been 'contemptuous of religion.'[4] Early in the following century, several prophecies alluded to crusading activity. The *Verses of Gildas*, probably written before 1320, linked existing prophecies of a successful crusade in the Holy Land with victory in Ireland. It claimed that the defeat of the 'stone walls of Ireland' was a necessary precursor to peace in Ireland, after which Edward II would be able to embark on a tour of Spain (where he would defeat the Moors), Egypt and Babylon, and then onwards to the final conquest of the Holy Land.[5] A roughly contemporaneous work, the *Prophecy of the Six Kings*, also suggested that the route to the Holy Land lay through Ireland.[6] In the early 1330s the Anglo-Irish tried to persuade the pope to call 'a crusade' against Irish heretics as, they said, they had burned churches, blasphemed, killed Christians and disrespected priests.[7] On these grounds they asked Pope John XXII to 'deign to call a crusade for the well-being of your soul and the souls of countless others who are fighting a just war against those evildoers' but their plea was ignored.[8] The prophecies relating to conquest in Ireland and onward success in the Holy Land were resurrected again under Edward III and, more enthusiastically, under Richard II, who appeared to be particularly susceptible to the message of prophecy.[9] Several prophecies were applied to

---

3 Colin Veach, 'Henry II and the ideological foundations of Angevin Rule in Ireland', *IHS* 42 (2018), 1–25, at 16; Hurlock, *Crusades*, p. 105. For the text of *Laudabiliter*, the disputed papal bull granting Ireland to Henry II in 1155, see Giraldus, *Opera*, v, p. 316. See also Maeve Callan, chapter 3, this volume.   4 Gervase of Tilbury, *Otia Imperialia*, pp 308–9.   5 The *Verses* survive in a manuscript of 1340 together with other prophetic works: BL Arundel MS 57, ff 4v–6v. The manuscript includes Thomas de Erseldoune's Prophecy of Edward II, f. 8v. Geoffrey of Monmouth, *Vita Merlini*, ed. and trans. Basil Clarke, *Life of Merlin: Vita Merlini* (Cardiff, 1973), p. 89. The interest in Merlin's prophecies and crusading was exemplified in TCD MS 496, a miscellany of the early fourteenth century that includes Geoffrey of Monmouth's commentary on Merlin's prophecy, a letter of the Fifth Crusade and a redaction of Oliver of Cologne's *Historia Damiatina*. I am grateful to Dr Thomas W. Smith for bringing this work to my attention. For a more detailed study, see his 'Oliver of Cologne's *Historia Damiatina*: a new manuscript witness in Dublin, TCD MS 496', *Hermathena* 194 (2017 for 2013), 31–62; Victoria Flood, *Prophecy, politics and place in medieval England: from Geoffrey of Monmouth to Thomas of Erceldoune* (Cambridge, 2016), p. 134; 'Merlin's prophecies of a goat and an eagle' in *The Brut, or the chronicles of England*, ed. Friedrich W.D. Brie (London, 1906), pp 73–4. Timothy Guard, *Chivalry, kingship and crusade: the English experience in the fourteenth century* (Woodbridge, 2013), p. 190. Flood, *Prophecy, politics and place*, p. 134.   6 An imperfect transcription of the prophecy from BL Harley MS 746 is published in Rupert Taylor, *The political prophecy in England* (New York, 1911), pp 160–4.   7 Callan, *Templars*, pp 25, 207–12. See further Maeve Callan, 'Making monsters out of one another in the early fourteenth-century British Isles: the Irish Remonstrance, the declaration of Arbroath, and the Anglo-Irish Counter-Remonstrance', *Eolas* 12 (2019), 43–63.   8 J.A. Watt, 'Negotiations between Edward II and John XXII concerning Ireland', *IHS* 10 (1956), 1–20.   9 T.M. Smallwood, 'The prophecy of the six kings', *Speculum* 60 (1985), 571–92. The English chronicler Thomas Walsingham (d. *c.*1422), for example, claimed that Richard II was very much in thrall to the Bridlington prophecies, which foretold that the

Richard during his reign;[10] Philippe de Mézières associated success in Ireland with the crusades; and the Wilton Diptych, arguably a crusading icon, seems to have depicted the island of Ireland in the orb atop the banner as a way of highlighting the role of Ireland in this vision of Richard II as saviour of the Holy Land.[11] Again, in 1421, the English parliament in Ireland suggested that Henry V of England ask the pope for permission to launch a crusade against the Irish because of their disobedience, but the request appears to have fallen on deaf ears.[12] Although the idea of a crusade – either directly against the rebellious Irish, or to the Holy Land via Ireland – was a persistent idea into the fifteenth century, at no time were practical measures ever taken to turn idea into reality and launch a holy war. As Maeve Callan commented, 'no pope called a crusade, at least not while England was a Catholic country'.[13]

A shift first came when Thomas, Lord Offaly (known as Silken Thomas, 1513–37), rebelled in the summer of 1534 (pl. 12.1). His motivations were varied, and included a desire to have his father, the ninth earl of Kildare (d. 2 Sept. 1534), recognized as deputy of Ireland by Henry VIII; opposition to Cromwellian political reform; internal faction; and Thomas' belief that his father would be executed by Henry VIII.[14] Claims were also made regarding religious grievances, though in reality he had no religious motivations. Religiously focused resistance was stirred up though by Emperor Charles V, nephew of Henry VIII's repudiated wife Catherine of Aragon, who sought to

cock (Richard II) was 'worthy to be emperor'. *Johannis de Trokelowe, et Henrici de Blaneforde monachum S. Albani, necnon quorundam anonymorum, Chronica et Annales*, ed. H.T. Riley (London, 1866), pp 233–4; Lesley Ann Coote, *Prophecy and public affairs in later medieval England* (Woodbridge, 2000), p. 128; Flood, *Prophecy, politics and place*, p. 146. 10 G.W. Coopland's introduction to Philippe de Mézières, *Letter to Richard II: a plea made in 1395 for peace between England and France*, trans. G.W. Coopland (Liverpool, 1975), pp ix–xxxiv; BL Cotton MS Claudius E VIII; Coote, *Prophecy and public affairs*, pp 153, 255; see also idem, 'The crusading bishop: Henry Despenser and his manuscript' in Nigel J. Morgan (ed.), *Prophecy, apocalypse and the day of doom* (Donington, 2004), pp 39–51; R.F. Yeager, '*Le Songe Vert*', BL Add. MS 34114 (the Spalding Manuscript), Bibliothèque de la ville de Clermont MS 249 and John Gower' in Simon Horobin & Linne R. Mooney (eds), *Middle English texts in translation* (York, 2014), pp 75–87, at p. 81. 11 J.J.N. Palmer, *England, France and Christendom, 1377–99* (London, 1972), pp 242–4. Nigel Saul, *Richard II* (London, 1999), pp 304–11; Christopher Tyerman, *England and the crusades, 1095–1588* (Chicago, 1988), pp 297–300; Maurice Keen, 'The Wilton Diptych: the case for a crusading context' in Dillian Gordon, Lisa Monnas & Caroline Elam (eds), *The regal image of Richard II and the Wilton Diptych* (London, 1997), pp 189–95; see also Dillian Gordon, *Making and meaning: the Wilton Diptych* (London, 1993); Michael J. Bennett, 'Richard II and the wider realm' in Anthony E. Goodman & James L. Gillespie (eds), *Richard II: the art of kingship* (Oxford, 1999), pp 187–204, at p. 203. 12 Elizabeth Matthew, 'Henry V and the proposal for an Irish crusade' in Brendan Smith (ed.), *Ireland and the English world in the late Middle Ages* (Basingstoke, 2009), pp 161–75. 13 Callan, *Templars*, p. 19. 14 Steven G. Ellis, 'FitzGerald, Thomas [*called* Silken Thomas], tenth earl of Kildare [*known as* Lord Offaly] (1513–1537)', *ODNB*; Brendan Bradshaw, 'Cromwellian reform and the origins of the Kildare rebellion, 1533–34', *TRHS* 27 (1977), 69–93; Felicity Heal, *Reformation in Britain and Ireland* (Oxford, 2003), pp 129–30. For Chapuys' report that Offaly believed his father had been killed, *CSP Spain* v, no. 164.

Crusading rhetoric and Anglo-Irish relations, c.1300–1600

make trouble for Henry in Ireland and who believed that Thomas had genuine religious motives. Steven Ellis has suggested that Thomas actually presented himself as a crusader to gain this imperial support for rebellion, and William Palmer has gone as far as to say that Thomas 'proclaimed his leadership a Catholic crusade'.[15] The imperial ambassador to England, Chapuys, certainly hoped that the rebellion would lead to a crusade against the English king.[16] He informed the emperor that Thomas was forcing townspeople to recognize the authority of the pope, the emperor and himself,[17] and Robert Cowley wrote to Cromwell that Silken Thomas and his followers had declared that they were 'of the Pope's sect and band'.[18] It is possible that these charges were exaggerated by those who sought to discredit the Geraldines, of whom Thomas was one, and that not everyone believed that this was a papally inspired rebellion. In the Annals of the Four Masters and Annals of Loch Cé, for example, in the accounts of the rebellion of Silken Thomas, there was no hint of religious motives, their scribes believing he was driven by the death of his father in London.[19] However, Thomas was fully aware of the benefit that papal support could bring, and at the end of the year dispatched his personal chaplain to Rome to remind Pope Paul III that Ireland had been a papal fief since the time of King John.[20] Although sympathetic, the pope did not see the Irish rebellion as a crusade, perhaps because it had begun before Henry VIII declared himself leader of the English Church in November 1534, or because Paul III talked of winning Henry back to Catholicism.[21] Ultimately the papacy never offered indulgences, a core component of crusade, to those who rebelled with Silken Thomas: indeed the only indulgences declared for fighting at this time were those issued by Thomas Cranmer, archbishop of Canterbury, who offered them for those who fought *against* the Irish rebels, not with them.[22] Thus, references to the rebellion of Silken Thomas as a crusade in historical assessments are unsupportable, and arise in part from the fact that Henry VIII's break with Rome and excommunication have coloured interpretation of the event.[23]

---

15 Steven G. Ellis, 'The Kildare rebellion and the early Henrician Reformation', *Historical Journal* 19 (1976), 807–30, at 812; William Palmer, *The problem of Ireland in Tudor foreign policy, 1485–1603* (Woodbridge, 1994), p. 45. 16 Heal, *Reformation*, p. 130. 17 *Calendar of letters, despatches, and state papers relating to the negotiations between England and Spain, preserved in the archives at Simancas, Vienna, Brussels and elsewhere.* 15 vols (London, 1862–1954) v, part 1, no. 86. 18 Robert Cowley to Thomas Cromwell, *c.* June 1534. *State Papers Henry VIII*, 5 parts in 12 vols (London, 1830–52), ii, p. 198. 19 *AFM* v, p. 1419–21; *Annals of Loch Cé*, ed. and trans. William H. Hennessy, 2 vols (London, 1871), ii, p. 285. 20 *Calendar of Letters… at Simancas*, v, pt. 1, p. 464, no. 164. 21 Michael Ó Siochrú, 'Foreign involvement in the revolt of Silken Thomas, 1534–5', *PRIA* 96C (1996), 49–66, at 57. 22 Dr Ortiz to the Empress, 20 June 1535. *CSP Spain* v, no. 176. 23 See, for example, Jefferies' reference to 'his crusade' and 'the crusade's impact' in Henry A. Jefferies, 'The early Tudor Reformation', 45.

168 *Ireland and the crusades*

In the wake of Silken Thomas' failed rebellion and the attainder placed on Kildare lands in 1536, his half-brother and heir, Gerald fitz Gerald, 11th earl of Kildare (d. 1585), became the nominal leader of opposition to English rule in Ireland. At the start of 1538, Gerald sent the bishop of Derry to Rome with letters requesting papal assistance in the form of ships, men and artillery, in protecting the Irish from 'the Antichrist' (Henry VIII), who would force the Reformation onto the churches in Ireland.[24] The pope was sympathetic to his plea, and said that he would call on all Christian princes to aid the Irish or, if they would not help, to ask them to secure financial aid through the granting of pardons.[25] But evidence that the Irish rebels sought papal backing for their actions beyond the purely practical is elusive at best. When in March of the following year the English captured the monk Ruaric O'Spellman, the bishop of Derry's messenger to the pope, they felt they had succeeded in hindering the rising rebellion, which they believed was driven by religion, but they appear to have misconstrued his reason for visiting the papal see.[26] Though O'Spellman was sent to ask the pope for assistance because the king's deputies in Ireland were refusing to recognize papal supremacy, as well as destroying churches and killing priests, he had actually been sent to ask for the authority to remove disloyal bishops and clergy, not for a crusade.[27] Thus, although there were concerns over the treatment of Catholics in Ireland and the refusal to acknowledge the supremacy of the pope, the solution sought here was administrative, not military.

Despite this, in the spring of 1539, the Geraldine League's planned conflict with Henry VIII was, according to Brendan Bradshaw, preached 'as a holy crusade' by the Franciscan observants of the Pale, who had been opposed to the Henrician Reformation since at least 1534.[28] Bradshaw also claimed that the friars launched a propaganda campaign on behalf of the rebellion, 'preaching it up as a crusade and promising eternal reward to those who should lose their lives while engaged on it. This was the news', he concluded, 'brought back by a Galway merchant in the early summer of 1539'.[29] According to the confession of this merchant, Thomas Lynche, in July 1539:

> The friars and priests of all the Yrishtree [*sic*], not only in O'Donnells country, but all other where I was, do preach daily that every man ought,

---

24 *Letters and papers, foreign and domestic, of Henry VIII*, ed. James Gairdner. 21 vols (London, 1864–1920), xiii, part 1, no. 77. **25** Ibid. **26** *Letters and papers, foreign and domestic*, xiv, no. 538. **27** *Letters and papers, foreign and domestic*, xiii, part 2, no. 1164. **28** Brendan Bradshaw, *The Irish constitutional revolution of the sixteenth century* (Cambridge, 1979), p. 137; see also his *The dissolution of the religious orders in Ireland under Henry VIII* (Cambridge, 1974), pp 208, 210–11. **29** Idem, 'The English reformation and identity formation in Ireland and Wales' in Brendan Bradshaw & Peter Roberts (eds), *British consciousness and identity: the making of Britain, 1533–1707* (Cambridge, 1998), pp 43–111, at p. 100.

Crusading rhetoric and Anglo-Irish relations, c.1300–1600

for the salvation of his soul, fight and make war against our sovereign lord the kings majesty, and his true subjects and if any of them shall so fight against the said majesty, or his subjects, die in the quarrel his soul, that shall be dead, shall go to heaven as the soul of Peter, Paul, and others which suffered death and martyrdom for God's sake.[30]

William Palmer argued that the pope was already encouraging a crusade against the excommunicate Henry, having instructed Cardinal Reginald Pole to persuade Francis I of France and the Holy Roman emperor, Charles V, to launch a crusade against him in December 1538.[31] But although the friars might have been talking in terms of holy war, there is no evidence in Lynche's report that the papacy supported the idea of turning the rebellion into a crusade, and papal backing was essential for a full crusade.

After the reigns of Edward VI (1547–53) and the Catholic Mary I (1553–8), rebellion against the English monarch on religious grounds, real or imagined, occurred again. In the 1550s, Shane O'Neill (c.1530–67), youngest son of the first earl of Tyrone, began to assert his authority in Ireland. Those he oppressed appealed to Elizabeth I, but, despite attempts to reason with him, no headway was made, and the queen made peace, acknowledging him as 'the O'Neill'; that is, she recognized him as chieftain of clan O'Neill. Ultimately, he continued to oppose the English, and by March 1566 the queen saw him as a danger.[32] It was only now that religion appeared in the story of Shane O'Neill's rebellion.[33] On 25 April 1566, O'Neill wrote to Charles IX of France asking for 5,000 men in return for making Ireland subject to France, and to the Cardinal of Lorrraine 'in consideration of his defence of the Romish faith'.[34] His appeal came to nothing, and on 2 June he was killed by the Scots at Cushendun; his pickled head was sent to the English in Dublin. His attempt to curry favour with the French was clearly part of a wider attempt to gain international assistance using whatever means necessary: he also wrote to the Scots and offered to repudiate his then wife, Katherine O'Donnell, in favour of taking James McDonald's widow as his fifth wife, marriages being one of his preferred ways to forge political alliances.[35]

---

30 Modernized spelling. *State papers of Henry VIII*, 5 parts in 12 vols (London, 1830–52), iii, p. 141.   31 Palmer, *The problem of Ireland*, p. 51.   32 Ciaran Brady, 'Politics, policy and power, 1550–1603' in Jane Ohlmeyer (ed.), *The Cambridge history of Ireland*, ii: *1550–1730* (Cambridge, 2020), pp 39–40.   33 Though it is interesting to note, in the context of crusade, that in 1560, when the O'Moore family met at Holy Cross abbey to swear an alliance before the holy relic there, in opposition to Elizabeth I, Shane O'Neill sent his rhymer to the meeting, aware of its importance. William J. Hayes, 'Holy Cross abbey', *Capuchin Annual* (1972), 286–301, at 298.   34 *CSP Ire.*, i, pp 298–9.   35 Mary O'Dowd, *A history of women in Ireland, 1500–1800* (London, 2005), pp 12, 25–7.

At the end of the 1560s, the rebellion of James fitz Maurice fitz Gerald (d. 1579) became the first Anglo-Irish conflict that could really be considered a crusade, although it took some time to achieve that status. Its origins lay in conflict between fitz Gerald's cousin, Gerald fitz James fitz Gerald, 14th earl of Desmond (c.1533–83) and English authority in Ireland. In August 1567, the earl was sent to the Tower of London by Sir Henry Sidney, the lord deputy of Ireland. He stayed there until the winter of 1570 and then, after a period of house arrest, returned to Ireland in March 1573. Following the earl of Desmond's re-arrest and escape, he set about reclaiming his lands and refused to back down, earning himself a declaration as a traitor in the summer of 1574. His opposition to English power, despite his protestations of loyalty, was driven by fear of the loss of his lands and authority. By September he had submitted to England's greater strength.

During the period of the earl of Desmond's incarceration, fitz Maurice took control of the Desmond family interests. He was strongly opposed to English influence in Ireland through men like John Perrot, and allied with other Anglo-Irish and Irish lords who were opposed to English rule. Fitz Maurice and his allies planned to rise up against the English government in 1569, to which end in February of that year he held an assembly in Dublin which declared that the Reformation had broken the terms of *Laudabiliter* (1155), the papal bull reputedly granting the English king Ireland, and as a result Ireland required a new, legitimate, ruler in place of Elizabeth I. He claimed that his motives were religious, and declared that his rebellion was a crusade intended to abolish Protestant worship in Ireland's towns, an idea which he appears to have developed under the influence of Irish Jesuits. On 12 May 1569 he wrote to the citizens of Cork to demand the expulsion of the Huguenots, a sentiment echoed by Archbishop MacGibbon to Phillip II of Spain, and by June he was in open rebellion.[36] He then wrote to Elizabeth I to explain his motives, which were that the queen unjustly ruled the Catholics of Ireland and England, but if those who opposed her could join together, they would be able to defeat this usurper. They would do this for Christ, 'under whose banner we fight'. Fitz Maurice defined himself as 'general captain in this holy war', and wrote of expelling 'false teachers and schismatical service'. Though the language he used was of holy war, there was no specific mention of an indulgence for supporters; instead, fitz Maurice declared that participants would gain 'honour, goods, and inheritance' as their reward.[37] His rebellion failed, however, when he was driven off

---

36 *CSP Ire.* i, p. 413; D.A. Binchy, 'An Irish ambassador at the court of Philip II', *Studies* 2 (1921), 353–74, 573–84. 37 *CCM* I, pp 397–9, no. 267.

Crusading rhetoric and Anglo-Irish relations, c.1300–1600   171

by Elizabeth's troops, and despite his rhetoric there was no suggestion that he had papal support at this point.

This did not deter fitz Maurice. On 25 February 1570, Elizabeth I was excommunicated by the papal bull *Regnan in Excelsis*, a decision taken partly in response to the first Desmond rebellion. This made her a legitimate target for Irish Catholics, something which might have spurred fitz Maurice to continue, despite his setbacks. Vehemently anti-Protestant, he claimed that Elizabeth I was forcing the Irish 'to forsake the Catholic faith by God unto his Church given and by the see of Rome hitherto prescribed to all Christian men'.[38] The English queen was described as a 'she-tyrant', who had 'lost her royal power by refusing to listen to Christ in the person of his vicar [the pope]'.[39] Fitz Maurice went on to call his enemies heretics, and to blame them for the end of peace in Ireland.

What gave his renewed plans for rebellion a threatening aspect was the planned involvement of the English mercenary Thomas Stukeley, who, it was reported in May 1571 and again in April 1572, was going to sail an army to Ireland.[40] James fitz Maurice revived his rebellion in the following year with no more success, and he was forced to submit to John Perrot, the lord president of Munster. In 1574 fitz Maurice went into exile, and the following year sailed to Europe to drum up support, offering the Irish crown to various Catholic rulers. He gained the support of Stukeley and, crucially, Pope Gregory XIII for an Irish invasion, the latter commissioning him to fight 'in defence of the true religion' in 1577.[41] Significantly, the pope also granted plenary indulgences for the expedition in 1578: at this point it could be said to be a crusade.[42]

Ultimately Stukeley's portion of the papal army was deflected to crusade in Morocco, where he died, but in the summer 1579 fitz Maurice landed his part of the papal army of Italian and Spanish troops at Smerwick, Co. Kerry. He disembarked, preceded by 'two friars bearing ensigns, and a bishop with a crozier staff and his mitre'.[43] Aid was promised in the form of fitz Maurice's ally the papal commissary and Catholic exile, Dr Nicholas Sanders, who wrote to the Irish people advising them that the rebellion was 'not the warr of men … but the warr of God', utilizing ideology to try and bring the fragmenting force together.[44] Fitz Maurice, waiting for this support to arrive, set off on pilgrimage to a nearby monastery in August 1579, and was killed *en route*

---

38 G.A. Hayes McCoy, 'Conciliation, coercion, and the Protestant reformation, 1547–71' in T.W. Moody, F.X. Martin & F.J. Byrne (eds), *A new history of Ireland*, iii: *Early modern Ireland, 1534–1691* (Oxford, 2009), pp 69–93, at p. 90. **39** Ibid., p. 105. **40** *CSP Ire.* i, pp 447, 469. **41** Paul E.J. Hammer, *Elizabeth's wars* (Basingstoke, 2003), p. 106; Robert King, *A primer of the history of the Catholic Church in Ireland*, 3 vols (Dublin, 1851), iii, pp 1262–4. **42** Robert Dudley Edwards, *Ireland in the age of the Tudors: the destruction of Hiberno-Noman civilisation* (London, 1977), p. 140. **43** *CSP Ire.* ii, p. 174. **44** King, *A primer*, iii, pp 1267–9.

by some Anglo-Irish opponents. Continuing under the leadership of the earl of Desmond, who had previously been reluctant to become involved, and his brother John, in November 1580 while encamped at Smerwick the rebels unfurled four ensigns depicting the 'Poopes banner' as a sign of their crusade, although in reality Desmond's motives were more about family strength than religious fervour.[45] At the beginning of the following month, the earl of Desmond was declared a traitor. In response, he launched a full-scale rebellion, which went on until he was captured and beheaded in November 1583. Although so much emphasis was put on the religious motivations for this war, and the papacy recognized it as a holy war, not everyone was convinced. The Annals of the Four Masters, compiled in the first years of the following century, saw the Desmond rebellion as a purely political revolt, and condemned the earl of Desmond and the Geraldines for rebelling against their lawful sovereign.[46]

The recusant James Eustace (1530–85), third Viscount Baltinglass, also revolted in the summer of 1580 in the belief that an excommunicated Elizabeth I could not be a legitimate ruler.[47] English contemporaries were aware of his use of religion to attract rebels: in July of that year Captain Zouche wrote to Walsingham that he thought the 'Baltinglass rebellion the more dangerous because he coloureth it with religion'.[48] Christopher Maginn refers to it as a crusade, and it was supported by Catholic priests and arguments in favour of the restoration of Catholicism, but it did not gain wider recognition, nor the support of the pope.[49]

Arguably, the motives of individual leaders, and of the men who followed them, mattered little in defining a rebellion as a crusade. What mattered was papal support, and the spiritual rewards that marked out a conflict as a crusade, and rebellion under fitz Maurice and the earl of Desmond had both. Fitz Maurice declared that he fought for the pope and he and his followers were granted 'a plenary indulgence as conceded to crusaders to all who take up arms against Elizabeth', the same that was granted to the earl of Desmond on 13 May 1580.[50] This grant made it unequivocal. This was a crusade in the pope's eyes, and he recognized the earl of Desmond as '*Dux Exercitus Catholicorum in Hibernia*'.[51] In the words of Declan Downey, 'the Geraldine War ... assumed the

---

45 Ibid., iii, pp 1272–5; report of Walter Raleigh in John Pope Hennessey, *Sir Walter Ralegh in Ireland* (London, 1883), p. 209. 46 Hurlock, 'The crusades to 1291', 533; *AFM* pp 1632, 1654–5, 1665, 1797. 47 Marcus Tanner, *Ireland's holy wars: the struggle for a nation's soul, 1500–2000* (London, 2001), p. 100. 48 *CSP Ire.* ii, p. 237. 49 Christopher Maginn, 'The Baltinglass rebellion, 1580: English dissent or Gaelic uprising?', *Historical Journal*, 47 (2004), 205–32, at 215. 50 For fitz Maurice's indulgence, see King, *A primer*, iii, p. 1264; BL Lansdowne MS 96, f. 53; for Desmond's, see King, *A primer*, iii, pp 1273–5; see also M. Benventura, 'The Geraldine war: rebellion or crusade?', *Irish Ecclesiastical Record* 103 (1965), 148–57. 51 *Spicilegium Ossoriense*, ed. Patrick Francis Moran (Dublin, 1874), p. 81.

Crusading rhetoric and Anglo-Irish relations, c.1300–1600

mantle of the first counter-Reformation military crusade in Ireland'.[52] In reality, it was the first crusade of any kind in Ireland. This also made it potentially a more dangerous rebellion, crusade allowing for a more brutal war where no quarter need be given. However, it arguably meant that crusading in Anglo-Irish relations ended almost as soon as it began, the failure of these uprisings damaging the utility of crusading rhetoric in Anglo-Irish conflicts, and leaving other rebel leaders uneasy about using holy war for what was, generally speaking, political rebellion. As a result, Lennon concluded that fitz Maurice's death in 1579 'set back the cause of militant Catholicism in Ireland'.[53]

The final and most widespread rebellion to engulf Tudor Ireland broke out in 1595 against the expansion of English rule from the Pale. Its leadership was assumed by Hugh O'Neill, second earl of Tyrone (c.1550–1616), who was declared a traitor in June of that year (pl. 12.2). Tyrone was aggrieved by his lack of political control, and felt the only way to achieve independence was to free himself from association with English power. He had perhaps also been prompted to openly rebel by Philip II of Spain.[54] Tyrone was joined by Hugh Roe O'Donnell of Tyrconnel (1572–1602) and his followers, but also found support among Irish Catholics who opposed the spread of English Protestantism. The conflict assumed the tone of a crusading holy war, and had an international element, because these men sought support from Catholic Spain. Although Nicholas Canny argued that in the early part of the rebellion Tyrone was suspicious of religious motives, as early as 1591, at Tyrone's behest O'Donnell was in contact with Philip II, and two years later Archbishop Edmund Mauguran of Armagh appealed to the Spanish court for assistance for a crusade.[55] Moreover, at this time there were still shipwrecked Spanish sailors from the failed Armada of 1588 living in Ireland who were regularly petitioning the Spanish government for aid against the English; Tyrone was protecting them, much to the anger of the English government.[56] In 1593 the exiled Irishman Don John de Lacey also suggested that a military Order of St Patrick, modelled on the Order of Santiago, be set up to aid in the liberation of Ireland.[57] In 1595, Tyrone and O'Donnell made a joint appeal to Philip

52 Declan Downey, 'Purity of blood and purity of faith in early modern Ireland' in Alan Ford & John McCafferty (eds), *The origins of sectarianism in early modern Ireland* (Cambridge, 2005), pp 216–28, at p. 219. 53 Colm Lennon, *Sixteenth-century Ireland: the incomplete conquest* (Dublin, 1994), p. 316. 54 Philip's secretary, Don Juan de Idiáquez, suggested that Philip write to O'Neill 'to induce him to enter into the confederacy [of Irish Catholics] openly', *CSP Spain*, iv, p. 611. 55 John J. Silke, 'The Irish appeal of 1593 to Spain: some new light on the genesis of the Nine Years War', *Irish Ecclesiastical Record* 22 (1950), 278–90; Nicholas Canny, 'O'Neill, Hugh [Aodh Ó Néill], second earl of Tyrone (c.1550–1616)', *ODNB*. See also Darren McGettigan, *Red Hugh O'Donnell and the Nine Years War* (Dublin, 2017). 56 William Camden, *History of the most renowned and victorious Princess Elizabeth* (1615) (4th ed. London, 1688), pp 446–7. 57 Micheline Kerney Walsh, 'The military order of St Patrick, 1593', *Seanchas Ardmhacha* 9 (1979), 274–85, at 277.

II for aid, and in return offered to become his vassals and make Archduke Albert Prince of Ireland. Philip was initially encouraging, and by the summer Tyrone had adopted the Catholic cause, promising to support those aiding 'God's just cause'.[58] Although Tyrone had initially revolted in defence of his rights, he was persuaded to turn his cause into a religious one by Jesuits and other priests. The Irish rebellion had taken on a distinctly pro-Catholic stance by this time, so much so that a booklet was issued in Rome referring to the 'Catholic League' fighting in Ireland.[59]

In August 1596, Tyrone and O'Donnell wrote to the pope claiming to be fighting in defence of the Old Faith. Both men claimed that they had gained this faith through their mother's milk – that is, they had been Catholic since birth – although until the mid-1590s Tyrone's adherence to Catholicism was not particularly in evidence.[60] It is possible that he converted to Catholicism only in the mid-1590s; that, at least, is when he started to employ religious rhetoric in his political statements. Certainly, in this year Tyrone began to demand freedom of religious choice, and in 1597 he insisted on 'free libertie of conscience' but not the supremacy of Catholicism.[61] In 1599 he wrote to the Irish towns to exhort them to imitate the example of the French who did 'go against their natural king, and maintained wars until he was constrained to profess the Catholic religion,' and called for the reform of the clergy and restoration of the spiritual authority of the pope.[62] However, he was inconsistent and not wholly wedded to the idea.[63] He appears to have been aware of the suspicion with which his new-found faith was greeted, and later wrote that religion 'was not the cause which first moved me to think of war' but that, since he had received such 'Divine aid that so far I have had glorious success', he had vowed to God to fight against heresy and for the restoration of Catholicism.[64] The generous interpretation would be that he had been through a genuine conversion; the cynical one being that this was a ploy to justify his adoption of the rhetoric of militant Catholicism, which he recognized as 'a coagulant' that would bring his supporters together.[65]

Following the disastrous English loss at Yellow Ford in 1598, the earl of Essex was dispatched to Ireland as its new governor. He handled the situation

---

58 *CCM* iii, p. 179, no. 244. 59 Bernardino Beccari, *Relatione della Guerra d'Hibernia, tra la lega de' catholici di quel regno, & l'asserta reina d'Inghilterra* (Rome, 1596). 60 J. Hagan, 'Some papers relating to the Nine Years War', *Archivium Hibernicum* 2 (1913), 280–1. 61 NA, SP 63/201, no. 114, printed in Hiram Morgan, 'The 1597 ceasefire documents', *Dúiche Néill: Journal of the O'Neill Country Historical Society* (1997), 14–15. 62 J.P. Meehan, *Fate and fortunes of Hugh O'Neill, earl of Tyrone and Rory O'Donnell, earl of Tyrconnell* (Dublin, 1886), pp 21–3. 63 Hiram Morgan, *Tyrone's rebellion: the outbreak of the Nine Years War in Tudor Ireland* (Woodbridge, 1993), pp 198, 204. 64 *The Irish war of defence, 1598–1600: extracts from the De Hibernia insula commentaries of Peter Lombard, archbishop of Armagh*, ed. Matthew Byrne (Cork, 1930), pp 39–41. 65 Seán Ó Faolain, *The Great O'Neill: a biography of Hugh O'Neill, earl of Tyrone, 1550–1616* (Dublin, 1942), p. 177.

Crusading rhetoric and Anglo-Irish relations, c.1300–1600

badly, losing many of his men and deciding to try and negotiate with Tyrone alone. His failure and suspected overreaching led to his arrest. It was after this that Tyrone decided to adopt what Hiram Morgan called 'the full faith and fatherland approach'.[66] He threatened those who would not support him with excommunication, and declared that he was fighting against heresy and for the Catholic faith. In November 1599, Tyrone sent a lengthy document to Elizabeth I, listing his demands before peace could be met. The first seven clauses stressed Catholic identity, and Tyrone claimed that his aim was to establish Catholicism in Ireland.

Support for Tyrone's religiously defined war from outside Ireland was slow to materialize, despite the promise of Father James Archer, a keen promoter of the rebellion as a Catholic crusade, that Spanish forces were coming in October 1598.[67] According to Peter Lombard's *De regno Hiberniae, sanctorum insula, commentarius*, written in 1600 as a propaganda tract to gain papal support by Tyrone's agent at the papal court, Tyrone was the one pushing to turn the rebellion into a crusade, asking the pope for a papal nuncio who would support him and recognition that his followers were crusaders. He was fulfilling a prophecy in saving Ireland for Catholicism, and thus deserved the pope's support.[68] Whatever the origin, the association of the rebellion with faith was, perhaps unsurprisingly, denied by the English, when in December 1598 Sir Thomas Norreys told the privy council that in Ireland 'religion is pretended as a cause', and that as a result priests were 'taking upon them great authority from the pope' and 'incited the whole province', having proclaimed Pope Pius V's bull in Ireland.[69] The Old Englishmen in Ireland also said that they had not suffered religious persecution, and the Palesman said that they were all Catholics and had been long before O'Neill's conversion.[70] English Catholics believed that Tyrone was only using religion as an excuse to gain support for his personal interests.[71] Nor was papal support unequivocal. In January 1601 Pope Clement VIII recognized that Tyrone led the Catholic army and encouraged him in his enterprise, but did not order the Irish clergy to support him.[72] That September, the much-delayed Spanish support arrived in the form of about 3,500 men who landed at Kinsale. The Spanish and their Irish allies faced mounting problems and following a series of problems with the siege, the weather, and their numbers, they surrendered in January 1602 (pl. 12.3).

---

66 Hiram Morgan, '"Never any realm worse governed": Queen Elizabeth I and Ireland', *TRHS* 14 (2004), 295–308, at 307; Canning, *The Old English in early modern Ireland*, p. 51.   67 *CSP Ire.* vii, p. 343; James Corboy, 'Father James Archer, S.J., 1550–1625(?)', *Studies* 33 (1944), 99–107, at 106.   68 P. Lombard, *De regno Hiberniae, sanctorum insula, commentarius* (Louvain, 1623), pp 462–3.   69 *CSP Ire.* v, p. 400.   70 Brady, 'Politics, policy and power', p. 82.   71 Thomas M. McCoog, *The Society of Jesus in Ireland, Scotland and England, c.1598–1606: 'Lest our lamp be entirely extinguished'* (Leiden, 2017), p. 226.   72 *Pacata Hibernia*, ed. T. Stafford (Dublin, 1810), ii, pp 667–8.

176   *Ireland and the crusades*

Although Tyrone's rebellion attracted only limited practical papal support in the form of the force which landed at Kinsale, half the size of the one which Tyrone had requested, the papacy did offer formal recognition of the rebellion as a crusade by offering an indulgence to those who fought. On 18 April 1600, pope Clement VII granted an indulgence to those who:

> have long struggled to recover and preserve your liberty, first under James Geraldine, of good memory, who endeavoured to throw off the yoke of slavery imposed on you by the English, deserters from the Holy Roman Church, – then under John Geraldine, cousin of the said James, – and lastly under our beloved son, Hugh O'Neale [*sic*], styled Earl of Tyrone, Baron Dungannon, and captain general of the Catholic army in Ireland: we grant to all of you who follow and assist the said Hugh and the Catholic army, if you truly repent and confess, and if possible receive the holy communion, plenary pardon, and remission of all sins, – as usually granted to those setting out to the war against the Turks for the recovery of the Holy Land.[73]

This was the second and last conflict that could be called a crusade in Ireland and its association with war in the East was explicit.

The greatest impact of Tyrone's decision to adopt the language of crusade and seek papal support was the end of political freedom for Ireland's native rulers. His 'faith and fatherland' argument made the last Tudor rebellion in Ireland about more than just the Tudor state versus discontented rebels: by trying to turn themselves into crusaders, the Irish had made themselves a legitimate target for complete destruction by the English forces. Sir Walter Raleigh's views on those who adopted the crusade – that they were motivated by Mohammed and the vanity of the pope – was shared by many of his contemporaries, and crusade was seen as a wholly illegitimate form of war.[74] In 1603, Tyrone surrendered, and he fled into exile four years later; in 1609, the Protestant settlement of Ulster began, and Irish dreams of Catholic resurgence were lost.[75]

In trying to turn politically motivated rebellion against the English in Ireland into a holy war, the Irish were simply using methods that the English

---

73 Lambeth Palace Library MS 608, f. 84.   74 Walter Raleigh, 'A discourse of the original and fundamental cause of natural, necessary, and unnatural war' in *Works of Sir Walter Ralegh* [*sic*], eds W. Oldys & T. Birch. 8 vols (Oxford, 1829), viii, pp 253–97. The only legitimate form of warfare for English Protestant thinkers was that called for by princes. Stephen Gosson, *The trumpet of warre: a sermon preached at Paules Crosse the seuenth of Maie 1598* (London, 1598), f. 29v.   75 Oliver P. Rafferty, *Catholicism in Ulster, 1603–1983: an interpretive history* (London, 1994), pp 8–11.

Crusading rhetoric and Anglo-Irish relations, c.1300–1600

had used against them from the mid-twelfth century onwards. But they succeeded in achieving something that the appeals of the 1330s and 1420s did not: the Irish finally secured papal backing for crusades in Ireland, fully supported by the papacy with the full remission of sins for those who fought. The papacy did not support the use of the crusade in Ireland before then because to do so would have meant using the full force of the Church against fellow Catholics, in what was essentially a series of disputes about rule, not religion. The fact that so many conflicts, and proposed conflicts, before that of James fitz Maurice used the language of crusade was a legacy of the twelfth-century conquest and the language used against the Irish, which portrayed them as irreligious and in need of firm rule. Similar language arose, to a lesser degree, in England's conflicts with the Welsh and the Scottish; in the latter case, the English had petitioned the pope to launch a crusade against the Scots in 1321 as part of the ongoing war, but met with no success.[76] That the language of crusading continued in Anglo-Irish relations is a reflection of the fact that the conquest of 1169 was never satisfactorily completed, and that English control was still disputed in the sixteenth century when the break with Rome allowed the Irish to turn the language of Anglo-Irish relations around, and use it against the English.

---

76 National Archives, C 47/27/12/3. Petition of the English ambassadors at Rome for the proclamation of a crusade.

13 / A Dublin 'crusader'

EMER PURCELL

'Everyone knows now that the cross-legged crusader theory is long since exploded.'[1] So wrote Arthur Vicars in the late nineteenth century; however, the tradition that one of the mummies in the crypt of St Michan's church is a crusader persists today.

St Michan's is located on Church Street, on the north side of Dublin city (pls 13.1 and 13.2).[2] In the medieval period the street was known as Oxmantown Street, and was the main thoroughfare leading to the town on the south bank. The name of the suburb, Oxmantown, reflects the tradition that the area was settled by the Ostmen when they were expelled from within the walls by the Anglo-Normans in 1170.[3] The traditional foundation date of St Michan's is 1095, but this is based on a sixteenth-century account by Meredith Hanmer.[4] The present church was built in 1683–6 and was to remain the only parish church on the north side of the river until the foundation of St Paul's and St Mary's in 1697.[5]

Where the tradition of a crusader mummy in St Michan's church originated has proven impossible to trace. The remains, still affectionately identified to visitors as a 'crusader' mummy, are tall and the legs are broken but crossed (pl. 13.3). Historically, crossed legs were thought to reflect the symbol of the crusades, the cross, and inferred that the individual had been on crusade, an interpretation which seems to have originated in the sixteenth century.[6] The tradition of the St Michan 'crusader' is particularly interesting considering that the crusades and crusaders feature so little in contemporary or near

---

1 Arthur Vicars, *An account of the antiseptic vaults beneath S. Michan's church Dublin* (Dublin, 1888), p. 6. Reviewed in *British Medical Journal* 2:1458 (1888), 1291–2. 2 The origins of St Michan and the early medieval church likewise are a something of a puzzle, for some initial considerations see Emer Purcell, 'Michan: saint, cult and church' in John Bradley, Alan Fletcher & Anngret Simms (eds), *Dublin in the medieval world* (Dublin, 2009), pp 119–40. 3 Emer Purcell, 'The expulsion of the Ostmen, 1169–1170: the documentary evidence', *Peritia*, 17–18 (2003–4), 273–94. Ostmen is used in late medieval Irish sources to refer to the descendants of the vikings who had settled in Ireland. 4 James Ware (ed.), *Ancient Irish histories: the works of Spencer, Campion, Hanmer and Marleburrough*. 2 vols (Dublin, 1809), ii, p. 194. 5 Henry, F. Berry (ed.), *The registers of the church of St Michan, Dublin, 1636–1685* (Dublin, 1907), iii, part 1, p. x; Maurice Craig, *Dublin, 1660–1860* (London, 1992). p. 41; H.J. Lawlor, 'Notes on the church of St Michan's, Dublin', *JRSAI* 16 (1926), 11–21, at 12. The church underwent substantial alterations in the nineteenth century. 6 Oliver Harris, 'Antiquarian attitudes: crossed legs, crusaders and the evolution of an idea', *Antiquaries Journal*, 90 (2010), 401–40. For a full discussion of the cross-legged phenomenon see Dave Swift, chapter 11, this volume.

A Dublin 'crusader'

contemporary Irish sources. One of the few sources where references to the crusades can be found are the annals that are said to have originated from a chronicle written in St Mary's abbey.[7] That abbey, a Cistercian house, was located on the east side of the Oxmantown suburb.[8] Another religious foundation in the suburb was the Dominican priory, and as Paul Duffy outlines, the Dominican order was associated in particular with the Cathar Crusade.[9]

Maurice Craig argued that the layout of the vaults of St Michan's tallies with the Renaissance plan of the church. He suggested that the new St Michan's – built in the 1680s – was probably larger than its medieval predecessor and that it was certainly broader.[10] He boldly stated in his account of the church that the 'crusader' is not a crusader and that the remains most likely date to the early modern period.[11] Tadhg O'Keeffe, on a visit to the church, has pointed out a number of features which suggest that the present St Michan's has a very complex architectural history.[12] Closer examination of the vaults led him to suggest that the entrance steps, located at the junction of the chancel and nave, might be older than the vaults themselves. They are set slightly to the east of the junction with the nave, suggesting that they could follow the alignment of an earlier church. The south side of the chancel wall is slightly longer than the north in order to accommodate these steps.

The skeletal remains in the crypt of St Michan's church were the subject of much discussion in the nineteenth century. Vicars was very clear in his analysis:[13]

> It is popularly received idea that these bodies are several hundred years old, and people go even so far as to say the body of a man with his legs crossed in the coffin nearest the wall is a crusader. The absurdity of this wild notion is obvious when we look at the coffins, which we have reasons for thinking are the original ones in which the bodies were first placed. They are of the ordinary shape of the present day, of which I believe I am correct in stating one of the earliest examples known is that of Lancelot, Bishop of Winchester, buried in 1626 in S. Saviour's Southwark, whose coffin was discovered in 1830 (Gent.'s Mag., Aug., 1830, p. 171). Everyone knows now that the cross-legged crusader theory is long since exploded.[14]

---

7 Hurlock, 'The crusades to 1291', 520; *CSMA*. 8 St Mary's was originally a Benedictine House but changed to Cistercian rule in 1148. 9 Paul Duffy, 'The exiled earl and soon-to-be saint', *HI* 24: 5 (2016), 16–19; see also Paul Duffy, chapter 5, this volume. 10 Craig, *Dublin*, p. 41. 11 Ibid., p. 41. 12 I visited the church with Professor Tadhg O'Keeffe, Department of Archaeology, UCD in 1995. 13 Laurence Tait, 'The anti-septic vaults at St Michan's', *British Medical Journal*, 2: 1460 (1888), 1416. 14 Vicars, *An account of the antiseptic vaults*, p. 6.

There was considerable debate as to why the remains were so well preserved. It was often attributed to the limestone in the walls, which might have allowed air to circulate more freely. Another suggestion was:

> that it is due to the tannin in the earthen floors of the vaults, as the ground on which S. Michan's is built was anciently a vast oak forest, and not very long ago known as Oxmantown Wood. Certain it is that the floor of the vaults does not show the slightest sign of damp, but, on the contrary, is of a pale yellow earth, fine and dry.[15]

Hanmer, writing in the sixteenth century, recorded another interesting tradition: that oak from woods on Oxmantown Green was used in the construction of the roof of Westminster Hall:

> From hence, William Rufus, Anno 1098, by licence of Murchad [Muirchertach Ua Briain] had that frame that made up the roofe of Westminster Hall, where no English spider webbeth or breedeth to this day.[16]

In 1832, the *Dublin Penny Journal* recounted a contemporary visit to the crypt, where one of the other mummies was said to be a nun:

> In one vault we are shown the remains of a nun, who died at the advanced age of 111; the body has now been thirty years in the mansion of death; and although there is scarcely a remnant of the coffin, the body is as completely preserved as if it had been embalmed, with the exception of the hair.[17]

In 1888 Lawson Tait wrote that:

> One of the mummies is said (by the attendant) to be a nun of the twelfth century, and the fingers of the body are perfectly pliable, so that mere desiccation does not account for the peculiar preservation of the bodies.[18]

We can see how this tradition evolved in the space of fifty years or so. In 1832 it seems she was interred for thirty years, but by 1888 one of the attendants was claiming that she dated back to the twelfth century.

15 Ibid., p. 10.   16 Hanmer, *Chronicle*, ii pp 194–5. However, Hanmer must be read with some caution on these matters.   17 Anon., 'St Michan's church', *Dublin Penny Journal* 2: 79 (1834), 209–10.   18 Tait, 'The anti-septic vaults at St Michan's'.

Oxmantown, like most localities, possessed its fair share of local legends. For example, Richard Stanihurst, writing in the sixteenth century, maintained that Little John, after the disbandment of Robin Hood and his merry men, came to live on Oxmantown Green. Allegedly he was often enticed by the local inhabitants to display his archery skills, and one day he shot an arrow from the bridge to Arbour Hill. Hence in Queen Elizabeth's time it was recorded that there 'standeth in Oxmantowne Green a little hillock named 'Little John's Shot'.[19] Stanihurst also recorded stories of a local man called Scaldbrother who was a nimble young thief who raided the streets of Oxmantown.[20] He avoided capture by retreating into a maze of caverns he had carved out for himself beneath Oxmantown Green; these became known as Scaldbrother's Hole.[21] According to Frederick Falkiner this legend continued to circulate among the boys of the Free School of King Charles, founded in 1663.[22] This school was located on the east side of Oxmantown Green. Nathaniel Burton, writing in the nineteenth century, related how these caverns, created by Scaldbrother, were later used as vats by the brewery located in Smithfield.[23] The legend of Scaldbrother persisted in the suburb for over four centuries. These traditions can be traced to late medieval/early modern sources. Unfortunately, I was unable to find any such references to the tradition of a crusader mummy in St Michan's, but one can see from the above how such a tradition could have taken root in this area.

The 'crusader' has most recently featured in the Irish media because its head was stolen in 2019.[24] The headlines that circulated around the 2019 robbery included RTÉ's report '800-year-old "crusader" at Dublin church decapitated' and the *Irish Times*' 'St Michan's reopens to public after restoration of crusader's head'.[25] News of the theft spread internationally, with an article in the *New York Times*: 'Stolen head of 800-year-old crusader is found by Dublin police'.[26] In actual fact, the thief himself returned both heads, and as part of the investigation the National Museum of Ireland carried out some conservation work on both skulls. Carol Smith of the National Museum of Ireland reports that during conservation of the 'crusader' head there was a very strong aromatic smell suggesting the use of embalming oils. The second skull

---

19 Liam Miller & Eileen Power (eds), *Holinshed's Irish chronicle: the historie of Ireland from the first inhabitation thereof, unto the yeare 1509 collected by R. Holinshed & continued till the yeare 1547 by R. Stanihurst* (Dublin, 1979), pp 50–1; Nathaniel Burton, *Oxmantown and its environs: or some suburban sketches of the eighteenth century* (Dublin, 1845), p. 15. 20 *Holinshed's Irish chronicle*: pp 50–1. 21 Ibid. 22 Frederick R. Falkiner, *The foundation of the hospital and free school of King Charles II, Oxmantown, Dublin* (Dublin, 1906), pp 24, 210. 23 Burton, *Oxmantown and its environs*, p. 16. 24 *RTÉ News*, 25 Feb. 2019, https://www.rte.ie/news/dublin/2019/0225/1032776-st-michans-crypt-crusader/, accessed 22 Dec. 2020. 25 *Irish Times*, 19 July 2019, https://www.irishtimes.com/news/social-affairs/religion-and-beliefs/st-michan-s-reopens-to-public-after-restoration-of-crusader-s-head-1.3951673, accessed 22 Dec. 2020. 26 *New York Times*, 6 Mar. 2091, https://www.nytimes.com/2019/03/06/world/europe/crusader-mummy-dublin-head.html, accessed 2 Apr. 2021.

stolen also gave off a similar smell and the head was also extremely heavy, which again might suggest embalming.[27] The presence of these oils meant that carbon-14 dating of the heads was not possible.

Curiously, this was not first time that a head was stolen from St Michan's crypts. It was recorded in the nineteenth century that:

> it seems that many years ago someone stole the head of John Sheares for a wager; and great was the wonderment caused at that time by its sudden disappearance. But through the agency of the late Dr. Madden, M.R.I.A., it was restored, and the remains of both brothers placed in lead and oak coffins in 1853.[28]

The Sheares brothers, John and Henry, were both United Irishmen who took part in the 1798 Rebellion and were interred in the crypts.[29]

Although the 'crusader' tradition was first rejected in the nineteenth century, it has had a long and lasting currency. And thus, in a way, the tradition has come to have acquired a validity of its own, and one which is dearly held by Dubliners, as was evident by the support and efforts of the local community when the head was stolen.[30]

As we have seen, traditions associating romantic medieval figures with the area were common in the early modern period. We have also seen clear evidence of the evolution of a narrative surrounding the figure of the purported nun whose antiquity is seen to have been exaggerated over the span of a few decades in the mid-nineteenth century. This is precisely the time when the Victorian fascination with the concept of the medieval was resulting in a revival of interest in ideas such as chivalry and crusade. Was the crossing of the legs of the St Michan's 'crusader' accidental? Or was it a deliberate action to add to the process of myth-making by somebody familiar with beliefs surrounding the cross-legged pose and crusaders? All that said, the age of the St Michan's 'crusader' cannot be conclusively gained through carbon-14 dating, leaving perhaps the slightest margin for doubt. The mystery of the origins of St Michan's church itself and of the tradition of the 'crusader' still prove of interest to the local community and scholars, and tourists are still drawn to visit the crypts.

It is perhaps beyond coincidence that the most enduring tradition relating to the crusades in Dublin is associated with a church that was purportedly established in 1095 – the very year of Pope Urban II's call to arms and the birth of the crusading movement.

---

27 Carol Smith, NMI (personal communication).　28 Vicars, *An account of the antiseptic vaults*, p. 9.　29 There is also a tradition that one of the supposed burial places of Robert Emmet is in the cemetery attached to St Michan's.　30 *Irish Times*, 19 July 2019.

14 / Epilogue: commanderies, crusades, frontiers

TADHG O'KEEFFE

In the opening paper in this collection, 'Ireland and the crusades: surveying the field', Edward Coleman discusses the historiography of two interlinked themes. The larger theme (though the lesser in terms of the volume of earlier literature) is the place of Ireland within the world of crusading. With this theme, the view from Ireland is outward: crusading activity, however it is defined, brought people *away* from where they lived. Ireland, prior to the Tudor period, was not a recognized crusading venue in itself (unlike, say, the Baltic lands, or southern France), but it was a place from which some individuals ventured as crusaders, and a place where former crusaders settled and could recount their experiences fighting for God. The other theme, which has a more substantial historiography, is the presence in medieval Ireland of the two great military-religious orders of crusader origin, the Knights Templar and Knights Hospitaller.[1] With this theme, the Irish perspective is inward: these orders came to Ireland, carrying with them some of the crusader *mentalité* (even if, as is likely, some of the members of the orders who came to Ireland had never actually been on crusade themselves). Looking to the future, it is reasonable to hope that this present volume and the earlier *Soldiers of Christ* edited volume, widely referenced herein, will together come to be regarded by future historiographers as key works in the study of these two matters.[2] One can be sure, though, that separately or together, these volumes will not contain the final words: tiresome though it is to repeat a familiar truism, more work is needed on almost all of the major issues which are discussed. My aim in this closing paper is to flag two such issues.

The first issue has an empirical base. It concerns the corpus of evidence that most directly connects Ireland to the crusades in Outremer, the land 'outside [beyond] the sea', meaning the land to the east of the Mediterranean:[3] the archaeology of the buildings of military-religious commanderies (or

---

1 The order of St Thomas of Acre had two possessions in Ireland, both pre-existing hospitals: Eric St John Brooks, 'Irish possessions of St Thomas of Acre', *PRIA* 58C (1956), 21–44. 2 Browne & Ó Clabaigh (eds), *Soldiers of Christ*. Note also the edited collection of papers on the Irish link with the so-called Albigensian Crusade: Duffy et al., *From Carrickfergus to Carcassonne*. 3 *Outremer* was a contemporary term describing the four Frankish states established in Syria and Palestine by the First Crusade (1096–9).

183

preceptories).[4] Some comments on how the Irish evidence compares with the evidence outside Ireland have already been published.[5] Here, I offer an expansion of those comments, less to arrive at a new narrative than to show the potential for one.

The second issue is more conceptual, and the discussion more reflective: the medieval frontier. Most historians would doubtless agree with the assertion that 'the crusading movement was from the first a frontier activity'.[6] Accordingly, the concept of frontier is encountered very frequently in the literature on medieval crusading, whether Levantine, Iberian or northern European/Baltic (although it is not a feature of the literature on the crusades against the Cathar heretics). I suspect that every university teacher of Ireland's Middle Ages, whether historian, archaeologist or historical geographer, who has brought a group of students to see the site of the Hospitaller commandery at Kilteel, Co. Kildare, located in the north-western foothills of the Wicklow mountains, has used the term 'frontier' in explaining why the Hospitallers were there in the first place. The concept is used for non-crusader medieval contexts too, of course, and it features especially prominently in the literature on medieval Ireland, where the focus has largely been on the island's internal frontiers, created by colonial expansion into native lands in the late twelfth and thirteenth centuries. In truth, 'frontier' is a very hackneyed concept by now. But overfamiliarity with it does not mean that it is a fully understood concept, nor does it mean that its value as an explanatory model has been exhausted. My discussion of the frontier in this closing chapter is a rumination on how the deployment of the concept, within and without the context of Christian crusading, might inform future discourse on Ireland's

See Alan V. Murray, 'Outremer' in Alan V. Murray (ed.), *The crusades: an encyclopedia* (Santa Barbara, 2006), iii, pp 910–12. For an interesting recent perspective on Outremer, see Uri Zvi Shachar, '"Re-orienting" *Estoires d'Outremer*: the Arabic context of the Saladin legend' in Laura K. Morreale & Nicholas L. Paul (eds), *The French of Outremer: communities and communications in the crusading Mediterranean* (New York, 2018), pp 150–78. Note how, although crusading provoked *jihad*, the Muslims of Outremer did not chronicle crusading as a specific event, or a distinct category of historical event, until the early sixteenth century: P.M. Holt, *The crusader states and their neighbours, 1098–1291* (London & New York, 2016), pp 17–18. **4** I have opted to use the term 'commandery' in preference to 'preceptory'. The nature of these establishments, with clarification of their functions, is usefully discussed in Jean-Marie Carbasse, 'Les commanderies: aspects juridiques et institutionnels' in Anthony Luttrell & Léon Pressouyre (eds), *La commanderie, institution des ordres militaires dans l'Occident médiéval* (Paris, 2002), 19–27. **5** Eamonn Cotter, 'The archaeology of the Irish Hospitaller preceptories of Mourneabbey and Hospital in context', in Browne & Ó Clabaigh, *Soldiers of Christ*, pp 103–23; Tadhg O'Keeffe & Pat Grogan, 'Building a frontier? The architecture of the military orders in medieval Ireland' in Browne & Ó Clabaigh, *Soldiers of Christ*, pp 81–102. Tadhg O'Keeffe & Paolo Virtuani, 'Reconstructing Kilmainham: the topography and architecture of the chief priory of the Knights Hospitaller in Ireland, c.1170–1349', *JMH* 46 (2020), 449–77. **6** Ann Williams, 'Crusaders as frontiersmen: the case of the order of St John in the Mediterranean' in Daniel Power & Naomi Standen (eds), *Frontiers in question: Eurasian borderlands, 700–1700* (Basingstoke, 1999), pp 209–27, at p. 209.

Epilogue: commanderies, crusades, frontiers   185

place within Europe. It is a rumination invited by the presence of the military-religious orders in Ireland,[7] but cannot be confined to them.

IRELAND IN EUROPE: ARCHAEOLOGY AND THE
MILITARY-RELIGIOUS ORDERS REVISITED

The discipline with the greatest potential to transform our knowledge of Ireland's crusader past through new data is, of course, archaeology. The reader might immediately assume me to mean, simply, that more archaeological investigation is needed on the military-religious sites in Ireland. The archaeology of those sites was discussed in three contributions to *Soldiers of Christ*.[8] It features less prominently in this volume because the earlier coverage was comprehensive; very little new work has been carried out in the seven years between that publication and this.[9] It hardly needs to be spelled out that geophysical investigations and targeted excavations would enhance our understanding of the sites. But recovering site-plans and dating sequences of buildings at military-religious order sites should not be the sole ambition of such work. There is also, for example, an 'economic archaeology' to be retrieved.[10] The investigation of other (non-Templar, non-Hospitaller) sites with crusader connections is no less desirable – by this I mean sites occupied by individuals who had been on crusade – but it is desirable only insofar as archaeological work at any medieval site is desirable: failing the discovery of souvenir items from overseas, it is inherently unlikely that archaeological work at properties associated with one-time crusaders will ever tell us much about their crusader lives.[11]

---

7 The relationship between frontier studies as a sub-field of medieval research in its own right, and the study of the military-religious orders (as the 'face' of the crusades), is rarely discussed in the literature. An important exception is Nikolas Jaspert, 'Military orders at the frontier: permeability and demarcation' in Jochen Schenk & Mike Carr (eds), *The military orders: culture and conflict in western and northern Europe* (London, 2017), pp 3–28.   8 Cotter, 'The archaeology of the Irish Hospitaller preceptories'; O'Keeffe & Grogan, 'Building a frontier?'; O'Conor & Naessens, 'Temple House', pp 124–51; for a re-reading of the Temple House structure as a chamber tower rather than a 'hall-house', see Tadhg O'Keeffe, *Medieval Irish buildings, 1100–1600* (Dublin, 2015), pp 167–8.   9 The exception is O'Keeffe & Virtuani, 'Reconstructing Kilmainham'.   10 The economy of the military orders in Ireland requires further study. The potential is shown in Margaret Murphy's important paper, 'Evidence for Templar agriculture in medieval Ireland' in Browne & Ó Clabaigh, *Soldiers of Christ*, pp 167–83. Differences between Hospitaller and Templar economies in Ireland require investigation; note how in Essex, for example, the Templars were 'staunch manorialists' and the Hospitallers 'predominantly farmers of rents and tithes' (Michael Gervers, '*Pro defensione Terre Sancte*: the development and exploitation of the Hospitallers' landed estate in Essex' in Malcolm Barber (ed.), *The military orders: fighting for the faith and caring for the sick* (London, 2016), pp 3–20, at p. 19). Do such differences have archaeological fingerprints?   11 A case in point is Trim, Co. Meath, where works associated with Geoffrey de Geneville (see McDonnell, this vol.) have been excavated: Alan R. Hayden, *Trim Castle, Co. Meath: excavations, 1995–8* (Dublin, 2000), *passim*; Finola O'Carroll,

But more archaeological work in Outremer itself has the potential to transform our understanding of the place of Ireland within the world of crusading. To be clear, it is not the structural or the material-cultural evidence from military-religious sites that might cast the most light on Ireland. The fact that the orders' missions in the far west of Europe did not compare with their missions in the far east of Europe[12] should disabuse us of any expectation of finding many material links. Rather, it is the burial record. Strontium and oxygen isotope analysis of excavated burials from the kingdom of Jerusalem has begun to reveal the likely birth-places in western Europe of those who settled permanently in the region.[13] For every individual who returned to (or settled in) Ireland having been on a crusade in the Holy Land, there was doubtless another who did not return. How many died in combat there and were buried there? It is entirely conceivable that some remained in Outremer, living and dying among other foreigners in one of the Frankish urban or rural settlements.[14]

Before turning back to Ireland, a certain clarity is needed in respect of the scope of archaeology in the study of the world of crusading. Looking to Outremer, the crusader venue where most archaeological work has been done, there is not one archaeology but multiple, imbricated, archaeologies. One such archaeology is specifically that of the acts of crusading. It pertains to the archaeological record which was created in the context of crusader warfare. This sub-field is dominated traditionally by the study of the castles, but that has certainly changed in recent years.[15] There are also archaeologies of the indigenous peoples of the region – Jews and Christians, as well as Muslims – independent of the context of war.[16] And there is also an archaeology of new European settlement in the region; not everybody of western European

'The Blackfriars preachers, Trim, Co. Meath and the legacy of Geoffrey de Geneville' in Małgorzata Krasnodebska-D'Aughton, Edel Bhreathnach & Keith Smith (eds), *Monastic Europe: medieval communities, landscapes and settlements* (Turnhout, 2019), pp 121–53. In neither case does the archaeology say anything about Geoffrey's crusader experience. The possibility that the gatehouse at Carrickfergus Castle, Co. Antrim, was inspired by structures encountered by Hugh de Lacy II while on crusade against the Cathars has been explored by Paul Duffy ('The architecture of defiance', *AI* 29: 1 (2015), 20–3; idem, 'From Carcassonne to Carrickfergus: the legacy of de Lacy's crusade experience in Britain and Ireland' in Duffy et al., *From Carrickfergus to Carcassonne*, pp 295–328, at pp 316–20). This is a rare instance in which such a claim can be made. **12** See, for example, Christie Majoros-Dunnahoe, 'Through the local lens: re-examining the function of the Hospitallers in England' in Jochen Schenk & Mike Carr (eds), *The military orders: culture and conflict in western and northern Europe* (London, 2017), pp 111–20. **13** See, for example, Piers D. Mitchell & Andrew R. Millard, 'Migration to the medieval Middle East with the crusades', *American Journal of Physical Anthropology* 140: 3 (2009), 518–25. **14** Ronnie Ellenblum, *Frankish rural settlement in the Latin kingdom of Jerusalem* (Cambridge, 1998). **15** Adrian J. Boas, *Crusader archaeology: the material culture of the Latin east* (London & New York, 1999); Mathias Piana & Christer Carlsson (eds), *Archaeology and architecture of the military orders: new studies* (Farnham, 2014). **16** A. Asa Eger (ed.), *The archaeology of medieval Islamic frontiers from the Mediterranean to the Caspian Sea* (Louisville, 2019).

Epilogue: commanderies, crusades, frontiers

descent who lived in the region – whether Frankish, Norman/Anglo-Norman, German or Italian – was a crusader, and not every 'western' settlement in the region was defended against possible Muslim aggression.[17] So, the archaeology of the military-religious orders constitutes, then, only one category within the broad field of 'crusader archaeology', even if it is, naturally, the dominant category in scholarship on crusader culture in western Europe.

There are two observations to make about military-religious archaeology. The first is that it is not a self-contained category (or, better phrased, a category with a discrete archaeological fingerprint). The Templars and Hospitallers, who were not the only military-religious orders but who dominate the conversation, were both monastic *and* military, so their built-works fall within the boundaries of the study of ecclesiastical architecture and castle architecture respectively, sometimes simultaneously. Each of those areas of research has its own history of work, its own modern research questions, and its own specialized language. To illustrate the point, the same corporate body – the Hospitallers in this case – was responsible for the hospital of St John and the other buildings within a complex in the heart of Jerusalem, on the one hand, and the extraordinary fortress of Crac des Chevaliers in Syria, on the other. The second observation follows naturally from the illustration just given. The archaeology of the military-religious orders is so dominated by the architectural evidence that it barely has an identity independent of architectural history. Thus, for example, the massive *Dictionnaire européen des orders militaires au moyen âge*, published just over a decade ago and containing entries by almost 240 writers, contains entries on the fortified and religious architectures of the orders but has no entry that specifically addresses the archaeology.[18]

We are still a long way off a comprehensive account of military-religious architecture in Ireland. None of the archaeological sites associated with the two orders in Ireland, including Mourneabbey, Co. Cork, which has seen archaeological excavation,[19] has seen investigation on the scale even close to what is desirable as a minimum. When such work is eventually carried out, we should anticipate it yielding more questions than answers. Unlike on a Cistercian site, for example, we simply cannot predict what buildings we might find on a Hospitaller or Templar site, much less their organization relative to each other.[20] I want to explore this issue further here.

---

17 Ellenblum, *Frankish rural settlement.*   **18** Nicole Bériou & Philippe Josserand (eds), *Prier et combattre: dictionnaire européen des orders militaires au moyen âge* (Paris, 2009).   **19** Cotter, 'The archaeology of the Irish Hospitaller preceptories', pp 106–17.   **20** Note Pál Ritoók's remark that 'it is not possible to identify a specifically Templar architecture in England. The architecture of their rural dwellings did not differ from manors of wealthy landlords or monastic granges such as those of the Cistercians' ('The architecture of the Knights Templar in England' in Malcolm Barber (ed.), *The military orders: fighting for the faith and caring for the sick* (London, 2016), pp 167–78, at p. 176).

The best evidence in Ireland for how a Hospitaller site was organized spatially and functionally is preserved in the early fourteenth-century *Registrum de Kilmainham* from the Hospitaller priory of Kilmainham, Co. Dublin.[21] It tells us that there was an inner and an outer enclosure. Formal, probably orthogonal, planning around a courtyard is attested to in the various entries pertaining to the priory's topography (pl. 14.1). Such planning, which seems to have allowed the priory's inner enclosure to resemble some actual crusader castles,[22] might have been a feature of Kilmainham alone, it being the chief house of the order in Ireland. We have no knowledge of the layout of the chief Templar house at Clontarf, but it too might have been a one-off, reflecting its contemporaneity with Kilmainham and its special status in Templar Ireland.

The physical remains at Temple House, Co. Sligo (Templar), the only military-religious order site in Ireland with substantial remains of domestic architecture, suggest that, as at Kilmainham, there was also some formal planning of an inner precinct involving a central courtyard: the surviving chamber tower (the so-called 'hall-house'), gate-tower and short stretch of curtain wall relate to each other spatially in a manner which suggests there was a small court.[23] If Temple House had indeed a courtyard plan, one cannot say that it intentionally reflected the claustral planning of contemporary monasteries: courtyards were features of all types of medieval settlement complex, and in such complexes the buildings were commonly parallel and perpendicular to each other.[24] Complicating matters, the remains at Mourneabbey, Hospitaller rather than Templar, which are the most extensive above-ground at any military order site in Ireland, offer no hints that there was any courtyard around which any of its buildings could have been distributed.[25]

The documentary record for an outer enclosure at Kilmainham, combined with the observed size of the area enclosed within a wall at Mourneabbey, and possibly also with the evidence that some of the other sites (Kilteel, most notably) were also extensive, leads one to imagine that the commandary precincts were larger spatially than those of most contemporary (earlier thirteenth-century) castles in Ireland, and that they possibly compared better with the larger bawn-walled castles of the later Middle Ages. That is not to suggest that they were crammed with buildings, but merely that they enclosed large areas. One is led towards the same conclusion about enclosure size (but not necessarily about building density) by the excavated evidence at Clerkenwell

---

21 O'Keeffe & Virtuani, 'Reconstructing Kilmainham'.   22 Ellenblum, *Crusader castles and modern histories*, 183–5.   23 For the plan, see O'Conor & Naessens, 'Temple House', pls 8, 9.   24 A case in point is Rincrew, Co. Waterford, a secular 'manorial' complex which was once identified incorrectly as a Templar castle: see Cotter et al., 'A blow to the temple', 163–78.   25 For the plan, see Cotter, 'The archaeology of the Irish Hospitaller preceptories', fig. 6.2.

Epilogue: commanderies, crusades, frontiers						189

(London) and South Witham (Lincolnshire), English sites of the Hospitallers and Templars, respectively.[26] Collectively, all of this evidence would suggest that the shapes of commanderies were variable.

In thinking about the plans of commanderies, we should separate those elements which were central to their 'institutional' functions – the churches and the domestic/administrative provisions – from elements such as the bakeries and the barns. The former buildings occupied the cores of commanderies, and those core spaces were probably neither large nor complex; the buildings associated with food production, or manufacturing, were not in the cores but outside them, often within outer enclosures (as seems to have been the case at Kilmainham). In eschewing the cloister garths as the spaces around which their commandery inner-precinct plans were to be organized, the Templars and Hospitallers arguably revealed their self-perception as soldiers who were monastics, as distinct from monastics who were also soldiers: they embraced the freedom to place their churches and residential/administrative structures wherever they wanted them, ignoring any imperative to follow claustral planning. Thus, a Hospitaller moving from one commandery to another would not expect to know his way around the new venue in the way that a re-locating Cistercian or mendicant friar would do.

Nonetheless, the practice of establishing commanderies in Europe, far from the Holy Land's theatre of war, might have led to some consistency. Continental sites, for example, show a common propensity to place the critical buildings side-by-side, and to incorporate the residential/administrative functions into multi-roomed, two-storeyed, blocks.[27] In some southern Scandinavian sites, long buildings run parallel to the churches, and it is not clear whether they were dormitories or hospitals, or indeed something else,[28] but the important point is that they and the churches associated with them were close together, sometimes side-by-side. Here, then, we are drawn back to Temple House. The remains there do not allow a reconstruction of the original layout, but it is conceivable that there was a small complex of buildings around a central courtyard and within a tight space, with a missing chapel and

---

26 Barney Sloane & Gordon Malcolm, *Excavations at the priory of the Order of the Hospital of St John of Jerusalem, Clerkenwell, London* (London, 2004); Philip Mayes, *Excavations at a Templar preceptory, South Witham, Lincolnshire 1965–67* (London, 2002).   **27** See, for example, Tréton Rodrigue, 'L'organisation topographique de la commanderie du Masdéu en Roussillon', *Archéologie du Midi médiéval* 28 (2010), 271–95; Damien Carraz & Sophie Aspord-Mercier, 'Le programme architectural d'un pôle seigneurial: la commanderie de Montfrin (Gard)', *Archéologie du Midi médiéval* 28 (2010), 297–315; Bellomo, Elena, 'The *cabrei* of the Order of Malta as an archaeological source: some notes on Piedmont' in Mathias Piana & Christer Carlsson (eds), *Archaeology and architecture of the military orders: new studies* (Farnham, 2014), pp 7–18.   **28** Christer Carlsson, 'Varne Hospitaller commandery: an archaeological field project' in Piana & Carlsson, *Archaeology and architecture of the military orders*, pp 19–27.

190   *Ireland and the crusades*

a missing hall to go with the chamber tower, and outside it a larger enclosure with less-formalized planning.

Finally, in this section, I want to comment on the churches of the military-religious orders. One of the striking features of the Kilmainham site, insofar as the *Registrum de Kilmainham* can be trusted to contain a fairly complete audit of structures, is the absence of a principal or focal church into which the entire community (including the corrodians) could gather. Instead, there were private chapels.[29] This underscores Kilmainham's essentially non-monastic character. There was an inner courtyard, and this was described as a *castrum* as late as the fourteenth century, suggesting that the compound was perceived by the Hospitallers themselves as primarily military. In 'castle-culture', to coin a phrase, chapels were not communal (and certainly were not parochial) but were places of private worship. It is still curious, though, that there was no church in the Kilmainham enclosure catering to its entire community. It is difficult to know whether Kilmainham was exceptional in this regard. At Mourneabbey are the ruins of a reasonably substantial and free-standing church inside the precinct. Also, at Crooke, Co. Waterford (Templar), there is enough evidence to suggest that the fragmentary church (smaller than that at Mourneabbey) was also free-standing within the complex. These two churches appear from their architecture to have been communal in a way that chapels were not communal, and so Mourneabbey and Crooke would seem to represent a different model from Kilmainham. Other sites, notably Tully, Co. Kildare (Hospitaller), and Hospital, Co. Limerick (Hospitaller), have relatively large churches that – in the latter case at least – might have been parochial, or at least accessible to those outside the commanderies (pl. 14.3). The caveat to assuming that they represent yet another variation is that we do not know the boundaries of the precincts (inner or outer) at those sites; these churches might have been outside the boundaries of the spaces to which the armed monastics had exclusive access. Unlikely as it might sound, at Kilmainham the parish church was outside the priory enclosure according to the documentary record, and archaeological evidence would allow one to suggest very tentatively the same at Kilteel, Co. Kildare (Hospitaller). Late in the Middle Ages, the Hospital church was incorporated in a complex of monastic-domestic structures of claustral character, but it was probably free-standing originally, so one cannot judge how it functioned in respect of both the Hospitaller community and the parochial community.

If there was – as I speculated above – some degree of consistency in the simplicity of planning in the cores of commanderies, was there a corresponding consistency in the plans of churches? The small corpus of surviving

---

29 O'Keeffe & Virtuani, 'Reconstructing Kilmainham'.

Epilogue: commanderies, crusades, frontiers

religious-military order churches in Ireland indicates that there was not. In studies of Templar architecture, circular-nave churches are often emphasized. They are known in England, the place to which one naturally looks in the first instance.[30] There are no examples in Ireland. Should we expect to find such a design were we to excavate a Templar site in Ireland? The answer is 'not necessarily'. The thesis that Templars built only round-nave churches, emulating the Holy Sepulchre, is an enduring one, but it was shown not to be true as long ago as 1954.[31] On the whole, wherever one looks in Europe, *local* architectural traditions were followed in church-building by the military-religious orders.[32] Thus, the heterogeneity that one observes in the churches of the two orders in Ireland is exactly as one would expect. That said, is there any to reason to think that, with more archaeological work, we might at least find some evidence of a transfer of architectural ideas into Ireland through Hospitaller or Templar channels? It is not improbable that the two orders 'carried' design or style ideas with them – in Provençe, for example, the adoption of Rayonnant Gothic from the Île-de-France is linked to the military-religious[33] – but there is no reason to think that they had any comparable impact on architectural 'style' in Ireland. Still, one could not rule out the possibility that the fortified Hospitaller priory at Kilmainham was influential in the development of *military* architectural style in Ireland in the 1170s.[34]

30 Ritoók, 'The architecture of the Knights Templar in England', pp 173–6. 31 Élie Lambert, 'L'architecture des Templiers', *Bulletin Monumental* 112 (1954), 7–60. 32 See, for example, Charles Higounet & Jacques Gardelles, 'L'architecture des ordres militaires dans le Sud-Ouest de la France', *Actes du 87e Congrès national des Sociétés savantes* (Poitiers, 1962), 173–94; for the same argument (including for the use of local labour) made in respect of Italy, see Nadia Bagnarini, 'I Templari nella Tuscia Viterbese: Vecchie Considerazioni e Nuove Prospettive di Ricerca. Storia ed Architettura' in Mathias Piana & Christer Carlsson (eds), *Archaeology and architecture of the military orders: new studies* (Farnham, 2014), pp 83–106. 33 Damien Carraz, 'Les ordres militaires, le comte et les débuts de l'architecture gothique en Provence', *Bulletin de la Société de l'histoire et du patrimoine de l'ordre de Malte* 13 (2003), 45–55. 34 I have argued elsewhere that a royal master mason worked on seigneurial commissions at Trim, and at Maynooth, Co. Kildare, in the mid-1170s (Tadhg O'Keeffe, *Ireland encastellated: Insular castle-building in its European context* (Dublin, 2021), pp 86–8). I have reflected on this further since this work was published. I suggest that the master mason – whom I argued might be identified as Maurice, who worked on Henry II's castles of Newcastle-upon-Tyne and Dover – was sent to Ireland by the king specifically to work on Trim, it being the fortress of his most trusted Anglo-Norman leader in Ireland, Hugh de Lacy, and that he also worked at Maynooth, for Maurice fitz Gerald, who was also in royal favour. The same mason is likely to have worked on St Thomas' priory in Dublin, founded in 1177 by Henry II as an act of reparation for his role in killing Thomas Becket. A mason with royal connections – probably the very same individual – seems to have been responsible in the late 1170s for the design of the great tower at Castleknock, Co. Dublin, owned by Hugh Tyrell, who, significantly, had became a tenant of the crown (ibid., p. 88). The Castleknock estate abutted the lands of the Kilmainham Hospitallers. The dates of the buildings known to have been inside the *castrum* at Kilmainham are not known, but that *castrum* was probably laid out in the 1170s, the decade in which the Hospitallers arrived in Ireland. If there was a royal master mason in the Dublin region, working on three baronial castles with the king's permission, it is very likely that he also worked at Kilmainham, and possibly also at Clontarf.

IRELAND AND OUTREMER:
REFLECTIONS ON MEDIEVAL FRONTIERS

Norman Housley once observed that 'the paradox of contemporary crusading studies (is) an unprecedented richness of research ... set against a background of confusion in terms of definition which only seems to deepen the more we discover'.[35] Few would dispute this. At the heart of the challenge is the distinction between, as Housley describes them, 'traditionalist' and 'pluralist' understandings of crusading, the former privileging the Levantine crusades as (in a sense) the 'authentic' crusades, and the latter allowing the term be used to describe all manner of armed conflict between medieval Catholicism and 'others', whether pagan, Muslim or heretic.[36] One might add that there is a similar 'background of confusion in terms of definition' of 'frontier'. The concept of the frontier has long been at the forefront of medieval scholarship in Ireland, implicitly if not explicitly, and recent work shows that it is still regarded as valuable.[37]

The words we use matter greatly. They shape discourse. When words and their definitions are largely modern – when they do not enjoy the imprimatur of usage and explanatory commentary in original sources, in other words – our need to police the boundaries of their meaning is all the stronger. In the preface to their now-classic edited collection from 1989, *Medieval frontier societies*, Robert Bartlett and Angus MacKay noted that their contributors did not engage in 'terminological or definitional debate about the nature of the frontier' but 'pursue[d] empirical issues and allow[ed] the frontier element in their analysis to speak for itself'.[38] To my mind, this is problematic.

---

35 Norman Housley, *Contesting the crusades* (Oxford, 2006), p. 2; see also Andrew Jotischky, *Crusading and the crusader states* (London, 2017), pp 1–4. 36 Housley, *Contesting the crusades*, pp 2–4; as an example of the latter, see Mikołaj Gładysz, *The forgotten crusaders: Poland and the crusader movement in the twelfth and thirteenth centuries* (Leiden, 2012), who describes the missions against the Mongols as 'defensive crusades'. 37 James Lydon, 'The problem of the frontier in medieval Ireland', *Topic: A Journal of the Liberal Arts* 13 (1967), 5–22; Patrick J. Duffy, 'The nature of the medieval frontier in Ireland', *Studia Hibernica* 22/3 (1982/3), 21–38; Tadhg O'Keeffe, 'Medieval frontiers and fortification: the Pale and its evolution' in F.H.A. Aalen & Kevin Whelan (eds), *Dublin, city and county: from prehistory to present* (Dublin, 1992), pp 57–77; idem, 'The frontier in medieval Ireland: an archaeological perspective', *Group for the Study of Irish Settlement Newsletter* (1995), 16–18; James Muldoon, *Identity on the medieval Irish frontier: degenerate Englishmen, wild Irishmen, middle nations* (Gainesville, 2003); Christopher Maginn, 'Gaelic Ireland's English frontiers in the late Middle Ages', *PRIA* 110C (2010), 173–90; Tom Finan, *Landscape and history on the Irish frontier: the king's cantreds in the thirteenth century* (Turnhout, 2016). 38 Robert Bartlett & Angus MacKay, 'Preface' in Robert Bartlett & Angus MacKay (eds), *Medieval frontier societies* (Oxford, 1989), pp v–vii, at p. v. More recently, in the same vein, Walter Pohl and Giles Constable have written extended essays on the medieval frontier(s) but did not problematize the concept: see, respectively, 'Frontiers and ethnic identities: some final considerations' in Flora Curta (ed.), *Borders, barriers, and ethnogenesis: frontiers in late antiquity and the Middle Ages* (Turnhout, 2005), pp 255–65, and 'Frontiers in the Middle Ages' in O. Merisalo (ed.), *Frontiers in the Middle Ages* (Louvain-la-Neuve, 2006), pp 1–28. For a more nuanced reading, see Jaspert, 'Military orders at the frontier'.

Epilogue: commanderies, crusades, frontiers

If frontiers speak for themselves, the best one can say is that they do so incoherently.

'Frontier' is a concept which, aside from being ill-defined, carries considerable historical and ideological baggage. The term is a relatively late one, appearing in the twelfth century in Spain, the thirteenth in Italy, and the fourteenth in north-western Europe.[39] Developed and used in military contexts originally, and therefore suited to the discourse on crusading, the concept it connotes is primarily *spatial*. There are two ways in which it has been deployed as a spatial concept in historical writing. In European historiography, it refers most frequently to a border or boundary, and is used therefore to describe the *linear* interfaces between spatially defined polities.[40] In historiography of North American origin, by contrast, 'frontier' refers most frequently to a zone – by its nature a perceptual space, a space born of culture, and of cultural fear of 'otherness', rather than politics – rather than a line or barrier.[41] These are very different interpretations. The European understanding is closer to how the concept was deployed in military contexts in the Middle Ages, but the North American understanding is closer to how the concept is now used by historians. Embedded in both is some assumption of conflict and contestation, which is, again, a carry-over from the medieval usage of the term. Places of conflict and contestation were everywhere and at a variety of scales in the Middle Ages, and places of supposed *frontier* contestation, according to historians, were often places where both notions of the frontier – the political and the cultural-perceptual – appear to have applied. And this was especially the case in medieval contexts described as 'crusader'. A good example is the late twelfth- and thirteenth-century Baltic region. There, the crusader 'frontier' – the space in which Christians sought to intrude their religion into the lands occupied by Slavs, Prussians, Lithuanians, Estonians, Finns and others – was simultaneously a place, or space, where 'missionaries saw … culture' (fitting the North American understanding of the concept) and 'rulers saw property' (fitting its European understanding).[42]

When deployed as a concept to describe and explain medium- and long-term patterns and processes of change across time and space, 'frontier' tends

---

39 Nora Berend, 'Preface' in Nora Berend & David Abulafia (eds), *Medieval frontiers: concepts and practices* (London 2016), pp x–xv, at p. xii. 40 Note, though, the provisos about the nature of medieval borders offered by Ronnie Ellenblum ('Were there borders and borderlines in the Middle Ages? The example of the Latin kingdom of Jerusalem' in Nora Berend & David Abulafia (eds), *Medieval frontiers: concepts and practices* (London 2016), pp 105–19). 41 The distinction is discussed by Daniel Power, 'Frontiers: terms, concepts, and the historians of medieval and early modern Europe' in Daniel Power & Naomi Standen (eds), *Frontiers in question: Eurasian borderlands, 700–1700* (Basingstoke, 1999), pp 1–12. 42 Burnam W. Reynolds, *The prehistory of the crusade: missionary war and the Baltic Crusades* (London, 2016), p. 173. For the Baltic Crusades see Alan V. Murray (ed.), *Crusade and conversion on the Baltic frontier, 1150–1500* (Aldershot, 2001).

to skirt questions of territorial sovereignty – which are questions about political boundaries – and to privilege instead cultural distinctions between geographical cores and peripheries.[43] One sees this in the historiography of medieval Europe, where the core-periphery distinction is central to the narrative of culture and society during 'the long twelfth century', the period in which crusading in the eastern Mediterranean region began.[44] Briefly, the cultural distinctions in question in the medieval period pertain to practices which might be economic (such practices are profoundly cultural), linguistic, artistic, or religious, or some combination of these and of other practices. Where is the geographical core in this core-periphery conceptualization? The Frankish lands, originally Carolingian and later Capetian, have long been thought of by historians as the core of the post-millennium, non-Byzantine, Christian world, the super-region from which cultural ideas diffused outwards in every direction. When Timothy Reuter remarked with a garnish of sarcasm that 'everything starts in France, from administration history, architecture and Arthurian romances, through chivalry, crusades and castles, to universities and water-mills',[45] he was listing activities and phenomena which were fundamentally cultural. A more generous imagining of a European spatial and cultural core in the eleventh and twelfth centuries would include Rome, given both the role of the papacy in pan-European affairs after the millennium and the evidence of a supposed renaissance of *Romanitas*, but in this reimagining the core is simply enlarged spatially (effectively reconstituting the early ninth-century empire as the cultural centre of post-imperial Europe).

Now, viewed today from this region of Europe in which *Romanitas* was reinvigorated in the eleventh century, contemporary (later-eleventh to thirteenth-century) Outremer would appear to have been a frontier *par excellence*, especially in the North American sense of the term. First, it was spatially distant, in a geographical sense, so travel was required to access it; the destination was certainly dangerous, but so too was the journey.[46] Second, it was populated by indigenous people – Muslim, Jewish and Christian – whose

---

43 David Abulafia, 'Introduction: seven types of ambiguity, *c.*1100–*c.*1500' in Nora Berend & David Abulafia (eds), *Medieval frontiers: concepts and practices* (London, 2016), pp 1–34, at pp 6–10.   44 J.D. Cotts, *Europe's long twelfth century: order, anxiety and adaptation, 1095–1229* (Basingstoke, 2013). The core-periphery model has also been used to explain the medieval Islamic frontiers of the eastern Mediterranean/western Asiatic region: see R. Brauer, 'Boundaries and frontiers in medieval Muslim geography', *Transactions of the American Philosophical Society* 85: 6 (1995), 1–73. For a critique of the model in this context, see A. Asa Eger, 'The archaeology of medieval Islamic frontiers: an introduction' in A. Asa Eger (ed.), *The archaeology of medieval Islamic frontiers from the Mediterranean to the Caspian Sea* (Louisville, 2019), pp 3–27, at pp 5–9.   45 Timothy Reuter, 'The "feudal revolution"', *Past and Present* 155 (1997), 177–95, at 187–8.   46 The fear of sea-travel to Outremer is highlighted in Caroline Smith, 'Saints and sinners at sea on the first crusade of Saint Louis' in Thomas F. Madden, James L. Naus & Vincent Ryan (eds), *Crusades – medieval worlds in conflict* (London & New York, 2010), pp 161–72.

Epilogue: commanderies, crusades, frontiers 195

recent histories were not shared by those in the 'core' lands, and, in the case of the Muslims, whose beliefs and activities so challenged the Western existential sensibility that intervention was deemed necessary (while also carrying penitential and other bonuses). In a sense, Ireland's physical disconnection from the same European core (and from England, which was integrated into that core from the late eleventh century) qualified it as an 'outremer' in its own right.[47] Contemporary colonial readings of Gaelic-Irish culture saw its geographical separation as central to its 'otherness'.[48]

From what has just been said, one might claim the concept of 'frontier' to be unproblematic. Indeed, one might even claim it to be a very useful concept, in that it offers a conceptual framework for a comparative history, justifying specifically the project of refracting the histories of Anglo-Norman lordship in Ireland and contemporary crusader occupation in Outremer through the same lens. But such a comparative history still requires the concept to be interrogated. The frontier does not, *pace* Bartlett and MacKay, 'speak for itself'.

To return to first principles, the concept of the frontier as deployed in historical writing about the Middle Ages continues to reveal a strong debt to the work of Frederick Jackson Turner, the *paterfamilias* of frontier studies. For Turner, 'frontier' connoted the meta-narrative of European expansion across the vastness of the North American continent in the nineteenth century: settlers crossed that vastness, meeting its challenges head-on, claiming ownership of the land, transforming its cultural character as they did so, and transforming their own identity – and creating the American democratic tradition – at the same time.[49] 'Frontier' similarly connotes meta-narratives in medieval historical research, such as that which describes some of the relationships of the core of Latin Christian Europe with some of Europe's peripheral regions, as explored in case studies in *Medieval frontier societies*, and subsequently in Bartlett's

---

47 In this context, one might note the insular eastern Mediterranean Hospitaller view of Outremer being Europe's western side, not its eastern (Anthony Luttrell, 'Malta and Rhodes: hospitallers and islanders' in Victor Mallia-Milanes (ed.), *Hospitaller Malta, 1530–1798: studies on early modern Malta and the Order of St John of Jerusalem* (Malta, 1993), pp 255–84, esp. p. 277). 48 For that disconnection and its cartographic imagining by Gerald of Wales, see Kathy Lavezzo, *Angels on the edge of the world* (Ithaca, 2006), pp 65–70. 49 Turner's seminal paper, 'The significance of the frontier for American history', is reprinted as the opening chapter of his *The frontier in American history* (New York, 1920), pp 1–38. For its deployment in medieval history see J.W. Thompson, 'Profitable fields of investigation in medieval history', *American Historical Review* 28 (1913), 490–504, and, in an explicit nod to Turner's idea of the 'closed frontier', Archibald Lewis, 'The closing of the mediaeval frontier 1250–1350', *Speculum* 33 (1958), 475–83. Note that these publications issued from North America. For a more recent discussion of the Turnerian genealogy of medieval frontier research, see R.I. Burns, 'The significance of the frontier in the Middle Ages' in Robert Bartlett & Angus MacKay (eds), *Medieval frontier societies* (Oxford, 1989), pp 317–39.

own classic account of the 'making' of medieval Europe.[50] As a meta-narrative, though, 'frontier' is open to post-modern critique.[51]

There is another way in which the concept merits critique, and careful reading of Turner's work reveals it. In the expanded Turnerian view, the frontier in nineteenth-century North America was the space where European settlers abutted indigenous Americans, where Christian culture abutted non-Christian culture, and where land brought into agricultural use abutted wilderness. While the comprehension of the American frontier is now more sophisticated,[52] there is a value in spelling out the nature of its original, late nineteenth-century, conceptualization, lest its baggage be carried into modern historical enquiry. The manner in which the concept of 'frontier' in medieval European scholarship borrows heavily from the Turnerian tradition is problematic from an ideological perspective. In the Turnerian view, the frontier is the outer boundary-zone of the agents and processes of civilization, and the spatial capturing of land is a positive transformative experience. A frontier, so imagined, always treats a periphery as a space to be transformed by a core. The dangers of associating crusading with improving or civilizing are self-evident.[53]

Leaving aside its dubious ideological framing, the Turnerian understanding of frontier underpins how the concept is understood in historical writing as uni-directional. Only one of the two 'parties' in a frontier zone is imagined as having ownership of that frontier. Thus, in an Irish context, the frontier is identified as having been colonial. It is understood to have expanded as colonial ownership (lordship) was secured through settlement, and to have retreated as the pattern was reversed; the transformation of the fourteenth century in Ireland was not, therefore, the expansion of a Gaelic-Irish frontier but, rather, the contraction of a colonial frontier.[54] To return to the themes of this volume, it is worth noting that, while the expansion of the colonial frontier in Ireland is understood to have been effected through military activity, it cannot be claimed that the military-religious orders played a significant role in that process, except perhaps in the late twelfth century when the chief houses of the two orders were established at the outskirts of Dublin (at Kilmainham and Clontarf). One could certainly argue that some of the

---

50 Robert Bartlett, *The making of Europe: conquest, colonization and cultural change, 950–1350* (London, 1993). 51 David Abulafia makes a similar point, without using the term 'meta-narrative': 'Introduction: seven types of ambiguity', pp 2–4. 52 See, for example, Kerwin Lee Klein, *Frontiers of the historical imagination: narrating the European conquest of native America, 1890–1990* (Berkeley & Los Angeles, 1997). 53 Daniel Gutwein & Sophia Menache, 'Just war, crusade, and *jihad*: conflicting propaganda strategies during the Gulf Crisis (1990–1991)', *Revue belge de philologie et d'histoire: Histoire médiévale, moderne et contemporaine* 80 (2002), 385–400; Ariel Koch, 'The new crusaders: contemporary extreme right symbolism and rhetoric', *Perspectives on Terrorism* 11:5 (2017), 13–24. 54 An exception is Christopher Maginn, 'Gaelic Ireland's English frontiers in the late Middle Ages', *PRIA* 110C (2010), 173–90.

Epilogue: commanderies, crusades, frontiers

military-religious order communities (in places like Kilteel, for example) were active, war-making, frontiersmen in more local frontier settings,[55] but the overall distribution of Hospitaller and Templar foundations in Ireland makes clear that these knights were not primarily involved in protecting, much less pushing out, the boundaries of colonial lordship. So, if the conquering of Ireland was perceived in terms of a crusade, a matter explored by Maeve Callan,[56] it is interesting that the very communities which had a direct connection with the great era-defining Levantine crusades were not really drafted into the process.

One purpose of this discussion of frontiers has been to edge the reader towards that very observation. There is another purpose, and it brings us away from the Hospitallers and Templars into a more general issue. The uni-directionality of the frontier model arguably obscures how places which are described by historians as 'frontiers' were centers as well as edges; they were often places which not only experienced change from the outside, but were places of outward agency and influence in themselves.[57] In Ireland, the tendency among medieval historians and archaeologists has traditionally been to see the frontier between colonials and natives as a theatre of aggression, following, as Jaspert put it, the perspective of the 'school of frontier strife' rather than that of the 'school of frontier harmony'.[58] There is a lesson for Ireland from the supposed frontier of Outremer: alongside the violence of colonial-native encounters was a harmony based on mutual recognition of opportunity. Irish medievalists might benefit from considering how the medieval Islamic *thughūr* functioned within crusades lands as a space of 'mixed populations and an active trading economy, with or without military engagement and religious motivation'.[59] Peace treaties between the Franks and the Muslims occured at a rate of one every two years between 1097 and 1291,[60] and during those periods there was trade, continuing a pattern that was established before the First Crusade.[61] The same lesson

---

55 See Virtuani, chapter 8, this volume.   **56** See Callan, chapter 3, this volume.   **57** Eger made this very point in respect of the crusader lands: 'The archaeology of medieval Islamic frontiers', pp 6–7. Turner, in a sense, recognised the inherent innovation of 'frontier societies' when he located the origins of American democratic tradition, and the constitutional right of Americans to bear arms, in the frontier *mentalité*. He did not see a concommitant innovation on the 'other side' of the North American frontier because there was none: the driving ideology of European expansion across North America was profoundly capitalist in the sense that land was capital and the *raison d'être* of European movement across the Continent was to take that land.   **58** Jaspert, 'Military orders at the frontier', p. 10. For an interpretation of medieval Ireland that veers towards the 'school of frontier harmony' perspective, see Tadhg O'Keeffe, 'Frontiers of the archaeological imagination: rethinking landscape and identity in thirteenth-century Roscommon, Ireland', *Landscapes* 19 (2018), 66–79.   **59** Brauer, 'Boundaries and frontiers in medieval Muslim geography'.   **60** Yvonne Friedman, 'Peacemaking: perceptions and practices in the medieval Latin east' in Conor Kostick (ed.), *The crusades and the Near East: cultural histories* (London, 2011), pp 229–57, at p. 232.   **61** Niall Christie, *Muslims and crusaders: Christianity's wars in the Middle East, 1095–1382, from the Islamic sources* (London, 2014), pp 73, 77.

might be learned from closer observation of the Iberian frontier, which would qualify as a crusading frontier in the 'pluralist' sense of the term.[62] There, urban foundations were used to populate the Christian frontier against the Muslims, and yet those very same towns not only provided homes to Moorish and Jewish minorities but had enshrined in their constitutions protections for the rights of those minorities, including to worship.[63] How does this relate to Ireland? Here we need to swap religious identity (as in the two examples given) for ethnic identity. One of the most striking features of the distribution of Anglo-Norman settlement in Ireland is the manner in which nucleated settlements and moated sites cluster in a north-south line between, roughly, Askeaton, Co. Limerick, and Kinsale, Co. Cork. This has been identified as a militarized frontier zone.[64] But the Anglo-Norman market settlements in that zone only make sense if reconstructions of their hinterlands include Gaelic-owned lands to the west. Was this much different, in principle, from what one finds in the Islamic worlds of Iberia and the eastern Mediterranean? Surely not. Is it inconceivable that, despite occcasional hostilies, the Hospitallers of Mourneabbey engaged benignly with the Gaelic-Irish as well as with other colonists?

CLOSING COMMENT

In the age of the crusades, Ireland was as far away as was any place in Europe from Jerusalem and its hinterland of Christian-fighter destinations. That Ireland should have a 'crusader history', as discussed in the chapters in this volume, is testimony to the central paradox of the great age of European crusades in Outremer. Insofar as 'Europe' existed as a single cognitive entity in the twelfth century, with Christianity as its glue, the crusader lands of the east, and the armed parties which headed towards to them, were central to its definition. Therein lies the paradox: twelfth-century Europe was defined in part by the 'otherness' of what was beyond it. The crusader lands were beyond Europe, in places of 'otherness',[65] but crusading was at the core of the European imagination, giving it a purposeful coherence which, as with Gregorian reform,

---

62 Housley, *Contesting the crusades*, pp 2–4.   63 Stephen Lay, *The Reconquest kings of Portugal: political and cultural reorientation on the medieval frontier* (Basingstoke, 2009), pp 147–8.   64 Terry B. Barry, 'The shifting frontier: medieval moated sites in counties Cork and Limerick' in F.A. Aberg & A.E. Brown (eds), *Medieval moated sites in north-west Europe* (Oxford, 1981), pp 71–85.   65 For the Baltic lands and the Christian-pagan frontier, see Linda Kaljundi, 'Waiting for the barbarians: reconstruction of otherness in the Saxon missionary and crusading chronicles, eleventh–thirteenth centuries', *Medieval Chronicle* 5 (2008), 113–27. Note, though, that Anti Selart has argued, citing archaeological work, that paganism had been 'supplemented' by Christian elements before any crusading activity took place in the region (*Livonia, Rus' and the Baltic Crusades*, trans. Fiona Robb (Leiden, 2015), p. 72).

Epilogue: commanderies, crusades, frontiers

transcended the politics of Europe's regions. Embodying this is the letter from Honorius III in December 1221 to the episcopate of France, England, Scotland, Ireland, Germany, Hungary, Tuscany and Lombardy, written after the failure of the Fifth Crusade and seeking new recruits for another attempt at crusading:[66] not all corners of Europe were included in the mail-shot, but the geography of the recipients underscores how different places, with different cultures and languages, were enfolded into the crusading project, giving them a contextual unity. Indeed, hostilities between traditional European foes could even be suspended when the matter of Jerusalem and its region was on the agenda, as if the greatest of European regional disputes were overshadowed by the greater challenge of reclaiming for Christendom – and for Europe – the origin-place of Christianity itself.

Such an interpretation presupposes that knowledge of events in the eastern Mediterranean, and of the efforts being made there by fighting Christians, were widespread in Europe in the twelfth century. In elite circles, of course, it certainly was widespread. Lower down the social hierarchy, knowledge presumably thinned out, but there were conduits by which almost everybody in medieval European society could have been aware of the great battles for that sacred landscape. The Cistercian voice on crusading was probably not widely heard, given the character of the Cistercian themselves, but the loss of Jerusalem in 1187, and with it the loss of the True Cross, certainly provided subject matter for monastic sermons which were probably widely heard.[67] It is likely, also, that those who had been on crusade and had returned safely made themselves known, and enjoyed some notoriety. The strongest testifiers to eastern conflict, though, were the Knights Templar and Knights Hospitaller, the two great military-religious orders of crusader-land origin. Located everywhere in Europe, it is barely conceivable that those who encountered these armed monastics did not know their historic and on-going link with the Holy Land. Exotic in the modern imagination, thanks to myths about strange ritual practices and the ongoing searches for the Holy Grail, their back-story possibly made them equally exotic and equally mysterious in the Middle Ages.

---

66 Thomas W. Smith, *Curia and crusade: Pope Honorius III and the recovery of the Holy Land, 1216–1227* (Turnhout, 2017), p. 175.   67 C. Matthew Phillips, 'Crucified with Christ: the imitation of the crucified Christ and crusading spirituality' in Madden, *Crusades: medieval worlds in conflict*, pp 25–33.

Bibliography

MANUSCRIPT SOURCES

ENGLAND

British Library, Arundel MS 57.
British Library, Cotton MS Claudius E VIII.
BL Cotton MS Vespasian AVI.
British Library, Harley MS 746.
British Library, Lansdowne MS 96.
Kew, The National Archives of the UK: C 54/198, mem. 27 (*Close Rolls*, 34 Edw. III).
Kew, The National Archives, C 47/27/12/3, Petition of the English ambassadors at Rome for the proclamation of a crusade.
Lambeth Palace Library, MS 608.

IRELAND

Dublin Diocesan Archives, *Liber niger Alani: a chartulary of the dioceses of Dublin and Glendalough, 12th–16th cent., compiled under the direction of archbishop John Allen, c.1530.*
Kilruddery House, Bray, Meath Estate Deed, bundle 162, Partition of the Manor of Great Bray, 1 Apr. 1666.
National Library of Ireland, NLI MS 13, *Collectanea de rebus Hibernicis (mainly ecclesiastical)* compiled by Archbishop William King and transcribed by Walter Harris, 1200–1700.
Trinity College Dublin, MS 347, MS 496, MS 700, MS 1061, MS 1440.

PRINTED PRIMARY SOURCES

Account roll of the priory of the Holy Trinity, Dublin 1337–46, ed. James Mills (Dublin, 1891).
'Ali ibn Tahir al-Sulami: The book of the jihad of 'Ali ibn Tahir al-Sulami (d. 1106): text, translation and commentary, ed. Niall Christie (London, 2016).
Annála Connacht: The Annals of Connacht (A.D. 1224–1544), ed. Alexander Martin Freeman (Dublin, 1944).
The annals of Clonmacnoise, being the annals of Ireland from the earliest period to A.D. 1408, trans. Conell Mageoghan (1627), ed. Denis Murphy (Dublin, 1896).
Annals of Inisfallen, ed. Seán McAirt (Dublin, 1951).
Annals of Loch Cé, trans. William H. Hennessy, *Rolls series* 54. 2 vols (London, 1871).
Annales Monastici: Annales Monasterii de Waverleia, ed. H.R. Luard, *Rolls series* 36. 5 vols (London, 1865).

Bibliography

The 'Annals of Multyfarnham': Roscommon and Connacht provenance, ed. and trans. Bernadette Williams (Dublin, 2012).

Annála Ríoghachta Éireann: Annals of the kingdom of Ireland by the Four Masters, from the earliest period to the year 1616. Edited from MSS in the library of the Royal Irish Academy and of Trinity College Dublin with a translation and copious notes, ed. and trans. John O'Donovan, with an introduction by Kenneth Nicholls. 7 vols (Dublin, 1990).

Bernard of Clairvaux: Sancti Bernardi Opera, eds Jean Leclercq, Charles Talbot & Henri-Marie Rochais. 8 vols (Rome, 1957–77).

Bernardino Beccari: Relatione della guerra d'Hibernia, tra la lega de' catholici di quel regno, and l'asserta reina d'Inghilterra (Rome, 1596).

The Brut, or the chronicles of England, ed. Friedrich W.D. Brie (London, 1906).

Calendar of Archbishop Alen's register c.1172–1534, ed. Charles McNeill (Dublin, 1950).

Calendar of the Carew manuscripts preserved in the archiepiscopal palace of Lambeth 1515–1624, eds J.S. Brewer & William Bullen. 6 vols (London, 1867–73).

Calendar of the close rolls preserved in the Public Record Office, Edward II. 4 vols (London 1892–8).

Calendar of the close rolls preserved in the Public Record Office, Edward III. 14 vols (London, 1896–1913).

Calendar of documents relating to Ireland preserved in her Majesty's Public Record Office, 1171–1307, ed. Henry S. Sweetman. 5 vols (London 1875–6).

'Calendar of documents relating to medieval Ireland in the series of ancient deeds in the National Archives of the United Kingdom', eds Brendan Smith & Paul Dryburgh, AH 39 (2006), 1–61.

Calendar of entries in the papal registers relating to Great Britain and Ireland: papal letters. 23 vols (Dublin, 1893–2018).

Calendar of the justiciary rolls or proceedings in the court of the justiciar of Ireland, preserved in the Public Record Office of Ireland, ed. James Mills. 3 vols (Dublin, 1905–14).

Calendar of letters, despatches, and state papers relating to the negotiations between England and Spain, preserved in the archives at Simancas, Vienna, Brussels and elsewhere. 15 vols (London, 1862–1954).

Calendar of letters and state papers relating to English affairs: preserved principally in the archives of Simancas: Elizabeth, 1587–1603, ed. Martin A.S. Hume. 4 vols (London, 1892–9).

Calendar of Ormond deeds, 1172–1603, ed. Edmund Curtis. 6 vols (Dublin, 1932–43).

Calendar of the patent rolls preserved in the Public Record Office, Edward III. 16 vols (London, 1891–1916).

Calendar of the patent rolls preserved in the Public Record Office, Henry III. 6 vols (London, 1901–13).

Calendar of state papers relating to Ireland in the reigns of Henry VIII, Edward VI, Mary and Elizabeth, 1509–1603, eds H.C. Hamilton, E.G. Atkinson & R.P. Mahaffy. 11 vols (London, 1860–1912).

Calendar of state papers, Spain. 13 vols (London, 1862–1954).

Cartulaire général de l'ordre des Hospitaliers de S. Jean de Jérusalem (1100–1310), ed. Joseph Delaville le Roulx. 4 vols (Paris, 1894–1906).

'Chartes données en Irlande en faveur de l'ordre de Cîteaux', ed. H. d'Arbois de Jubainville, Revue Celtique 7 (1886), 81–6.

Chartularies of St Mary's abbey, Dublin with the register of its house at Dunbrody and Annals of Ireland, ed. John T. Gilbert. 2 vols, Rolls series 80 (London, 1884).

The Civil Survey AD 1654–56, ed. R.C. Simington. 10 vols (Dublin, 1931–61).

The Coucher book of Furness abbey, eds J.C Atkinson & J. Brownbill. 2 vols (Manchester, 1886–1919).

Decrees of the ecumenical councils, ed. Norman P. Tanner. 2 vols (London, 1990).

The deeds of the Normans in Ireland/ La geste des Engleis en Yrlande: a new edition of the chronicle formerly known as The song of Dermot and the earl, ed. Evelyn Mullally (Dublin, 2002).

Documents of the affairs of Ireland before the king's council, ed. G.O. Sayles (Dublin, 1979).

Documents of the Christian church, ed. Henry Bettenson (London, 1943).

'Documents relating to the suppression of the Templars in Ireland', ed. G. MacNiocaill, *AH* 24 (1967), 183–226.

The Dublin Guild Merchant Roll c.1190–1265, eds Philomena Connolly & Geoffrey Martin (Dublin, 1992).

Extents of Irish monastic possessions, 1540–1541: from the manuscripts in the Public Record Office, London, ed. Newport B. White (Dublin, 1941).

Geoffrey of Monmouth: *Life of Merlin: Vita Merlini*, ed. and trans. Basil Clarke (Cardiff, 1973).

Gerald of Wales (Giraldus Cambrensis):

—, *Autobiography of Gerald of Wales*, ed. and trans. H.E. Butler (Woodbridge, 2005).

—, *Expugnatio Hibernica: the conquest of Ireland*, ed. and trans. A.B. Scott & F.X. Martin (Dublin, 1978).

—, *The history and topography of Ireland: Topographia Hibernica*, ed. and trans. John J. O'Meara (Mountrath, 1982).

—, *The journey through Wales: the description of Wales*, trans. Lewis Thorpe (London, 1978).

—, *Opera*, ed. J.S. Brewer, James F. Dimock & George F. Warner, *Rolls series* 21. 8 vols (London, 1861–91).

Gervase of Canterbury: *The historical works of Gervase of Canterbury*, ed. William Stubbs, *Rolls series* 71. 2 vols (London, 1879).

Gervase of Tilbury: *Otia Imperialia: recreation for an emperor*, ed. and trans. S.E. Banks & J.W. Binns (Oxford, 2002).

The great parchment book of Waterford, ed. Niall Byrne (Dublin, 2007).

The history of William Marshal, eds A.J. Holden, S. Gregory & D. Crouch, Anglo-Norman Text Society, 3. 3 vols (London, 2002–6).

Holinshed's Irish chronicle: The historie of Ireland from the first inhabitation thereof, unto the yeare 1509 collected by R. Holinshed and continued till the yeare 1547 by R. Stanihurst, eds Liam Miller & Eileen Power (Dublin, 1979).

Irish historical documents, 1172–1922, eds Edmund Curtis & R.B. McDowell (London, 1943, repr., 1968).

Irish exchequer payments, 1270–1446, ed. Philomena Connolly (Dublin, 1998).

Jean de Joinville: *Jean de Joinville and Geoffrey de Villehardouin: chronicles of the crusades*, trans. Caroline Smith (London, 2008).

The Annals of Ireland by Friar John Clyn, ed. and trans. Bernadette Williams (Dublin, 2007).

John of Trokelowe: *Johannis de Trokelowe, et Henrici de Blaneforde monachum S. Albani, necnon quorundam anonymorum chronica et annales, regnantibus Henrico tertio, Edwardo primo, Edwardo secundo, Ricardo secundo et Henrico quarto*, ed. H.T. Riley, *Rolls series* 28, part 3 (London, 1866, repr. Cambridge, 2013).

Letters and papers, foreign and domestic, of Henry VIII, ed. James Gairdner. 21 vols (London, 1862–1932).

Liber cartarum prioratus Sancti Andree in Scotia, ed. Thomas Thompson (Edinburgh, 1841).

The martyrology of Tallaght, eds R.I. Best & H.J. Lawlor (London, 1931).

Matthew Paris: *Matthaei Parisiensis, monachi Sancti Albani chronica maiora, 1200–59*, ed. H.R. Luard. 7 vols (London, 1872–83).

Odo of Deuil: *De profectione Ludovici VII in Orientem*, ed. V.G. Berry (New York, 1948).

Pacata Hibernia or a history of the wars in Ireland during the reign of Queen Elizabeth taken from the original chronicles, ed. T. Stafford. 2 vols (Dublin, 1810).

Ordnance Survey letters relating to Co. Dublin, by Eugene O'Curry, Royal Irish Academy, MS 14 C. 23 (Dublin, 1837).

Patrologia Latina, ed. J.P. Migne. 221 vols (Paris, 1844–64).

Peter Lombard: *De regno Hiberniae, sanctorum insula, commentarius* (Louvain, 1623).

—, *The Irish War of Defence, 1598–1600: extracts from the De Hibernia insula commentaries of Peter Lombard, archbishop of Armagh*, ed. Matthew Byrne (Cork, 1930).

Bibliography

Peter of les Vaux-de-Cernay: *The history of the Albigensian Crusade*, ed. and trans. W.A. Silby & M.D. Silby (Woodbridge, 1998).

Peter the Venerable: *The letters of Peter the Venerable*, ed. Giles Constable. 2 vols (Cambridge, MA, 1967).

Philippe de Mézières: *Letter to Richard II: a plea made in 1395 for peace between England and France*, trans. G.W. Coopland (Liverpool, 1975).

Pontifica Hibernica. Medieval papal chancery documents concerning Ireland, 640–1261, ed. Maurice P. Sheehy. 2 vols (Dublin, 1962–5).

Pontificum romanorum vitae, qui fuerunt inde exeunt saeculo ix ad finem saeculi xiii, ab aequelibus conscriptae, quas ex archive pontifici, Bibliothecae Vaticanae aliarumque codicibus, adiectis suis cuique ex annalibus et documentis graviorbus editae, ed. J.M. Watterich, 2 vols (Leipzig, 1862 repr. 1966).

The proceedings against the Templars in the British Isles, ed. Helen Nicholson. 2 vols (Farnham, 2011).

'Provincial and diocesan decrees of the diocese of Dublin during the Anglo-Norman period', ed. Aubrey Gwynn, *Archivium Hibernicum* 11 (1944), 31–117.

Il purgatorio di San Patrizio, documenti letterari e testimonianze (secc. XII–XVI), ed. G.P. Maggioni, R. Tinti & P. Taviani (Florence, 2018).

Records of the borough of Leicester 1196–1327, ed. M.E. Bateson (London, 1899).

Regesta pontificum Romanorum (AD 1198–1304), ed. A. Potthast. 2 vols (Berlin, 1874–5).

Register of the hospital of St John the Baptist without the New Gate, Dublin, ed. Eric St John Brooks (Dublin 1936).

Die Register Innocenz' III. 14 vols (Graz, Cologne, Vienna, Rome, 1964–2018).

Registrum de Kilmainham: Register of chapter acts of the hospital of Saint John of Jerusalem in Ireland, 1326–1339, under the grand prior, Sir Roger Outlawe, with additions from the times of his successors, Sir John Mareschall, Sir John Larcher and Sir John FitzRichard, grand priors of Ireland, edited from the Bodleian MS. Rawl. B. 501, ed. Charles McNeill (Dublin, 1932).

The registers of the church of St Michan, Dublin, 1636–1685, ed. Henry F. Berry, Parish Register Society (Dublin, 1907), vol. 3.

Robert of Torigni: *The chronicle of Robert of Torigni*, in *Chronicles of the reigns of Stephen, Henry II, and Richard I*, ed. Richard Howlett, Rolls series 82. 4 vols (London, 1889), vol. 4.

Sean MacRuaidhrí Mac Craith, *Caithréim Thoirdhealbhaigh*, ed. and trans. Standish Hayes O'Grady, Irish Texts Society 26–7. 2 vols (London, 1929).

Sigebert of Gembloux: *Chronica*, Monumenta Germaniae Historica, Scriptores 6, ed. L.C. Bethmann (Hannover, 1844), pp 268–474.

The song of the Cathar wars: a history of the Albigensian Crusade, ed. and trans. Janet Shirley (Farnham, 1996).

Spicilegium Ossoriense: being a collection of original letters and papers illustrative of the history of the Irish church from the Reformation to the year 1800, ed. Patrick Francis Moran (Dublin, 1874).

State papers published under the authority of His Majesty's commissioning, Henry VIII. 12 vols (London, 1830–52).

Statuta capitulorum generalium ordinis Cisterciensis ab anno 1116 ad annum 1786, ed. Joseph-Marie Canivez. 8 vols (Louvain, 1933–41).

Statutes and ordinances and acts of the parliament of Ireland: King John to Henry V, ed. H.F. Berry (Dublin, 1907).

Stephen Gosson: *The trumpet of warre: a sermon preached at Paules Crosse the seuenth of Maie 1598* (London, 1598).

Vetera monumenta Hibernorum et Scotorum historiam illustrantia qae ex Vaticani, Neapolis ac Florentiae tablularis deprompsit, 1216–1547, ed. Augustinus Theiner (Rome, 1864).

Walter Bower: *Scotichronicon by Walter Bower in Latin and English*, ed. D.E.R. Watt. 9 vols (Aberdeen, 1987–1998).

Walter Raleigh: *Works of Sir Walter Ralegh*, eds W. Oldys & T. Birch. 8 vols (Oxford, 1829).

William Camden: *History of the most renowned and victorious Princess Elizabeth* (1615) (4th ed. London, 1688).

William of Rishanger:

—, *Willelmi Rishanger quondam monachi S. Albani et quorundam anonymorum, chronica et annales regnantibus Henrico tertio et Edwardo primo, AD 1259–1307*, ed. H.T. Riley, *Rolls series* 28 (London, 1865).

—, *The chronicle of William de Rishanger, of the barons' wars: the miracles of Simon de Montfort*, ed. James Orchard Halliwell-Phillipps (London, 1840).

INTERNET RESOURCES

CELT: Corpus of Electronic texts, https://celt.ucc.ie//published.html

CIRCLE: A calendar of Irish chancery letters, c.1244–1509, https://chancery.tcd.ie/content/welcome-circle

SECONDARY SOURCES

Abulafia, David, 'Introduction: seven types of ambiguity, *c.*1100–*c.*1500' in Nora Berend & David Abulafia (eds), *Medieval frontiers: concepts and practices* (London, 2016), pp 1–34.

al-Dawoody, Ahmed, *The Islamic law of war* (New York, 2011).

al-Ghazal, Sharif Kaf, 'The origin of bimaristans (hospitals) in Islamic medical history', Foundation for Science, Technology and Civilisation (2007).

Alansari, A. & K. Hirao, 'The impact of bimaristans design on design factors of therapeutic buildings' *International Design Journal* 7 (2017), 59–66.

Ambler, Sophie Thérèse, *The Song of Simon de Montfort: England's first revolutionary and the death of chivalry* (London, 2019).

Amundsen, D.W., *Medicine, society, and faith in the ancient and medieval worlds* (Baltimore, 1996).

Anon., 'St Michan's church', *Dublin Penny Journal* 2: 79 (1834), 209–10.

Asa Eger, A. (ed.), *The archaeology of medieval Islamic frontiers from the Mediterranean to the Caspian Sea* (Louisville, 2019).

Asa Eger, A. 'The archaeology of medieval Islamic frontiers: an introduction' in A. Asa Eger (ed.), *The archaeology of medieval Islamic frontiers from the Mediterranean to the Caspian Sea* (Louisville 2019), pp 5–9.

Ashbridge, Thomas, *The crusades: the war for the Holy Land* (London, 2012).

—, *Greatest knight: the remarkable life of William Marshal, the power behind five English thrones* (London, 2015).

Bagnarini, Nadia, 'I Templari nella Tuscia Viterbese: Vecchie Considerazioni e Nuove Prospettive di Ricerca. Storia ed Architettura' in Mathias Piana & Christer Carlsson (eds), *Archaeology and architecture of the military orders: new studies* (Farnham, 2014), pp 83–106

Baldwin, John W., 'Master Stephen Langton, future archbishop of Canterbury: the Paris schools and Magna Carta', *EHR* 12 (2008), 811–46.

—, *Paris, 1200* (Stanford, 2010).

Bárány, Attila, 'Crusades and crusading in Hungarian historiography' in Lévai Csaba (ed.), *Europe and the world in European historiography* (Pisa, 2006), pp 129–48.

Barrow, G. Lennox, 'The Knights Hospitaller of St John of Jerusalem at Kilmainham', *Dublin Historical Record* 38 (1985), 108–12.

Bibliography

Barry, Terry B., 'The shifting frontier: medieval moated sites in counties Cork and Limerick' in F.A. Aberg & A.E. Brown (eds), *Medieval moated sites in north-west Europe* (Oxford, 1981), pp 71–85.

Bartlett, Robert, *The making of Europe: conquest, colonization and cultural change, 950–1350* (London, 1993).

—, *Gerald of Wales: a voice of the Middle Ages* (Stroud, 2006).

Bartlett, Robert & Angus MacKay, 'Preface' in Robert Bartlett & Angus MacKay (eds), *Medieval frontier societies* (Oxford, 1989), pp v–vii.

Barquero Goñi, Carlos, 'The Hospitallers and the kings of Navarre in the fourteenth and fifteenth centuries' in Helen Nicholson (ed.), *The military orders, ii: Welfare and warfare* (Aldershot, 1998), pp 348–54.

Barber, Malcolm, *The new knighthood: a history of the Order of the Temple* (Cambridge, 1993).

—, *The Cathars: dualist heretics in Languedoc in the high Middle Ages* (London, 2000).

—, 'The reputation of Gerard de Ridefort' in Judith Upton-Ward (ed.), *The military orders, iv: On land and sea* (Aldershot, 2008), pp 111–19.

Becker, Patricia, 'An analysis of the Dublin Guild Merchant Roll, c.1190–1265' (MPhil, TCD, 1996).

Beglane, Fiona, *Anglo-Norman parks in medieval Ireland* (Dublin, 2015).

Bellomo, Elena, 'The cabrei of the Order of Malta as an archaeological source: some notes on Piedmont' in Mathias Piana & Christer Carlsson (eds), *Archaeology and architecture of the military orders: new studies* (Farnham, 2014), pp 7–18.

Bennett, Michael J., 'Richard II and the wider realm' in Anthony E. Goodman & James L. Gillespie (eds), *Richard II: the art of kingship* (Oxford, 1999), pp 187–204.

Benventura, M., 'The Geraldine war: rebellion or crusade?', *Irish Ecclesiastical Record* 103 (1965), 148–57.

Berend, Nora, 'Frontiers' in Helen J. Nicholson (ed.), *Palgrave advances in the crusades* (Basingstoke, 2005), pp 148–71.

—, 'Preface' in Nora Berend & David Abulafia (eds), *Medieval frontiers: concepts and practices* (London, 2016), pp x–xv.

Bériou, Nicole & Philippe Josserand (eds), *Prier et combattre: dictionnaire européen des ordres militaires au moyen âge* (Paris, 2009).

Biller, Peter, 'William of Newburgh and the Cathar mission to England', *Studies in Church History. Subsidia* 12 (1999), 11–30.

Binchy, D.A., 'An Irish ambassador at the court of Philip II', *Studies* 2 (1921), 353–74, 573–84.

Bird, Jessalyn, 'Crusaders rights revisited: the use and abuse of crusader privileges in early thirteenth-century France' in Ruth Mazo Karras, Joel Kaye & E. Ann Matter (eds), *Law and the illicit in medieval Europe* (Philadelphia, 2008), pp 133–46.

—, 'Paris masters and the justification of the Albigensian Crusade', *Crusades* 6 (2007), 117–55.

Bird, Jessalyn, Edward Peters & J.M. Powell (eds), *Crusade and Christendom: annotated documents in translation from Innocent III to the fall of Acre, 1187–1291* (Philadelphia, 2013).

Boas, Adrian J., *Crusader archaeology: the material culture of the Latin east* (London & New York, 1999).

Bonnefoy, Aine, 'The role of Vaucouleurs in the careers of Geoffrey de Geneville and his sons', https://www.academia.edu/29384540/The_role_of_Vaucouleurs_in_the_careers_of_ Geoffrey_de_Geneville_and_his_sons. Unpublished paper.

Bourgeois, Frank, 'La théorie de la guerre juste: un héritage chrétien?', *Études théologiques et religieuses* 81 (2006), 449–74.

Bourgeois, Nicolas, 'Les Cisterciens et la croisade de Livonie', *Revue historique* 635 (2005), pp 521–60.

Boyce, D. George, *Nationalism in Ireland* (London, 1995).

Bradley, John, Cóilín Ó Drisceoil & Michael Potterton (eds), *William Marshal and Ireland* (Dublin, 2017).

Bradshaw, Brendan, *The dissolution of the religious orders in Ireland under Henry VIII* (Cambridge, 1974).

—, 'Cromwellian reform and the origins of the Kildare rebellion, 1533–34', *TRHS* 27 (1977), 69–93.

—, *The Irish constitutional revolution of the sixteenth century* (Cambridge, 1979).

—, 'The English reformation and identity formation in Ireland and Wales' in Brendan Bradshaw & Peter Roberts (eds), *British consciousness and identity: the making of Britain, 1533–1707* (Cambridge, 1998), pp 43–111.

Brady, Ciaran, 'Politics, policy and power, 1550–1603' in Jane Ohlmeyer (ed.), *The Cambridge history of Ireland, ii: 1550–1730* (Cambridge, 2020), pp 39–40.

Brauer, R., 'Boundaries and frontiers in medieval Muslim geography', *Transactions of the American Philosophical Society* 85: 6 (1995), 1–73

Breen, Aidan, 'Ua Conairche, Christian (Gilla-Críst)', *DIB*.

Brooks, Eric St John, 'The de Ridelesfords', *JRSAI* 81 (1951), 115–38.

—, 'The de Ridelesfords', *JRSAI* 82 (1952), 45–61.

—, 'Irish possessions of St Thomas of Acre', *PRIA* 58C (1956), 21–44.

Brown, Daniel, 'Power and patronage across the North Channel: Hugh de Lacy, St Andrews and the Anglo-Scottish crisis of 1209 [Part 1]', *Scottish Historical Review* 94 (2015), 1–23.

—, *Hugh de Lacy, first earl of Ulster: rising and falling in Angevin Ireland* (Woodbridge, 2016).

Browne, Martin & Colmán Ó Clabaigh (eds), *Soldiers of Christ: the Knights Hospitaller and the Knights Templar in medieval Ireland* (Dublin, 2016).

—, *Households of God: the regular canons and canonesses of St Augustine and Prémontré in Ireland* (Dublin, 2019).

Brown, R. Allen, *Normans and the Norman conquest* (Dover, NH, 1985).

Buck, Andrew D., 'Settlement, identity, and memory in the Latin East: an examination of the term "crusader states"', *EHR* 135 (2020), 271–302.

Bull, Marcus, *Knightly piety and the lay response to the First Crusade: the Limousin and Gascony c.970–1130* (Oxford, 1998).

—, *Eyewitness and crusade narrative: perception and narration in accounts of the Second, Third and Fourth Crusades* (Woodbridge, 2019).

Bull, Marcus & Damien Kempf (eds), *Writing the early crusades: texts, transmission and memory* (Woodbridge, 2014).

Burgtorf, Jochen, Paul Crawford & Helen J. Nicholson (eds), *The debate on the trial of the Templars (1307–1314)* (Farnham, 2010).

Burns, R.I., 'The significance of the frontier in the Middle Ages' in Robert Bartlett & Angus MacKay (eds), *Medieval frontier societies* (Oxford, 1989), pp 317–39.

Burton, Nathaniel, *Oxmantown and its environs: or some suburban sketches of the eighteenth century* (Dublin, 1845).

Butler, R.D., *Some notices of the castle and of the eccesiastical buildings of Trim* (Naas, 1978).

Byrne, Aisling, 'Translating the crusades in late medieval Ireland' in Aisling Byrne & Victoria Flood (eds), *Crossing borders in the insular Middle Ages* (Turnhout, 2019), pp 161–77.

Byrne, Niall, *The Irish crusade: a history of the Knights Hospitaller, the Knights Templar, and the Knights of Malta, in the south-east of Ireland* (Dublin, 2007).

Caffery, Paul, 'Visual culture of Hospitaller knights of the priory of Ireland' in Martin Browne & Colmán Ó Clabaigh (eds), *Soldiers of Christ: the Knights Hospitaller and the Knights Templar in medieval Ireland* (Dublin, 2015), pp 151–66.

Callan, Maeve, *The Templars, the witch, and the wild Irish: vengeance and heresy in medieval Ireland* (Dublin, 2015).

—, 'Making monsters out of one another in the early fourteenth-century British Isles: the Irish remonstrance, the declaration of Arbroath, and the Anglo-Irish counter-remonstrance', *Eolas* (2019), 43–63.

Bibliography

Canning, Ruth A., *The Old English in early modern Ireland: the Palesmen and the Nine Years War, 1594–1603* (Woodbridge, 2019).

Canny, Nicholas P., 'The ideology of English colonization: from Ireland to America', *William and Mary Quarterly* 30 (1973), 575–98.

—, 'O'Neill, Hugh [Aodh Ó Néill], second earl of Tyrone (*c.*1550–1616)', *ODNB*.

Carbasse, Jean-Marie, 'Les commanderies: aspects juridiques et institutionnels' in Anthony Luttrell & Léon Pressouyre (eds), *La commanderie, institution des ordres militaires dans l'Occident médiéval* (Paris, 2002), 19–27

Carlin, M., 'Medieval English hospitals' in L. Granshaw & R. Porter (eds), *The hospital in history* (London, 1989), pp 21–41.

Carraz, Damien, 'Les ordres militaires, le comte et les débuts de l'architecture gothique en Provence', *Bulletin de la Société de l'histoire et du patrimoine de l'ordre de Malte* 13 (2003), 45–55.

Carraz, Damien & Sophie Aspord-Mercier, 'Le programme architectural d'un pôle seigneurial: la commanderie de Montfrin (Gard)', *Archéologie du Midi médiéval* 28 (2010), 297–315

Carroll, M.J., *The Knights Templar in Ireland* (Bantry, 2006).

Casey, Denis, 'Irish involvement in the First and Second Crusades? A reconsideration of the eleventh- and twelfth-century evidence', *Crusades* 13 (2014), 119–42.

Cassidy-Welch, Megan (ed.), *Remembering the crusades and crusading* (London, 2017).

Cassidy-Welch, Megan & Anne E. Lester, 'Memory and interpretation: new approaches to the study of the crusades', *JMH* 40 (2014), 225–36.

Christer, Carlsson, 'Varne Hospitaller commandery: an archaeological field project' in Mathias Piana & Christer Carlsson (eds), *Archaeology and architecture of the military orders: new studies* (Farnham, 2014), pp 19–27

Christie, Niall, *Muslims and crusaders: Christianity's wars in the Middle East, 1095–1382, from the Islamic sources* (London, 2014).

Church, Stephen, *King John: England, Magna Carta and the making of a tyrant* (London, 2015).

Clay, R.M. *The medieval hospitals of England* (London, 1909).

Clinton, Mark, *Carrickmines Castle: the rise and fall* (Bray, 2019).

Cole, P.J., *The preaching of the crusades to the Holy Land, 1095–1270* (Cambridge, MA, 1991).

Coleman, Edward, 'The crusader's tale' in Cherie Peters & Sparky Brooker (eds), *Tales of medieval Dublin* (Dublin, 2014), pp 92–101.

—, '"Powerful adversaries": the Knights Templar, landholding and litigation in the lordship of Ireland' in Martin Browne & Colmán Ó Clabaigh (eds), *Soldiers of Christ: the Knights Hospitaller and the Knights Templar in medieval Ireland* (Dublin, 2016), pp 184–94.

Colfer, Billy, *Arrogant trespass: Anglo-Norman Wexford, 1169–1400* (Dublin, 2002)

—, *The Hook peninsula, County Wexford* (Cork, 2004).

Collins, Tracy, 'Timolin: a case study of a nunnery estate in later medieval Ireland,' *Anuario de estudios medievales* 44: 1 (2014), 51–80.

Congar, Yves, 'Henri de Marcy, abbé de Clairvaux, cardinal-évêque d'Albano et légat pontifical', *Analecta Monastica* 5 (1958), 1–90.

Connolly, Philomena, *Medieval record sources* (Dublin, 2002).

Constable, Giles, 'The alleged disgrace of John of Salisbury in 1159', *EHR* 69 (1954), 67–76.

—, 'Frontiers in the Middle Ages' in O. Merisalo (ed.), *Frontiers in the Middle Ages* (Louvain-la-Neuve, 2006), pp 1–28

Cooke, Nicole A., *Fake news and alternative facts: information literacy in a post-truth era* (Chicago, 2018).

Coote, Lesley Ann, *Prophecy and public affairs in later medieval England* (Woodbridge, 2000).

—, 'The crusading bishop: Henry Despenser and his manuscript' in Nigel J. Morgan (ed.), *Prophecy, apocalypse, and the day of doom* (Donington, 2004), pp 39–51.

Corboy, James, 'Father James Archer, S.J., 1550–1625(?)', *Studies* 33 (1944), 99–107.

Cosgrove, Art (ed.), *A new history of Ireland, ii: Medieval Ireland, 1169–1534* (Oxford, 1993).

—, 'The writing of Irish medieval history', *IHS* 27 (1990), 97–111.

Cotter, Eamonn, 'The archaeology of the Irish Hospitaller preceptories of Mourneabbey and Hospital in context' in Martin Browne & Colmán Ó Clabaigh (eds), *Soldiers of Christ: the Knights Hospitaller and the Knights Templar in medieval Ireland* (Dublin, 2016), pp 103–23.

Cotter, Eamonn, Paul MacCotter & Tadhg O'Keeffe, 'A blow to the temple: the "monastic castle" at Rincrew (Co. Waterford) reinterpreted', *Journal of Irish Archaeology* 24 (2015), 163–78.

Cotts, J.D., *Europe's long twelfth century: order, anxiety and adaptation, 1095–1229* (Basingstoke, 2013).

Coulson, Charles, *Castles in medieval society: fortresses in England, France, and Ireland in the central Middle Ages* (Oxford, 2003).

Cowan, Ian B., P.H.R. Mackay & Alan Macquarrie (eds), *The Knights of St John of Jerusalem in Scotland* (Edinburgh, 1983).

Craig, Maurice, *Dublin, 1660–1860* (London, 1992).

Crotty, Gerald, 'Heraldry in medieval Ireland I: prolegomena', *Peritia* 24–5 (2013–14), 313–47.

Crouch, David, *William Marshal* (London, 2016).

—, 'Marshal, William [called the Marshal], fourth earl of Pembroke (*c*.1146–1219), soldier and administrator', *ODNB*.

D'Alton, John, *The history of County Dublin* (Cork, 1838).

Davies, Mary, *Bray*, Irish Historic Towns Atlas, no. 9 (Dublin, 1998).

—, *That favourite resort: the story of Bray, Co. Wicklow* (Bray, 2007).

De Gussem, Jeroen, 'Bernard of Clairvaux and Nicolas of Montiéramey: tracing the secretarial trail with computational stylistics', *Speculum* 92 (2017), 190–225.

Delaborde, H.F., 'Un frère de Joinville au service de l'Angleterre, Geoffroy, sire de Vaucouleurs', *Bibliothèque de l'école des chartes* 54 (1893), 334–43.

Demurger, Alain, *Chevaliers du Christ: les ordres religieux-militaires au moyen âge, XIe–XVIe siècle* (Paris, 2002).

Dollman, Francis, *Examples of ancient domestic architecture* (London, 1858).

Down, Kevin, 'Colonial society and economy' in Art Cosgrove (ed.), *A new history of Ireland, ii: Medieval Ireland, 1169–1534* (Oxford, 1993), pp 439–91.

Downey, Declan, 'Purity of blood and purity of faith in early modern Ireland' in Alan Ford & John McCafferty (eds), *The origins of sectarianism in early modern Ireland* (Cambridge, 2005), pp 216–28.

—, 'Continuity, legitimacy and strategy: the titular priors of Ireland – Romegas, González, Wyse and Brochero – and their relations with the Spanish monarchy, 1576–1625' in Martin Browne & Colmán Ó Clabaigh (eds), *Soldiers of Christ: the Knights Hospitaller and the Knights Templar in medieval Ireland* (Dublin, 2016), pp 61–80.

Dressler, Rachel, 'Cross-legged knights and the signification of English medieval tomb sculpture', *Studies in Iconography* 21 (2000), 91–121.

Dryburgh, Paul & Brendan Smith (eds), *Handbook of medieval Irish records in the National Archives of the United Kingdom* (Dublin, 2005).

—, 'Calendar of documents relating to medieval Ireland in the series of ancient deeds in the National Archives of the United Kingdom', *AH* 39 (2006), 1–61.

Dudley Edwards, Robert, *Ireland in the age of the Tudors: the destruction of Hiberno-Noman civilisation* (London, 1977).

Duffy, Patrick J., 'The nature of the medieval frontier in Ireland', *Studia Hibernica* 22/3 (1982/3), 21–38.

Duffy, Paul, '"Ung sage et valent home": Hugh de Lacy and the Albigensian Crusade', *JRSAI* 141 (2011), 66–90.

—— 'The church of Bearach, the grange of Baldoyle and the town of the dark stranger,' in Seán Duffy (ed.), *Medieval Dublin XV* (Dublin, 2015), pp 89–118.

——, 'The architecture of defiance', *AI* 29: 1 (2015), 20–3.

——, 'The exiled earl and soon-to-be saint', *HI* 24: 5 (2016), 16–19.

——, 'From Carcassonne to Carrickfergus: the legacy of de Lacy's crusade experience in Britain and Ireland' in Paul Duffy, Tadhg O'Keeffe & Jean-Michel Picard (eds), *From Carrickfergus to Carcassonne: the epic deeds of Hugh de Lacy on the Albigensian Crusade* (Turnhout, 2018), pp 295–328.

——, 'Preliminary excavation report for 6–13 Stephen Street Upper, 7–19 Longford Street and 71–75 Aungier Street, Dublin 2, Licence Ref. 17E0212' (Unpublished report, NMS Archives, 2019).

Duffy, Paul, Tadhg O'Keeffe & Jean-Michel Picard (eds), *From Carrickfergus to Carcassonne: the epic deeds of Hugh de Lacy on the Albigensian Crusade* (Turnhout, 2018).

Duffy, Paul & Daniel Brown, 'From Carrickfergus to Carcassonne: Hugh de Lacy and the Albigensian Crusade' in Paul Duffy, Tadhg O'Keeffe & Jean-Michel Picard (eds), *From Carrickfergus to Carcassonne: the epic deeds of Hugh de Lacy during the Albigensian Crusade* (Turnhout, 2018), pp 9–30.

Duffy, Seán, *Ireland, 600–1169: an island of saints and scholars?* (London, 1993).

—— 'The problem of degeneracy' in James Lydon (ed.), *Law and disorder in thirteenth-century Ireland: the Dublin parliament of 1297* (Dublin, 1997), pp 87–106.

—— (ed.), *Robert the Bruce's Irish wars: the invasion of Ireland, 1306–1329* (Stroud, 2002).

Duggan, Anne, 'The making of a myth: Giraldus Cambrensis, *Laudabiliter*, and Henry II's lordship of Ireland', *Studies in Medieval and Renaissance History* 4 (2007), 107–70.

——, '*Totius christianitatis caput*: the pope and the princes' in Brenda Bolton & Anne Duggan (eds), *Adrian IV, the English pope (1154–59): studies and texts* (Aldershot, 2003), pp 138–55.

——, 'The power of documents: the curious case of *Laudabiliter*' in Brenda Bolton & Christine Meek (eds), *Aspects of power and authority in the Middle Ages* (Turnhout, 2007), pp 251–75.

Dunne, Laurence, 'Murder, pillage and destruction: archaeological finds from medieval Tralee' in Griffin Murray (ed.), *Medieval treasures of Co. Kerry* (Tralee, 2010), pp 61–72.

Dunning, Patrick J., 'Pope Innocent III and the Irish kings', *Journal of Ecclesiastical History* 8 (1957), 17–32.

——, 'The letters of Innocent III to Ireland,' *Traditio* 18 (1962), 229–53.

Du Noyer, George, 'Notice of the cross-legged sepulchral effigies existing at Cashel', *Archaeological Journal* 2 (1846), 121–31.

Dutton, Kathryn, 'French crusading and political culture under Geoffrey, count of Anjou and duke of Normandy, 1129–51', *History* 29 (2015), 419–44.

Edbury, Peter, 'The crusader states' in David Abulafia (ed.), *The new Cambridge medieval history* (Cambridge, 1999), v, pp 590–606.

Edington, Susan & Sarah Lambert (eds), *Gendering the crusades* (Cardiff, 2001).

Eliav-Feldon, Miriam, Benjamin Isaac & Joseph Ziegler (eds), *The origins of racism in the West* (Cambridge, 2018).

Elisséeff, Nikita, 'The reaction of the Syrian Muslims after the foundation of the first Latin kingdom of Jerusalem' in M. Shatzmiller (ed.), *Crusaders and Muslims in twelfth-century Syria* (Leiden, 1993), pp 162–72.

Ellenblum, Ronnie, *Frankish rural settlement in the Latin kingdom of Jerusalem* (Cambridge, 1998).

——, *Crusader castles and modern histories* (Cambridge, 2007).

—, 'Were there borders and borderlines in the Middle Ages? The example of the Latin kingdom of Jerusalem' in Nora Berend & David Abulafia (eds), *Medieval frontiers: concepts and practices* (London, 2016), pp 105–19.

Ellis, Steven G., 'The Kildare rebellion and the early Henrician Reformation', *Historical Journal* 19 (1976), 807–30.

—, 'Centre and periphery in the Tudor state' in Norman L. Jones & Robert Tittler (eds), *A companion to Tudor Britain* (Oxford, 2008), pp 133–50.

—, 'FitzGerald, Thomas [*called* Silken Thomas], tenth earl of Kildare [*known as* Lord Offaly] (1513–1537)', *ODNB.*

Eogan, James, 'A betagh settlement at Attyflin, Co. Limerick' in Christiaan Corlett & Michael Potterton (eds), *Rural settlement in medieval Ireland in the light of recent archaeological excavations* (Bray, 2009), pp 67–78.

Falkiner, C.L., 'The hospital of St John of Jerusalem in Ireland', *PRIA* 26C (1907), 275–317.

Falkiner, Frederick R., *The foundation of the hospital and free school of King Charles II, Oxmantown, Dublin* (Dublin, 1906).

Falls, Cyril, *Elizabeth's Irish wars* (Syracuse, 1997).

Fichtenau, Heinrich, *Heretics and scholars in the high Middle Ages, 1000–1200* (University Park, PA, 1998).

Field, Sean & Cecilia Gaposchkin, 'Questioning the Capetians, 1180–1328', *History Compass* 12 (2014), 567–85.

Finan, Tom, *Landscape and history on the Irish frontier: the king's cantreds in the thirteenth century* (Turnhout, 2016).

Fitzgerald, Walter, 'Timolin', *Journal of the County Kildare Archaeological Society* 2 (1899), 413–25.

Flanagan, Marie Therese, *Irish society, Anglo-Norman settlers, Angevin kingship: interactions in Ireland in the late twelfth century* (Oxford, 1989).

—, *Irish royal charters: texts and contexts* (Oxford, 2005).

—, 'Irish royal charters and the Cistercian order' in M.T. Flanagan & J.A. Green, *Charters and charter scholarship in Britain and Ireland* (New York, 2005), pp 120–39.

—, *The transformation of the Irish Church in the twelfth and thirteenth centuries* (Woodbridge, 2010).

—, 'St Malachy, St Bernard of Clairvaux and the Cistercian order', *Archivium Hibernicum* 68 (2015), 294–311.

Flood, Victoria, *Prophecy, politics and place in medieval England: from Geoffrey of Monmouth to Thomas of Erceldoune* (Cambridge, 2016).

Flori, Jean, 'Ideology and motivations in the First Crusade' in Helen J. Nicholson (ed.), *Palgrave advances in the crusades* (Basingstoke, 2005), pp 15–36.

Fonnesberg-Schmidt, Iben, *The popes and the Baltic Crusades, 1147–1254* (Leiden, 2007).

Forey, Alan, 'The military orders and holy war against Christians in the thirteenth century', *EHR* 104 (1989), 1–24.

—, *The military orders: from the twelfth to the early fourteenth centuries* (Basingstoke, 1993).

Forni, A., 'La "nouvelle prédication" des disciples de Foulques de Neuilly: intentions, techniques et réactions' in A. Vauchez (ed.), *Faire croire: modalités de la diffusion et de la réception des messages religieux du XIIe au XVe siècle* (Rome, 1981), pp 19–37.

Frame, Robin, 'The justiciar and the murder of the MacMurroughs', *IHS* 18 (1972), 223–30.

—, *Colonial Ireland, 1169–1369* (Dublin, 1981).

—, *Ireland and Britain, 1170–1450* (London, 1998).

—, 'Exporting state and nation: being English in medieval Ireland' in Len Scales & Oliver Zimmer (eds), *Power and the nation in European history* (Cambridge, 2005), pp 143–65.

Bibliography

France, John, *The crusades and the expansion of Catholic Christendom, 1000–1714* (London, 2005).

—, 'Crusading warfare' in Helen J. Nicholson (ed.), *Palgrave advances in the crusades* (Basingstoke, 2005), pp 58–80.

Friedman, Yvonne, 'Peacemaking: perceptions and practices in the medieval Latin east' in Conor Kostick (ed.), *The crusades and the Near East: cultural histories* (London, 2011), pp 229–57.

Gaposchkin, Cecilia, *The making of Saint Louis: kingship, sanctity, and crusade in the later Middle Ages* (Ithaca, 2008).

—, *Invisible weapons: liturgy and the making of crusade ideology* (Ithaca, 2017).

Gervers, Michael (ed.), *The Second Crusade and the Cistercians* (New York, 1992).

—, 'Donations to the Hospitallers in England in the wake of the Second Crusade' in Michael Gervers (ed.), *The Second Crusade and the Cistercians* (New York, 1992), pp 155–61.

—, '*Pro defensione Terre Sancte*: the development and exploitation of the Hospitallers' landed estate in Essex' in Malcolm Barber (ed.), *The military orders: fighting for the faith and caring for the sick* (London 2016), pp 3–20.

Gittos, Brian & Moira Gittos, *Interpreting medieval effigies: the evidence from Yorkshire, to 1400* (Oxford, 2019).

Gładysz, Mikołaj, *The forgotten crusaders: Poland and the crusader movement in the twelfth and thirteenth centuries* (Leiden, 2012).

Gordon, Dillian, *Making and meaning: the Wilton Diptych* (London, 1993).

Graves, James, 'On the cross-legged effigies of the county of Kilkenny', *Transactions of the Kilkenny Archaeological Society* 2 (1852), 63–4.

Greene, Joshua, *Moral tribes: emotion, reason, and the gap between us and them* (New York, 2013).

Griffiths, R.A., 'Langstrother [Longstrother], Sir John (d. 1471), administrator and prior of the hospital of St John of Jerusalem in England', *ODNB*.

Griffith-Jones, Robin & David Park, *The Temple church in London. History, architecture and art* (Woodbridge, 2010).

Guard, Timothy, *Chivalry, kingship and crusade: the English experience in the fourteenth century* (Woodbridge, 2013).

Gutwein, Daniel & Sophia Menache, 'Just war, crusade, and jihad: conflicting propaganda strategies during the Gulf Crisis (1990–1991)', *Revue belge de philologie et d'histoire: Histoire médiévale, moderne et contemporaine* 80 (2002), 385–400.

Gwynn, Aubrey, *The Irish church in the eleventh and twelfth centuries* (Dublin, 1992).

Gwynn, Aubrey & R. Neville Hadcock, *Medieval religious houses: Ireland* (London, 1970).

Hadcock, R. Neville, 'The Order of the Holy Cross in Ireland' in J.A. Watt, J.B. Morrall & F.X. Martin (eds), *Medieval studies: presented to Aubrey Gwynn, SJ* (Dublin, 1961), 44–54.

Hagan, J., 'Some papers relating to the Nine Years War', *Archivium Hibernicum* 2 (1913), 280–1.

Hagger, Mark S., *The fortunes of a Norman family: the De Verduns in England, Ireland and Wales, 1066–1316* (Dublin, 2001).

Hamarneh, S., 'Development of hospitals in Islam', *Journal of the History of Medicine and Allied Sciences* 17 (1962), 366–84.

Hammer, Paul E.J., *Elizabeth's wars* (Basingstoke, 2003).

Harbison, Peter, 'In memoria', *Irish Arts Review* 28: 4, 110–13.

Haren, Michael, 'Two Hungarian pilgrims' in Michael Haren & Yolande de Pontfarcy (eds), *The medieval pilgrimage to St Patrick's Purgatory: Lough Derg and the European tradition* (Enniskillen, 1988), pp 129–68.

—, '*Laudabiliter*: text and context' in M.T. Flanagan & J.A. Green (eds), *Charters and charter scholarship in Britain and Ireland* (Basingstoke, 2005), pp 140–63.

Harnack, Adolf von, *Militia Christi: die christliche religion und der soldatenstand in den ersten drei jahrhunderten* (Tübingen, 1905).

Harris, Oliver, 'Antiquarian attitudes: crossed legs, crusaders and the evolution of an idea', *Antiquaries Journal* 90 (2010), 401–40.

Hartland, Beth, 'Vaucouleurs, Ludlow and Trim: the role of Ireland in the career of Geoffrey de Geneville (*c.*1226–1314)', *IHS* 32 (2001), 457–77.

—, 'The household knights of Edward I in Ireland', *Historical Research* 77 (2004), 161–77.

Hartstone, Albert, 'Notes on a recumbent effigy in Timolin churchyard', *Journal of the County Kildare Archaeological Society* 1 (1892), 131–4.

Hayden, Alan R., *Trim Castle, Co. Meath: excavations, 1995–8* (Dublin, 2000).

Hayden, J. Michael, *Crutched friars and croisiers: the canons regular of the order of the Holy Cross in England and France* (Rome, 2013).

Hayes, William J., 'Holy Cross abbey', *Capuchin Annual* (1972), 286–301.

Hayes McCoy, G.A., 'Conciliation, coercion, and the Protestant reformation, 1547–71' in T.W. Moody, F.X. Martin & F.J. Byrne (eds), *A new history of Ireland, iii: Early modern Ireland, 1534–1691* (Oxford, 2009), pp 69–93.

Heal, Felicity, *Reformation in Britain and Ireland* (Oxford, 2003).

Heng, Geraldine, *The invention of race in the European Middle Ages* (Cambridge, 2018).

Hennessey, John Pope, *Sir Walter Ralegh in Ireland* (London, 1883).

Hélary, Xavier, 'Les rois de France et la Terre Sainte de la Croisade de Tunis à la chute d'Acre (1270–1291)', *Annuaire-Bulletin de la Société de l'histoire de France* 118 (2005), 21–104.

Hickey, Elizabeth, *Skryne and the early Normans* (Drogheda, 1994).

Higounet, Charles & Jacques Gardelles, 'L'architecture des ordres militaires dans le Sud-Ouest de la France', *Actes du 87e Congrès national des Sociétés savantes* (Poitiers, 1962), 173–94.

Hodgson, Natasha, *Women, crusading and the Holy Land in historical narrative* (Woodbridge, 2007).

Hodgson, Natasha, Katherine Lewis & Matthew Mesley (eds), *Crusading and masculinities* (London, 2019).

Holt, P.M., *The crusader states and their neighbours, 1098–1291* (London & New York, 2016), pp 17–18.

Horden, P., 'The earliest hospitals in Byzantium, Western Europe, and Islam', *Journal of Interdisciplinary History* 35 (2005), 361–8.

Housley, Norman, 'Crusades against Christians: their origins and early development, *c.*1000–1216' in Peter W. Edbury (ed.), *Crusade and settlement* (Cardiff, 1985), pp 17–36.

—, 'Jerusalem and the development of the crusade idea, 1099–1128' in B.Z. Kedar (ed.), *The Horns of Hattin* (Jerusalem, 1992), pp 27–40.

—, 'The thirteenth-century crusades in the Mediterranean' in David Abulafia (ed.), *The new Cambridge medieval history* (Cambridge, 1999), v, pp 569–89.

—, *Contesting the crusades* (Oxford, 2006).

—, 'An English proposal for a crusade against the Irish, *c.*1329–31' (Unpublished paper, 2017).

Hunt, John, *Irish Medieval figure sculpture, 1200–1600*. 2 vols (Dublin, 1974).

Hunyadi, Zsolt, *The Hospitallers in the medieval kingdom of Hungary, c.1150–1387* (Budapest, 2010).

—, 'The military activity of the Hospitallers in the medieval kingdom of Hungary (thirteenth to fourteenth centuries)' in K. Borchardt, N. Jaspert & H.J. Nicholson (eds), *The Hospitallers, the Mediterranean and Europe* (Aldershot, 2007), pp 193–203.

Hurlock, Kathryn, 'The crusades to 1291 in the annals of medieval Ireland', *IHS* 37 (2011), 517–34.

—, *Wales and the crusades, c.1095–1291* (Cardiff, 2011).

—, *Britain, Ireland and the crusades, c.1000–1300* (Basingstoke, 2013).

Bibliography

Hurlock, Kathryn & Paul Oldfield (eds), *Crusading and pilgrimage in the Norman world* (Woodbridge, 2015)

Isaac, Benjamin, *The invention of racism in classical antiquity* (Princeton, 2004).

Jaspert, Nikolas, 'Military orders at the frontier: permeability and demarcation' in Jochen Schenk & Mike Carr (eds), *The military orders: culture and conflict in western and worthern Europe* (London, 2017), pp 3–28

Jefferies, Henry A., 'The early Tudor Reformation in the Irish Pale', *Journal of Ecclesiastical History* 52 (2001), 34–62.

Jensen, Gillian Fellows, *Scandinavian personal names in Lincolnshire and Yorkshire* (Copenhagen, 1968).

Jensen, Janus Møller, 'King Erik Emune (1134–1137) and the crusades: the impact of crusading ideology on early twelfth-century Denmark' in Kurt Villads Jensen (ed.), *Cultural encounters during the crusades* (Odense, 2013), pp 91–104.

Jensen, Kurt Villads, 'Denmark and the crusading movement: the integration of the Baltic region into medieval Europe' in Allan I. Maclnnes, F. Pederesen & Thomas Riis (eds), *Ships, guns and Bibles in the North Sea and Baltic states, c.1350–1700* (East Linton, 2000), pp 185–205.

Jones, Andrew W., 'Fulk of Neuilly, Innocent III, and the preaching of the Fourth Crusade', *Comitatus* 41 (2010), 119–48.

Jonin, Pierre, 'Le climat de croisade des chansons de geste', *Les cahiers de civilisation médiévale* 27 (1964), 279–88.

Josserand, Philippe, *Église et pouvoir dans la péninsule Ibérique: les orders militaires dans le royaume de Castille (1252–1369)* (Madrid, 2004).

Jotischky, Andrew, *The Carmelites and antiquity: mendicants and their pasts in the Middle Ages* (Oxford, 2002), pp 281–6.

Jotischky, Andrew, *Crusading and the crusader states* (London, 2017).

Joynt, M., *Contributions to a dictionary of the Irish language* (Dublin, 1976).

Kahl, Hans-Dietrich, 'Crusade eschatology as seen by St Bernard in the years 1146 to 1148' in Michael Gervers (ed.), *The Second Crusade and the Cistercians* (New York, 1992), pp 35–47.

—, 'Die kreuzzugseschatologie Bernhards von Clairvaux und ihre missionsgeschichtliche auswirkung' in Dieter R. Bauer & Gotthard Fuchs (eds), *Bernhard von Clairvaux und der beginn der moderne* (Innsbruck, 1996), pp 262–315.

Kalinke, Marianne E. (ed.), *Norse romance I: the Tristan legend* (Cambridge, 1999).

Kaljundi, Linda, 'Waiting for the barbarians: reconstruction of otherness in the Saxon missionary and crusading chronicles, eleventh–thirteenth centuries', *Medieval Chronicle* 5 (2008), 113–27.

Kendi, Ibram X., *Stamped from the beginning: the definitive history of racist ideas in America* (New York, 2016).

—, *How to be an antiracist* (New York, 2019).

Keen, Maurice, 'The Wilton Diptych: the case for a crusading context' in Dillian Gordon, Lisa Monnas & Caroline Elam (eds), *The regal image of Richard II and the Wilton Diptych* (London, 1997), pp 189–95.

Kienzle, Beverly M., *Cistercians, heresy and crusade in Occitania, 1145–1229: preaching in the Lord's vineyard* (York, 2001).

—, 'Preaching the cross: liturgy and crusade propaganda', *Medieval Sermon Studies* 53 (2009), 11–32

King, Robert, *A primer of the history of the Catholic Church in Ireland.* 3 vols (3rd ed. Dublin, 1851).

Klein, Kerwin Lee, *Frontiers of the historical imagination: narrating the European conquest of native America, 1890–1990* (Berkeley & Los Angeles, 1997).

Knowles, David & R. Neville Hadcock, *Medieval religious houses: England and Wales* (2nd ed. London, 1971).

Koch, Ariel, 'The new crusaders: contemporary extreme right symbolism and rhetoric', *Perspectives on Terrorism* 11: 5 (2017), 13–24.

Lambert, Élie, 'L'architecture des Templiers', *Bulletin Monumental* 112 (1954), 7–60

Lankester, Philip J., 'The thirteenth-century military effigies in the Temple church' in Robin Griffith-Jones & David Park (eds), *The Temple church in London: history, architecture, art* (Woodbridge, 2010), pp 93–134.

Lawlor, H.J., 'Notes on the church of St Michan's, Dublin', *JRSAI* 16 (1926), 11–21.

Lavezzo, Kathy, *Angels on the edge of the world* (Ithaca, 2006).

Lay, Stephen, *The reconquest kings of Portugal: political and cultural reorientation on the medieval frontier* (Basingstoke, 2009).

Leask, Harold G., 'Herbert Wood', *JRSAI* 86 (1956), 109.

—, 'An altar tomb at Athassel abbey, Co. Tipperary,' *JRSAI* 76 (1946), 215–18.

Leclercq, Jean, 'Deux épîtres de saint Bernard et de son secrétaire' in J. Leclercq (ed.), *Recueil d'études sur saint Bernard et ses écrits* (Rome, 1966), ii, pp 313–18.

—, 'L'encyclique de saint Bernard en faveur de la croisade' in J. Leclercq (ed.), *Recueil d'études sur saint Bernard et ses écrits* (Rome, 1987), iv, pp 227–46.

—, 'Pour l'histoire de l'encyclique de saint Bernard sur la croisade' in J. Leclercq (ed.), *Recueil d'études sur saint Bernard et ses écrits* (Rome, 1987), iv, pp 247–63.

—, 'Recherches sur la collection des épîtres de saint Bernard', *Les cahiers de civilisation médiévale* 55 (1971), 205–19.

Lennon, Colm, *Sixteenth-century Ireland: the incomplete conquest* (Dublin, 1994).

—, 'The medieval manor of Clontarf, 1171–1540' in Seán Duffy (ed.), *Medieval Dublin XII* (Dublin, 2012), pp 189–205.

Lester, Anne E., 'A shared imitation: Cistercian convents and crusader families in thirteenth-century Champagne', *JMH* 35 (2009), 353–70.

Lewis, Archibald, 'The closing of the mediaeval frontier, 1250–1350', *Speculum* 33 (1958), 475–83.

Lewis, C.P., 'Lacy, Gilbert de (fl. 1133–1163)', *ODNB*.

Lippiatt, Gregory E.M., *Simon V of Montfort and baronial government, 1195–1218* (Oxford, 2017).

—, 'Simon de Montfort, les Cisterciens et les écoles: le contexte intellectuel d'un seigneur croisé (1187–1218)', *Les cahiers de civilisation médiévale* 61 (2018), 269–88.

Lydon, James, 'Richard II's expeditions to Ireland', *JRSAI* 93 (1963), 135–49.

—, 'The problem of the *frontier* in *medieval Ireland*', *Topic: A Journal of the Liberal Arts* 13 (1967), 5–22.

—, *The lordship of Ireland in the Middle Ages* (Dublin, 1972).

—, 'The years of crisis, 1254–1315' in Art Cosgrove (ed.), *A new history of Ireland*, ii: *Medieval Ireland, 1169–1534* (Oxford, 1993), pp 179–204.

—, 'The impact of the Bruce invasion, 1315–27' in Art Cosgrove (ed.), *A new history of Ireland*, ii: *Medieval Ireland, 1169–1534* (Oxford, 1993), pp 275–302.

—, 'Medieval Wicklow: "a land of war"' in Ken Hannigan & William Nolan (eds), *Wicklow: history and society* (Dublin, 1994), pp 151–89.

Lloyd, Simon, *English society and the crusade, 1216–1307* (Oxford, 1988).

Luttrell, Anthony, 'Malta and Rhodes: hospitallers and islanders' in Victor Mallia-Milanes (ed.), *Hospitaller Malta, 1530–1798: studies on early modern Malta and the Order of St John of Jerusalem* (Msida, Malta, 1993), pp 255–84.

Mackay, Ronan, 'Geneville (Joinville), Geoffrey de', *DIB*.

MacLellan, Rory, 'Abandoning piety and pugnacity? New military orders in the sixteenth and seventeenth centuries' in Nicholas Morton (ed.), *The military orders*, vii: *Piety, pugnacity and property* (London, 2019), pp 208–17.

Bibliography

—, *Donations to the Knights Hospitaller in Britain and Ireland, 1291–1400* (London, 2021).

MacNiocaill, Gearóid, 'À propos du vocabulaire social irlandais du bas Moyen Âge', *Études Celtiques* 12 (1970), 512–46.

MacShamhráin, Ailbhe, *Church and polity in pre-Norman Ireland: the case of Glendalough* (Maynooth, 1996).

MacShamhráin, Ailbhe, James Moynes, Peter Harbison & Seán Duffy (eds), *Medieval Ireland: an encyclopedia* (London, 2005).

Maddicott, John R., *Simon de Montfort* (Cambridge, 1994).

Maginn, Christopher, 'The Baltinglass rebellion, 1580: English dissent or Gaelic uprising?', *Historical Journal* 47 (2004), 205–32.

—, 'Gaelic Ireland's English frontiers in the late Middle Ages', *PRIA* 110C (2010), 173–90.

Maier, Christoph T., *Crusade propaganda and ideology: model sermons for the preaching of the cross* (Cambridge, 2000).

—, 'The roles of women in crusade: a survey', *JMH* 30 (2004), 61–82.

Maillet, Laurent, 'Un maître spirituel de l'Occident chrétien, Adam, abbé de Perseigne', *Revue Historique et Archéologique du Maine* 9 (2009), 97–120.

—, 'Les missions d'Adam de Perseigne, émissaire de Rome et de Cîteaux (1190–1221)', *Annales de Bretagne et des Pays de l'Ouest* 120 (2013), 100–16.

Majoros-Dunnahoe, Christie, 'Through the local lens: re-examining the function of the Hospitallers in England' in Jochen Schenk & Mike Carr (eds), *The military orders: culture and conflict in western and northern Europe* (London, 2017), pp 111–20.

Malkki, Janne, Katja Ritari, Tuomas Lehtonen & Kurt Villads Jensen (eds), *Medieval history writing and crusading ideology* (Helsinki, 2005).

Manning, Conleth, 'The Athassel tomb', *Irish Arts Review* 224 (2005), 132–5.

—, 'Hervey Morres and the "Montmorency imposture"', *HI* 28: 2 (2020), 22–5.

Martin, F.X., 'Gerald as Historian' in *Expugnatio Hibernica: the conquest of Ireland*, ed. and trans. A.B. Scott & F.X. Martin (Dublin, 1978), pp 278–82

—, 'Ireland in the time of St Bernard, St Malachy, St Laurence O'Toole', *Seanchas Ardmhacha* 15 (1992–3), 1–35.

—, 'Allies and an overlord, 1169–72' in Art Cosgrove (ed.), *A new history of Ireland*, ii: *Medieval Ireland, 1169–1534* (Oxford, 1993), pp 67–97.

Marvin, Laurence W., *The Occitan war, a military and political history of the Albigensian Crusade, 1208–1219* (Cambridge, 2008).

Massey, Eithne, *Prior Roger Outlaw of Kilmainham, 1314–1341* (Dublin, 2000).

Matthew, Elizabeth, 'Henry V and the proposal for an Irish Crusade' in Brendan Smith (ed.), *Ireland and the English world in the late Middle Ages* (Basingstoke, 2009), pp 161–75.

Mayer, Hans E., 'Henry II of England and the Holy Land', *EHR* 97 (1982), 721–39.

Mayes, Philip (ed.), *Excavations at a Templar preceptory, South Witham, Lincolnshire, 1965–67* (Leeds, 2002).

McCoog, Thomas M., *The Society of Jesus in Ireland, Scotland and England, c.1598–1606: 'Lest our lamp be entirely extinguished'* (Leiden, 2017).

McCutcheon, Clare, *Medieval pottery from Wood Quay, Dublin* (Dublin, 2006).

McGettigan, Darren, *Red Hugh O'Donnell and the Nine Years War* (Dublin, 2017).

McIlreavy, David, 'Walter de Ridelesford', *DIB*.

McInnes Gracie, David, *Militia Christi: the Christian religion and the military in the first three centuries by Adolf von Harnack* (Philadelphia, 1982).

MacIvor, Dermot, 'The Knights Templar in county Louth', *Seanchas Ardmhacha* 4:1 (1960–1), 72–91.

McNeal Dodgson J. & J.J.N. Palmer, *Domesday Book: index of persons* (Chichester, 1992).

McNeill, Charles, 'The Hospitallers at Kilmainham and their guests', *JRSAI* 54 (1924), 15–30.

McNeill, Charles, 'Harris: Collectanea de rebus Hibernicis', *Analectica Hibernica* 6 (1934), 248–450.

McQuarrie, Alan, *Scotland and the crusades, 1095–1560* (Edinburgh, 1985).

Meehan, J.P., *Fate and fortunes of Hugh O'Neill, earl of Tyrone and Rory O'Donnell, earl of Tyrconnell* (Dublin, 1886).

Miller, A.C., 'Jundi-Shapur, bimaristans, and the rise of academic medical centres', *Journal of the Royal Society of Medicine* 99 (2006), 615–17.

Mitchell, Piers D. & Andrew R. Millard, 'Migration to the medieval Middle East with the crusades', *American Journal of Physical Anthropology* 140: 3 (2009), 518–25.

Moore, Michael, *Archaeological inventory of County Waterford* (Dublin, 1999).

Morgan, Hiram, *Tyrone's rebellion: the outbreak of the Nine Years War in Tudor Ireland* (Woodbridge, 1993).

—, 'The 1597 ceasefire documents', *Dúiche Néill: Journal of the O'Neill Country Historical Society* (1997), 14–15.

—, '"Never any realm worse governed": Queen Elizabeth I and Ireland', *TRHS* 14 (2004), 295–308.

Morton, Nicholas E., *Encountering Islam on the First Crusade* (Cambridge, 2016).

—, *The medieval military orders: 1120–1314* (Harlow, 2013).

Mourad, Suleiman A. & James E. Lindsay, *The intensification and reorientation of Sunni jihad: ideology in the crusader period: Ibn ʿAsākir of Damascus (1105–1176) and his age, with an edition and translation of Ibn ʿAsākir's 'The forty hadiths for inciting jihad'* (Leiden, 2013).

Muldoon, James, *Identity on the medieval Irish frontier: degenerate Englishmen, wild Irishmen, middle nations* (Gainesville, FL, 2003).

Murphy, Margaret, 'From swords to ploughshares: evidence for Templar agriculture in medieval Ireland' in Martin Browne & Colmán Ó Clabaigh (eds), *Soldiers of Christ: the Knights Hospitaller and the Knights Templar in medieval Ireland* (Dublin, 2016), pp 167–83.

Murphy, Margaret & Michael Potterton, *The Dublin region in the Middle Ages* (Dublin, 2010).

Murphy, Sean J., 'Herbert Wood, archivist and historian (1860–1955)', https://www.academia.edu/41278716/Herbert_Wood_Archivist_and_Historian_1860–1955. (Unpublished paper).

Murray, Alan V. (ed.), *Crusade and conversion on the Baltic frontier, 1150–1500* (Aldershot, 2001).

Murray, Alan V., 'Outremer' in Alan V. Murray (ed.), *The crusades: an encyclopedia* (Santa Barbara, 2006), iii, pp 910–12.

Naus, James, *Constructing kingship: the Capetian monarchs of France and the early crusades* (Manchester, 2016).

Newman, E.L., 'Medieval sheep-corn farming: how much grain yield can each sheep support?', *Agricultural History Review* 50 (2002), 164–80.

Nic Ghiollamhaith, Aoife, 'Dynastic warfare and historical writing in North Munster, 1276–1350', *Cambridge Medieval Celtic Studies* 2 (1981), 73–89.

Ní Cheallacháin, Muireann, 'Preliminary report on excavations at Ardee, Licence No. 21E0124' (Unpublished report, NMS Archives, 2021).

Nicholson, Helen J., 'The Knights Hospitaller on the frontiers of the British Isles' in Jürgen Sarnowsky (ed.), *Mendicants, military orders and regionalism in medieval Europe* (Aldershot, 1999), 47–58.

—, *The Knights Hospitaller* (Woodbridge, 2001).

—, *The Knights Templar: a new history* (Stroud, 2001).

—, 'Serving king and crusade: the military orders in royal service in Ireland, 1220–1400' in Marcus Bull & Norman Housley (eds), *The experience of crusading*, i: *Western approaches* (Cambridge, 2003), pp 233–52.

—, 'Margaret de Lacy and the Hospital of Saint John at Aconbury, Herefordshire' in Anthony Luttrell & Helen J. Nicholson (eds), *Hospitaller women in the Middle Ages* (Aldershot, 2006), pp 153–77.

—, 'The testimony of Brother Henry Danet and the trial of the Templars in Ireland' in Iris Shagrir, Ronnie Ellenblum & Jonathan Riley-Smith (eds), *Laudem Hieroslymitani*. Subsidia 1 (Aldershot, 2008), pp 411–23.

—, *The Knights Templar on trial: the trial of the Templars in the British Isles, 1308–1311* (Stroud, 2009).

—, 'The trial of the Templars in Ireland' in Jochen Burgtorf, Paul Fleming Crawford & Helen Nicholson (eds), *The debate on the trial of the Templars: 1307–1314* (Farnham, 2010), pp 225–36.

—, 'The changing face of the Templars', *History Compass* 8 (2010), 653–67.

—, 'The military orders in Wales and the Welsh March in the Middle Ages' in Peter W. Edbury (ed.), *The military orders*, v: *Politics and power* (Farnham, 2012).

—, 'The Hospitallers' and Templars' involvement in warfare on the frontiers of the British Isles in the late thirteenth and early fourteenth centuries' in Jürgen Sarnowsky (ed.), *Ordines militaris colloquia Torunensia historica* (Toruń, 2012), 105–19.

—, 'The military-religious orders in the towns of the British Isles' in Damien Carraz (ed.), *Les ordres militaires dans la ville médiévale (1100–1350)* (Clermont-Ferrand, 2013), pp 113–26.

—, 'A long way from Jerusalem: the Templars and Hospitallers in Ireland *c.*1172–1348' in Martin Browne & Colmán Ó Clabaigh (eds), *Soldiers of Christ: The Knights Hospitaller and the Knights Templar in medieval Ireland* (Dublin, 2016), pp 1–22.

—, *The everyday life of the Templars: the Knights Templar at home* (Stroud, 2017).

—, 'Evidence of the Templars' religious practice from the records of the Templars' estates in Britain and Ireland in 1308' in Iris Shagrir, Benjamin Z. Kedar & Michel Balard (eds), *Communicating the Middle Ages*. Subsidia 11 (London, 2018), pp 50–63.

—, 'The surveys and accounts of the Templars in England and Wales, 1308–13' in G.E.M. Lippiatt & Jessalyn L. Bird (eds), *Crusading Europe: essays in honour of Christopher Tyerman*. Outremer 8 (Turnhout, 2019), pp 181–209.

—, 'Holy warriors, worldly war: military-religious orders and secular conflict', *Journal of Medieval Military History* 17 (2019), 61–79.

—, 'The Hospitallers in medieval Britain' in Jurgen Sarnowsky, Krystof Kwiatkowski, Hubert Houben, Laszlo Posan & Attila Barany (eds), *Studies on the military orders, Prussia, and urban history* (Debrecen, Hungary, 2020), pp 41–55.

—, 'Negotiation and conflict: the Templars' and Hospitallers' relations with diocesan bishops in Britain and Ireland' in Thomas W. Smith (ed.), *Authority and power in the medieval church, c.1000–1500* (Turnhout, 2020), pp 371–89.

Ní Mhaonaigh, Máire, *Brian Boru: Ireland's greatest king?* (Stroud, 2007).

Nolan, Tom, 'The order of the Knights Templar in the Waterford area', *Decies* 14 (1980), 52–60.

O'Brien, Elizabeth, 'Pre-Norman ecclesiastical sites in the half barony of Rathdown' (MA, UCD, 1980).

—, 'Ballyman,' *Medieval Archaeology* 29 (1985), 214.

—, 'Churches of south-east county Dublin' in G. MacNiocaill & P.F. Wallace (eds), *Keimelia* (Galway, 1988), pp 504–24.

—, 'Final report on excavations at Ballyman, E182 (1979–86)' (Unpublished report, NMS Archives, 2000).

O'Brien, Jacqueline & Peter Harbison, *Ancient Ireland: from prehistory to the Middle Ages* (London, 1996).

O'Carroll, Finola, 'The Blackfriars preachers, Trim, Co. Meath and the legacy of Geoffrey de Geneville' in M. Krasnodebska-D'Aughton, E. Bhreathnach & K. Smith (eds), *Monastic Europe: medieval communities, landscapes, and settlements* (Turnhout, 2019), pp 121–53.

O'Carroll, Finola, Denis Shine, Mark McConnon & Laura Corrway, 'The Blackfriary button', *Ríocht na Midhe* 27 (2016), 30–6.

O'Carroll, Finola, Ian Kinch & Laura Corrway, 'Digging the past, growing the future: the Blackfriary project', *Ríocht na Midhe* 29 (2018), 27–38.

O'Connell, Philip, 'Kells, early and medieval: part II', *Ríocht na Midhe* 2 (1960), 8–22.

Ó Corráin, Donnchadh, 'Island of saints and scholars: myth or reality?' in Oliver P. Rafferty (ed.), *Irish Catholic identities* (Manchester, 2013), pp 32–61.

—, *The Irish church, its reform and the English invasion* (Dublin, 2017).

Ó Clabaigh, Colmán, *The friars in Ireland, 1224–1540* (Dublin, 2012).

—, 'Prayer, politics and poetry: Cambridge, Corpus Christi College MS 405 and the Templars and Hospitallers at Kilbarry, Co. Waterford' in Martin Browne & Colmán Ó Clabaigh (eds), *Soldiers of Christ: the Knights Hospitaller and the Knights Templar in medieval Ireland* (Dublin, 2016), pp 206–17.

O'Conor, Kieran & Paul Naessens, 'Temple House: from Templar castle to New England mansion' in Martin Browne & Colmán Ó Clabaigh (eds), *Soldiers of Christ: the Knights Hospitaller and the Knights Templar in medieval Ireland* (Dublin, 2016), pp 124–51.

Ó Cuív, Brian (ed.), 'A fragment of Irish annals', *Celtica* 14 (1981), 83–104.

O'Doherty, J.F., 'Rome and the Anglo-Norman invasion of Ireland', *Irish Ecclesiastical Record* 42 (1933), 131–45.

O'Dowd, Mary, *A history of women in Ireland, 1500–1800* (London, 2005).

Ó Faolain, Seán, *The Great O'Neill: a biography of Hugh O'Neill, earl of Tyrone, 1550–1616* (Dublin, 1942).

Ó Floinn, Ragnall, 'Papal bullae found in Ireland', *Ulster Journal of Archaeology* 74 (2017–18), 162–74.

O'Keeffe, Grace, 'The Hospital of St John the Baptist in medieval Dublin: functions and maintenance' in Seán Duffy (ed.), *Medieval Dublin IX*, pp 166–82.

O'Keeffe, Tadhg, 'Medieval frontiers and fortification: the Pale and its evolution' in F.H.A. Aalen & Kevin Whelan (eds), *Dublin, city and county: from prehistory to present* (Dublin, 1992), pp 57–77

—, 'The frontier in medieval Ireland: an archaeological perspective', *Group for the Study of Irish Historic Settlement Newsletter* (1995), 16–18.

—, *Medieval Irish buildings, 1100–1600* (Dublin, 2015).

—, *Tristernagh priory, Co. Westmeath: colonial monasticism in medieval Ireland* (Dublin, 2018).

—, 'Frontiers of the archaeological imagination: rethinking landscape and identity in thirteenth-century Roscommon, Ireland', *Landscapes* 19 (2018), 66–79.

—, *Ireland encastellated: Insular castle-building in its European context* (Dublin, 2021).

O'Keeffe, Tadhg & Rhiannon Carey Bates, 'Colonial monasticism, the politics of patronage, and the beginnings of Gothic in Ireland: the Victorine cathedral priory of Newtown Trim, Co. Meath', *Journal of Medieval Monastic Studies* 6 (2017), 51–76.

O'Keeffe, Tadhg & Paolo Virtuani, 'Reconstructing Kilmainham: the topography and architecture of the chief priory of the Knights Hospitaller in Ireland, *c.*1170–1349', *JMH* 46 (2020), 449–77.

O'Keeffe, Tadhg & Pat Grogan, 'Building a frontier? The architecture of the military orders in medieval Ireland' in Martin Browne & Colmán Ó Clabaigh (eds), *Soldiers of Christ: the Knights Hospitaller and the Knights Templar in medieval Ireland* (Dublin, 2016), pp 81–102.

O'Malley, Gregory, *The Knights Hospitaller of the English langue 1460–1565* (Oxford, 2005).

—, 'Authority and autonomy: relations between Clerkenwell, Kilmainham and the Hospitaller central convent after the Black Death' in Martin Browne & Colmán Ó Clabaigh (eds), *Soldiers of Christ: the Knights Hospitaller and the Knights Templar in medieval Ireland* (Dublin, 2016), pp 23–46.

O'Neill, James, *The Nine Years War, 1593–1603: O'Neill, Mountjoy and the military revolution* (Dublin, 2018).

Ordman, Jilana, 'Was it an embarrassment of rewards?: possible relationships between religious devotion among participants in the Second Crusade, 1145–1149, and their losses in the field' in E. Weber (ed.), *Seduction: the art of persuasion in the medieval world*. Essays in Medieval Studies 30 (2014), pp 113–40.

Bibliography

Orme, Nicholas & M. Webster, *The English hospital, 1070–1570* (New Haven & London, 1995).

Ó Riain, Diarmuid, 'An Irish Jerusalem in Franconia; the abbey of the Holy Cross and Holy Sepulchre in Eichstät', *PRIA* 112C (2012), 219–70.

Ó Riain, Padraig, *Dictionary of Irish saints* (Dublin, 2011).

Orpen, G.H., *Ireland under the Normans, 1169–1333*. 4 vols (Oxford, 1911–20; repr. Dublin, 2005).

Ó Siochrú, Michael, 'Foreign involvement in the revolt of Silken Thomas, 1534–5', *PRIA* 96C (1996), 49–66.

O'Sullivan, Aidan, 'Wood in archaeology', *AI* 4: 2 (1990), 69–73.

Otway-Ruthven, A.J., 'The organisation of Anglo-Irish agriculture in the Middle Ages', *JRSAI* 81 (1951), 1–13.

—, 'The partition of the de Verdon lands in Ireland in 1332', *PRIA* 66C (1967–8), 401–55.

Palmer, J.J.N., *England, France and Christendom, 1377–99* (London, 1972).

Palmer, William, *The problem of Ireland in Tudor foreign policy, 1485–1603* (Woodbridge, 1994).

Patterson, Linda, Luca Barbieri & Ruth Harvey (eds), *Singing the crusades: French and Occitan lyric responses to the crusading movements, 1137–1336* (Cambridge, 2018).

Paul, Nicholas L., *To follow in their footsteps: the crusades and family memory in the high Middle Ages* (Ithaca, 2012).

—, 'In search of the Marshal's lost crusade: the persistence of memory, the problems of history and the painful birth of crusade romance', *JMH* 40 (2014), 292–310.

—, 'The fruits of penitence and the laurel of the cross. The poetics of crusade and conquest in the memorials of Santa Maria de Ripoll' in Torben K. Nielsen & Iben Fonnesberg-Schmidt (eds), *Crusading on the edge: ideas and practice of crusading in Iberia and the Baltic region, 1100–1500* (Turnhout, 2016), pp 245–73.

Paul, Nicholas & Suzanne Yeager (eds), *Remembering the crusades: myth, image and identity* (Baltimore, 2012).

Pegg, Mark, *A most holy war: the Albigensian Crusade and the battle for Christendom* (Oxford, 2008).

Perkins, Clarence, 'The Knights Templar in the British Isles', *EHR* 25 (1910), 209–30.

Phillips, C. Matthew, 'Crucified with Christ: the imitation of the crucified Christ and crusading spirituality' in Thomas F. Madden, James L. Naus & Vincent Ryan (eds), *Crusades – medieval worlds in conflict* (London & New York, 2010), pp 25–33.

Piana, Mathias & Christer Carlsson (eds), *Archaeology and architecture of the military orders: new studies* (Farnham, 2014).

Picard, Jean-Michel, 'Aquitaine et Irlande dans le haut moyen age' in Jean-Michel Picard (ed.), *Aquitaine and Ireland in the Middle Ages* (Dublin, 1994).

—, 'The colour purple: cultural cross-fertilisation and translation in early medieval Ireland' in E. Bremer, J. Jarnut, M. Richter & D. Wasserstein (eds), *Language of the people – language of religion: medieval Judaism, Christianity and Islam* (Munich, 2007), pp 241–9.

—, 'Transmission and circulation of French texts in medieval Ireland: the other Simon de Montfort' in Paul Duffy, Tadhg O'Keeffe & Jean-Michel Picard (eds), *From Carrickfergus to Carcassonne: the epic deeds of Hugh de Lacy during the Albigensian Crusade* (Turnhout, 2018), pp 129–50.

Pohl, Walter, 'Frontiers and ethnic identities: some final considerations' in Flora Curta (ed.), *Borders, barriers, and ethnogenesis: frontiers in late antiquity and the Middle Ages* (Turnhout, 2005), pp 255–65

Potterton, Michael, 'French connections in late medieval Ireland: the case of Geoffrey de Geneville (c.1226–1314)', *Explorations in Renaissance Culture* 39 (2013), 59–81.

Potterton, Michael & Margaret Murphy, 'Agriculture in the Tara/Skreen region, c.AD 1179–1660' in Muiris O'Sullivan, Christopher Scarre & Maureen Doyle (eds), *Tara: from the past to the future* (Dublin, 2013), pp 391–400.

Power, Daniel, 'Frontiers: terms, concepts, and the historians of medieval and early modern Europe' in Daniel Power & Naomi Standen (eds), *Frontiers in question: Eurasian borderlands, 700–1700* (Basingstoke, 1999), pp 1–12.

Prescott, Elizabeth, *The English medieval hospital, 1050–1640* (London, 1992).

Prestwich, Michael, *Edward I* (New Haven, 1988).

Purcell, Emer, 'The expulsion of the Ostmen, 1169–1170: the documentary evidence', *Peritia* 17–18 (2003–4), 273–94.

—, 'Michan: saint, cult and church' in John Bradley, Alan Fletcher & Anngret Simms (eds), *Dublin in the medieval world* (Dublin, 2009), pp 119–40.

Purkis, William J., *Crusading spirituality in the Holy Land and Iberia, c.1095–c.1187* (Woodbridge, 2008).

—, 'Introduction. Material religion in the crusading world', *Material Religion* 14 (2018), 433–7.

—, '"Zealous imitation": the materiality of the crusader's marked body', *Material Religion* 14 (2018), 438–53.

Rae, Edwin C., 'Irish sepulchral monuments of the later Middle Ages: part I: the Ormond Group', *JRSAI* 100 (1970), 1–38.

—, 'Irish sepulchral monuments of the later Middle Ages: part II: the O'Tunney atelier', *JRSAI* 101 (1971), 1–39.

Rafferty, Oliver P., *Catholicism in Ulster, 1603–1983: an interpretive history* (London, 1994).

Rawcliffe, Carole, *Medicine for the soul* (Stroud, 1999).

Rees, William, *A history of the order of St John of Jerusalem in Wales and on the Welsh border, including an account of the Templars* (Cardiff, 1947).

Regout, Robert, *La doctrine de la guerre juste de saint Augustin à nos jours d'après les théologiens et les canonistes catholiques* (Paris, 1935).

Reuter, Timothy, 'The "feudal revolution"', *Past and Present* 155 (1997), 177–95.

Reynolds, Burnam W., *The prehistory of the crusade: missionary war and the Baltic Crusades* (London, 2016).

Riley-Smith, Jonathan, *The crusades, Christianity, and Islam* (New York, 2008).

—, *The Knights Hospitaller in the Levant, c.1070–1309* (Basingstoke, 2012).

Rist, Rebecca, *The papacy and crusading in Europe, 1198–1245* (London, 2009).

Ritoók, Pál, 'The architecture of the Knights Templar in England' in Malcolm Barber (ed.), *The military orders: fighting for the faith and caring for the sick* (London, 2016), pp 167–78.

Rodrigue, Tréton, 'L'organisation topographique de la commanderie du Masdéu en Roussillon', *Archéologie du Midi médiéval* 28 (2010), 271–95.

Roquebert, Michel, *La religion cathare le bien, le mal et le salut dans l'hérésie médiévale* (Paris, 2001).

Rubin, Miri, *Charity and community in medieval Cambridge* (Cambridge, 1987).

St Lawrence, John Edward, 'The Liber miraculorum of Simon de Montfort: contested sanctity and contesting authority in late thirteenth-century England' (PhD, University of Texas, 2005).

Saul, Nigel, *Richard II* (London, 1999).

Schabel, Chris, 'The myth of the White Monks' "mission to the orthodox": Innocent III, the Cistercians, and the Greeks', *Traditio* 70 (2015), 237–61.

Scott, A.B., 'Latin learning and literature in Ireland 1169–1500' in Dáibhí Ó Cróinín (ed.), *A new history of Ireland, i: Prehistoric and early Ireland* (Oxford, 2005), pp 934–5.

Scott, Brendan, 'The Knights Hospitaller in Tudor Ireland: their dissolution and attempted revival' in Martin Browne & Colmán Ó Clabaigh (eds), *Soldiers of Christ: the Knights Hospitaller and the Knights Templar in medieval Ireland* (Dublin, 2016), pp 47–60.

Scott, George Digby, *Stones of Bray* (Dublin, 1913).

Seaver, Matthew & Maeve Sikora, 'Miscellany', *JRSAI* 149 (2019), 166–70.

Bibliography

Selart, Anti, 'Popes and Livonia in the first half of the thirteenth century: means and chances to shape the periphery', *Catholic Historical Review* 100:3 (2014), 437–58.

—, *Livonia, Rus' and the Baltic Crusades* (Leiden, 2015).

Setton, Kenneth (ed.), *The history of the crusades.* 6 vols (Madison, Wisconsin, 1969–89).

Shachar, Uri Zvi, '"Re-orienting" *Estoires d'Outremer*: the Arabic context of the Saladin legend' in Laura K. Morreale & Nicholas L. Paul (eds), *The French of Outremer: communities and communications in the crusading Mediterranean* (New York, 2018), pp 150–78.

Sheehy, Maurice, 'The Bull *"Laudabiliter"*: a problem in medieval diplomatique and history', *Journal of the Galway Archaeological and Historical Society* 29 (1961), 45–70.

Shields, Hugh, 'The "Lament for Simon de Montfort": an unnoticed text of the French poem', *Medium Ævum* 41 (1972), 202–7.

Shine, Denis, Ashley Green, Finola O'Carroll, Stephen Mandal & Bairbre Mullee, 'What lies beneath: chasing the Trim town wall circuit', *AI* 30: 1 (2016), 34–8.

Silke, John J., 'The Irish appeal of 1593 to Spain: some new light on the genesis of the Nine Years War', *Irish Ecclesiastical Record* 22 (1950), 278–90.

Simms, Katharine, *Medieval Gaelic sources* (Dublin, 2009).

Sloane, Barney & Gordon Malcolm, *Excavations at the priory of the Order of the Hospital of St John of Jerusalem, Clerkenwell, London* (London, 2004).

Smallwood, T.M., 'The prophecy of the six kings', *Speculum* 60 (1985), 571–92.

Smith, Brendan, 'The medieval border: Anglo-Irish and Gaelic Irish in late thirteenth and early fourteenth century Uriel' in Raymond Gillespie & Harold O'Sullivan (eds), *The borderlands: essays on the history of the Ulster-Leinster border* (Belfast, 1989), pp 41–54.

— (ed.), *The Cambridge history of Ireland*, iv: 600–1550 (Cambridge, 2017).

Smith, Caroline, 'Saints and sinners at sea on the first crusade of Saint Louis' in Thomas F. Madden, James L. Naus & Vincent Ryan (eds), *Crusades – medieval worlds in conflict* (London & New York, 2010), pp 161–72.

Smith, Thomas W., 'Oliver of Cologne's *Historia Damiatina*: a new manuscript witness in Dublin, Trinity College Library MS 496', *Hermathena* 194 (2017 for 2013), 31–62.

—, *Curia and crusade. Pope Honorius III and the recovery of the Holy Land, 1216–1227* (Turnhout, 2017).

Sommerfeldt, John R., 'The Bernardine reform and the crusading spirit', *Catholic Historical Review* 86 (2000), 567–78.

Soukup, Pavel, 'Pilgrimage elements in crusades with Czech participation in the twelfth century' in Daniel Doležal & Hartmut Kühne (eds), *Wallfahrten in der europäischen Kultur* (Frankfurt am Main, 2006), pp 53–64.

Spencer, Stephen, 'Emotions and the other: emotional characterizations of Muslim protagonists in narratives of the crusades' in Simon Parsons & Linda Patterson (eds), *Literature of the crusades* (Woodbridge, 2018), pp 41–54.

Stalley, Roger, *The Cistercian monasteries of Ireland* (New Haven, 1987).

—, 'A misunderstood gothic masterpiece: the Cantwell effigy at Kilfane, Co. Kilkenny' in Etienne Rynne (ed.), *Figures from the past* (Dún Laoghaire, 1987), pp 209–22.

Stancliffe, Clare, 'Red, white and blue martyrdom' in Dorothy Whitelock, Rosamund McKitterick & David N. Dumville (eds), *Ireland in early medieval Europe* (Cambridge, 1982), pp 21–46.

Stokes, G.T., 'Calendar of the "Liber niger Alani" (Continued)', *JRSAI* 7 (1897), 404–22.

Streusand, Douglas E., 'What does jihad mean?', *Middle East Quarterly* 4: 3 (1997), 9–17.

Suard, François, 'Chanson de geste traditionnelle et épopée de croisade', *Au carrefour des routes d'Europe: la chanson de geste* (Aix-en-Provence, 1987), i, pp 1033–55.

Sumption, Jonathan, *The age of pilgrimage: the medieval journey to God* (Mahwah, NJ, 2003).

Svenungsen, Pål Berg, 'Norway and the Fifth Crusade: the crusade movement on the outskirts of Europe' in Elizabeth Jane Mylod, Guy J. Perry & Thomas W. Smith (eds), *The Fifth Crusade in context: the crusading movement in the early thirteenth century* (London, 2017), pp 218–29.

Sweetman, P. David, 'Archaeological excavations at St John's priory, Newtown, Trim, Co. Meath', *Ríocht na Mídhe* 8 (1990/1), 89–104.

Tait, Laurence, 'The anti-septic vaults at St Michan's', *British Medical Journal* 2: 1460 (1888), 1416.

Tamm, Marek, 'The Livonian crusade in Cistercian stories of the early thirteenth century' in T.K. Nielsen & I. Fonnesberg-Schmidt (eds), *Crusading on the edge: ideas and practice of crusading in Iberia and the Baltic region, 1100–1500* (Turnhout, 2016), pp 365–89.

Tamminen, Mikka, *Crusade preaching and the ideal crusader* (Turnhout, 2018).

Tanner, Marcus, *Ireland's holy wars: the struggle for a nation's soul, 1500–2000* (London, 2001).

Taylor, Rupert, *The political prophecy in England* (New York, 1911).

Thatcher, Oliver J. & Edgar Holmes McNeal (eds), *A source book for mediæval history: selected documents illustrating the history of Europe in the Middle Age* (New York, 1905).

Thomas, Hugh M., *The English and the Normans: ethnic hostility, assimilation, and identity, 1066–c.1220* (Oxford, 2003).

Thompson, J.W., 'Profitable fields of investigation in medieval history', *American Historical Review* 28 (1913), 490–504.

Tibble, Steve, *The crusader armies* (New Haven, 2018).

Tipton, Charles, 'Peter Holt: turcopolier of Rhodes and prior of Ireland', *Annales de l'Ordre Souverain Militaire de Malte* 22 (1964), 82–5.

—, 'The Irish Hospitallers during the Great Schism', *PRIA* 69C (1970), 33–43.

Tolan, John, *Saracens: Islam in the medieval European imagination* (New York, 2002).

Toll, C., 'Arabic medicine and hospitals in the Middle Ages: a probable model for the military order's care of the sick' in Helen Nicholson (ed.), *The military orders, ii: Welfare and warfare* (Aldershot, 1998), pp 35–43.

Trotter, D.A., *Medieval French literature and the crusades* (Geneva, 1988).

Turner, Frederick Jackson, 'The significance of the frontier for American history', *The frontier in American history* (New York, 1920), pp 1–38.

Turner, Kathleen, *If you seek monuments: a guide to the antiquities of the barony of Rathdown* (Dublin, 1983).

Tyerman, Christopher, *England and the crusades, 1095–1588* (Chicago, 1988).

—, *The invention of the crusades* (Toronto, 1998).

—, *God's war: a new history of the crusades* (London, 2006).

—, *How to plan a crusade* (London, 2015).

Vander Elst, Stefan, *The knight, the cross and the song: crusade propaganda and chivalric literature, 1100–1400* (Philadelphia, 2017).

Veach, Colin, *Lordship in the four realms: the Lacy family, 1166–1241* (Manchester, 2014).

—, 'Henry II and the ideological foundation of Angevin rule in Ireland', *IHS* 42 (2018), 1–25.

Vicars, Arthur, *An account of the antiseptic vaults beneath S. Michan's church Dublin* (Dublin, 1888).

Vincent, Nicholas, 'Angevin Ireland' in Brendan Smith (ed.), *The Cambridge history of Ireland, i: 600–1550* (Cambridge, 2018), pp 185–221.

—, *Magna Carta, a very short introduction* (Oxford, 2012).

Virtuani, Paolo, 'The Knights of St John of Jerusalem in medieval Ireland (*c.*1169–1378)' (PhD, UCD, 2014).

Bibliography

—, 'Unforgiveable trespasses: the Irish Hospitallers and the defence of their rights in the mid-thirteenth century' in Martin Browne & Colmán Ó Clabaigh (eds), *Soldiers of Christ: the Knights Hospitaller and the Knights Templar in medieval Ireland* (Dublin, 2016), pp 195–205.

von Güttner-Sporzyniski, Darius, 'Recent issues in Polish historiography of the crusades' in Judith Upton-Ward (ed.), *The military orders, iv: On land and by sea* (Aldershot, 2008), pp 13–21.

Walsh, Micheline Kerney, 'The military order of St Patrick, 1593', *Seanchas Ardmhacha* 9 (1979), 274–85.

Walton, Julian, *The royal charters of Waterford* (Waterford, 1992).

Watson, Sethina, 'The origins of the English hospital', *TRHS* 16 (2006), 75–94.

Watt, J.A., 'Negotiations between Edward II and John XXII concerning Ireland', *IHS* 10 (1956), 1–20.

—, 'The Anglo-Irish colony under strain, 1327–99' in Art Cosgrove (ed.), *A new history of Ireland*, ii: *Medieval Ireland, 1169–1534* (Oxford, 1993), pp 352–96.

Weiler, Björn, '*Negotium terrae sanctae* in the political discourse of Latin Christendom, 1215–1311', *International History Review* 25 (2003), 1–36.

Williams, Ann, 'Crusaders as frontiersmen: the case of the order of St John in the Mediterranean' in Daniel Power & Naomi Standen (eds), *Frontiers in question: Eurasian borderlands, 700–1700* (Basingstoke, 1999), pp 209–27.

—, 'Heresy in Ireland in the thirteenth and fourteenth centuries' in Seán Duffy (ed.), *Princes, prelates and poets in medieval Ireland* (Dublin, 2016), pp 339–51.

Wood, Herbert, 'The Templars in Ireland', *PRIA* 26C (1907), 327–77.

—, 'The public records of Ireland before and after 1922', *TRHS* 13 (1930), 17–49.

Yeager, R.F., '*Le Songe Vert*, BL Add. MS 34114 (the Spalding Manuscript), Bibliothèque de la ville de Clermont, MS 249 and John Gower' in Simon Horobin & Linne R. Mooney (eds), *Middle English texts in translation* (York, 2014), pp 75–87.

Index

Ab Iorwerth, Llwelyn, 81, 103
Abbeydorney (Co. Kerry), 44
Abulafia, David, 196n51
Acre (Israel/Palestine), 96, 99, 101, 102, 134
Africa, 69
Aillardi, 74
Ainy (Co. Limerick), 118, 133, 158
al-Andalus, 38
al-Din, Sultan Nar, 131
al-Ghazali, Abu Hamid, 39
al-Mansourah (Egypt), 99
al-Sham [Bilad], 38
al-Sulami, Ali ibn Tahir, 38, 39
Albert VII, archduke of Austria, 174
Aldredus Palmerus, 72
Alen, John, archbishop of Dublin, 134, 141
Alexandria (Egypt), 98
Alphonse, count of Poitiers, 97
Aldredus Palmerus, 72
Alured, 135
Aluredo, 141
Amalfi (Italy), 129
Amalric, king of Jerusalem, 61n40
America, North, 195, 196, 197n57
scholarship, 193, 194, 195, 196
Americas, the, 69
Angevin (adj.), 16, 84, 89, 122, 138
Anglo-Norman(s) (adj.), 16, 17, 18, 21, 23, 25, 27, 29, 31, 32, 35, 49, 50, 51, 58, 70, 71, 75, 76, 86, 92, 93, 95, 109, 111, 113, 117, 122, 133, 157, 164, 178, 187, 191n34, 195, 198
Anglo-Saxons, 58n28
Anjou (France), 48, 58n27, 61n40, 97, 101, 106
Annals of the Four Masters, 167, 172
Annals of Inisfallen, 31
Annals of Loch Cé, 167
Annals of Multyfarnham, 85
Aquitaine (France), 58n27
Aragon (Spain), 50, 81, 122, 166
Arbour Hill, Dublin, 181

archbishops/archbishoprics
Armagh, 25, 27n45, 50, 65, 173
Cashel, 27n45, 50, 62, 103
Dublin, 21, 25, 27, 50, 53, 79, 101, 114, 115, 119, 125, 134, 140n26, 141, 143, 146
Tuam, 53
Archdall, Mervyn, 21
Archer, Father James S.J., 175
Ardagh (Co. Longford), 65
Ards peninsula (Co. Down), 110
Arklow (Co. Wicklow), 126
Askeaton (Co. Limerick), 198
assassins, the, 99
Athassel (Co. Tipperary), 161, pl. 11.5
Athy (Co. Kildare), 127
Attyflynn (Co. Limerick), 148
Australia, 69
Avignon (Dép. Vaucluse, France), 67
Ayyubid caliphate, the, 97, 99

Babylon, 165
Bahriyyas, the, 99
Baibars, Sultan, 99, 101, 123
Baldongan (Co. Dublin), 112, pl. 7.2
Baldoyle (Co. Dublin), 148
Baldwin, archbishop of Canterbury, 76
Baldwin IV, king of Jerusalem, 61
Baldwin, John, 83
Ballemunder, 142
Ballimany, 142
Ballycorus (Co. Dublin), 136n2, 142
Ballyhoge (Co. Wexford), 110
Ballyhoge (Co. Wexford), 110
Ballymacorus (?Co. Dublin), 136, 140, 141, 142, 148, 152
Ballyman (Co. Dublin), 136, 138, 139, 140, 141, 142, 143, 145, 146, 147, 148, 149, 150, 151, 152, pls 10.1, 10.2, 10.3
Baltic, the, 107, 183, 184, 193, 198n65
Baltinglass (Co. Wicklow), 62
Banagh, Jordano, 141
Bangor (Co. Down), 44

224

Index

Barbarossa, Frederick, Holy Roman emperor, 63, 94
Barber, Malcolm, 139
Barnasligan (Co. Dublin), 143
Bartlett, Robert, 192, 195
Baziège (*Dép.* Haute-Garonne), 84, pl. 5.2
Beaubec (*Dép.* Seine-Maritime), 48
Beaubec [Bey More] (Co. Meath), 49
Becket, Thomas, archbishop of Canterbury, 53, 62n42, 63, 64, 138, 191n34
Bective (Co. Meath), 48
Berengaria of Navarre, wife of Richard I, 159
Bernard, of Clairvaux, 25, 39, 41, 42, 43, 44, 46, 47, 49, 50, 51, 80, 107, pl. 2.1
Beverley (Yorkshire), 74
'Bevis of Hampton', 31
Bey More [Beaubec] (Co. Meath), 49
Béziers (*Dép.* Hérault), 78 [spelling]
bimaristans, 131
Bird, Jessalyn, 83
bishops/bishoprics, Ireland
    Ardagh, 65
    Armagh, 44
    Connor, 44, 65
    Derry, 168
    Down, 44, 65
    Glendalough, 149n
Black Book of the exchequer, 63
Black Death, 34, 156
Blund, Henry, archbishop of Dublin, 50
Bohemia, 42, 43, 45
Bordeaux (*Dép.* Gironde), 77, 78
Boru, Brian, 16, 51
Bourgeois, Nicolas, 46
Bradshaw, Brendan, 168
Bray (Co. Wicklow), 136, 144, 146, 150n97, 152
Bradley, Brother, 150
Bramber (Sussex), 81
Bray (Co. Wicklow), 136, 144, 145, 146, 152
Braydock, Philip, 78
Breakspear, Nicholas [Adrian IV], 55
Bridlington prophecies, the, 165n9
Bristol, 73
Britain, 52, 55, 72, 113, 120, 122, 136, 138, 156, 160
British Museum, 85

Brittany (France), 46
Broghton family, 113
Bruce, Edward, 66, 124, 125
Bruce, Robert, 65, 124, 125
Bruce wars, the, 127, 156
Bunratty Castle (Co. Clare), 64
Burgundy (France), 83
Burton, Nathaniel, 181
Butler, family, 21
    Theobald Walter, 157, 158n10
    Thomas, prior of Ireland, 114
Byrne, Aisling, 31, 34, 128, 138, 171, 174, 202, 203, 207, 213
Byrne, Niall, 138
Byzantium/Byzantine, 46, 194

Cairo (Egypt), 98, 99
Callan, Maeve, 17, 31, 36, 109, 115, 141, 166, 197
Cambridge Corpus Christi MS 405, 117
Canny, Nicholas, 173
Canterbury (Kent), 78, 79
Canterbury, see of/archbishops of, 53, 55, 81, 89, 101, 167
Cantwell [de Kentewall] family, 157, 159, 162
Capetian (adj.), 81, 89, 99, 194
Carcassonne (*Dép.* Aude), 79, 81, pl. 5.1
Cardiff (Wales), 73
Carlow, region, 127
Carolingian (adj.), 25, 194
Carrick-on-Suir (Co. Tipperary), 108, 112
Carrickfergus (Co. Antrim), 186n11
Carrickgollogan (Co. Dublin), 136, 141, 142, 146, 147
Carriklydan, 146
Cashel (Co. Tipperary), 159, 160, 161
cathedral, St John the Baptist (Church of Ireland), 159
    council of, 60
    diocesan library, 140n26
    effigy, 159, 160, 161,
Castelnaudary (Aude), 81, 110
Castile (Spain), 50, 116
Castleknock (Co. Dublin), 124, 191n34
Catalonia (Spain), 48, 77
Cathars, the, 16, 18, 30, 47, 56, 57, 77, 78, 79, 80, 82, 89, 92, 179, 184, 186n11

Catherine of Aragon, 166
Cavan, Co., 130
Champagne (France), 48, 93, 94, 96, 103
Chapuys, Eustace, 166n14, 167
Charles II, king of England (1660–85), 181
Charles V, Holy Roman emperor, 166, 169
Charles IX, king of France (1560–74), 169
Charles, count of Anjou, 97, 106
Cheminon (Marne), 97
Chronica Majora, 123
Chester (England), 81
Chichester (Sussex), 135, pl. 9.3
Chronicon of Sigebert de Gembloux, 55n14
Cîteaux (*Dép.* Côte-d'Or, France), 49
civil war, English, 58n27
Clairvaux (*Dép.* Aude, France), 42, 44, 45, 46, 49
Clerkenwell (London), 122, 188–9
Climethedta, 144
Clonkeen (Co. Dublin), 151
Clonmore (Co. Dublin), 142, 146, 147, 152
Clonoulty (Co. Tipperary), 20n11, 35
Clontarf, Battle of, 16
Clontarf (Co. Dublin), 16, 20, 148, 188, 191n34
Clumore, 142, 143
Clunard (?Clonard, Co. Meath), 73
Cogadh Gáedel re Gallaib, 16
Coleman, Edward, 17, 34, 36, 111, 137, 183
Cooley, Co. Louth, 92, 148
Commenus, Manuel, emperor of Byzantium, 46
Connacht, 49, 50, 86, 111, 117, 126, 127
Conradin of Hohenstaufen, 122
Constable, Giles, 55, 56, 192n38
Constantine, emperor, 55, 134
Cork, city, 170
'Cornubiensis', 71
Cornwall (England), 73
Cotswolds, the, 73
Cotter, Eamonn, 158
Counter-Remonstrance, 65, 67, 68; *see also* Remonstrance
Courson, Robert, 80, 83
Cowley, Robert, 167
Cox, David, 88n51

Crac des Chevaliers (Syria), 129, 187
Craig, Maurice, 179
Cranmer, Thomas, archbishop of Canterbury, 167
Créton, Jean, 155
Crooke (Co. Waterford), 118, 137, 190, pl. 7.1
crusade, concept and ideology, 15, 16, 17, 22, 23, 24, 27, 30, 39, 43, 47, 50, 51, 56, 57, 80
crusade, culture and experience, 16, 25, 29, 30
crusader lands, 24, 30, 123, 129, 132, 133, 156, 186, 193
crusaders, 13, 16, 18, 27, 28, 29, 30, 31, 32, 34, 37, 56, 70, 73, 78, 79, 80, 81, 83, 84, 89, 96, 98, 99, 101, 102, 104, 105, 106, 108, 111, 161, 164, 167, 172, 175, 176, 178, 179, 181, 182, 183, 184, 186, 193, 195, 198
crusades, 15, 16, 19, 21n12, 22, 23, 24, 25, 26, 27, 28, 29, 31, 32, 36, 37, 42, 43, 45, 46, 47, 48, 50, 51, 54, 56, 60, 62, 65, 66, 67, 68, 69, 78, 79, 80, 81, 83, 84, 89, 91, 92, 93, 95, 96, 97, 98, 99, 100, 101, 102, 104, 105, 106, 109, 110, 111, 120, 145, 154, 156, 161, 162, 164, 165, 166, 167, 168, 169, 170, 171, 172, 173, 175, 176, 177, 178, 179, 182, 183, 185, 186, 192, 194, 197, 198, 199
 Albigensian, 12, 18, 30, 48, 57, 75, 78, 79, 80, 81, 82, 84, 89, 92, 95, 96, 97, 110, 179, 183n1
 Aragon, 122
 Baltic, 193
 Barons' crusade, 100
 eastern Europe, 46
 Franco-papal crusade, 122
 in Spain, 60
 of Louis IX, 31, 91
 Spain, 60, 121
 First, 16, 29, 31, 38, 57n22, 107, 129, 183n3, 197
 Second, 29, 41, 42, 43, 44, 45, 46, 96
 Third, 30, 47, 70, 75, 96, 108, 134
 Fourth, 47, 48, 96
 Fifth, 31, 50, 80, 96, 165n5, 199
 Seventh, 93, 96–9
 Eighth, 18, 31, 91, 93, 99–102
 Ninth, 18, 101

Index

227

crusading, 12, 16, 17, 18, 19, 22, 24, 27, 28, 31, 32, 46, 60n39, 70, 73, 75, 91, 93, 99, 104, 105, 106, 110, 111, 120, 121, 133, 134, 154, 156, 160, 161, 162, 164, 165, 166, 173, 177, 182, 183, 184, 186, 192, 193, 194, 196, 198, 198, 199
Cushendun (Co. Antrim), 169
Cyprus, 98, 113

d'Alton, John, 21
d'Auxonne, Béatrice, 94
Dalkey (Co. Dublin), 145, 152
Damascus (Syria), 131
Damietta (Egypt), 98, 99
Davies, Mary, 145
de Beaumont, Amicia, 82
de Bermingham, Peter, 64
de Bleden, Stephen, 73
de Braose family, 82
 Gilbert, 81
 William, 81, 82, 89
de Burgh family, 155
 Richard, 86
de Burley, Thomas, prior of Ireland, 127
de Bykenore, Alexander, 119, 153
de Clahull, Hugh, 21
de Clare, Aífe, 57
de Clare, Richard (Strongbow), 20, 21, 57, 58, 60, 92, 110, 111, 118, 142, 144, 158
de Clare, Thomas, 64, 102
de Cogan, Richard, 144
De consideratione, 46, 47, 47,
de Erseldoune, Thomas, 165n5
de Feypo family, 87
 Adam, 87
 Christiana 88
 Richard [I], 87, 88
 Richard [II], 87, 88
 Richard [III], 87
de Freynet, Gilbert, 78
de Geneville family, 104
 see also de Joinville
 Geoffrey, 18, 91, 92, 93, 94, 95, 96, 97, 98, 99, 100, 101, 102, 103, 104, 105, 106, 185n11, 186n11, pls 6.1, 6.3
 Simon, 94

de Hackett, William, 159, 160, 162
de Howth, John, 146
de Joinville family, 93, 94, 96,
 Geoffrey III, 96
 Geoffrey IV, 96
 Geoffrey V, 96
 Jean, 18, 91, 96, 97, 98, 99, 100, 101, 102, 103, 104, 105, 106
 Matilda, wife of Geoffrey de Geneville, 104
 Simon, father of Jean de Joinville, 94, 96
 Simon, son of Geoffrey de Geneville, 103
 Walter, 103
de Kentewall, Thomas, 157
de Lacey, John, 173
de Lacy family, 48, 82, 86, 87, 90, 92, 93, 95, 110, 111
 Gilbert, 92, 108, 110
 Hugh I, 48, 89, 92, 93, 191n34
 Hugh II, 16, 18, 30, 48, 79, 80, 81, 82, 83, 84, 85, 86, 87, 88, 89, 92, 95, 110, 111, 186n11
 John, 81
 Margaret, 92
 Matilda (aka Maud), 20n11, 94, 105
 Walter, 48, 87, 89, 93, 94
 William Gorm, 89
De laudenovae militiae, 39, 47,
de Lindsey, Thomas, 137
de Lissebon family, 146, 147
 Aunger, 146
 John, 145, 146, 152
 Walter, 141
 William, 146
de Marcy, Henry, abbot of Clairvaux, 47
de Marisco, Christina, 144n52, 152n106
 Geoffrey, 158, 159, 162
de Mézières, Philippe, 166
de Montfort family, 48, 104
 Bertrade, 82n24
 Simon, 18, 48, 79, 81–90, 92, 110, pl. 5.1
 Simon II, 96, 104
de Pembridge, John, 66
de Pencoyt, Geoffrey, 64, 66
de Perseigne, Adam, abbot, 51
de Prendergast, Maurice, 34n82, 108

De regno Hiberniae, sanctorum insula, commentarius, 175

de Ridelesford, Walter, 144, 145, 152

de Stapelbrugge, Stephen, 137

de Ros, William, 124

de Sandford, Fulk, archbishop of Dublin, 125

del Aqua, Walter, 124

des Vaux-de-Cernay, Guy, 48
Pierre, 51

de Verdon, John, 93

de Vescy, William, 102

Dictionnaire européen des orders militaires au moyen âge, 187

Diet of Frankfurt, 43

Donation of Constantine, 55

Dorset, 95

Dover (Kent), 191n34

Down, Kevin, 149

Downey, Declan, 172

Dressler, Rachel, 161

Drumlane (Co. Cavan) 130

du Noyer, George, 159

Dublin
All Hallows priory, 148
castle, 66, 94, 155,
Christ Church cathedral, 151, 158, 160, pl. 11.3
city, 16, 18, 21, 36, 57, 66, 67, 70, 72, 73, 74, 75, 76, 78, 79, 102, 111, 120, 124, 125, 134, 145, 155, 169, 170, 176, 178, 181, 182, 196
county/region, 20, 66, 116, 127, 140, 142, 144, 145, 147,
Dublin Penny Journal, 180
Guild Merchant Roll, 18, 70, 72, 73, 74, 75, pl. 4.1
Holy Trinity priory, *see* Christ Church cathedral
Hospital of St John the Baptist, Newgate, 134, pl. 4.2
marches, 17, 146, 152,
St Mary's abbey, 179
St Mary's church, 178
St Michan's church, 18, 178, 179, 180, 181, 182, pls 13.1, 13.2, 13.3

St Patrick's cathedral, 65

St Patrick's parish, 72

St Paul's church, 178

St Peter's church, pl. 11.1

St Thomas's priory/abbey, 191n34

synod (1186), 62

Trinity College, 158

Duffy, Paul, 18, 29, 75n17, 179

Duggan, Anne, 55, 59n31, 61n38, 63, 109

Dú[i] More, 143

Duiske abbey, Graiguenamanagh (Co. Kilkenny), 160

Dunstable annalist, 82

Duvenaldus *palmerius de* Limeric, 76

Edessa (Turkey), city of, 41

Edward I, prince/king of England (1272–1307), 29, 30, 31, 91, 93, 96, 100, 101, 102, 103, 104, 105, 123, 124, 126, 127, 144n52

Edward II, king of England (1307–27), 63, 65, 68, 104, 114, 125, 165,

Edward III, king of England (1327–77), 20, 67, 104, 114, 115, 162, 163, pls 11.6, 11.7

Edward IV, king of England (1461–70), 116, 169

Edwardus *Palmerius,* 72

Egypt, 97, 98, 99, 165

Eleanor of Aquitaine, 58n27

Eleanor of Castille, 102

Eleanor of Provençe, 94

Elias, son of Siward the goldsmith, 72

Elizabeth I, queen of England, 120, 169, 170, 171, 172, 175, 181

Ellis, Stephen, 167

England, 22n20, 25, 29, 30, 33n81, 34n82, 35, 42, 45, 46, 50, 52, 53, 55, 56, 58, 61, 62n42, 63, 65, 73, 74, 77, 78, 81, 82, 85, 89, 91, 92, 93, 94, 100, 101, 103, 104, 105, 108, 109, 113, 114, 115, 116, 117, 119, 120, 122, 123, 124, 125, 131, 132, 133, 137, 144n52, 166, 167, 170, 177, 187n20, 191, 195, 199

Eogan, James, 148

Epirus (Greece), 123

Essex, earl of, 174, 175

Europe, Eastern, 24, 43, 44, 46

Eustace, James, third Viscount Baltinglass, 172

Index

229

Evesham (Worcestershire, England), 84, 85, 86, 87, 88, 96, pl. 5.3
Evreux (*Dép.* Eure), 82
Exeter family, 86
    Jordan, 85, 86
    Stephen, 85, 86
Expugnatio Hibernia, 54, 57, 58, 60, 61, 155

Falkiner, Caesar Litton, 17, 19, 20, 21, 22, 28, 37
Falkiner, Frederick, 181
Ferrers, William, count of Derby, 82
Fethard (Co. Tipperary), 89
First Barons' War, 82
fitz Gerald
    family (the Geraldines), 21, 59, 167, 172
    Gerald (d. 1583), 170
    Gerald (d. 1585), 168
    James (Geraldine) (d. 1579), 170, 171, 172, 173, 176, 177
    John (Geraldine) (d. 1536), 176
    Maurice (d. 1176), 59, 191n34
    Maurice (d. 1286), 114
    Maurice (d. 1356), 33
    Thomas (d. 1537), 117, pl. 12.1
fitz Osbert family, 158, 162
fitz Ralph, Richard, 65
fitz Richard, Robert, 158, 162
fitz Roger, William, master of the Hospital, 20, 36, 114, 123, 126, pl. 8.1
Flanders (Belgium), 74, 77, 103
Flandrensis, 71
Forey, Alan, 121
Forni, Alberto, 50
France, 18, 29, 30, 31, 41, 42, 46, 48, 49, 50, 51, 52, 57, 58, 62, 77, 78, 79, 80, 82, 89, 91, 92, 93, 94, 97, 99, 100, 103, 104, 105, 107, 113, 139, 158, 169, 183, 194, 199
Francigena, 71
Free School, King Charles, 181
Frowyck, Prior John, 119
Fulk of Anjou, 61n40
Fulk of Neuilly, 47

Galgethel *palmer filius* Reinaldi, 74
Gallen (Gailenga), barony, 86

Galway, city, 78, 168
Gascony (France), 77, 78
Geoffrey, count of Anjou, 58n27
Geoffrey of Monmouth, 165n5
Gerald [the Cathar], 77
Giraldus Cambrensis, 34n82, 54, 55, 57, 58, 59, 60, 61, 62, 63, 68, 73, 109, 155, 165, 195n48
German empire, the, 24
Germany, 25, 42, 45, 77, 199
Gerrard, Chris, 136
Gervase of Canterbury, 58
Gervase of Tilbury, 68, 165
Gillibertus se[...] *militis*, 75
Glencree (Co. Wicklow), 150, 151
Glendalough (Co. Wicklow), 142, 149
Glenmalure (Co. Wicklow), 102, pl. 7.2
Glenmondyr, 142
Glenmunare, 142
Glenmunder (Co. ?), 136, 140, 142, 143, 147, 151, 152
Glenmunare, 149
Glennmuneri, 142
Glenwhery, 151
Glinne Munire, 142, 143
Gloucestershire, 110
Gowran (Co. Kilkenny), 157, 158n11
Granard (Co. Longford), 65
Greene, Joshua, 52n2
Gregorian reform, the, 57, 198
Grey, Henry, Lord of Ruthin, 116
Grissaphan, George, 119
Gwynn, Aubrey, 22, 130

Hadcock, Neville, 22, 130, 134
Hanmer, Meredith, 178, 180
Heraclius, patriarch of Jerusalem, 61, 62n42
Haren, Michael, 59n31
Harris, Oliver, 161
Harris, Walter, 21, 140n26
Haverfordwest (Pembrokeshire), 73
Henry, count of Champagne, 46
Henry I, king of England (1100–35), 59, 133
Henry II, king of England (1154–89), 20, 32, 44, 53, 54, 55, 56, 57, 58, 60, 61, 62, 63, 64, 66, 68, 69, 77, 89, 92, 108, 109, 110, 111, 138, 157, 165, 191n34

230   *Ireland and the crusades*

Henry the Young King (d. 1183), 30
Henry III, king of England (1216–72), 27,
    29, 30, 92n4, 94, 95, 96, 100, 101, 104,
    105, 114
Henry IV, king of England (1399–1413), 115
Henry V, king of England (1413–22), 32, 166
Henry VII, king of England (1485–1509), 117
Henry VIII, king of England (1509–47), 120,
    166, 167, 168, 169
Henry, Lord Grey of Ruthin, 116
Herefordshire (England), 87
Historia Damiatina, 165n5
Holt, Brother Peter, 114
Holy Cross abbey (Co. Tipperary), 169n33
Holy Grail, the, 199
Holy Land, the, 16, 17, 23, 27, 29, 30, 32, 36,
    42, 46, 50, 56, 62, 70, 71, 72, 73, 76, 79,
    80, 93, 99, 101, 102, 106, 107, 110, 113, 120,
    122, 123, 126, 128, 129, 131, 132, 133, 134, 138,
    139, 156, 161, 165, 166, 176, 186, 189, 199
Holy Roman empire, the, 94, 105
Holy Sepulchre, Jerusalem, 191
holy war, 31, 32, 38, 39, 46, 56, 110, 115, 128,
    164, 166, 169, 170, 172, 173, 176; *see also*
    jihad
Hospital (Co. Limerick), 35, 118, 158, 160, 162,
    190, pls 11.2, 14.3
hospitals, 17, 108, 110, 112, 118, 119, 129, 130,
    131, 132, 133, 134, 135
Housely, Norman, 67n68, 192
Huguenots, 170
Humbert of Romans, 95
Hundred Years War, 89
Hungary, 24n31, 116, 199
Hurlock, Kathryn, 17, 28, 29, 31, 109, 115

Île-de-France, 191
Inch (Co. Down), 65
Irish Public Record Office, 19
Irish Times, 181
Isabella, Queen of France, 10, 159
Islam, 30, 40, 68, 132, 194n44, 197, 198,
Ivory, Thomas, 17, 118

Jaspert, Nikolas, 197
Jericho, Israel/Palestine, 71

Jerpoint Abbey (Co. Kilkenny), 160, pl. 11.4
Jerusalem
    city of, 27n47, 30, 38, 42, 44, 56, 61, 62,
        71, 76, 97, 99, 107, 120, 129, 131, 132,
        134, 138, 187, 198, 199
    Hospital of St John, 32, 35, 92, 129, 131,
        132
    kingdom of, 29, 38, 101, 186
Jews, 16, 56, 186, 194, 198
Jihad, 38, 39, 40, 184n3; *see also* Holy War
Johannes Flandrensis le Riddire, 75
John, king of England (1199–1216), 61, 62n45,
    63, 66, 70, 76, 79, 81, 82, 83, 89, 92, 94,
    110, 142, 144, 158, 159, 167
John of Salisbury, 55, 59, 63
John of Howth, 145
John Scotus Eriugena, 25
Jordan, river, 71

Kahl, Hans-Dietrich, 42
Keating, James, 116, 117
Kells, Co. Meath, 92, 93
Kells-Mellifont, Synod of (1152), 44, 57
Kendi, Ibram, 52n2
Kenilworth (Warwickshire), 96
Kienzle, Beverly Mayne, 80
Kilbarry (Co. Waterford), 35, 117, 118, 128, 137
Kilbixy (Co. Westmeath), 130
Kilcloggan (Co. Waterford), 118, 137
Kilfane (Co. Kilkenny), 157, 159, 160
Kilkenny, Co., 157
    Hospital of St John the Baptist, 110
    St Mary's church, 161
Killerrig (Co. Carlow), 127
Killure (Co. Waterford), 118
Kilmainham (Co. Dublin), 20, 21, 36, 37, 73,
    92, 102, 108, 115, 116, 118, 119, 127, 132, 133,
    134, 159, 162, 163, 188, 189, 190, 191, 196,
    pl. 14.1
Kilmainhambeg (Co. Meath), 93
Kilmainhamwood (Co. Meath), 92
Kilsaran, Co. Louth, 92, 149
Kilteel (Co. Kildare), 127, 136, 184, 188, 190,
    197, pl. 8.2
King, William, archbishop of Dublin, 21
Kinsale (Co. Cork), 175, 176, 198, pl. 12.3

Index

231

Kitab al Jihad, 38

Knights Hospitaller, 16, 17, 19, 20, 21, 22, 23, 28, 32, 33, 34, 35, 36, 37, 70, 81, 93, 101, 102, 107, 108, 109, 110, 111, 112, 113, 114, 115, 116, 117, 118, 119, 120, 121, 122, 123, 124, 125, 126, 127, 128, 129, 131, 132, 133, 134, 135, 137, 140n26, 152n105, 159, 162, 183, 184, 185, 187, 188, 189, 190, 191, 195n47, 197, 198, 199

Knights Templar, 16, 20, 21, 28, 30, 32, 34, 35, 36, 40, 68, 70, 92, 100, 101, 107, 108, 109, 110, 111, 112, 113, 114, 115, 116, 117, 118, 119, 120, 121, 122, 124, 129, 132, 136, 137, 138, 139, 140, 141, 142, 143, 144. 145, 146, 147, 148, 149, 150, 151, 152, 153, 161, 162, 183, 185, 187, 188, 189, 190, 191, 197, 199

Kyteler, Alice, 33

Lancelot, bishop of Winchester, 179

Langton, Stephen, archbishop of Canterbury, 78, 81, 82, 83, 84, 89, 90

Langton, Walter, 78

Languedoc, France, 18, 24, 30n56, 56, 78, 79, 84

Larcher, Brother John, 114, 127,

Lateran Council,
Third (1179), 56
Fourth (1216), 50

Laudabiliter [et Satis], 54, 55, 57, 59, 60, 61, 62, 63, 64, 65, 66, 67, 68, 69, 109, 165n3, 170

Laurac (Aude), 110

le Brun, Fromond, 142

Le Dalgin, 146

le Gros, Raymond, 73

le Jay, Master Brian, 124

le Poer, Richard More, 127, 128

Leask, Harold, 161

Leclercq, Dom Jean, 42, 45

Ledrede, Richard, bishop of Ossory, 33, 65, 66, 67, 68

Leicester (England), 74

Leicester Guild Roll, 74

Lennon, Colm, 173

León, Spain, 50

Liber miraculorum, 87, 88, 89

Liffey, river, 111

Limerick
city, 57, 73, 76, 78, 117,
king of, 50

Lippiatt, Gregory, 83

Lismore (Co. Waterford), 44, 53

'Little John', 181

Liffey, river, 21, 111, 115, 125

Lippiatt, Gregory, 48, 83

Litany of Saints, 142

Lombard, Peter, 175

London (England), 73, 170

Longespée effigy, Salisbury, 158

Lorraine (France), 169

Lough Cé (Co. Roscommon), 86

Louis VII, king of France (1137–80), 41, 58n27, 59, 60

Louis IX, king of France (1214–70), 31, 82, 91, 93, 97, 98, 99, 100, 101, 104, 105, 106

Louth, Co., 149

Low Countries, the, 24

Lucca (Italy), 100

Ludlow Castle (Shropshire), 96

Luighne, cantred, 86

Lyde, barony (England), 88

Lydon, James, 106

Lynche, Thomas, 168, 169

Mabillon, Dom Jean, 42

McDonald, James, 169

MacGibbon, Maurice, archbishop of Cashel, 170

MacLellan, Rory, 120

mac Murrough, family, 66, 102
Diarmait, 45, 46, 49, 57, 60
brothers [Art & Murchertach], the, 64, 66

MacNiocaill, Geraoid, 140

Madden, Dr, 182

Maginn, Christopher, 172

Magna Carta, 83, 84, 89, 90

Malachy [Ua Morgair, Máel Máedóc], of Armagh, 25, 44, 45, 51, pl. 2.2

Mamluks, the, 99, 101

Manning, Con, 158, 161

Margaret of Provençe, 100

Markward of Anweiler, 56

Marseilles, 97

Marshal, Isabel 110
    William the elder, 30, 110
    William the younger, 86
    Richard, 114

Martin, F.X., 59, 60, 61

Martyrology of Donegal, 143

Martyrology of Tallaght, 142, 143

Mary, queen of England (1153–8), 120, 169

Matilda, daughter of Henry I, 58n27

Matthew, Elizabeth, 31

Mauguran, Edmund, archbishop of Armagh, 173

Maurice 'the engineer', 191n34

Maynooth (Co. Kildare), 191n34

Mortimer, Roger, 104

McNeill, Charles, 23

McDonnell, Ciarán, 18

McIlreavy, David, 17

Meath
    ancient kingdom, 93
    county, 92, 124
    lordship, 87, 89, 93, 94, 95, 106

Mediterranean, the, 16, 18, 23, 39, 72, 107, 111, 112, 113, 115, 121, 134, 183, 194, 195n47, 198, 199

Mellifont (Co. Louth), 27, 44, 48, 50, 51, 79, 80, 103

Merlin, 165n5

Midi-Pyrenees (France), 79

Moors, the, 165, 198

Morgan, Hiram, 175

Morocco, 171

Mourneabbey (Co. Cork), 35, 187, 188, 190, 198

Murphy, Margaret, 35, 113, 138, 139, 147, 148, 149, 185n10

Muslim (adj.), 31, 38, 39, 99, 131, 132, 187

Muslims, 15, 16, 27, 38, 39, 46, 47, 56, 60, 61, 68, 98, 99, 107, 122, 184n3, 186, 192, 194, 195, 197, 198

Navarre, Spain, 50, 116

Nest, daughter of Rhys ap Tawdr, 59

New Ross (Co. Wexford), 78

New York Times, 181

Newman, E.L., 149

Newcastle-upon-Tyne, 191n34

Newtown Trim (Co. Meath), 134, 135, pls 9.1, 9.2

Nicholaus *palmerius filius* Aillardi, 74

Nicholson, Helen J., 17, 32, 34, 70, 121, 122, 138

Nicolas of Clairvaux, 45, 46

Nile, river, 98

Nobber, Co. Meath, 92

Norensis, 71

Normandy (France), 24, 48, 52, 53, 58n27, 77, 82

Norragh (Co. Kildare), 158

Norreys, Thomas, 175

O'Brien, Elizabeth, 143, 151

O'Briain, Brian Ruad, 64

O'Brien, Brian Bán, 33

Ó Clabaigh, Colmán, 35, 117

O'Conairche, Christian, 51

O'Conor, Kieran, 35

O'Connor family, 64

O'Donnell, Katherine, 169

O'Heney, Muirges, archbishop of Cashel, 62

O'Keeffe, Tadhg, 18, 35, 36, 179

O'Malley, Gregory, 33, 34

O'Moore family, 169n31

O'Neill family, 169
    Dónal, 65
    Hugh, 32, 173, 179, pl. 12.2
    Shane, 169

O'Spellman, Ruaric, 168

O'Toole family, 66, 126
    Adam Duff, 78
    Adducc Dubh, 66, 67, 68, 69
    Lawrence, archbishop of Dublin, 25, 53

Occitania, 79, 80, 82, 83, 84, 86, 89

Odo of Deuil, 41

Odo of Wirmis, 139

Old Man of the Mountain, the, 99

Oliver of Cologne, 165n5

Order of St Lazarus, 132

Order of St Patrick, 173

Otto IV, Holy Roman emperor, 68

Ottoman Turks, 31, 41, 123, 176

Otway-Ruthven, Jocelyn, 140

Index 233

Outlaw, prior of Kilmainham, 23, 33, 35, 114, 116, 125, 159, 162
Outremer, 16, 18, 92, 183, 184n3, 186, 194, 195, 197, 198
Owenmore, river, 111
Oxmantown, 178, 179, 180, 181

Palestine, 62, 183n3
Palmer, William, 167, 169
Paparo, John, cardinal, 57
Paris (France), 33, 48, 80, 81, 82, 83, 94, 97
    abbey of St Victor, 82
    Ste-Chapelle, 97
Paris, Matthew, 123
Patricius *miles*, 76
Perrot, John, 170, 171
Peter II of Aragon, 81
Peter *Palmerus*, 72
Phillip II [Augustus], king of France (1190–1223), 81
Phillip II, king of Spain, 170
Picard, Jean-Michel, 17, 85
Pignatelli, Bernardo, 44
Pipe, barony (England), 88
Pisa (Italy), 44
Pium et sanctum propositum, 50
Pole, Cardinal Reginald, 169
Pontigny (*Dép.* Yonne), 82
popes
    Anacletus (*c*.79–*c*.92), 134
    Sylvester I (314–35), 55
    Leo IX (1049–54), 56
    Alexander II (1061–73), 53
    Urban II (1088–99), 15, 31, 56, 182
    Eugenius III (1145–53), 41, 43, 44, 50, 51
    Adrian IV (1154–9), 54, 55, 59, 60, 63, 64, 66, 68 pl. 3.1
    Alexander III (1159–81), 53, 54, 56, 63, 68, 69
    Calixtus III, Antipope (1188–78), 63
    Innocent III (1198, 1216), 27, 46, 47, 48, 50, 51, 79, 80, 81, 82, 118, 143
    Honorius III (1216–27), 46, 199
    Gregory IX (1227–41), 46
    Innocent IV (1243–54), 46
    John XXI (1276–7), pl. 1.1
    John XXII (1316–34), 63, 67, 69, 165
    Clement VII (1523–34), 175, 176
    Pope Paul III (1534–49), 167
    Pius V (1566–72), 175
    Gregory XIII (1572–85), 171
Potterton, Michael, 147
Prestwich, Michael, 93
Prophecy of the Six Kings, 165
Provençe (France), 191
Prussia, 107
Purbeck (Dorset), 95
Purcell, Emer, 18

Quantum praedecessoresnostri, 43
Quia major, 50, 79
Quoniam ea, 60
Quran, 38

Radulf *Palmer*, 72
Radulphus *Palmerus le Tannur*, 73
Rae, Edwin, 158
Ranulf, earl of Chester, 82, 84
Rathmichael (Co. Dublin), 145
Rathmore (Co. Kildare?), 119
Rawson, Prior John, 117
Raymond VI, count of Toulouse, 79, 81
Raymond VII, count of Toulouse, 79
Register of the Hospital of St John the Baptist, 72
Registrum de Kilmainham, 21, 23, 33, 113, 119, 188, 190
Regnan in Excelsis, 171
Reiner *palmer*, 74
religious orders
    Augustinians (canons regular), 24
    Benedictines, 46, 47, 107
    Cistercians, 17, 24, 44, 45, 46, 47, 48, 49, 51, 62, 65, 80, 97, 189, 199
    Fratres Cruciferi ('crutched friars'), 17, 129, 133, 134
    mendicants (incl. Dominican friar preachers, Franciscan friars minor), 24, 27n45, 31, 51, 66, 78, 79, 81, 95, 100, 101, 103, 168, 169, 171, 179, 189
    St Thomas of Acre, 34, 108, 109, 110, 112, 120, 183n1
    see also Knights Hospitaller; Knights Templar

234   *Ireland and the crusades*

Remonstrance, 63, 64, 65, 66, 67; *see also* Counter-Remonstrance
Renneville (Haute-Garonne), 110
Reuter, Timothy, 194
Revel, Hugh, 123
Rhodes, island of, 33n81, 114, 115, 116
Riccardi, bankers, 100
Richard of Cornwall, 100
Richard I (the Lionheart), king of England (1189–99), 30, 75, 76, 159
Richard II, king of England (1377–99), 155, 165, 166
Richard of Cornwall, 100
Richard of Exeter, 86
Riley-Smith, Jonathan, 12n1, 122
Rincrew (Co. Waterford), 138, 188n24
Rindown Castle (Roscommon), 103, 126
Ritoók, Pál, 187n20
Robert I, count of Artois, 97, 98, 99
Robert *Palmer*, 72
Robin Hood, 181
Rochais, Henri, 42
Roger *Palmerus*, 72
Rogerus Cniht, 75
Roman empire, the, 55
Roman Church ['Rome'], the, 15, 46, 50, 55, 64, 89, 164, 167, 168, 171, 176, 177
Romanitas, 194
Rome, city, 15, 44, 167, 168, 174, 194
    Lateran, the, 50
Romsey (Hampshire), 159
Roscommon
    castle, 86, 103
    Dominican friars at, 103
    region, 100
    town, 86
RTÉ, 181
Rum, the, 39

St Andrew, church of, 84
St Augustine, 39
St Brigid, 35
St Dominic (Dominic de Guzmán), 79, 95
St Helena, 134
St John Brooks, Eric, 72
St Lawrence, John, 86

St Patrick's Purgatory (Co. Donegal), 119
St Sillán, 142, 143
St Wulfsige, 88
Sander, Nicholas, 171
Santiago, Order of, 173
Santiago de Compostella, 71
Saintonge (France), 77, 78
Saladin, 30, 61n40, 62
Salerno (Italy), 129
Salisbury (Wiltshire), 158
Sandwich (Kent), 73
Saracens, 62, 139
Satis Laudabiliter, 59, 60, 63, 68, 69
Savoyard(s), 94, 105
Scaldbrother, 181
Scotus Eriugena, John, 25
Scandinavia, 24, 189
Schottenklöster, 25
Scotland, 25, 65, 73, 100, 108, 112, 121, 124, 149, 199
Second Barons' War, 84, 88, 89, 90, 94
Sedulius Scottus, 25
Selart, Anti, 198n65
Shankill (Co. Dublin), 145, 146
Sheares, John, 182
Sheares, Henry, 182
Sheehy, Maurice, 59, 60
Shropshire, 96
Sibyl, queen of Jerusalem, 61n40
Sicily, 38, 56, 97
Sidney, Sir Henry, 170
Simnel, Lambert, 117
Siward the goldsmith, 72
Skyrne, barony, 87
Slavs, the, 46, 193
Sligo, 100
Smerwick (Co. Kerry), 171, 172
Smith, Carol, 181
Smith, Thomas W., 165n5
Smithfield, Dublin, 181
'Song of Dermot and the earl', 58
South Witham (Lincolnshire), 189
Southwark, St Saviour's, 179
Southwell (Nottinghamshire), 159
Spain, 31, 34, 48, 49, 56, 60, 68, 69, 121, 128n39, 165, 170, 173, 193

Index

235

Spanish Armada, 173
Stachfythenan (Co. Kildare), 125
Stalley, Roger, 157 , 160
Stanihurst, Richard, 181
Statutes of Pamiers, 83, 89, 90
Stephen, king of England (1135–54), 58n27
Strade (Co. Mayo), 85, 86
Strongbow; *see* de Clare, Richard
Stukeley, Thomas, 171
Swift, Dave, 18
Swift, Catherine, 18
Sussex (England), 73
Syria, 39, 183n3, 187

Tachehemeder, 144, 145
Tait, Lawson, 180
Talbot, family, 21
    Thomas, prior of Kilmainham, 115, 116
Taloun, Richard, 151
Tany, William, 123
Tara, Hill of, 93
Taylor, Clare, 78
Temple House (Co. Sligo), 35, 111, 150, 185n8,
    188, 189
Theobald, count of Champagne, 97
Thomas, abbot of Mellifont, 50, 51, 142
Thomas, clerk of Strongbow, 142
Thomas, duke of Lancaster, 114–15
Thomas, Hugh, 58
thughūr, 197
Timolin (Co. Kildare), 158
Tipperary, Co., 157
Topographia Hibernica, 61, 62
Torphichen (West Lothian), 124
Toulouse (*Dép.* Haute-Garonne), 79, 81, 110,
    pl 5.1
Tralee (Co. Kerry), 160
Tre Fontane (Rome), abbey of, 44
Treaty of Montreuil, 193
Trim (Co. Meath), 91, 92, 94, 95, 103, 104,
    105, 185n11
    'Blackfriary', Dominican, 95, 100, 104,
        105, 185n11, pl. 6.3
    castle, 95, 185n11, 191n34, pl. 6.2
    friary, Franciscan, 100
    Sheep Gate, pl. 6.2

Tristams saga ok Ísöndar, 75, 76
Tristan, Jean, 101
Tully (Co. Kildare), 190
Tunis, 101
Tunisia, 99
Turner, Frederick Jackson, 195, 196, 197
Turstinus *palmer*, 74
Tyrconnell, 143
Tyerman, Christopher, 26
Tyrell, Hugh, 191n34

Ua Briain, Domnall Mór, 76
    Muirchertach, 180
Ua Conairche, Gilla Críst, bishop of
    Lismore, 44, 51, 53
Ua Conchobair, Áed, 49
Ua Dubthaig, Cadhla, archbishop of Tuam,
    53
Ua Máel Muaid, Ailbe, abbot, 62
Uí Neill, the, 64
Ultonia, 73

Vatican, the, 103
Vaucouleurs (Meuse), 94, 97, 100, 103
Veach, Colin, 82
Verses of Gildas, 165
Vézelay (*Dép.* Yonne), 41, 42
Vicars, Arthur, 178, 179
Vikings, 15, 52, 178n3
Villa Laprihd (?Leopardstown, Co. Dublin), 73
Vineam Dominiu Saboath, 50
Virtuani, Paolo, 17, 34, 36, 106n125
Vox in excelsio, 137

Waldesians, 47
Walensis, 71
Wales, 25, 61, 73, 74, 89, 91, 82, 100, 103, 108,
    115, 121
Wall family, 158
Wallace, William, 124
Walsh, Brother John, 128
Walsingham, Thomas, 165n9, 172
Walter le Bachelor, 20n11
Walter *palmerius*, 74
Walter *filius Palmeri*, 74
Walter the Templar, 20

Warbeck, Perkin, 117
Waterford,
  city, 35, 57, 73, 78, 127,
  county, 20, 34n82, 111, 149
  Waterford Charter Roll, 162, 163, pls 6.1, 11.6, 11.7
Watson, Sethina, 133
Wends, the, 43
Westminster, 102
  medieval hall, 180
Wexford, Co., 20, 34n82, 111, 118, 149
  town, 57
Wicklow, region, 127
Willelmus *filius* Herberti *militus*, 75–6
William I, king of Scotland (1165–1214), 81
William II (Rufus), king of England (1087–1100), 180

William of Newburgh, 77
William of Tudela, 78
William of Tyre, 71
Willelmus *crucesignatus*, 75
Willelmus *palmerius*, 74
William *palmerius de* Beuerle, 74
Willelmus *palmerius filius* Torkil, 74
Wilton Diptych, 166
Winchester (Hampshire), 73
Wladislas, duke of Bohemia (1140–58), 43
Wood, Herbert, 17, 19, 20, 21, 22, 28, 37, 140, 141n34
Wogan, John, 124, 149

Yellow Ford, Battle of, 174

Zouche, John, captain, 172